D0934476

# BOLTON
## *and*
# WODEHOUSE
## *and*
# KERN

# BOLTON
*and*
# WODEHOUSE
*and*
# KERN

## The Men Who Made Musical Comedy

# LEE DAVIS

# H

James H. Heineman, Inc.

New York

ISBN 0-87008-145-4

*Photo Insert credits:*
Page 1, Page 3 (TOP), Page 12 (TOP LEFT), Page 13 large photo:
COURTESY OF THE MUSEUM OF THE CITY OF NEW YORK
Page 2 (TOP): COURTESY OF PETER MARBURY
All other photos: COURTESY OF THE BOLTON LIBRARY

*Text design by Beth Tondreau Design / Mary A. Wirth*

Printed in the United States of America

JAMES H. HEINEMAN, INC.
475 Park Ave.
New York, NY 10022

# Acknowledgments

*To my son Chris*
*who, like the trio,*
*is bringing a unique and creative freshness*
*to the American Theatre*

This is the trio of musical fame,
    Bolton and Wodehouse and Kern:
Better than anyone else you can name,
    Bolton and Wodehouse and Kern.
Nobody knows what on earth they've been bitten by,
All I can say is I mean to get lit an' buy
  Orchestra seats for the next one that's written by
    Bolton and Wodehouse and Kern.

    —ATTRIBUTED TO GEORGE S. KAUFMAN BY
    GUY BOLTON AND ANNE KAUFMAN SCHNEIDER

# *Contents*

# *Credits*

It was Thanksgiving Day, 1980, in Remsenburg, Long Island. I had been sent by Peggy Bolton-Burrowes, Guy Bolton's daughter, to fetch Lady Ethel Wodehouse and bring her to the Bolton house, where the three of us would share a holiday dinner.

The Wodehouse estate was entire then; a developer has since fragmented it. The house was large and white and Georgian, a calm accumulation of angles and windows fronting an astonishing garden, manicured as meticulously as those of Versailles. Dotted, like small way stations among the shrubs, were feeding paraphernalia to sustain the myriad wildlife that crossed and recrossed the side yard with the determination of noontime crowds in Manhattan.

I rang the doorbell, and the sounds of dogs filled the afternoon: yelps, barks, squeals, the scratching of feet on floors, the thudding of bodies against doors. The maid ushered me into a large, modest, organized living room. The vestige of a fire still smoldered in the fireplace; the room was lined with tall windows and books and mementos of P. G. Wodehouse.

In a chair at the far end of the room sat Lady Ethel. She couldn't be ninety-four, I thought. No one of ninety-four can look like that. Her hair bore not a whisper, not a notion of gray. She was slim; her eyes were hidden behind small, heavy glasses, and her hands, delicate, manicured, with hardly a trace of age, were constantly and lightly in motion, like the fluttering of wings.

"How are you?" I asked.

"Terrible. Terrible," she shook her head. "Can't see. Can't hear. Can't walk. But I certainly can dance." The eyes twinkled. Animation lit the face for a moment, then faded.

It was only the first of many dizzying plunges and exhilerating ascents that afternoon.

We drove slowly through the autumn leaves. In five minutes, we were at the Bolton residence, a scant three-quarters of a mile away. It was, in contrast to Plum and Ethel's, a little more rumpled, slightly more unkempt, a shade less formal. Peggy was standing nervously in the doorway, charm and grace and willingness overflowing her, as if the container of herself was far too inadequate to hold her inexhaustible supply of enthusiasm, wonder, and generosity. Her body had taken on a certain comfortable abundance; the Bolton eyes, like the eyes of birds, unblinking and brown, peered through glasses that had slipped to the end of her nose. Glamour glimmered behind the glasses; folds of blonde hair flowed over her shoulders.

"Ethel," she said. "How are you today?"

"Feel terrible," answered Lady Ethel. "Can't walk. Can't, etc. . . ."

"Well, now, you must do what you want. Just relax. Just—relax."

In the Bolton living room of forest green and mahogany, a fire crackled and roared, filling in spaces left by paintings that had been packed, books that had been boxed; the house, like a turned tumbler, was slowly being emptied of the Bolton belongings.

Much of it had been transferred to my home, and a year of cataloging would bring some sort of order to it, an almost well-told story that would ultimately form the basis of this book. Guy Bolton's death had triggered its trajectory. He and P. G. Wodehouse were both patients of my father, one of the local doctors in Remsenburg and its environs. As a teenage caddy, I had carried these two impressive gents' clubs around the golf course of the Westhampton Country Club. It seemed that they were always in deep and unintelligible conversation, which might have accounted for the modest success of their game. But they were immortals, and they had brushed my life, and I felt a special bond to them. And the notice of Guy Bolton's passing in 1979 made it nearly imperative that someone should set him in his rightful place in the history of the American Musical Theatre.

On Thanksgiving Day of 1980, however, Lady Wodehouse was the center of attention. Settling into an armchair, she held out her arms to an army of dogs that immediately surrounded her, licking at her proffered hands, rubbing against her legs, threatening to topple the table that Peggy had set in front of her to receive tea and whatever followed.

"Now we're going to have tea and cake at four and then cocktails at five and then dinner at six and don't I sound like a Prussian general giving the orders," said Peggy, warming herself before the fire. It was already quarter to five, and tea had just appeared.

"Daddy would have been coming out of his study now," mused Peggy, "blinking like an owl because he'd probably fallen asleep more than he'd written. He'd do that, you know."

"Do what?" asked Lady Ethel.

"Fall asleep when he was writing. When he was in his nineties. Goodness. It's a wonder he and Plummy could hold pens, much less write. Do you remember the walks?" She turned to Lady Ethel, trying to find some memories for me, attempting to coax the past up through the tunnels of time in her.

"Walks. Yes, walks," answered Lady Ethel, distractedly.

"What do you suppose they talked about?" prodded Peggy.

"Writing. That's all Plummy and Guy ever talked about."

"Do you remember—"

"Oh, my dear. Memory's gone. That's the first to go, you know that. Used to remember everything. Used to party. Used to dance. Loved to bet."

"Yes!" Peggy leaned forward, encourged, nudging the gates open. "One morning, at Le Touquet. I must have been seventeen. I was down at the beach. I was always at the beach. And you came over a rise all decked out in your gown and your jewelry, coming back from the casino, and—do you remember that?"

The eyes lit behind the glasses. "Days the color of champagne," she said, remembering.

"We'll have some at cocktail time," said Peggy.

"That's now, isn't it? Let's have it now," urged Lady Ethel, reaching out to conduct her canine chorus.

And so it went, for eleven years. Before she died, Lady Ethel Wodehouse gave me multiple, valuable interviews.

And no one was more diligent about finding details and memories and people for me than Peggy Bolton-Burrowes. We sat at café tables in Antibes, Marbella,

Portofino, in restaurants and hotel lobbies in Switzerland and, on her rare visits to America, in my living room, reliving the lives of Guy Bolton, P. G. Wodehouse, and Jerome Kern.

And no less obliging and kind was Betty Kern Miller, who welcomed me into her home in Kentucky, built and decorated like the homes of Eva and Jerome and Betty Kern in Bronxville and Beverly Hills—neatly white with black trim, bursting with books and bookshelves and punctuated by rare furniture. She let me into Jerome Kern's life by allowing me to sit at his precious Bluthner piano, to leaf through his correspondence, to peruse his manuscripts. But mostly she opened her mind and her memory to me over a series of days of intense recording in which we attempted to re-create, for a moment, one of the true geniuses of Broadway, the father not only of Betty Kern Miller but of the modern American musical.

If only Wodehouse's stepdaughter, Leonora, were alive, I could then thank all three of the daughters; but my deepest gratitude goes to the two who survive, well and graciously.

It was through them, in fact, that I had access to some three hundred scripts of important musicals and plays created by these men, including some that are available in no other libraries, many with penciled notations that indicated personal involvements and developments. Scene sketches, correspondence, contracts—all became part of the research for the book.

Much more was put at my disposal: diaries, pencil sketches, photographs of the great men at work and at play were all supplied by Peggy Bolton-Burrowes and Betty Kern Miller.

Extensive research was conducted at the Lincoln Center Library, the New York Public Library, The Library of the Motion Picture Academy, the Motion Picture Library of the University of California (particular thanks to its curator Ned Comstock), and the Theatre Collection of the Victoria and Albert Museum in London.

Beyond this, years were spent in exhaustive interviews with nearly one hundred friends, acquaintances, associates, employees, and enemies of the trio of musical fame. Some of the interviewees carried scars and anger. Venerable British composer Vivian Ellis refused to see me, but he gave me a vitriolic earful in an hour-long telephone conversation; ditto Françoise Bolton, the embittered widow of Guy's tragic son Guybo; Ira Gershwin spoke lovingly of Plum and Jerry, but not at all about Guy. Nevertheless, he readily made available the Ira Gershwin–P. G. Wodehouse correspondence, never before published.

Still others were universally cooperative and informative. June, the glamourous British musical comedy star, was a lifelong lover of Guy Bolton, and she supplied much balance and insight. In 1982, I asked for and received some time with her. She lived then in New York City, on the Upper East Side, in a neatly arranged studio apartment that was one-third occupied by a large hospital bed. She had just recovered from pneumonia, and a private nurse attended her. Her voice had all but left her, and she only spoke four sentences in the hour and a half we spent together.

She was small and frail; her skin was nearly translucent. She was immaculately, neatly attired in a peignoir; her hair was freshly brushed and tied with a ribbon. Her eyes were utterly blue and seemingly bottomless. She was one of the most strikingly beautiful women I have ever seen.

Waving me to a couch, she greeted me from her wheelchair. On a tray in front of her, tied neatly with another ribbon, was a pile of correspondence, copies of all of the letters that Guy had written to her. The originals had been entrusted to her close friend, actress Irene Worth.

We greeted each other, warmly and silently, and she looked me squarely in the eyes. "You're going to write about Guy?" she asked, in a small and strained voice.

"Yes," I replied.

She brought her hands almost together, then moved them apart, then back together again, then apart, in silent applause.

"Read them," she asked me. "Now." And she waited in patient silence as I scanned each of the multitude of letters she was presenting to me. I asked her twice, while I was reading, "Why didn't you and Guy marry?" She refused to answer either time.

I finished the letters, replaced their ribbon, and fitted them gently into my briefcase.

She smiled. "He loved me," she said, intensely. "Guy loved me." And tears, like first rain, ran down her face.

The nurse, obviously concerned, moved toward June, who waved her off. Turning to me, she reached out and gripped my hands in a strong and affectionate dismissal, and smiled.


That was an unusual interview. Others were less emotionally informative, but rich in facts. Myrna Loy, Lord Sidney Bernstein, Leonore Gershwin, and Miriam (Mrs. Tim) Whelan brought the Hollywood years of these three men gloriously alive. Vivienne Segal retraced the Princess years with wit and insight. Keenan Wynn brought the Great Neck years of his father and Bolton and Wodehouse into focus. Irving Caesar was invaluable in reconstructing the theatre of the twenties. In England, Sir John Gielgud, Wendy Toye, Mona

Lister, Millie (Mrs. Toby) Rowland, Peter Cotes, and others cast sharp light on the London theatre scene and the lives of the three; Edward Cazelet was ceaselessly kind and cooperative in supplying Wodehouse family information; and finally, Richard Usborne, Alfred Simon, Gerald Bordman, Stanley Green, Robert Kimball, Miles Krueger, and David Jasen supplied the historical perspective that was needed to bring credibility to the personal and therefore suspect nature of all biographical research.

To the following, who gave me their time and memories, my gratitude: George Abbott, Clinton Atkinson, Adele Astaire, Fred Astaire, Louis Aborn, Dr. Bernard Berger, Lord Sidney Bernstein, Françoise Bolton, Gerald Bordman, Vivian Byerley, Cornelia Bessie, Ingrid Bergman, Irving Caesar, Edward Cazelet, Camilla Cazelet, Alison Colvil, Peter Cotes, Andrew Crookston, Reginald Denham, Lady Frances Donaldson, Vivian Ellis, June Clyde Freeland, Mrs. Eleanor Freedley Johnson, Sir John Gielgud, Ira Gershwin, Leonore Gershwin, Countess Elsie Lee Gozzi, Stanley Green, Julie Harris, Kitty Carlisle Hart, Robert Kimball, Robert Hiden, June (Hillman), George de Jongh, Mrs. Bert Kalmar, Bert Kalmer, Jr., David Jasen, Dean Kay, Edwin Lester, Viveca Lindfors, Mona Lister, Jo Loesser, Peter Lubbock, Robert Lantz, Myrna Loy, Dr. Edward MacLellan, Cecil Madden, Ferde Mayne, Sueo Miyajawa, Marni Nixon, Olive O'Neill, Merielle Perry, Bert Pollack, Michael Price, Margaret Ramsey, Sir Michael Redgrave, Helene Reynolds, Mrs. Richard Rodgers, Mrs. Toby Rowland, Sidney Sheldon, Alfred Simon, Vivienne Segal, Ann Smith, Laurel Baker Tew, Geoffrey Toone, Wendy Toye, Frederick Toye, Jr., Ray Tudor, Richard Usborne, June Vasselais, Roger Vasselais, Douglas Watt, Ethel Watt, Joan Kemp-Welch, Allen Whitehead, Audrey Wood, Keenan Wynn, Lady Ethel Wodehouse, Andrew Lloyd Webber, Robert Wright and George Forrest.

Scanning the list, it is impossible not to notice how many have died since the book was begun. So much for the hazards of attempting to re-create a time passed.

Finally, my gratitude to Amy Umland, who, as a college student, helped me in the cruel and endless task of cataloging the Bolton library. My most profound thanks for the unswerving faith in this project of James Heineman, a valued friend, a man more thoroughly schooled in Wodehouse and Wodehousiana than anyone else I know, and a publisher of inestimable foresight and courage. And lastly, my everlasting thanks to Susan Schwartz, an editor of endless talent, insight, precision, and compassion.

Lee Davis
Westhampton, N.Y.
June 1992

*The wondrous lovely madness of the night went out of American life with the Twenties. You are a lucky man if you got a taste of it.*

—GEORGE JEAN NATHAN,
in Allen Churchill's
*The Theatrical Twenties*

# THE NOT VERY DISTANT PAST

*Two animated figures in an autumn landscape. One, Pelham Grenville Wodehouse, a Matterhorn of a man, a moving mountain bundled brightly against the cold, wearing a golf cap in defiance of sense or season, walks slightly behind his companion of multiple years and myriad ventures.*

*The companion, Guy Bolton, slightly smaller, slightly more animated, slightly more angular, his firmly chiseled profile still affirming the fact that he was once many women's finest fantasy, swings his arms as if he were conducting some hidden orchestra, possibly playing* an overture to one of the shows the two wrote, long ago, with George Gershwin or Cole Porter. Or Jerome Kern.

"Look at them," says Guy, noticing the smallest flick of a lace curtain, the tiniest movement of a face behind a breath-fogged window pane. "Behind their windows. Setting their watches."

The two octogenarians stroll stolidly through avenues of autumn leaves in the small, tree-thick village of Remsenburg, Long Island. It is precisely 2:00 P.M., and they are traveling at precisely the same pace and over precisely the same route as that of yesterday, last week, last month, last year.

The precision in their habits has nothing whatever to do with their perception of reality.

"We're such punctual chaps. Gives them an anchor," says Plum, smiling. "Remember Colonel Savage? Punctuality personified."

"We gave him what for."

"And what he wanted."

"Nobody could give that old goat what he really wanted. He only got what he deserved when somebody sued him."

"Listen," says Plum, changing the subject as if he were taking a sharp right turn, "I've tried reading Shelley again, you know."

"Yes?" Guy sparkles inwardly. He has just had *The Olympians,* his book about Shelley, accepted by World Publishing.

"Loved 'Ozymandias.' Always have. But now, 'The Revolt of Islam.' Hope you won't be offended, old chap. But—"

"But?"

"Have you ever been beaten about the head with a sand bag?"

Guy laughs, low in his throat, appreciatively.

They turn a corner. Guy's peke, Squeaky, chatters on ahead, yipping at the ghost of something, and then careering back toward them.

"What was Morrie Gest's real name?" asks Plum.

"Oh lord, Plummy, I can't remember anything anymore. Anything I really want to remember anymore."

They proceed in pregnant silence.

"Something Jewish. Dark and musical. Moish—"

"Moisha Gerhonovitch!" Guy's brown eyes light.

"That's it, chap!" Plum, always the support for Guy, encourages him still more. "Married Belasco's daughter. Ugly as sin."

"Reine," chuckles Guy. "Reine Belasco. David with his turned-around collars and Reine with her turned-around morals."

"And Bessie Marbury. Dear, elephantine Bessie."

"*Benignly* elephantine Bessie."

"Of course."

They are only partway in Remsenburg now. Their memories have leaped the gap, have stretched and settled them back in the Princess Theatre, in the early teens.

"Well, all Bessie ever wanted was to be an agent anyway," muses Guy, brushing a fallen leaf from his lapel. "She did go after Ray whenever he wouldn't listen to us."

"Nose to bosom," muses Plum, remembering the confrontations between Bessie Marbury and Ray Comstock in the producer's office at the Princess.

"All producers are cheats, aren't they?" Guy's question is really a conclusion.

"Cheating was a religious experience with them," answers Plum anyway. "Only Belasco dressed the part."

They proceed for a moment in contemplative silence.

"Good lord," says Plum, stopping for a moment and confusing Squeaky. "Do you realize that I met Jerry in 1906? The same year that *Mr. Popple of Ippleton* opened?"

"Good lord is right," agrees Guy.

"Seymour Hicks. That was the bloke. With Charlie Frohman, in London. Doing all those shows with girls in the title: *Shop Girl, A Runaway Girl, The Earl and the Girl*—"

"What was he doing at the Aldwych that year?"

"*The Babes and the Baron.*"

"Did I ever tell you," Guy, warmed by the wind and tantalized by the talk, begins to regain his memory. "Did I ever tell you that Hicks collaborated in 1905 with Cosmo Hamilton?"

"Cosmo—!"

"The same." Guy can chuckle now. Long ago, without a smile, he divorced his first wife because of her celebrated affair with Hamilton.

"If we *wrote* that, we'd be pilloried. Why do you suppose that life behaves so badly compared to fiction?"

"Because people do?"

"I suppose. I suppose," muses Plum, turning his face to the westering sun. "It was always so good in those days. So much fun. Popping in and out of managers' offices. Running up the lyrics. Dashing off that rot for *Vanity Fair*."[1]

*Although the past may not repeat itself,*
*it does rhyme.*

—MARK TWAIN

# 1

# Overture
## 1881–1903

The breeze blew in steadily from the English Channel. It always did at Deal; its windmill wasn't one of those frozen figures, blue-and-white china images on a stolid sideboard. It whirled, crazily and relentlessly, its arms a blur and its bit biting downward.

Ivy Bolton's hat had blown off and she was holding it in her hand. Her younger brother Guygo, for all his charm, was a bundle of insecurities. The two were about to meet with their father, Reginald. The deadline had arrived, and, as usual, Guygo was late and vacillating.

Maybe, he told her, his round brown eyes alert and questioning, maybe he should do a crayon. Maybe father would be more receptive to his drawings than his poems.

Guy Bolton was seven and a half years old this mild and tender summer of 1890, and Ivy, at a mature ten and a half, was more than an older sister. A mentor, a shield against the world and their father, she had, to him, arms as wide as the windmill, and as impressive.

No, she said, a poem is better. She promised to help him, if he would show her his poem. It was important to produce something for their father, and on a regular basis, if only to forestall his disappointment and anger. Here on the coast of Kent, where they loved the summers and the holidays and their times together, the three had formed the Downs Art Club. Every fortnight, each of them — Reginald Pelham Bolton (president), Ivy Bolton (editor) and Guy Bolton (treasurer) — would deliver a poem or a piece of a poem or a drawing or a fragment of a drawing.

The bylaws of the club were drawn up a year earlier by their father, Reginald, and carefully copied in flawless calligraphy by him into its portfolio. Their style and their content revealed more about their father than either child was able to divine from his actions:

> The intention of the club is to promote the study and practice of art, and the improvement of our spelling.

> While grammar and nonsense are to be upon equal terms, the former will, it is hoped, fill the book, while the latter is to be confined to a page at a time.

> The Club is to be select; it will not admit any one under the rank of Knight. Perhaps an Editor may be permitted, if he comes in at the side door, and doesn't use the knocker!

> Remarks and criticisms are allowed, but only to those members who are willing to have similar criticism applied to their own productions.

> No quarrelling will be countenanced, except among the subjects in the stories.

> The portfolio will serve the purpose of a record of our efforts, and will not only preserve them, but show the gradual improvement which always follows practice and painstaking.

> If the book becomes interesting, we will instead of charging compound interest to those people who may be interested in it, lend it to them free of charge.

> And when we have filled it, we will put it carefully by, as a reminder in future years of happy hours spent together in the days of childhood which are so short, and yet fly so fast, never to come again. [1]

The wistfulness that crossed Reginald Pelham Bolton's sharply etched face informed the bylaws of the club. Only four years before, on June 19, 1886, Jamie (nicknamed Rex), the youngest of his three children, had died of consumption, after suffering terribly. Kate Bolton entered in her diary that night, "Our little Rex fell asleep. Jesus called a little child unto him."

And from then until she died in 1891, in their home and Guy's birthplace, Broxbourne, Herts, forty miles north and west of London, Kate resumed the steady drinking she had temporarily abandoned when Jamie became ill. Reginald tried to draw her back to them, hiding all of the cooking wine and drinking liquor, but Kate by now had drifted into the final phases of alcoholism, and when there was nothing else, she drank cologne.

Reginald's womanizing was the reason she gave herself and the world; but who knew what really gnawed at her? She had, after all, two other children: Ivy, the oldest, born May 18, 1879, and Guy, born November 23, 1882. But her narrowing, softened world had no space in it for the reality of a family. And so, Guy and Ivy experienced two wrenching losses nearly at once and learned early the virtue of erecting inner walls of protection against hurt.

Small wonder that the Downs Art Club became a haven, a world within a world. Ivy wrote of gentle subjects: sunsets and flowers and the flowing of fences toward the horizon. Guy's efforts tended toward the gory, but no more so than those of any boy his age.

And now, as Kate's drinking deepened, so did Reginald's depression. Toward the end of that same summer of 1890, he too began to withdraw from the children. Ivy, understanding, accepted it stoically. But, confused and unable to define his confusion, Guy began to resent his father's silences and to chafe at his father's presence.

The summer that had begun so brightly turned dark and, what was worse, lonely. Taller than most of the other children his age in Deal, less coordinated, Guy was far less sure of himself than they were. He wanted many friends very badly, but he was afraid to breach the barriers that would lead him out of loneliness and into these friendships.

As August waned, Ivy encouraged him to seek out one companion, who stayed with his parents at Deal's only summer hotel. Guy obeyed, wordlessly. In later years, he recalled threading his way through the lanes leading to the beach, planning an afternoon with a friend he never named.

The journey, he remembered, began jauntily enough. But once he reached the front doors, his nerve and his purpose deserted him. Well-dressed adults in pin-striped flannels and bobbing birdhats flowed through the door and filled the porch. Guy sidestepped them, retiring to an indentation in the exterior wall of the hotel. There, he wedged himself into the hollow, hoping to fuse with the facade and remain invisible until his friend appeared.

But the friend, who never knew that Guy was there, never came. And as the afternoon wore on, there became no need to remain invisible, for no one he knew recognized him or called his name.

"Did you have a good time?" asked Ivy when he returned for dinner.

"We had a lot of fun," lied Guy. "Walked on the beach. Had adventures."[2]

Pelham Grenville Wodehouse struggled into the world prematurely. Eleanor Wodehouse was on vacation in Surrey on October 15, 1881, the day of his birth. She had planned to deliver her third son when she arrived in Hong Kong, where her husband Henry Ernest—known as Ernest—and her other two sons were already living. But there he was, making more noise on a sustained basis than he probably would for the rest of his ninety-six years.

"[Eleanor] had a small gift for drawing and painting and a romantic taste in Christian names . . ." notes Frances Donaldson in her definitive Wodehouse biography. "Her eldest son, Philip Peveril (he was born on the Peak in Hong Kong, [and no educated young British girl of that age had *not* read Sir Walter Scott's *Peveril of the Peak*]) was known as Peveril; her second, Ernest Armine, was called Armine; her third, Pelham Grenville, quickly became known as Plum or Plummie; her fourth, Richard Lancelot, was called Dick. . . . There is no other evidence that Eleanor was a very imaginative person."

Or terribly devoted to her children, either. Although Plum traveled back to Hong Kong with his mother, he had no chance whatever to pick up either the language or the customs. At the age of two, he and his brothers were shipped back to England to spend the rest of their youths in various boarding schools in various locations.

Certainly, it was the custom in those days for those who lived in the colonies to send their children back to boarding schools in England (Kipling is one of the most famous examples), but once *their* children were out of sight, Eleanor and Ernest Wodehouse seemed to excise them from their minds, also. At best, they saw them once every six or seven years. "We looked upon mother more like an aunt," wrote Plum later. "She came home very infrequently."[3]

So, family life for the Wodehouse boys became a mixture of manufactured warmth from strangers caring for somebody else's discarded children and nonstop elation during the high and heady holidays spent with grandparents and aunts and uncles. It didn't begin to make up for the love and fun that Plum and his brothers read about in the stories at school. But there were compensations. Plum and his older brother Armine had much in common and naturally grew close. They both loved art. They both loved walking. They both realized the value of solitude, where Plum first began to fill in the blank places in his life with created stories. Neither of them complained about their situation. In fact, they made the most of it and looked forward to the two weeks they would spend every summer (along with Peveril the Enigmatic) at Ham Hill, Grandmother Wodehouse's home overlooking the river Teme.

Actually, it was the hill on which the house was situated that they looked forward to more than Grandmother Wodehouse, for she was, by all accounts, a strange lady. "Did you ever notice," said Armine to Plum one August day as they sat on the mound of ground that had once, during the Civil War, contained Cavaliers and Roundheads, "Grandma looks a little like a monkey?"

"But a kindly one." Even at the age of seven, Plum was loathe to give offense to others, even if they weren't present.

A year later, Peveril developed a weak chest, and the best place for treatment in the 1880s was the Channel Islands. So, off they went, all three of them in a package, to Elizabeth College, a hundred-boy public school on the island of Guernsey. There they boarded at the headmaster's house.

Guernsey was a place of rolling greenness and blue bays, burnished skies and brilliant mornings. Armine and Plum strolled the hills and made up stories. Only Plum wrote them down. Somehow, it must have seemed to him that the only true permanency in life at that time was that which found its way to paper.

Fannie Kern was well into her seventh pregnancy, but she was not about to let it spoil a trip to the racetrack. Even though January of 1885 was one of the coldest New York had experienced in years, and the twenty-seventh was a day much like all the others that month, Fannie and Henry decided that, despite Fannie's girth, they were going to travel from their mid-town Manhattan apartment to the races at Jerome Park in the Upper Bronx. It was a fashionable place, much more so than Belmont Park, which had just opened in the outer boroughs.

So they went and enjoyed the crisp and exciting and profitable afternoon. Sometime during the carriage ride back to their apartment at Sutton Place and Fifty-sixth Street, Fannie began to feel the onset of labor. They made it home in time, and Jerome David Kern arrived, as peremptorily as he would in later life, upon the scene. The third of three sons who survived infancy, he would be Fannie and Henry Kern's last and most talented child.

Nearby were Henry's successful stables (some biographers say he was also at the time the head of the Street Sprinklers' Association; some say he wasn't)[4] and next door lived a young boy named Louis A. Hirsch, who would someday grow up to be a Broadway composer.

Not much is known about Jerome Kern's childhood, except that he was a slim and sensitive boy whose increasingly well-to-do parents democratically sent his brothers and him to public school.

Very early in his life, Jerry, as his brothers Joseph and Edwin called him, began to play the piano. Before long, he played well enough to give eight-handed concerts — with his mother and two brothers — for his father.

His mother, a lover of theatre, decided on his tenth birthday to introduce her son to it. She took him to a show whose name he couldn't recall in later years.

Perhaps that was because the Broadway season of 1894–95 was a good but not remarkable one. It contained Victor Herbert's first effort, *Prince Ananias,* a flop which had closed before Jerry's birthday, and its hit was Charles Hoyt's hilarious comedy, *A Milk White Flag,* which, considering an incident that would occur early in Kern's career, very well might have been the show they saw.

Mother and son came home from Broadway with colorful memories. For Jerry, they would remain long beyond that day. At the tender age of ten, Kern was hooked.

Within a year, he would be back in a theatre, seeing Victor Herbert's first hit, *The Wizard of the Nile,* then returning home and playing parts of the score on the piano for his school chums.

His adolescence opened steadily and rewardingly before him. He lived in New York and New York was where the theatre was, and he would go there as often as he could. His family could afford it; it was only a streetcar ride away. . . .

And then Henry Kern decided to go into the clothing business. He was going to be richer still, and they were going to buy their first house, a three-story brick one with a wooden dependency in the rear, in the middle of a good German-Jewish neighborhood, just a short way from D. Woolf and Company, where Henry would be — again, history is vague — a partner? an employee?

They'd love it in Newark.

Newark?

Yes, Newark.

A long, long ferry ride from Broadway.


Deal, like Dover and other Channel towns, had its treasures for Guy and Ivy: the geometry of sailboats gleaming on wind hollowed waters, the staircase slopes to the sea, the bell in the town tower, rung on the hour to tell the fishermen the time.

When, years later, Guy went back, he wrote to Ivy, "The place is utterly unchanged, except for one newish, not very aggressive hotel. The bell that used to jump up and down on top of the tower to tell the time to the fishermen is still there and it still jumps."[5]

And there, too, he finally confessed to her, was the indentation in the wall of the summer hotel, where he waited for a companion who never appeared.

After their mother died, their father only visited Deal on weekends, leaving Ivy and Guy in the care of their German nurse. They liked Nana; they missed their mother. Guy remembered her before the drinking began, before her head was shaved because she could no longer care for herself. He would sit on her lap, and she would look at him lovingly, and ask, "Who stole Mommy's eyes?" and she would reach for his, for they were the same—wide, unblinking, and brown—and he would see himself, magnetic, mischievous, enigmatic.

Now the eyes were no more, the game at an end. He had not really stolen his mother's eyes, only borrowed them. He would tell her that and she would hug him, the strange sweetness of her breath and the softness of her hair circling him in safety.

But Nana loved him, too, and while her breath didn't smell like his mother's, he liked sitting on Nana's lap and studying her strange Indian countenance. Germans weren't supposed to look that way. Nana's ancestors had, in some forgotten time, mixed with Gypsies.

Nana would read to him and help him with his school work. He needed help. He wasn't particularly successful at school, either academically or socially. He still towered over his classmates in Broxbourne, and this set him apart. It was really only Ivy and Nana who sought him out.

And then, one September day in 1892, only a year after Kate died, Reginald married Ethelind, an American woman living in Broxbourne. She was the woman Kate said caused the alcoholism that brought about her death.

Ethelind was anything but beautiful. She had long, angular features and a foreboding countenance; she did nothing to soften her sometimes clumsy and often unfriendly actions. Although the accounts are sketchy, it seems that she kept the children at arms' length, and perhaps more than that.

From that time until Reginald's death in 1944, Guy believed that his father hated him. Despite the lovingness of the Downs Art Club and its bylaws, despite the painstaking sketches that Reginald had provided for Guy and Ivy, and despite Ivy's assurances to the contrary, Guy persisted in this belief.

An uncertain and sensitive child, he mistook his father's preoccupation for hatred, and Reginald was a preoccupied man. A scholar, an inventor, an engineer, a traveler, he was hardly ever home for a sustained period of time.

His trips took him increasingly to America. His own father was an American, and the Bolton family's roots were partly in Savannah, Georgia. Under glass, Reginald preserved a deed issued under the seal of King George, in which Robert Bolton in October 1772 had rented a plot of land in Georgia to one William Handley for the spicy sum of one peppercorn.

Clear business heads, it appeared, didn't run in the Bolton family.

They never would.[6]


Plum and Armine, swept like leaves around the concentric currents that contained their parents, gravitated toward their father, when he was there. He was blue-eyed and tall and taciturn, and Plum was slowly and certainly becoming that way, too.

But as quickly as he sometimes appeared, Ernest disappeared, leaving the boys in the care of distant people. And then, Armine, too, disappeared. Ernest decided that his four boys (Dick, the youngest, had now appeared upon the scene) should have different careers and be sent to different schools. Peveril remained on Guernsey, at Elizabeth College. Armine went to Dulwich, in southeast London. Dick, after distinguishing himself as the child croquet champion of Gloucestershire, went to Cheltenham College, where he became a German scholar. And Plum was sent to Malvern House, a Navy preparatory school situated in Kearnsey, Kent, near Dover—a short way down the beach from Deal.


Jerry Kern entered the Thirteenth Avenue School in Newark with confidence. His parents were unfailingly supportive of him, filling him with the boldness of spirit that neither young Guy Bolton nor young P. G. Wodehouse shared. And even at that age, Jerry had charm, and he could play the piano like no boys he knew or who knew him. Besides, his father was doing better than ever financially and was expanding Woolf and Company from clothing to clothing and furniture. For this well-loved and well-cared-for young man, life was good and it held every possibility of becoming better.

By the time Jerry entered Newark High School in the fall of 1899, he didn't miss Broadway at all; he was too busy. During his first year of high school, he began playing the piano and the organ at assemblies. Faculty and students listened intently and with pleasure. This was no ordinary key plunker. This was a talented, personable, self-assured musician.

In January of 1901, the seniors of Newark High School invited Jerry, a junior, to join the class show. On the night of March 8, 1901, he made his first entrance into show business on a velocipede, upon which he made several circuits of the stage before trading the unicycle for a piano, where he launched enthusiastically and confidently into an opening ragtime medley.

The audience, awed at this multitalented performer listed in the program as "J. D. Kern, as Mr. Weary Willie,"[7] applauded wildly and demanded several encores.

Elated, Jerry moved from the piano to offstage right. Not satisfied with merely stopping the show, he was running it, too, as one of the stage managers.

Reverends ran rampant among Guy and Ivy's ancestors: one fought for George Washington and was decorated by him; one witnessed the Draft Riots from his church in lower New York City during the Civil War; one—Reverend Robert Bolton—built a magnificent mansion called Pelham Priory, which still stands in Pelham Manor, a diminutive but elite hamlet in Westchester County, north of New York City.

In 1893, Reginald's brother, Reverend Winter Bolton, served as pastor of the Church of the Redeemer in Pelham. In September of that year, in Broxbourne, Ethelind gave birth to a son who died in infancy. Reginald, realizing that there was little now to link them to Broxbourne, packed the family belongings, Ethelind, Ivy, Guy, and Nana and moved everyone across the Atlantic and into his brother's rectory.

Within a month, he and Ethelind strayed on to New York City, leaving the children and Nana behind. Guy and Ivy were miserable in Westchester. Deal was an ocean and a world away; father visited very little and then less and less. When she wasn't with their father, Ethelind went to see her relatives in Washington, D. C., where she had been born; when Reginald had some rare spare time, he went there, too. And so, it was again Nana and Ivy and Guy and loneliness, a continuing quartet.

The two children were sent first to the public school in New Rochelle, where their odd accents immediately set them apart.

On a spring day in 1894, when Ivy was seventeen and Guy was twelve, Ivy entered his room. He was packing.

"Where are you going?" Ivy was alarmed. Her younger brother was not ordinarily given to spontaneous actions.

"Away."

"But *where?*"

"Any place. I don't care."

"You can't just go any place. You have to know *where* you're going. Besides—" Ivy was older, and more practical, "Father will be angry."

"He's *always* angry." It wasn't true, except to Guy, who now turned to Ivy, his intense brown eyes full upon her. "Come with me, Ivy. I'll take care of you."

Ivy thought. It was *she* who should be taking care of her dreamer of a brother.

Guy closed his suitcase, asking her once more to come, assuring her that it would be fun and different.

What he proposed *was* exciting, like the stories he used to write for the Downs Art Club.

"Wait for me." And she ran to her room and packed a suitcase.

So the two travelers departed and got no farther than the next town before relatives realized they were missing. In the end, Ivy was secretly happy to conclude the trip. Guygo, for all his bravado, seemed to have no sense of direction.

Reginald, as Ivy had predicted, was furious. There was no homecoming for the prodigals, only punishment. So, perhaps realizing that things would never really get better in Pelham if he challenged his father, Guy would decide to follow Reginald's footsteps into engineering. Ivy, tasting the outside world and finding it either bitter or bland, would enter a convent with the Maryknoll Sisters in Peekskill, New York, where she would remain for the rest of her life. [8]


Plum was no Navy candidate. His eyesight was too bad, his grades were too low, and he missed Armine too much. One vacation trip to Dulwich convinced him that this was where he should be, and he pleaded long distance with his father to let him transfer there. His father consented.

And so began the happiest part of Plum's youth, very possibly the only time he entered into the society of others with enthusiasm and abandon. At Dulwich, he was a player on both the football and cricket teams, a boxer of some threat, a school prefect, a member of the Classical Sixth ("The classical side . . . as it turned out, . . . was the best form of education I could have had as a writer," he would later say), [9] and the editor of the literary magazine, the *Alleynian.* "He was, in fact, one of the most important boys in the school," wrote William

Townend, his study mate and lifelong friend, to Wodehouse's other important biographer, David Jasen.

And to Jasen himself, Plum remarked, "Except for Alec Waugh, I seem to be the only author who enjoyed his schooldays. To me, the years between 1894 and 1900 were like heaven."

Part of this enjoyment might have been attributed to his parents' return from Hong Kong. Ernest, suffering from sunstroke, was recycled, and for the first time in fifteen years, the family became a family.

Sort of.

Ernest tried. Eleanor's idea of motherhood ran to large doses of discipline and distantness. But, as remote as she was from her children, she was extremely affectionate toward her husband, indulging him, cajoling him, allowing him to think he was in charge while she took charge. Plum, the eternal observer, while not actually embracing her lessons in domesticity, noticed them. The embracing would come later.

He and Armine spent their happiest hours with their father, taking long walks with him, laughing at his jokes—which were inventive and plentiful— and carrying his clubs when he played golf.

But, the family life the boys craved was again short-lived. Maybe Ernest and Eleanor thought they had had enough of domesticity after a year. Possibly they were restless. Perhaps they felt that, with only one life to live, they deserved to live it away from London.

Whatever the reason, they soon quit Dulwich for Shropshire, leaving the boys once more in the care of others.

Plum was now writing regularly, although Arthur Herman Gilkes, Dulwich's famous headmaster, had a few reservations about the talent and character of this budding genius. At the end of the winter term of 1899, Gilkes sent off this airy evaluation of Plum to Eleanor and Ernest:

> He is a most impractical boy . . . often forgetful; he finds difficulty in the most simple things and asks absurd questions, whereas he can understand the most difficult things. . . . He has the most distorted ideas about wit and humour; he draws over his books in a most distressing way, and writes foolish rhymes in other people's books. One is obliged to like him in spite of his vagaries. . . .[10]

One wonders how much indigestion Gilkes got from eating those words in later years.

Schooldays sped to an end. Undaunted by his headmaster, Plum published his first paid-for piece, an essay on "Some Aspects of Game Captaincy" for the February 1900 issue of *Public School Magazine.*

Armine was off to Oxford. Plum expected to follow him.

"You want to write?" asked his father one summer day in 1900 in Shropshire.

"Yes," answered Plum, succinctly.

"What else?"

"That."

"That alone?"

"That alone."

"Not the type of work for a responsible young man," opined Ernest, echoing and foreshadowing countless judgments of countless fathers of countless writer-sons. "Good for the spare time and holidays." He leaned back, crossing his hands in the role of the perfect Victorian father. "Got an honest job for you."

"I thought—" ventured Plum.

"Oxford? Afraid not," answered his father, honestly distressed. "My pension only allows one son at Oxford. No," he leaned forward enthusiastically, "you'll start next month as a clerk. Good position. Fine future. At the London branch of the Hong Kong and Shanghai Bank."

Jerry impressed everybody. His schoolchums. His teacher of theory and orchestration at the New York College of Music. Everyone but his father.

"You're getting older," he said to the young Kern. "What do you want to do?"

"I want to compose."

"You can do that at night. In the daytime, you'll work in the business."

"But—"

"You'll be successful. You'll see."

In 1897, Reginald and Ethelind Bolton bought a house at 638 West 158th Street in Manhattan. It was a huge, rambling structure located on the northernmost edge of a wandering tract of land owned by the family of John James Audubon. Audubon had been dead since 1851, and his home—where Morse had tested his first successful electrical transmitter—was crumbling to dust. Between the Audubon ruins and the new Bolton home ranged an enormous garden that would become famous for years as a pocket of bucolic beauty in the midst of deepening caverns of concrete. Reginald puttered in that garden daily, and one day stumbled into some old Indian relics. He preserved them not only in his library, but between the covers of a book titled *Indian Life of Long Ago*.

Writing, it turned out, was also part of Reginald's voluminous catalog of accomplishments. He also invented sporadically, tended to his business, and managed some time for his wife. His company, R. Bolton and Co., Engineers, sold heavy equipment, designed other heavy equipment, and made a lot of money.

Reginald's patents for a hydraulic governor, the Bolton and Hartley air compressor, an electric crane-gearing, an electrical rock-boring and hammering apparatus, and perhaps the very first air conditioner that worked swelled the Bolton wealth.

Young St. George Guy Reginald Bolton became used to the amenities of life, and his father's ways of acquiring them were not lost on him. He enrolled in the engineering course at Pratt Institute in Brooklyn, believing his father when he told him that he couldn't make a living at writing. Very well. He would do what his father did: practice engineering and write on the side.

But a year at Pratt convinced Guy that engineering was no fun at all. Now he knew where his father's dour expression came from.

He transferred to the Atelier Masquery on East Twenty-third Street, where he received a degree in architecture. By 1900, he was working as an architectural designer for his father. Two years later, he moved on to other architectural firms. Later in life, he would take friends and admirers to the Soldiers' and Sailors' Monument on Riverside Drive and up the Hudson River to West Point, to the Hotel Thayer.

"I designed these," he would say, and these two structures—one an up-thrust tube guarded by military statues, the other a jailhouse masquerading as a blockhouse masquerading as a hotel—constitute the major evidence of Guy Bolton's architectural career—those and the minute and detailed drawings that he did of his first stage sets and the architectlike lists of props and lights that he would soon leave to legions of stage managers.

As he moved from youth to manhood, Guy began to write more than he designed. When, in 1904, the magazine *Smart Set* accepted his first story—a maudlin melodrama about a man sacrificing himself to keep a dog from drowning—architecture dimmed to black. The freedom, the reward, the acknowledgment that the boy who had once pressed himself into the indentation of a hotel wall in Deal could achieve on the pages of a popular magazine were irresistible.

Plum barely endured the tedium of his work at the Hong Kong and Shanghai Bank. His salary was eighty pounds a year, not enough to support him, even in squalor. His father had to match that amount to allow him to occupy a small bed-sitting room off Markham Square, which he later described to biographer David Jasen as "horrible lodgings off the King's Road."

There, he did what he would do, in one variation or another, for the rest of his life: escape from dull reality into bright fantasy. He elbowed his way through the thickets of the bank, barely able to wait for the Elysium of his lodgings and the clear air that surrounded the act of writing.

"I wrote everything in those days," he said to Jasen, "verses, short stories, articles for the lowest type of weekly paper, only a very small portion of them ever reaching print."[11]

But he was writing, that was the point. And publishing. And looking forward to publishing again.

Ultimately, all of this activity, plus the law of averages, plus the genius of the man, plus the presence of William Beach-Thomas, whom he had known as a headmaster at Dulwich and who was now an assistant editor on the London *Globe,* resulted in a quandary of major proportions: to exist in agony or to trade his job at the bank for the insecurity of writing intermittent humorous items for the newspaper.

By all accounts, Plum hesitated for a fraction of an instant before deciding.

"On September 9, 1902," he wrote in his diary, "having to choose between the *Globe* and the Bank, I chucked the latter and started out on my wild lone as a freelance. This month starts my journalistic career."[12]


Jerry Kern couldn't believe his ears. Hadn't he, as *still* an undergraduate of Newark High School (he would never be a graduate — a not uncommon state for young men in those days) composed the music for the Newark Yacht Club's satire of *Uncle Tom's Cabin?*

And hadn't they filled the Kreuger Auditorium for it?

And hadn't he climbed up on the stage and gathered bouquets from the audience?

And hadn't the critics in the newspapers called his music "catchy and up to date . . . [and] much better than some of the music heard in many of the comic operas on the stage today . . ."?

And hadn't the very father who was dictating his future to him now sent him off to Heidelberg to study music for four months?

And hadn't—

"Makes no difference. You're a son of mine, you work in the business," said his father. Or something like that. Jerry in future years remembered the impact more than the words.

Shortly after he began work, he was sent by his father to the Bronx to deal with an Italian family who, Henry Kern had heard, had just received a consignment of new pianos from Italy. It might, he reasoned, be a good business move to carry a couple of pianos in the store. It would make his son happy, too.

Up to the Bronx journeyed Jerry. He arrived just in time for lunch. The talk flowed. The food flowed. The wine flowed. Before he left, Jerry had signed a purchase order for considerably more than two pianos.

The next day, they began to arrive at Woolf and Company's warehouse. Jerry and his father were there. "You can't imagine," Jerry loved to relate in later years, "what it looks like for two hundred pianos to come off vans."

Henry turned to Jerry. "Son," he said (according to Kern biographer Michael Freedland), "I think I'm going into the piano business. As for you, I think you should become a musician."[13]

# 2

# Warn Curtain

## 1903–1910

Guy had ripened into an extraordinarily handsome young man. He was no longer taller than those around him; in fact, he was somewhat shorter. But he was nevertheless striking, in the sharp, chiseled features of his jutting jaw, the melting brownness of his eyes, the aristocratic bearing of his body.

He chafed at living with his father and Ethelind, at not entirely doing what he wished to do, at being uptown in Riverdale, when he might be downtown, where the lights were and the ladies were and the promise was.

Neatly, immaculately dressed, witty, informed, unflaggingly interested, he dazzled the damsels who deigned to cross the line from lower Manhattan to Washington Heights, where Reginald and Ethelind lived. He trained the audible echoes of his British upbringing into carefully cultivated verbal surprises, slipped into conversation effortlessly so that they astonished by their precious rarity. It set him apart, yet made him desirable.

He would never lack the company of women from that time forward.

In 1907, his first cousin, Julie Alexander Currie, arrived in New York from San Francisco to visit relatives and acquire some Eastern culture. Her dazzlement with her only slightly older male cousin was answered in kind.

It was like an eighteenth-century romance, trembling into melodrama. Guy was remarkably handsome; Julie was extravagantly beautiful. Both were, in a sense, away from their roots, waiting for wonder and looking for love. Julie was nineteen; Guy was twenty-one; they were naive enough to be out of a story by Booth Tarkington.

And so, true to form, Guy suggested that they run away, for no good reason—she wasn't pregnant and neither family would have disapproved—and marry, which they did, in October 1908. Also true to form, they didn't run very far. The two expatriates fled a mere ten miles, tied the conjugal knot, and settled on Staten Island, a short trolley and ferry ride from Washington Heights.

For two years, Guy played the dutiful husband, working at his father's office, designing, writing at night. In August, a son, Richard Montgomery, was born, and Guy and Julie left Staten Island for New York, settling into an apartment on West Ninety-first Street. They enjoyed Manhattan, the excitement, the growing nature of it, the possibilities.

The theatre.


It shouldn't have been possible, but it was. Plum, towering over six feet now, his clear blue eyes framed by the iron-rimmed spectacles that he would wear for the rest of his life, perceived that he was growing bald. Think of it. Only twenty-two years old. Blast.

He sighed philosophically. Sighing was all he could do and all he *would* do in any crisis from that time forward. No sense in fretting over what couldn't be fixed. And most misfortune couldn't be fixed.

By 1903, Plum's byline was becoming widespread and well known. *Punch* and the *Daily Express* were publishing his humorous sketches and verses regularly. He had begun to write a series of school books, his first prose to be issued in book form. His first novel, *The Pothunters,* had run as a serial in *Public School Magazine* and had been published by A&C Black the previous year.

His second novel, *A Prefect's Uncle,* had been released this year, and there was yet another, *Tales of St. Austin's* ready to roll into the presses.

All of them were about boys under the age of eighteen—probably the only human beings Plum could either identify with or understand in 1903. Their popularity was due in part to the fact that they were free from moralizing—a trait they shared with their creator.

Plum had little time to socialize during his first years in London, and gave no indication of any inclination to do so, even if he had the time. Socializing waited until the arrival of Herbert W. Westbrook, who appeared at 23 Walpole Street, where Plum was then living, with a letter of introduction from a mutual friend at the bank.

Westbrook was an aspiring writer. To have another writer come to him for advice when he had only been plying his trade for three years must have been bewildering to Plum. Nevertheless, showing the relentless poise that would confound his acquaintances later in life, he not only gave Westbrook advice; he gave him encouragement.

In return, Westbrook offered him lodgings at Emsworth House, a small preparatory school on the border of Hampshire and Sussex, very near Portsmouth. Westbrook was an assistant master there, and he convinced Plum that the atmosphere would be much more conducive to writing than the more distracting excitement of London.

By all accounts, Plum had a delicious time at Emsworth, writing, clowning a bit with Westbrook, playing cricket with the boys, turning out much material for the *Globe* and for himself.

Westbrook, it turned out, was more than a mere usher into Emsworth. A borrower who didn't repay his debts and a lender who never expected recompense, a man with artistic ambitions and hardly any talent to realize them, an idler who was universally liked, he became the prototype of Plum's famous character of Ukridge in *Love Among the Chickens.*

Ambivalent about his new-found association, Plum moved to a house of his own in Emsworth in 1904—a home he would buy six years later.

That summer, on a five-week holiday from the *Globe,* he made his first trip to America and, after meeting the famous boxer Kid McCoy, increased his income and his popularity by writing a series about a boxer named Kid Brady.

It was in New York on that first trip in 1904 that Plum became intrigued by the workings of the criminal mind. He never did understand those workings, but that didn't stop him from nurturing an abiding preoccupation with outlaws for the rest of his life.

In fact, his very first excursion into the theatre would involve a lyric about the joys of jail, obviously written by a man who had never been there.


"I want the curly-headed kid with the glasses," some of the customers would say, and Jerry Kern, obliging, charming, yet always aware of the precise effect he was having upon his audiences, would sit at the piano in Wanamakers department store, where he worked as a song plugger for Lyceum Music at the princely sum of seven dollars a week. His job as a plugger was to play what the customers wanted in the way that they wanted, so long as Lyceum published it. His employer had already released the first two Kern melodies to see the certainty of print, "At the Casino" and "In a Shady Bungalow," and although Jerry was happy with the fact, he was less happy with the publisher. It was too small.

The big one was Witmark, which handled the big names—Victor Herbert, Gustav Luders, and Ernest Ball. And Ball also plugged Witmark songs by playing the piano at Wanamakers.

In fact, Jerry was between two giants in that department store. The other was Jean Schwartz, who would go on to write such standards as "Chinatown, My Chinatown" and "Rock-a-bye Your Baby With a Dixie Melody." Because these two were often called off to some producer's office or some theatre or another, Jerry was getting increased exposure at Wanamakers, and he began to play songs other than Lyceum's, timing them judiciously.

One day, when Ernest Ball appeared late, he heard one of his original melodies coming from young Kern's corner of the music department.

Jerry opined to his bemused fellow composer that it was a nice tune.

Ball agreed. But he also observed that Lyceum didn't publish it. He went on to observe that since Lyceum didn't publish *his* tunes, it didn't publish the *best* tunes.

It was the sort of conversation for which Jerry had hoped. He had been angling for an introduction at Witmark. He slid gracefully into another Ball tune.

Ball, shrugging out of his overcoat, eyed the brash young boy with the curly hair and the undeniable talent. And then, for reasons that might have had something to do with self-protection, he suggested that the young man take his tunes to another, older company, T. B. Harms, which was currently being resurrected by another young man named Max Dreyfus. Dreyfus, he added, was looking for new talent, and Witmark wasn't.

"Whoever heard of Max Dreyfus?" asked Jerry, reaching for his coat.

"Whoever heard of Jerome Kern?" echoed Ball, busying himself at the keyboard.

Jerry had only been bandying. He was not in the habit of passing up any opportunities whatsoever. Without hesitation, he sought out the dilapidated offices of T. B. Harms, on East Twenty-second Street.

One look at Max Dreyfus and Jerry knew he was home. Dreyfus inspired confidence even if his surroundings didn't. Sartorially splendid, in the habit of coming to work in a morning coat and top hat, which he carefully and casually and theatrically threw across the piano in his office, he had imagination, grace, and a nose for new talent.

The thin, balding, ambitious publisher and the short, curly-haired, ambitious composer hit it off from the beginning.

In a very short time Jerry was on his way to Broadway, thanks to Max Dreyfus, who placed his songs within earshot of the right people. Two of these people were the supershowmen of the time, Joe Weber and Lew Fields. They had just bought Seymour Hicks and Walter Slaughter's British failure, *An English Daisy.*

Broadway audiences at the turn of the century, much like those of the 1980s, went crazy over anything British. Good enough, thought Weber and Fields. If the two of them tucked up *An English Daisy* and brightened it by shoving in some interpolations by American composers, they might make a winner out of a loser.

They were wrong, but when *An English Daisy* opened on January 18, 1904, at the Casino, two of Jerry's songs were in the score. Two days short of his twentieth birthday, Jerome Kern had arrived on Broadway.

Meanwhile, Max Dreyfus was working overtime, giving his protégé double and triple exposure. Jerry began to work as a rehearsal pianist and as a tour accompanist for such luminaries as Marie Dressler and Edna Wallace Hopper. Wherever he went, he never lost the opportunity to suggest a Kern interpolation.

In the midst of this, according to Jerry's biographers David Ewen and Gerald Bordman, Jerry made his first trip to London. But Andrew Lamb, in his 1985 monograph *Jerome Kern in Edwardian England* places Jerry in the West End in the 1905–6 season. His proof includes Jerry's intense involvement in 1904 with a New York production that needed a bushel of interpolations.

The show was *Mr. Wix of Wickham.* Its producer was Edward Rice, a sort of David Merrick of the early American Musical Theatre. The writer of the original book and the original score was an Englishman, Herbert Darnley. Rice was convinced that the major reason for the show's failure in England was Darnley's score.

Max Dreyfus introduced Jerry to Rice, who immediately took to this bright youngster who wrote pretty and original melodies. For Jerry, no matter how vaunting his ambition, was a charmer, too, and would remain so for all of his life. His brashness was bred of certainty. He knew he was good, and what was the sense of denying the truth?

When *Mr. Wix of Wickham* opened at the Bijou on September 19, 1904, half the show's twenty-three numbers carried the signature of Jerome D. Kern, and six of them involved not only Kern music but Kern lyrics. Jerry wrote the lyrics to twenty-two songs between 1904 and 1907, when he decided to leave the words to others. Each of them had a delightful touch of whimsy and an intelligence that informed the music wisely and refreshingly.

*Mr. Wix of Wickham*'s Susan was typical:

> Susan is a pretty girl,
> With suitors by the score,
> There's nothing wrong in that,
> But there's a fellow lives next door—
> Makes my life a misery, I fear I'm going daft,
> Every night like a busy bee, he warbles down the
>     shaft:
> "Susan,
> No time I'm losin'
> That's why I'm usin'
> This way to say,
> That I love you dearly, Susan,
> And I'm all confusion,
> Because I'm choosin'
> My fiancée."
>
> Beastly wise while I'm snoozin'.
> Recently I bought some records for my gramophone,
> Started it a-going and then shuddered with a groan,
> Coming from the wheezing thing, was that old,
>     lovesick croon;
> I could do a highland fling on the author of this
>     tune:
> "Susan . . . etc."
>
> I'm going to move away,
> I'll have to very soon.
> I'm going, I'll confess to you, upon my honeymoon.
> Susan wears my diamond ring,
> And she's my bride to be,
> And that chap will no more sing,
> When Susan marries me,
> "Susan . . . etc."[1]

*Mr. Wix of Wickham* was blasted by the critics, with ample reason. It wasn't only Darnley's score that had sunk the show the first time around; it was all of it. *Mr. Wix* staggered on for forty-one performances and then mercifully fell silent.

But before it did, Alan Dale, the respected critic of the *American,* said a few things in print that gave a leg up to Jerry's career.

He was not as disenchanted with the show as were his colleagues. ". . . A pleasing entertainment," he pronounced it, "containing much that is pretty, and something that is humorous, a few good people, two or three 'dizzy blondes' and a dozen catchy airs."

The "catchy airs" he was referring to were not those of Darnley. ". . . Its music, by Jerome D. Kern," he went on, "towers in such an Eiffel way, above the average hurdy-gurdy, penny-in-the-slot, primitive accompaniment to the musical show that criticism is disarmed and Herbert Darnley's weak and foolish 'book' sterilized."[2]

Propelled by the power of the press, work poured into Jerry's eager arms. *The Silver Slipper,* another British musical, needed some interpolations. *An English Daisy,* still hanging on, needed some more.

Max moved T. B. Harms closer to the theatres in which the scores it published were heard. In 1905 the firm opened new offices at 126 West 44th Street. Jerry, coming into an inheritance from his grandfather, bought in as a partner.

Encouraged by Max, Jerry boarded a boat for England to explore the source of the British shows into which he had lately poured so many interpolations. What he saw and experienced in the summer and fall of 1905 delighted him.

The 1905–6 season was a bright one in the West End, dominated by the work of three men: Charles Frohman, an American producer who shared Broadway showgoers' blind acceptance of anything British; George Edwardes, whose taste in titles was always predictable (*The School Girl, A Country Girl, The Girl from Kay's,* etc.); and the same Seymour Hicks who had been indirectly responsible for the vehicle that had introduced Jerry, as a composer, to Broadway.

In London, Jerry shuttled back and forth, from the celebrated and elaborate shows by George Edwardes at his two flagship theatres, the Gaiety and Daly's, to St. Martin's Lane and the Duke of York's, Charles Frohman's flagship, and to the Vaudeville Theatre, operated jointly by Frohman and Seymour Hicks. By July of 1905, Jerry was under contract to Charles Frohman and Seymour Hicks to produce twelve songs a year for the next three years.

That very summer, he bolstered, melodically, a faltering theatre piece in which Hicks was starring, *The Catch of the Season,* with a book by Hicks and popular playwright Cosmo Hamilton, and a score by Herbert E. Haines.[3]

Hicks, like Edwardes, had a habit of doing shows with names that brought on the girls — *The Shop Girl, A Runaway Girl, The Earl and the Girl,* for instance — and his taste in composers often forced him to bring on the interpolaters. This was good news for Jerry. He was fulfilling his contract to the actor/manager/writer/producer with aplomb.

In 1909, Douglas J. Wood produced the Greek pageant at New York's respected Architectural League, of which Guy Bolton was a member. In 1910, he read Guy's story in *Smart Set*, liked it, and told Guy so. Wood also, it seemed, had an idea for a play and wondered if Guy would care to collaborate on it with him.

Guy knew nothing about writing plays, and his only contact with the theatre had been as an enthusiastic audience member. But he had learned architecture and learned it well and hadn't much cared for it. Playwriting intrigued him, and learning and making a living in a profession he liked intrigued him even more.

Julie was pregnant again; in November, she would give birth to a daughter, Katherine Louisa, who would thereafter and mysteriously go by the name of Joan.

Everything was blissful then; when you're that young, immortality is imaginable. Guy imagined his immortality would be helped by the presence of Douglas Wood, and with logical reason: Wood was only a year older than Guy; his rise on the stage had been meteoric, partly because of his talent, partly because of the contacts his famous mother had been able to supply. Under the stage name of Ida Jeffreys-Goodfriend, she had been a disciple of Ibsen and had gained stardom when she took over Fanny Davenport's mantle as leading lady of the Augustin Daly Stock Company.

Her son Douglas made his debut in 1899 at the age of eighteen, playing the role of the bridegroom in *The White Horse Tavern.* David Belasco saw him in that and took him on as an apprentice. Wood went on to play with the great Richard Mansfield and to be called by the *Dramatic Mirror* a "rising young actor" in 1909.

In 1910, the year he came to Guy with his idea for a play, he was important enough in the New York theatre to refuse to appear for a curtain call in a play called *The Battle.* His reason was compelling: he'd been shot in the third act and felt that resurrecting himself for a curtain call would shatter the verisimilitude of the evening.

So, young as he was, Douglas Wood had clout, a clear understanding of his craft, and a dedication to reality. What he needed was a writer to record his ideas. Guy eagerly accepted the job. They spent hours, then days, then days and evenings at the Thirty-ninth Street Theatre, a small house owned by Sam and Lee Shubert.

At the moment, a French farce, *The Million,* produced by Colonel Henry Savage, was rehearsing. It was in trouble; the out-of-town reviewers had been less than lukewarm.

Wood brought Guy into this inner, morose circle.

And, although the evidence is circumstantial, it seems that Guy, like Jerry in his early days, was called in to do some interpolating. Unlike Jerry, he didn't have T. B. Harms to record the evidence publicly.

However, until his death, Guy kept a typescript of *The Million,* with painstakingly detailed stage manager's notes written by hand.

The handwriting is his.[4]

When *The Million* finally opened, on October 23, 1911, it had been doctored so much, the theatre must have resembled a hospital. And the *Dramatic Mirror* noted in its review, "*The Million . . .* had its first out of town production several weeks ago, since when it has received a thorough combing out at the hands of some reviser . . . changed from the Latin Quarter of Paris [to] New York City . . . on Second Avenue, the Bowery, and Pelham Road. The change is . . . commendable. There were weak act endings that seem to have had a building up by the stage manager. . . ."

Fascinating.

*Nobody Home,* the first of the Princess musicals that Guy would write with Jerome Kern, four years later, would be transplanted from London to New York. And, although the interiors of some of Guy's later plays would be wanting, the curtain lines would be unfailingly brilliant, punctuations that were pauses for the interior scene endings, tantalizing tags for preliminary act endings, and full stops for finales. Every career has a pattern to it, and Guy's seems to have established itself slightly before his first public theatre credit.

In 1904, Plum was hopelessly, abidingly smitten by the London theatre. So, when Owen Hall, an actor/manager, came to him one December day and, on the strength of his verse in *Punch,* asked him to write an extra lyric for a Frank Curzon musical with music by Elizabeth Frederika Lehmann called *Sergeant Brue,* he accepted with alacrity.

When the show opened on December 10 at the Strand, Plum was in the audience. The song, "Put Me in My Little Cell," with its distinctly Wodehousian rhymes and reasons — "There are pleasant little spots my heart is fixed on,/ Down at Parkhurst or at Portland on the Sea,/ And some put up at Holloway and Brixton,/ But Pentonville is good enough for me" — was a huge success.

Plum went back the following Monday night and noted in his diary, "Encored both times. Audience laughed several times during each verse. This is fame."[5]

It was money, too. Hall paid him five guineas, the equivalent of a week's wages on the *Globe.*

Life was exhilerating. "On this, the 13th of December, 1904, time 12 P.M., I set down that I have *arrived,*" he enthused. "Letter from Cosmo Hamilton congratulating me on my work and promising commission to write lyrics for his next piece. . . ."[6]

The commission didn't arrive, at least not immediately. Plum turned his talents back to writing short stories for the *Strand,* sending off comic verses to *Vanity Fair,* and churning out yet another school book, *The Head of Kay's.*

Several months went by without a syllable from Cosmo Hamilton. Pity. He'd thought the theatre was crying for his talents.

It would, very shortly. And the messenger bearing the cries would be none other than Jerry Kern's London benefactor, Seymour Hicks.

After doing three interpolations for Frohman and Hicks's *The Catch of the Season,* Jerry returned to New York and T. B. Harms. There, an old schoolmate, Edward Laska, found him wearing — according to Laska's later memory — a straw hat with no top and drawing — again according to Laska — on an unlit cigar. Bizarre as it seems, it could have been Jerry in one of his antic moments. No one liked a practical joke or an eccentric situation more than Jerry. He would gain as much fame among his friends for his practical jokes as he would in the world for his melodies.

Laska had a lyric that played around with the currently popular word "spoon." He asked Jerry if he could do anything with it. Jerry could and did, immediately.

The two went off to see Laska's producer and were told to cool their heels. When two other later arrivals were ushered in ahead of them, Jerry erupted, grabbed Laska, and headed for Charles Frohman's office.

Although Frohman was out, his assistant, Alf Hayman, agreed to listen to their song. He liked the melody but not the lyric. Laska, eager to please, said he'd rewrite it.

Once more, Jerry pulled him aside. "The hell you will," he whispered. "We don't make changes for assistants."

Once more they stormed out and within a few minutes stormed into the Shubert office.

"We want to see Lee Shubert," announced Jerry in his most charming and assertive voice, adding untruly, "we're protégés of Reginald De Koven."

Jerry knew that Lee Shubert had just produced a successful De Koven show, and, sure enough, the ruse worked. They were ushered into the office of one of the most difficult-to-see producers on Broadway, a man noted for the multiple calluses on his heart.

The two broke through more than that office's guardian-secretaries that afternoon. Shubert liked both music and lyrics and agreed to insert the song into a new Eddie Foy show that was currently in rehearsal. The show was none other than Seymour Hicks's *The Earl and the Girl.*

The song, "How'd You Like to Spoon with Me?," became a hit, and on the strength of this, the Shuberts asked Jerry to write another interpolation in yet another Seymour Hicks production, this time with a slightly—very slightly—different title, *The Babes and the Baron.*[7]

Right after *this* show opened, Jerry left again for England, this time to fulfill his contract with Frohman and Hicks and to interpolate three songs into the Herbert Haines score of their latest venture, *The Beauty of Bath.* The time hadn't quite arrived for Jerry to write a main score. When that time came, conceivably because of his early experience as a supplier of the best songs in somebody else's score, he would allow no interpolaters.


It had been so long since he'd heard from Cosmo Hamilton, his only contact on the West End, that Plum was stunned when he received a note from Seymour Hicks to report to the Aldwych Theatre. On the recommendation of Hamilton, he was to begin work supplying lyrics to shows that Hicks and Charles Frohman were about to produce. The pay would be two pounds a week, and Plum could begin work immediately on a show that was to open on March 19: *The Beauty of Bath.*

Fetching his old chum Westbrook, Plum went off to the Aldwych that February afternoon. "Need a bit of support for this," he explained to Westbrook nervously, as they neared the theatre. "Hope it isn't an inconvenience."

Inconvenience? To meet Seymour Hicks? Was Plum crazy?

Hicks, looking and acting like an Edwardian Noel Coward, greeted them at the stage door.

"Young American composer I want you to meet," he said. "You'll be working with him. Need three songs. Think you can do it?"

Before Plum could even nod, Hicks turned and bid the two speechless men follow him.

They entered the stage area, and there, in a small circle of light, his shirt sleeves rolled up, a possibly winning poker hand consuming his attention, his curly hair catching the light, sat Jerome David Kern.

And so, two-thirds of the trio that would eventually write theatre history met and began to work. They produced three songs, but only one of them, "Oh, Mr. Chamberlain!" (which took a satirical swipe at British politician Joseph Chamberlain, noted at the time for his protective-tariff policies), was a success. When the show opened, on March 19, the song received six encores, much laughter, and a great deal of space in the press.

That afternoon, then, was a momentous one for Plum, and, in a quieter way, for Jerry, too. Later, Plum would remember the meeting in detail: "When I finally managed to free [Jerome Kern] from the card table and was able to talk to him, I became impressed," he recalled. "Here, I thought, was a young man supremely confident of himself—the kind of person who inspires people to seek him out when a job must be done."8

The contrast between Plum and this self-assured composer became immediately apparent to Westbrook as he and Plum exited from the Aldwych that afternoon. "On leaving the stage door," Westbrook remembered, "Plum was so stunned with joy and excitement that he walked a mile along the Strand without him [sic] knowing where he was or whether he was coming or going."9

He was coming, all right. Into his own, as was Jerry.

It would be ten years before they'd collaborate again, but they wouldn't forget each other in the interim.

# 3

# Curtain Up

## 1906–1914

$B$y 1906, Plum Wodehouse had become enough of a friend of Seymour Hicks and his wife, whose stage name was Ellaline Terriss, to spend blissful holidays with them in the country. There he would absent himself for hours in a small plantation of trees, writing.

Spurred on by his success in the theatre, Plum now put his powers of self and outer observation to work and graduated from books about boys to books about semiadults.

With the money he made, he bought Seymour Hicks's car, a splendid Darracq. It was just the transportation for an up-and-coming writer, and on November 17, 1906, Plum penned in his diary, "Bought a motor for 450 pounds from Seymour Hicks. Lord help me!"[1]

He needed at least that much support, apparently. After only one hasty lesson from the producer, Plum set out by himself for Emsworth, ended up in a hedge, walked away from the car, took a train to London, and drove neither his Darracq nor any other car ever again.

The accident damaged neither the automobile nor the friendship; when Hicks

32

took *The Beauty of Bath* from the Aldwych to his own Hicks Theatre in December, he brought Plum along as his chief lyricist.

In 1906 Jerry met important people who would make a difference in his life. Backstage at *The Beauty of Bath,* he was introduced not only to Plum Wodehouse but to the diminutive and dapper director Edward "Teddy" Royce—who would ultimately direct a huge handful of Kern shows—and George Grossmith, Jr., a multiple-threat talent. Before rehearsals of that show were over, Grossmith and Jerry would write a little march called "Rosalie," which would find its way into two New York shows before the season was over—Grossmith's own *The Spring Chicken* and, with reworked lyrics by Harry B. Smith, Charles Frohman's *The Laughing Husband.*

The young composer was now in demand on both sides of the Atlantic. Interpolation, he found, carried with it a six-thousand-mile commute.

By the end of August, he had written three songs for Frohman's New York production of a London hit, *The Little Cherub.* Only one song, "Meet Me at Twilight," survived the tryout tour.

There were three lyricists working on the show, but Jerry was taken by the work of only one of them. A cigar-chomping, rotund, former press agent, he talked with a Manchester accent and wrote the kind of lyrics Jerry liked. In 1906, he was known as Michael Elder Rourke. When Jerry next worked with him at the Princess Theatre in 1914, he would be known as Herbert Reynolds.

The 1906–7 season spun dizzily on. For the Shuberts, Jerry interpolated one song into *Lady Madcap,* a—what else?—English musical. His professional life wasn't entirely a garden of delights. *The White Chrysanthemum* and *The Orchid* both closed out of town, burying his contributions.

No matter. *Fascinating Flora,* a musical with a predictable story about a raving beauty who is torn between saving a dull marriage and setting out on a career in grand opera contained almost a dozen of his songs and two of his lyrics.

The lyrics were to music by Fred Fisher, a prolific and popular composer of, among many songs, "Come Josephine in My Flying Machine," "Peg O' My Heart," and "Chicago." Kern and Fisher wrote two songs together, "I'd Like to Make a Smash Hit 'Mit You" and "Right Now." Neither are likely to be preserved in the Kern canon, as the chorus to "Right Now" attests:

Sweet love like honey,
Always needs a spoon, dear,
And the time for spooning is now.
Right now.
Don't tell me "Not yet, honey, but soon, dear,"
Not tomorrow, not day after,
But now.[2]

The two would never collaborate again, and the next time they met would be in a courtroom, on opposite sides of a lawsuit.

If Jerry's lyrics for *Fascinating Flora* were eminently forgettable, his music was not, and that music made a lasting impression upon one of the producers of the show: a young, eager, smiling, nervous newcomer from Buffalo named Ray Comstock. He would figure in the later life of Jerry, too, in an important way.

In the early winter of 1907, Plum wrote on in Threepwood and created his second most lovable character, Psmith ("The 'P' is silent, as in pshrimp").[3] Published in a magazine called *The Captain,* it did nothing to diminish either his literary standing or his bank account.

The next project did. That same year, Plum let his better judgment out for an airing and collaborated with Herbert Westbrook on a Wilkie Collins-type tale titled *Not George Washington.* A thinly disguised double autobiography, it will never rank in the forefront of Plum's work. But its most interesting effect was to throw the two together for another, *theatrical* collaboration, this time with the sister of Baldwin King-Hall, the owner of Emsworth House.

It was no better than *Not George Washington.* Plum summed it all up in his diary entry of November 11, 1907: "'The Bandit's Daughter,' a musical sketch by Herbert Westbrook *and* P. G. Wodehouse, music by Ella King-Hall, produced at the Bedford Music Hall, Camden Town. A frost!"[4]

Whether this first theatrical venture not under the auspices of Seymour Hicks had anything to do with Plum's parting from the producer is a mystery. He did leave his first theatrical mentor, though, in December 1907 and joined the Gaiety Theatre as resident lyricist.

The year 1907 began well enough for Jerry. He published five of his songs, and his interpolations dotted Broadway like running lights. He had a few here with Frohman, a few there with the Shuberts, and a couple with Klaw and Erlanger.

Then, in October, Colonel Henry Savage imported Franz Lehar's *The Merry Widow* to the Great White Way, and suddenly, standards for songwriters on Broadway soared. The limited-range, almost spoken melodies that character-ized British musical theatre gave way to full range, sustained melody lines. The new trend didn't bother Jerry. He could write both. He could write just about anything and had, ever since high school.

And then tragedy struck, as it often does, in multiple blows.

On December 30, his mother was rushed to Saint Barnabas Hospital in Newark. The next day, she died of gastric dilatation and peritonitis. From that date forward, Jerry would refuse to celebrate New Year's Eve in any way.

His father, ailing before his mother, was forced to retire from the presidency of Woolf's. That summer he decided to move from their home in Newark to their summer cottage in Spring Lake, New Jersey. Perhaps it made his final months a little more pleasant, perhaps not. Heat broke all records in the East that summer, and Henry died on August 13, 1908, of pernicious anemia and exhaustion.

Jerry's youth had come to an abrupt end.

No record has been left of the impact of his parents' deaths upon him, except for his refusal, for the rest of his life, to accept invitations to New Year's parties. Like the two men with whom he would soon change the face of the American Musical Theatre, he was a private person. Unlike them, his youth had been a secure one, filled with affection and the certainty of a family. With the family gone, he turned to the security of work and the certainty of success.

Jerry and his brothers sold the family property in Newark as quickly as they could, and he moved to an apartment at 107 West 68th Street in Manhattan, close to his friends, his work, and the theatre.

George Grossmith was in town, and the two collaborated on two interpola-tions for Frohman's British *Girls of Gottenberg,* and one of Jerry's five songs in Frohman's American *Fluffy Ruffles,* in which Grossmith also starred.

One of the girls of Gottenberg was a pretty and paralyzingly sensuous little lady named Edith Kelly. Jerry filled in his personal spaces by squiring her to the best night spots in town. She was grateful; he was in love.

Plum made his second voyage to America in May of 1909, taking a single room at a literary gathering place, the Hotel Earle in Greenwich Village. His

American publisher A. E. Baerman found it for him, and Plum would stay there whenever he made his subsequent trips to America, at least until 1914.

Living in the same hotel was ace literary agent Seth Moyle, who became Plum's first American representative. He quickly placed two of Plum's short stories in *Cosmopolitan* and *Collier's.*

Well now, thought Plum. *This* is the place to be, all right. He cabled the *Globe,* resigning forthwith. Westbrook could carry on the tradition.

Actually, Westbrook carried on more than that. He married Ella King-Hall, their collaborator on the disastrous *The Bandit's Daughter.*

Plum stayed on at the Earle, pounding out stories. The first flush faded, then disappeared. By the beginning of 1910, it was apparent that the displaced humorist would have to eat his cable and return to London and the *Globe.*

Coming back to England, he bought Threepwood for 200 pounds, furnished it with one bed, one table, one chair, several dogs, and a typewriter. Back in the bookwriting atmosphere he loved, he produced, first, a batch of short stories for the *Strand,* then *Psmith in the City*—which could have been subtitled *Plum at the Bank*—and *A Gentleman of Leisure,* the seminal and prophetic novel upon which many subsequent ones would be modeled. Set in a Shropshire mansion, it featured, among others, a lovable but dimwitted peer, a formidable aunt, a pretty but also dimwitted girl—and a butler.

But what delighted Plum most about *A Gentleman of Leisure* was that it attracted American producer William A. Brady, who thought it was material that could easily be turned into a theatre piece. In collaboration with playwright John Stapleton, Plum returned to New York and the Hotel Earle and began work on transforming the book into a play.


Jerry was back in England in the spring of 1909. Life was slower here than in America. He had been elated by Julia Sanderson's singing of his interpolations in *Kitty Grey* that winter and depressed by the newspaper stories—and personal confirmation—that Edith Kelly was about to follow the example of other Florodora beauties and become the beautiful consort of a doting millionaire. Edith had picked herself a swell one, none other than Frank Gould. Jerry couldn't fight that.

So, when Lauri de Frece and Tom Reynolds suggested that the three young blades take a boat ride up the Thames, drop in on James Blakely, an actor friend, and then go on to a few pubs in Walton-on-Thames, he accepted.

The best pub in that picturesque village was The Swan, and that was where they headed, to cheer up their American friend, who, by then, needed work as well as bucking up. He had spent his entire inheritance—$30,000—in one year on his faithless Edith.

With all of this in his mind, it seems a little less than believable that he would fall in love at first sight with The Swan's owner's daughter, Eva Leale. Second or third sight, or fourth lager, seems more like it.

Not that she wasn't worth the undivided attentions of this young and rising composer. Sweet of face and retiring of nature, she had unwavering eyes and a warm and winning way, an intelligence that didn't threaten and a bearing that didn't beckon.

Her contrast to the hourglass-figured, seductive affirmation of Edith Kelly couldn't have been lost on Jerry. Nor could the contrast of her personality to his have been lost on her. Enchanting but brash, mercurial in temperament and hedonistic in habit, given to drinking large amounts of lager and sleeping till noon, he was this village girl's opposite in behavior, if not in spirit. Besides, in heels, she was an inch taller than his own five feet six inches.

Nevertheless, six hours later, whether in inebriated excess or emotional certainty, Jerry confided to the astonished Eva Leale that he was going to marry her.

And he did, but not right away. First, he had to convince her that he really *was* a well-known composer. He did this by playing the piano for her and sending her sheet music with his name on it, circled.

Then, he had to get past her formidable father, who opened all of her mail. Jerry succeeded by being his own charming self—and inserting secret notes within his letters.

Finally, he had to convince her that he had enough money to marry her. He did this by sending her a cable. No one had ever sent her a cable before.

All of this occupied the spring and summer of 1909. In early September, Jerry sailed for America, where he again turned to interpolations. One of the Frohman shows for which he supplied songs was *The Echo,* coproduced by the man who would ultimately produce most of Jerry's later shows, Charles Dillingham.

It wasn't until October of 1910 that he returned to England and Eva. Asking her father in the most proper British way for her hand, Jerry realized yet another driving desire. He and Eva were married on October 25, 1910, in a small parish church near Walton.

They returned to New York, a city that momentarily dazzled Eva. But she was as game as Jerry. Skirting the resistance of his maid, she quickly established herself as the head of his household and the holder of his deepest and gentlest affections.[5]

The world of musical Broadway was still a world of operetta in the 1910–11 season; the waltzes and the harmonies and the plot complications of *The Merry Widow* still echoed in the ears of producers and audiences. Victor Herbert's *Naughty Marietta,* Karl Hoschna's *Madame Sherry,* Ivan Caryll's *The Pink Lady,* written by Americans, might just as easily have come from someplace in Middle Europe.

Opulence was the operative word. Ninety-member choruses, forty-piece orchestras, five-act operettas. That was what audiences wanted, and that was what the producers gave them.

When the Shuberts decided to open their new theatre, the Winter Garden, they planned a gala, triple bill consisting of a ballet, a one-act opera, and a revue.

And the composer they picked to write the bulk of the score of the revue was Jerome Kern. It was his biggest assignment since *Mr. Wix of Wickham,* seven years earlier.

The revue and the show in which it rested opened on March 20, 1911. Titled *La Belle Paree* and listed in the program as "A Jumble of Jollity in Two Acts and Eleven Scenes," it contained the largest amount of music by Jerome Kern in one show yet to appear on Broadway.

Toward the end of the program, a young singer who had just graduated from Dockstader's Minstrels joined a blackface maid, played by Stella Mayhew, to belt out a Kern tune called "Paris Is a Paradise for Coons." After opening night, the song was moved toward the beginning of the program and reprised, largely because of the hysterical audience response to the delivery by the young singer, whose name was Al Jolson.

When, in 1911, Guy Bolton and Douglas Wood settled down to work on their play at the Thirty-ninth Street Theatre, they found themselves in medias res and in heady company besides. Colonel Henry W. Savage was the resident and roaring producer, but other producers who knew and had worked with Wood stopped by.

David Belasco, of the ministerial garb and flowing locks and melodramatic posture, who was devoted to "art" as long as he could understand it, dropped in. Ray Comstock and Morrie Gest, who were managing Bert Williams and George Walker, the two leading black comedians of the time, and who owned a raft of out-of-town theatres, looked in as they were looking around for their own New York house.

In 1911, attending the theatre was a social occasion, and those who were wealthiest loved to attend special benefit performances that only they could afford. To see and be seen was the purpose of these affairs, and one of the brightest of the Friday afternoon soirees was the annual benefit for the Bide-A-Wee Society for stray cats and dogs.

The ladies of the committee, among them Mrs. Stuyvesant Fish, Mrs. George J. Gould, Mrs. Orme Wilson, and Mrs. John Jacob Astor, assisted by Mrs. William Saeke Hofstra and Mrs. Ulysses S. Grant, were honored this year to have not only Douglas J. Wood as star and director of a brand new play he had written with a dashing, brown-eyed but unknown young man, but Wood's famous mother, Mrs. Ida Jeffreys-Goodfriend, playing an important role.

And so, on Friday afternoon, November 17, 1911, at 2:30 P.M., the curtain rose on *The Drone,* a modern comedy by Douglas J. Wood and Guy Bolton, presented for the very first—and mercifully last—time on any stage.

It was a play without an identity. Called a comedy, it had enough melodrama in it to keep generations of actors playing lecherous landlords and actresses portraying gentle heroines employed for a century of seasons. Its title, *The Drone,* was apt; the characters never said in two words what they could say in twenty.

The ladies, however, loved it. They sat rapt while the plot spun around them. Concerned with the fortunes of the Mather family of East Shoreham, Connecticut, and the machinations of the patriarch, George Mather, to cheat the New York and Northern Railroad out of barrels of money by buying up all the land it would have to cross, it creaked forward with ferocious uncertainty.

George, the scurrilous Mather, was offset by N. D. Hollingsworth (played by Wood), a man to be loved by both the audience and George's daughter Margery.

Complications arrived by the freightcarload, but by the final curtain, endearing, youthful idealism won out over aged greed, and the ending left only a few dry eyes in the audience and on the stage.

Departing, having worked his goodness and shown the family the light, Hollingsworth gives Margery a farewell present of a ring. But she has other ideas about the jewelry's significance:

MARGERY:        (*Shyly, as she is about to put on the ring*)
                Would you mind putting it on *this* hand?
                (*A pause*)

| | |
|---|---|
| HOLLINGSWORTH: | (*With a sudden fierce eagerness*) Do you mean—? |
| MARGERY: | Here—on this finger. |
| HOLLINGSWORTH: | Do you mean—you have changed your mind? |
| MARGERY: | I mean—I saw you just now for the first time and—I fell in love at first sight. (*He crushes her in his hands*) |

CURTAIN

The society ladies applauded wildly. As the curtain calls multiplied, Douglas Wood stepped forward and, silencing the audience with two upraised hands, announced in quiet and impressive tones that he could not, in all justice, claim credit for most of the play. The bulk of the writing had been done by his collaborator, Guy Bolton.[6]

Guy loved the applause, the accolades, the blame. Bitten fatally, he decided to give up architecture for a year and devote his time entirely to playwriting.

Julie was overjoyed. Pretty, vivacious, dazzling, and dazzled by the atmosphere of the theatre, she eagerly embraced the new life. It would embrace her, too, in a very short time, in a way she hadn't planned.

Plum, back in London to work and tend to his dogs, didn't get to see the Broadway opening of his *A Gentleman of Leisure* on August 24, 1911, but he *did* catch up with it later when it was touring. He met its leading man, Douglas Fairbanks, Sr., then a young actor who had not yet confounded movie audiences with his surreal swoops across rooftops and dizzying descents down hanging Oriental tapestries.

When the play was revived in Chicago two years later, retitled *Thief for a Night,* it would star another comer, John Barrymore.

The possibility exists that Plum was hurt by Westbrook's marriage to Ella King-Hall, but the evidence is circumstantial and tenuous. Ella was fifteen years older than he and was probably more admired than loved by Plum. But, perhaps feeling left out, he formed an attachment to a widow, Mrs. Lillian Armstrong, in 1909, and went off on weekends and holidays from then until 1914 to spend mysterious and unrecorded times with her and her daughter Bubbles.

In 1912, he wrote *The Prince and Betty,* published in America as a combination crime and love story and in England as merely a love story. (Plum saved the crime part and would publish it in 1915 in England under the title *Psmith Journalist.*)

*The Prince and Betty* contained the first of many love scenes that are odd amalgams of beauty and impossibility: ". . . knowing that there's someone who is fonder of you than anything . . . [is] like strawberries and cream in a new dress by moonlight, on a summer night, while somebody plays the violin far away in the distance so that you can just hear it," he wrote, tenderly and implausibly.

Plum was apparently no more comfortable writing love scenes than he was living them.

Small matter, again. The theatre beckoned once more in the person of Lawrence Grossmith, the brother of lyricist-entertainer George Grossmith, Jr. Lawrence had just inherited three thousand pounds and was willing to squander it on his career. He came to Plum with a request for a long sketch that might be extended into a one-act play.

Plum dug into his bag of stories for the *Strand* and came up with one he and Westbrook had done called "Rallying Round Old George." He turned it into *Brother Alfred,* gave half the credit and his fee to Westbrook, and delivered it to Lawrence Grossmith, who loved it.

The track record of Wodehouse and Westbrook as theatrical collaborators remained unblemished. *Brother Alfred* opened April 8, 1913, at the Savoy and closed after a run of two weeks.

*La Belle Paree,* the revue that contained a sizable smattering of Jerome Kern tunes, rolled happily into the summer of 1911 and then bounced onto the road. Jerry went on to interpolate two songs into Nora Bayes's newest show, *Little Miss Fix-It,* and when Florenz Ziegfeld presented his second annual *Follies* in 1911, Jerry had his first—among many to come—songs in a Ziegfeld production.

In addition, Charles Frohman could always be counted on to provide holes in his productions for Kern interpolations; his American production of the Carl Ziehrer operetta, *The Kiss Waltz,* contained a bounteous bunch, and a half dozen other Frohman ventures that season featured Jerry's work.

But it was the Shubert Brothers who gave Jerry his first main score on Broadway. Originally titled *The Girl and the Miner* ("Girl" shows were just as popular in New York as they had been in London when Plum and Jerry first met), it eventually emerged in Philadelphia as *The Red Petticoat*. The show, a sort of featherbrained cross breeding of *Sweeney Todd* and *The Girl of the Golden West*, gathered mixed reviews from the New York critics. It closed after sixty-one performances.

But, success or failure, it was a beginning for Jerry. Producers were finally willing to give the kid with the curly hair and the glasses a chance to score his own show.

Julie and Guy moved to a larger apartment at 348 Central Park West in the middle of 1912. With two children and a budding playwright in residence, they needed space.

Their world widened. Guy plunged into his earliest theatrical efforts with the energy that youth, a disregard for consequences and a bravado bred of blindness could give. He and Julie went to the theatre as often as they could and met a multitude of theatrical figures.

Guy wasn't immune to the fact that there were beautiful women both backstage and onstage. With casts that numbered in the nineties, operettas and musicals employed girls galore. Guy's Edwardian demeanor and a habit he had of locking solely into whomever was with him won the heart and body of more than one young chorine.

And Julie, thrown into this glamorous world where reality was not always the rule but happy endings usually were, let her eyes rove until they rested on a tall, marvelously constructed and seductive British playwright, author of, among other like works, "The Blindness of Virtue."

His name was Cosmo Hamilton.

Plum had had a chum on the *Globe* in 1907 named Charles Bovill. That same year, Bovill had written some lyrics for *The Gay Gordons*. Now he had been commissioned to write a revue for the Empire Theatre.

He asked Plum to come along on the job. It would be an ideal opportunity to leave the horrible old hotel into which the humorist and his dogs had moved after selling Threepwood, which had turned into a financial burden. Bovill suggested that Plum move into *his* posh and roomy and conducive-to-collaboration flat in Prince of Wales Mansions, Battersea.

And so the two collaborated, not only on the revue but on a series of sketches. *Nuts and Wine,* as the revue was called, opened to warm notices at the Empire on

January 4, 1914; the series of sketches began publication in the *Strand* in London and the *Delineator* in America.

On the 23d of the same month, *The Man Upstairs,* a collection of Plum's short stories, was published. He felt secure enough to take time out for another trip to America.

For Jerry, it was back to interpolations, temporarily. He loved to drop in on Billie Burke, who was readying Arthur Wing Pinero's *The Amazons* for an April opening. "He'd . . . sit at a small piano in the wings," the future Mrs. Ziegfeld would later write, "strumming a special arrangement which sounded like mandolin music while Shelley Hull pretended to play on stage and while I sang."[7]

Frohman let him in on Leo Fall's *The Doll Girl,* which eventually opened in August with more Kern than Fall tunes, and no credit in the program for Jerry.

Jerry, however, was not about to let this go unnoticed. If he didn't get credit in the program, he'd get it in the press. A few calls to a few columnists produced a deluge of interviews with Jerry carrying such titles as "Native Song Writer Gives Foreign Composers' Scores New Brilliancy" and "New Maker of Melodies Talks About His Trade."

The last article, appearing in the New York *World,* was a brilliant, if slightly blind, rationale for interpolation. The reasons, Jerry explained, that imported musicals needed reworking in New York were twofold:

First, he posited, no one of any importance in London arrived at the theatre until the play was an hour old. So, the first hour in most European operettas consisted of throwaway material that had to be jettisoned to satisfy New York audiences.

Jerry neglected to notice—at least in print—that New York musicals were built the same way for the same reason. Overtures were endless, with countless first and second endings. Forty years later, Guy would explain to director Clinton Anderson that *Oh, Lady! Lady!!,* the last of the trio's shows for the Princess, was written with a long opening chorus ". . . to take care of late comers."[8]

Jerry's second reason was equally tenuous. In German theatre particularly, he noted, the leading ladies were prima donnas who could sing difficult melody lines, whereas Broadway stars usually couldn't. A quick listen down the street to a Victor Herbert operetta would have drowned out that particular argument.

It wasn't until later in the article that Jerry revealed his role in writing most of the music of *The Doll Girl*. He made certain that readers of the piece knew what the show's program didn't tell them. After all, anonymity was not a posture that Jerome Kern was willing to abide for very long. Nor would he have to. *The Doll Girl*'s libretto had been written by the musical theatre's most prolific book writer, Harry B. Smith. Before he died in 1936, Smith would write the books for 123 musicals and supply the lyrics for several thousand songs. His voice wasn't a small one, and he liked Jerry's music.

Furthermore, he liked Jerry. And Jerry liked him. Smith collected rare stamps. Very well, Jerry began a collection of rare books that would remain his abiding and sometimes obsessive hobby for the rest of his life. Smith's wife, Irene, once a prima donna, appreciated the inventiveness of Jerry's tunes. Jerry loved her immediately.

With Eva, they became a friendly foursome.



Cosmo Gordon Hamilton—the very same Cosmo Hamilton who had written the libretto of *The Beauty of Bath*—was not only a renowned playwright in 1913; he was an activist for sexual freedom. In England and in America, he had toured as a lecturer advocating the teaching of sex-hygiene to children, a subject about as popular in the provinces that year as war.

His views on sexual freedom extended, logically enough, to the institution of marriage. He wrote, fearlessly, "The American woman never marries for love. The self-supporting American woman never marries at all. Or if she does marry, she never has any children."[9]

That kind of sentiment outrages some women and excites others. Julie apparently was affected in the latter way. Once she met and got to know Cosmo Hamilton, she realized that his opinions regarding sexual mores were not confined to the printed page.

Guy confronted her. The young and ambitious playwright regarded himself as sophisticated and sexually liberated, but, as was the case with many men in 1913, this particular freedom of expression was reserved for husbands, not wives. He was aware of Julie's meetings with Cosmo Hamilton, and he wanted them to end.

Julie defied him and continued to see Hamilton. What had occurred between the Englishman and her was too exciting to be sordid, too secret to matter that much.

She didn't realize her husband's thoroughness in research, which now expanded into the hiring of a private detective to spy on the clandestine meetings of

Julie and Hamilton. Once he had established that they were having an affair, he moved out of their Manhattan apartment and into the Hotel Gramatan in Bronxville.

Julie wavered, but not a great deal. There were reconciliations and comings and goings, threats and confrontations. The resolution of the conflict could wait, thought Guy, until he finished the first play that would be wholly his.

Ironically, its subject was divorce.


In the summer of 1914, with war rumbling in Europe's backyard, Plum Wodehouse once again boarded a ship for New York. There, he worked out an amicable arrangement with an old friend, Norman Thwaite. Thwaite had an apartment at 43 East Twenty-seventh Street; he worked on the *New York World* until two in the morning and slept for most of the rest of the day.

Plum could write at will, and he needed to. His income had remained about the same, but his spending seemed to have increased. So, he was not at all thrilled when Thwaite proposed a blind date. Besides, Lillian Armstrong was back in England and very much on Plum's mind.

Thwaite persisted, ticking off the virtues that Plum's date possessed: her widowhood, her beauty, her Britishness, and Thwaite's certainty that they were remarkably suited to each other.

He was right. They suited each other just fine—from August 3, 1914, until the day Plum died.

The blind date's name was Ethel Newton Rowley, and she was four years younger than Plum. Born on May 23, 1885, in King's Lynn, she was an only child, reared by her grandmother. She had married, in 1903, at eighteen, Joseph Arthur Leonard Rowley, who was bound for India.

She joined him there, and they had a daughter born on March 12, 1905, whom they named Leonora.

In 1910, Rowley, an engineer, drank contaminated water from a well near a site he was overseeing. He died soon afterward, and Ethel and Leonora returned to England a short time after that.

Ethel didn't wear her widow's weeds overlong. Shortly after arriving in London, she met and married twenty-seven-year-old John Wayman, whose role in her life remained deliberately misty; in fact Ethel was introduced to Plum in 1914 as the Widow Rowley. However, she did eventually tell him— and hardly anyone else—that she and Wayman were married on January 28, 1911, at the St. George's Registry Office, and that he presented himself as a company director, living on Eaton Square, at 47 Chester Terrace (now Chester Row).

That much of the story is verifiable, and it was on Eaton Square that he and Ethel resided in momentary wedlock. Whether he told her before or after their marriage that he was the son of a coachsmith and his illiterate wife, grew up in the poor suburb of Vauxhall, and was not a company director but a worker on the London *Globe*'s "By the Way" column, is unclear.

It couldn't have been the happiest of marriages. Eighteen months after it took place, Wayman was declared bankrupt, and shortly after that, he died. No reason was given in his published obituary.

The mystery of it apparently mattered not at all to the instantly smitten Plum; it was Ethel's present, not her past, that fascinated him. The reserve and embarrassment that had until then distanced the retiring author from others seemed to melt away before Ethel's commanding presence.

Perhaps it was this presence; perhaps it was the fact that she was not particularly attractive; perhaps it was her zest for life and a wonderful way she had of putting everything in its proper place at its proper time and seeing that it stayed there that demolished Plum's defenses and made life without her unthinkable.

At any rate, life in New York that summer became, for Plum, days spent with Ethel, evenings spent with his writing apparatus, and an occasional hello or goodbye to Thwaite. The two lovers passed the time at Long Beach, Long Island, swimming, commuting there and back on the Long Island Railroad— even then a test of the strength of a romantic mood. Within two months, they had decided to marry.

Plum had only $100 in the bank on September 30, 1914, when he and Ethel walked up the aisle of the Little Church Around the Corner, off Madison Avenue on Twenty-ninth Street. The minister, late to the ceremony because he had just made a killing on the stock market, was richer in capital, but not in genius or joy that day.

Soon after the ceremony, the newlyweds moved into a small bungalow in Bellport, Long Island, a spot Plum, in his excursions on the LIRR, had found compatible with his taste for isolation and beauty.

"The typical Wodehouse heroine changed after Plum got married," notes Frances Donaldson. "She put on more flesh and blood. She was no longer someone who believed that to be in love was to live on a perpetual diet of strawberries and cream, eaten to the sound of soft music; sometimes she even behaved in the manner of real life."

Shortly after the marriage, Plum's fortunes changed for the better when he was hired by *Vanity Fair,* the smartest magazine in New York. He was soon writing most of the magazine, under various pseudonyms.

In 1914, and forever thereafter, Plum had great resilience and patience, enduring without comment the long and tedious ride from the country to the city on the Long Island Railroad. But Ethel found the tiny, gingerbread town of Bellport confining. She was naturally gregarious, loved the parties that Plum loathed, and so convinced him that they needed an apartment in New York as well as the bungalow in Bellport. They found one, at 375 Central Park West, which provided the basis for Plum's *nom de magazine,* C. P. West.

Life had turned from frost to bliss. And it would get better, because of the decision by *Vanity Fair* editor Frank Crowninshield to make Plum the magazine's drama critic.

Jerry did some more anonymous interpolations for Charles Frohman in the fall of 1913, but with very little joy. His sights were set on a project of the Shubert Brothers, a French farce, adapted musically, to be called *Oh, I Say!* Once again, Jerry would do the main score, and Harry B. Smith the lyrics.

*Oh, I Say!* flopped. "A farce with musical interruptions" was one critic's opinion, followed by no notice at all of Jerry's music.[10]

The show left New York and went on the road with a changed identity, but even the titillating title *Their Wedding Night* couldn't draw audiences.

The idea for *The Rule of Three,* Guy's first solo comedy, came from his notebooks: seven years before, he had read a review by Alan Dale, Jerry Kern's champion, of the French playwright Sardou's *La Piste,* produced in New York as *The Love Letter.*

Dale was delighted with divorce as a topic for farce, and wondered, ". . . how on earth it is that our numerous dramatists can sit still and let a foreigner positively crowd them to death on this divorce topic. What more prolific and teeming subject is there than that of American divorce, and why, why should it be a Frenchman who sees it first?" So, Guy dipped into Sardou (both *La Piste* and *Divorcona*) and composed *The Rule of Three.*

In his room in Bronxville, he worked without relief, establishing the six- and seven-day, eight-hour-a-day writing schedule to which he would adhere for the rest of his life.

The affair between Julie and Cosmo Hamilton now acquired epic and public proportions. Guy wrote on, and bitterness crept into the play, along with a certain raciness difficult to discern today.

Guy readied *The Rule of Three* at the end of 1913 and delivered it to the producers, Douglas J. Wood and Henry Savage, who read it, approved, and introduced Guy to a man by the name of Bickerton. Bickerton headed a young and adventurous company called the New Era Producing Company. He and Guy worked on shaping the farce about divorce, which would be the company's second production, into shape for an audience.

On Monday, February 16, 1914—a snowy evening that, combined with a transit strike, was hardly a night for theatregoing—*The Rule of Three* opened at the Harris Theatre, on 42nd Street, west of Broadway.

The sprightliness of the Vermont hotel in which Guy had set his comedy thawed semifrozen spirits that night. The goings on were the stuff of French farce—couples changing partners; a woman who has been married three times and who has a daughter who is delighted that her father, papa, and daddy are all in the hotel at the same time; and a matchmaker who manipulates everybody into a happy ending.

Sardou had done that already. What Guy did was to spice it with bright lines and funny situations. He allowed his characters in the beginning of the play to utter aphorisms from the books of quaint sayings he maintained in his library until the end of his life. Such gems as "Woman purposes—but man proposes" or "Marriage is the net in which the jade snares the jaded" were dotted copiously through the evening, enough so for him to allow his matchmaker to ultimately counter, "My dear . . . my appetite for cynical aphorisms is limited."

"I made those up while I was taking my last night's tub," splutters the quotations spouter.

"That makes it all the worse," adds Mrs. Flower, the matchmaker. "It's both indecent and neglectful to think of anything but soap under those circumstances."

The evening was full of stage tricks and sight gags salted with slapstick, such as a device Mrs. Flower uses to quiet her opponent: a combination chewing gum, molasses, and glue that makes talking impossible. Guy liked this invention so much he lifted it intact and used it in two later plays.

It all added up to an evening of moderately mindless fun, and when the final curtain fell and the curtain calls ended, the cries of "Author!" rose from the audience. No author came forward. Instead, Will Archer, a former Weber and Fields comedian who played a meddling bellhop, ran on, crying, "Mr. Guy Bolton! Author! Mr. Guy Bolton!"

No one appeared.

Archer turned to the audience. "Guess he ain't here," he mused and then added, "Well, anyway, I'd like to express my appreciation for the author's appreciation of the audiences's appreciation."[11]

If ever spontaneous lines sounded written, they were these, and it may be that Guy, once again clinging to an indentation that would hide him from possible rejection, wrote them for Archer, just in case.

The next morning, the reviews were kind. The *Sun* called it amateurish (it was) and the *Journal* pronounced it ". . . a bright and amusing farce of the quiet kind . . ." (it was) and lauded Guy for being ". . . clever in construction, funny in situation and bright in lines" (he was).

This, plus the daring arrangement of the "Rule of Three [Marriages]," plus the supposedly risqué lines, buoyed sales at the box office and filled the gossip columns, making Guy a spokesman for modern living styles.

It was a case of art imitating life imitating art. Once the play was safely set, Guy turned his attention to his wife and that other advocate of modern thought, Cosmo Hamilton. He set up a nocturnal raid on the couple. This tacky practice of catching adulterating adults *in flagrante delicto* was a humiliating necessity, since the only grounds for divorce in New York State in those days were adultery.

Hamilton, caught in the net of his own advocacy, made immediate plans to leave for London. In late November 1914, Justice Isaac N. Mills, sitting in Supreme Court in Mount Vernon, signed a final divorce decree, awarding young Joanie to Julie and Dickie to Guy.

Guy moved back into the Central Park West apartment; Julie, with Joanie, left on a boat for England to join Cosmo Hamilton. And from that day forward, until the day she died, in 1967, Joanie would never call Guy "Father."

He stayed restlessly on in New York, trying out ideas, basking in his new notoriety, tasting his freedom by frequenting the stage doors of various musicals with voluminous and voluptuous choruses.

While this was happening, the relationship between Dickie and his father deteriorated. In July, Guy sailed with him to England. There, he turned his son over to Julie, who was now married to Cosmo Hamilton.

When Guy excised Julie from his life, he also excised his affection and responsibility for the children. In 1914, there was only room for work in his life, and he would find success in two ways: first, in an answer to a letter he mailed from the Hotel Russell in London in July and, second, in the person of a young composer with whom he would write his first musical comedy libretto at the end of that same year.

*Chapter*

# 4

# Opening Chorus
## 1914–1915

What was most important in show business, Jerry Kern realized early on, was keeping your name before the managers and the public. When, in 1914, Charles Frohman asked Jerry to contribute some songs to flesh out the Paul Rubens score for *The Girl from Utah,* he demanded billing. When the producer agreed to take it under advisement, Jerry and Eva sailed off on a European holiday. Rehearsals wouldn't begin until July. Interpolations were never needed until the last minute. They could spend the early summer of 1914 in Europe.

When Guy went to England in the summer of 1914 to gather his thoughts, to find in the peace of Deal what he couldn't find in the shards of his shattered marriage, he took along a suitcase full of reading material. Most of it consisted of plays, among them *Nowadays* by George Middleton.

Middleton was an experienced playwright and writer. By 1914, he had had nine plays produced. All of them were of high literary quality, and none of them had been a success.

A tall, scholarly-looking, gentle man who took to wearing pince-nez that made him seem more severe than he really was, Middleton was four years older than Guy. Born in Paterson, New Jersey, he was married to the daughter of Michigan's liberal governor William La Follette. Fola Middleton was a charismatic and colorful woman who was decades ahead of her contemporaries in her ideas concerning women's rights, and she had been his inspiration and model for the central character of *Nowadays*.

Guy read the play and was intrigued by it. It was clumsily constructed, and the plot was as predictable as the sunrise, but the characters were richly drawn, their conflicts were real and believable, and, most of all, the playwright's ideas regarding modern man and woman were similar to his own. As much as he had objected to the conduct of Julie and Hamilton, Guy had to admit that if they had been characters in a play he had written, they would have behaved exactly as they had behaved.

What he also had to admit was that there were weaknesses in his own playwriting. Sardou had, after all, supplied the characters and the situations for *The Rule of Three. The Drone,* for all its noble purpose, had been populated by people who mattered only to each other. And now, here was George Middleton, who, for all his lack of understanding of what made a scene work on a stage, did know how to create characters who would matter to an audience.

When he arrived in London, Guy took out a piece of hotel stationery, dipped his pen into the inkwell, and wrote the letter that would propel him, in three short years, into the vanguard of American playwriting.

> My Dear Mr. Middleton [he wrote], I want to send you a line to tell you with what pleasure I have just read your Feminist play. It is laid out on a broader plane than anything of the kind— . . . and the able character delineation and the *human charm* [emphasis his] of it lift it well above any possible charge of mere didaction.
>
> It ought to be played. I hope it will be, and I hope that I shall see it. With sincere congratulations,
>
> > Cordially yours,
> > Guy Bolton[1]

The wishes for the play went unrealized. It never saw the light of a leiko, but it became the catalyst for the collaboration of the two writers. And as such, it was probably as important as if it had been produced.

Middleton answered Guy's letter immediately, and the two met in New York shortly after Guy's return. They hit it off instantly. Middleton found Guy warm, frank, and private. Guy found Middleton private, frank, and warm. They were certain they could work together.

But not quite yet.


Jerry and Eva returned to their new apartment at 226 West Seventieth Street at the beginning of July 1914. They would stay there for two years, and the years would be among the most important of Jerry's life.

Restless, tired of being the eternal interpolater, Jerry was ablaze with new ideas. He was noticed in the summer of 1914, but he felt he wasn't well noticed. The time had come for more recognition. And Jerry saw that it happened.

Charles Frohman agreed to give Jerry billing, along with Rubens, for his four-song contribution to *The Girl from Utah*. When the show opened at the Knickerbocker on August 24, a lilting production number, "Same Sort of Girl," became the most instantly popular Kern song. But another number, a quiet, lovely Jerome Kern ballad haunted those who heard it and became, in time, the show's most memorable melody. "They Didn't Believe Me" had, in the words of Alec Wilder, in his definitive study of American popular music, *American Popular Song: The Great Innovators, 1900–1950*, ". . . [a] melodic line [that] is as natural as walking. Yet its form is not conventional even by the standards of that time. . . . I can't conceive how the alteration of a single note could do other than harm the song. It is evocative, tender, strong, shapely. . . ."

There wasn't a cliché in the song. Furthermore, it locked into Herbert Reynolds' lyrics so well, both seemed to be of a piece.

Musicians and composers, realizing this, looked with new eyes at Jerry. Victor Herbert, the acknowledged composer-king of Broadway in 1914, told his fellow members of the newly formed ASCAP, "That man will one day inherit my mantle."[2]

It was enough to make a young composer have faith in himself and his ideas, and these ideas were only a year away from full-blown realization.


The first obstacle to Guy's immediate collaboration with George Middleton was a play of his own called *The Fallen Idol*. He had actually written it right after *The Drone*. Elated by his success with the society ladies, he had plunged into turning out a turgid, overwrought, and overwritten paean to art and love and youth.

Under the title *Suttee* (a Brahman word meaning the sacrifice of a wife on the funeral pyre of her dead husband), the play was given a tryout in May 1913 at another Friday afternoon gathering of the Bide-A-Wee Society. Its reception was considerably less enthusiastic than that given *The Drone.*

But, after six months of rewriting, Guy felt he had a viable script. He and Douglas J. Wood made the rounds of the producers' offices.

Nobody was interested.

Finally, they called on Joe Weber, the rotund half of the great comedy team that had produced *An English Daisy,* the show that had first introduced Jerome Kern's music to Broadway in 1904. Weber and Fields had by now split up and gone into separate production ventures. Fields had always had a clearer head than Weber and so was a better producer by far. But Weber's name and frame loomed large enough to snare coproducers like Ziegfeld, who taught him how to mount a show, if not how to choose one.

Weber was looking for prestige material. With the same blind eye that was rapidly sapping his reputation and bank account, he welcomed Wood and Bolton, capitulated to their youthful enthusiasm and the obvious fundraising contacts of Wood, and accepted the play for production.

Elated beyond dreams, Guy went home and penciled across his title page "GUY BOLTON'S FIRST PLAY!" (It was actually his third, but it was first in his affections.) He worked lovingly on the script, using his architectural background to sketch scene plots, laboriously penning property plots by hand, coloring in elevations of each set. He would do this only once more—in his first collaboration with George Middleton. After that, he relinquished the foothold he still had in architecture.

The play went into rehearsal. Maybe, if something more monumental hadn't occurred that fall of 1914, it might have succeeded, though a reading of the script does nothing to support this idea.

The distraction that sidetracked the salvation of *A Fallen Idol* was musical, and music to Guy's ears.


Charles Frohman was no music critic, but he was no fool, either. If Victor Herbert thought so highly of Jerry, he could, too. He gave Jerry another main score.

He and Klaw and Erlanger had plans to follow *The Girl from Utah* at the Knickerbocker, which the triumvirate had just bought, with a new musical fashioned for the talents of Marie Cahill, a corpulent comedienne who resembled a female Joe Weber, and Richard Carle, the scarecrow British comedian who delivered his lines through his adenoids.

Jerry knew Carle; he had sung a Jerome Kern interpolation in *The Spring Chicken.* Jerry knew *of* Marie Cahill. She had a reputation for laying waste to the shows in which she starred and dragging in any old interpolation by any old interpolater that struck her fancy. In 1904, in an operetta called *It Happened in Nordland,* she had engaged in a wild confrontation with Victor Herbert over just such an outrage.

The prospects of another star-composer confrontation seemed more than merely possible. But Jerry had people he could depend on at his side. Frohman was there, although he was only coproducing this show with Klaw, Erlanger, and Daniel V. Arthur, Marie Cahill's husband. Harry B. Smith was writing the lyrics. They hadn't hired a librettist yet, but that was unimportant. The songs and the plots in 1914 musicals seldom matched, anyway.


Soon after Guy's successful farce, *The Rule of Three* opened, Marie Cahill and her husband went to see it. They'd read the gossip columns about its racy lines and situations; they'd heard how bright and clever the writing was; they hoped that the accolades were partially true and that its young playwright would be just as eager to please as the composer they'd hired, and probably as inexpensive, and certainly less proud of himself.

What they saw and heard that evening they liked.

Within a week they'd engaged Guy Bolton to write the libretto for *Ninety in the Shade,* as their new musical was now titled.

He was new and untried and had only seen operettas. Youth and bad examples convinced him he could do as well as that and probably better. Still, he was only three years into playwriting, with only one play produced, and he would be working with some of the most formidable talents of the day. His hand must have shaken, even slightly, as he signed.

In early November 1914, nine years after P. G. Wodehouse met Jerome Kern backstage at the Aldwych, Guy Bolton shook hands with Jerome Kern backstage at the Knickerbocker. They were the same height, Guy noted in his diary.[3] They could look at each other eye to eye.

But would they *see* eye to eye? Jerry was surrounded by the producers and the stars. Guy stood by himself. Not in years had he stood quite so completely by himself.

The young composer drew closer to him and suggested they go off by themselves to talk. That afternoon, they exchanged ideas and forged a partnership. They were men of few words but much energy. One was a genius; the other appreciated genius. Both instinctively knew what worked on a stage before an audience. The two took to each other, in mutual trust and agreement.

Guy had conferences with Cahill and Carle, with the producers, with the director, a young man named Robert Milton, and with the dance designer, Julian Alfred. And Jerry prepared him for each new step.

The show progressed by pieces. Guy delivered an outline. Jerry decided where the music should go. Cahill argued. Julian Alfred decided where the dances should go. Cahill argued. The set and costume designers took over. Cahill argued with them.

It was much more exciting for Guy than *The Fallen Idol,* which was beginning to fall both apart and by the wayside. It must have seemed ironic to Joe Weber, one of the clown princes of the musical stage in the nineteenth century, to see that his primary venture into serious drama was being diluted by its author's involvement with — of all things — the musical stage.

Working with Jerry and Harry Smith — and even that screaming tyrant Marie Cahill — kept Guy's adrenaline pumping. More than that, he had ample opportunity to test his instincts. He easily picked up on Cahill and Carle's strengths and wrote for them. He became aware of their weaknesses and avoided them. He realized, sometimes before Jerry did, where a song was needed.

Later, in an article printed in the *New York American,* Guy would recall that his method of placing songs was simple: "I counted back," he said, "to the last song, and then counted forward to the next one."

Of course it wasn't that simple, and both Jerry and Guy knew it. Guy's natural theatrical savvy, which would assert itself most often when he was writing musicals and least often when he was writing plays — was at work in a nascent form.

There was also, for both young men, an added dimension of shared adventure and experiment. Even at this early date, according to Guy's recollection, Jerry was concerned with an effort to inject verisimilitude into a musical. It's possible that he saw, in the uniting of his talent to that of a young, theatrically unblemished and malleable playwright like Guy, a golden opportunity to test the feasibility of interrelating music, lyrics, and libretto, of fusing the music into the show, rather than tacking it onto it.

Whatever the motivation, it worked, on both a business and a personal level. From the very first, Guy liked Jerry. His experience and self-assurance went beyond his years. Guy needed that confidence now.

And he liked Jerry's songs. Guy knew little about music, but he did know talent. He knew that the melodies that poured so effortlessly from Jerry had substance as well as charm, much like the man himself.

Guy watched and learned. Jerry studied his music's effect on the cast, on anyone who listened to it. "You never know what effect a melody will have until you try it on an audience," Guy remembered Jerry telling him. "Or a lyric. A lyric that reads well doesn't always play well."[4]

When the cast and crew of *Ninety in the Shade* entrained for Syracuse, on Monday, December 28, 1914, Guy wasn't aboard. He was forced by an impending opening to stay behind with *The Fallen Idol.* But when *Ninety in the Shade* opened at Syracuse's Empire Theatre a few days later, on New Year's Eve, he was there, basking in the applause, the music, the favorable reviews, and the hysteria afterward.

Cahill and Carle were expected by their audiences to do a spoof a night. *Ninety in the Shade,* on its opening night out of town, had no spoof, and the two expected it by the end of the Syracuse engagement. So, Guy wrote "The Triangle," a send-up of the modern problem play for the two stars. It had nothing whatsoever to do with the already complicated plot of *Ninety in the Shade.* But, placed before an expectant audience, it worked.

Nevertheless, Jerry's sense of verisimilitude was offended by it as it originally stood. The longer they stayed in Syracuse, he muttered to Guy, the more the musical began to resemble standard operetta. Material flew in and out with no more motivation than the whims of the stars. Rather than merely accepting the illogical insertion of a routine from nowhere, the two constructed a musical bridge which spanned the space between story and specialty. Guy paved it with his first lyric, and as the lyric faded into the routine, Jerry carried the melody under "The Triangle" as a waltz underscoring.

And that worked, too.

Everything, however, didn't. On the morning of opening night in Syracuse, Jerry handed Marie Cahill a new song, "All That I Want," and by that night she still hadn't learned all of its lyrics. And she never had to. The song was sliced from the show in Syracuse.

"The Comic Side," a burlesque of the Mexican War by six chorus boys, was a sequence everyone thought would be a hilarious hit. It turned out to be a dismal flop and ended up in the Syracuse theatrical graveyard, too.

But "Whistling Dan," an unpretentious number with a catchy Kern melody (he would later reuse it as the title tune of *Leave It to Jane*) which Marie Cahill performed while the girls whistled in the background, was an instant crowd pleaser and critic catcher.

Meanwhile, back at the Comedy Theatre, *The Fallen Idol* opened. It had a strong cast. Weber had assembled the best for what would be his worst: veteran actor David Powell played Grebble, a young sculptor; David Bruning, in what one critic described as "a makeup that reminded us of Warfield's von Barwig in *The Music Master,*"[5] did a bravura job with the part of the villainous Victor Valdecinni, a musician; Janet Beecher gracefully underplayed the part of Christine, his American wife (and mistress of the mind but not the body of Grebble); and Marie Chambers, an unknown, was a resounding hit in the comedy part of Mrs. Atwater.

But they were no match for the play, a melange of overwriting and under-characterization. The plot concerned the troubles caused by the marriage of a forty-five-year-old pianist (Valdecinni) who plays and speaks rhapsodies and is the victim of a strange, creeping paralysis that seems to affect everything but his vocal chords, and a twenty-five-year-old American girl (Christine).

Christine is in love with Grebble, a designer of monuments (Guy used his sketches of the Soldiers and Sailors Monument for the play). Valdecinni has an illegitimate son by a Parisian model, and Grebble forfeits his commission for the monument to pay off the model and save Christine from scandal. Christine can't leave Valdecinni because she married him for better or worse, so Valdecinni has a change of character and poisons himself with pills just before the final curtain.

The critics and the audience were colder than the corpse of Valdecinni. Reviewers' reactions varied from a kindly *succès d'estime* to "palpable theatrical trickery" to *Vogue's* devastating but accurate analysis: "The actors are required to deliver polysyllabic periods at moments when living people would express themselves in simple speech. Life itself is more reticent and modest than Mr. Bolton's counterfeit presentment of it."

Guy's intuitiveness about writing to George Middleton was right. He knew that he was skilled at curtain lines and theatrical effects. *The Fallen Idol* had some interesting ones, particularly a double recognition scene that involved the flinging into the fire of a picture of Valdecinni's child. But he was also aware that the only skill he seemed to have with his characters was in letting them chew the scenery into spaghetti.

*The Fallen Idol* expired after nine performances.

Meanwhile, *Ninety in the Shade* seemed to be spinning out of control. Everybody wanted to get into the act and the script.

Clare Kummer, a good playwright and a terrible composer, was brought in by Marie Cahill to provide some interpolated interludes. Jerry looked on in silent fury, while Guy tried his best to open up the story for the interludes. More and more, the tired and tested formulas of operetta found their way into the story and then overwhelmed it, blowing up the bridges that Jerry and Guy built.

On January 25, 1915, two nights after the opening of *The Fallen Idol, Ninety in the Shade* premiered at the Knickerbocker. The reception was not nearly as warm as the title. In fact, the *New York Clipper*, usually a benign welcomer of whimsy, came down hard: "Lack of tuneful melodies, forced comedy, and a mediocre book is the chief reason for its failure to arouse interest. Both stars worked hard on the opening night, but their efforts were in vain, and before the first act had progressed very far the piece dwindled down to about zero."

Other critics were a cut kinder, but only that. The *Dramatic Mirror*, echoing but improving upon the *Clipper*'s opinion, recorded the ". . . decidedly pleasing temperature, though it never rises to the alluring heights of its title," and the *World* compared it favorably with earlier Gaiety musicals.

What interest there was centered chiefly on the exotic locale and the pretty girls. The plot, worked over by many unseen hands by this time, was absolutely out of operetta, complete with mistaken identity, savage savages, civilized civilians, and marching military men. The modern touches were offered by the presence of millionairess Polly Bainbridge (Miss Cahill), who travels to the Philippines to marry Willoughby Parker (Carle), a dealer in hemp.

Philippine revolutionaries and a widow of a planter whose sexual inclinations and the lack of research on Guy's part earn her the nickname of "The Hot Tamale," tangle and retangle, until Polly, convinced that Parker is more interested in women than in hemp or her, goes off into the tropical sunset on the arm of a charming sea captain named Bob Mandrake.

There were some witty lines, and in musicals of the time—in contrast to straight plays—characterization was the quality looked for last. Brightness, breezy observations, and snappy tag lines were the order of the night. And those, Guy found, he could supply effortlessly.

Furthermore, despite the hysteria of the closing weeks of rehearsals, it had been fun. In *Ninety in the Shade,* Guy began a practice that would give him and his collaborators many giggles during writing and rehearsals: that of anointing chorus girls and boys with punned names. Only one was tried this time, but that was just a beginning: a long forgotten chorine named Amperito Ferrer played a character called Lettice Romaine.

Jerry's songs, while not up to the promise of "They Didn't Believe Me," were heavily rhythmical and eminently danceable. Many of them would find their way into future Kern shows. Like Plum and Guy, Jerry never really threw anything away.

Still, while the critics found Miss Cahill "delightfully demure" and liked Carle because he "simply acted himself," they generally turned thumbs down on the book and the music.

The producers kept the show open through January, but demand for tickets had trickled down to a mere mist in February, when the drama critic of *Vanity Fair,* a young and witty gent named P. G. Wodehouse, dealt it a final, gentle coup de grace:

> Our lawyer tells us that as we did not pay for our seat, an action for damages against the perpetrators of "Ninety in the Shade" will not be; so we must be content with a strongly worded protest. If Mr. Guy Bolton wrote the book as it is served up to the public at the Knickerbocker, he is to be censured; if as from a not small acquaintance with the inner workings of musical comedy productions we are inclined to suspect his original book was mangled and disintegrated to suit the purposes of Miss Cahill and Mr. Carle, he is to be commiserated with. . . .

Plum apparently knew, and possibly from more than one source. He had been in London with Carle and Kern. No proof exists that Jerry fed him inside information about the evolution or convolution of the book of *Ninety in the Shade,* but it is plausible since he had, as he claimed in print, a ". . . not small acquaintance with the inner workings of musical comedy productions. . . ."[6]

When, on February 27, the ticketholders arrived for the fortieth performance, they were told that Miss Cahill was ill and the performance was cancelled. Actually, there was an actors' revolt taking place. The players hadn't been paid in a week and wouldn't go on until they were.

Erlanger, looking like an eager gnome, mounted a chair backstage and talked to the company, assuring them that he would personally guarantee everybody's salary if they played that night. He went on to assure them that although *Ninety in the Shade* would close that week, it would open in Philadelphia the following week and go on the road after that. And everybody would have a job. But too many cast members had worked for Erlanger before, and called his bluff. The show closed after the matinee, never to open again.

It would be the last starring vehicle for Marie Cahill and the last popular role for Carle. Cahill would go into vaudeville and Carle into obscurity. Youth was the attraction of the day, and neither of these former stars was young.

But Kern and Bolton were, and although they hadn't been paid their royalties for two weeks, they were anything but discouraged. Guy hadn't had a show that had paid off its investment yet, so he didn't know what he was missing. Jerry had, but he was not particularly proud of this show. He did, however, like the young librettist with the strong profile and the quiet countenance, and he foresaw the beginnings of a partnership that would benefit both of them.

*If* he could catch him.

As soon as *Ninety in the Shade* opened, Guy was off on another venture: his adaptation, with Joseph Noel, of Jack London's *The Sea Wolf.*

Noel was a grizzled and wizened newspaper man who had once had a fling at gold mining. When he was a reporter for the *Oakland* (California) *Herald* and the *San Francisco Bulletin* and *Examiner,* he had met and become close friends with London, Ambrose Bierce, and a raft of other West Coast journalists.

In 1910, he had come East, turned to playwriting, and in 1912 had a hit on Broadway called *The Marriage Knot.* He would write eleven more plays and have six of them produced in New York before he turned to writing his memoirs. In 1914, while *Ninety in the Shade* was in rehearsal, Klaw and Erlanger put him in touch with Guy Bolton.

But the meeting is shrouded in mystery. *Someone* collaborated with Guy on *The Sea Wolf,* but the evidence indicates that it *wasn't* Noel. It wasn't even someone of the same *sex* as Noel. Indications are that Guy had planned the play long before he *met* Noel.

Guy's plan, preserved in an outline, was to set the story almost entirely aboard Wolf Larsen's ship. But in his papers is a letter and detailed scenario of the first act, which is set in an opium den.

The letter, on the stationery of the Little Theatre of Philadelphia, is dated Sunday, October 25, 1914, before the opening of either *Ninety in the Shade* or *The Fallen Idol.* It's from a woman who addresses Guy affectionately and closes in the same manner:

> Dear Brother Guy: — I am enclosing the rough copy of the first act for you to revise. I didn't have it done into play shape because I felt it was useless to pay for good typing twice and I am sure you will want to change at least part of it.

I think I have the idea and when typed properly it will run to the thirty sides. All I left out was the storm in Act I, and I rather felt that detracted from the big storm in the third act, and I didn't think Brodie would be quick witted enough to turn the lights out exactly as a flash of lightning. You can however use the storm if you think it best.

I had the professor dissapear [sic] with Maud because it made the shanghaiing of Humphrey easier.

I shall start right in on the second act now so as to get it to you this week. If I get "stumped" in this act I shall bring it over to you, but—please don't feel you have to take me to lunch every time I come to New York. I went this time because—well because I wanted too [sic] and I certainly enjoyed it but—don't let it be a duty!

I want to write to Jane so I shall let this be merely a short note and so with hopes for a succesful [sic] play and advance royalties soon!

I am hastily<br>Sister Peggy[7]

The mystery woman now fades from the scene. Speculation about her can be fun and dangerous: Was she a young, aspiring playwright, dazzled by this *bon vivant* from New York? Or was she an *established* playwright who was taking the young and untried but dashingly handsome writer/architect under her practiced wing, to teach him the craft he was so eager to learn? And to receive in return enough payment to assume anonymity?

And what about Noel? Where did he come in or go out?

Unless some cache of letters surfaces, the answers will never be known. What *is* known is that the acting copy of the play emerged almost word for word as Sister Peggy wrote it.

*The Sea Wolf,* publicly by Guy Bolton and Joseph Noel, stays fairly close to the original novel but concentrates on the love story between Maude Brewster (uncertainly played by Jane Salisbury) and Wolf Larsen (wonderfully wrought by veteran actor Charles Dalton). Maude is shanghaiied by Larsen and dragged aboard his ship. She resists his advances, he's blinded by fire, and they all end up marooned on a picturesque island, where the sightless Larsen wanders off a cliff to his death.

Every stop on the melodrama organ is pulled out. Act 2 ends with a storm at sea. Act 3 ends with the burning of Larsen's boat. Fidelity to the theatre of a hundred years earlier is marked by the use of incidental music while the heroine struggles in the arms of the villain.

The incidental music was composed by none other than Jerome D. Kern, who probably figured that it was easiest to keep track of Guy by working with him. The music will never be included in any medley of Jerome Kern favorites; no trace of it has ever been found in the boxes and trunks of compositions left after Jerry's death. Only the program credit attests to the fact that it ever existed.

*The Sea Wolf* opened on March 11, 1915, at the Pansoris Theatre in Hartford, Connecticut, and closed the week of March 15 at the Tremont Theatre in Boston. It *had* to close; it, like *The Fallen Idol,* was too bad to be true.

Again, no matter. Jerry realized in Guy what Guy was only beginning to admit. His talent was for farce and cleverness. Serious subjects were the province of others. His and Jerry's worlds were musical ones, and something important in the musical theatre was about to happen, at a small theatre that was about to be closed by its owners, the Shuberts, and its manager, F. Ray Comstock.

# Crossover:

# THE
# NEAR PAST

"Wonder what the world would have been like if Ray Comstock had never been born?" muses Plum, as the sun disappears momentarily behind a dime-size cloud.

"Less noisy," answers Guy, not missing a beat.

"Less contentious," adds Plum.

"Less profitable for us," admits Guy.

"Yes, I suppose so," sighs Plum, adjusting his cap as the sun emerges again. "If you believe in fate and that sort of excuse for bad behavior, it was bloody fortuitous, our being alive at the same moment, wasn't it?"

"Like the spokes on a wheel," adds Guy.

"Yes, and the Princess was the axle."

"And Bessie was the grease."[1]

# Chapter 5

# Interlude: Birth of a Princess; Birth of a Notion

Back in Toledo in the early 1900s, young F. Ray Comstock had acquired a reputation among his colleagues at the Auditorium Theatre for his "sheer grit and pertinacity." He looked ambitious. He sounded ambitious. He launched ambitious projects, one of which was to establish himself as a theatrical producer and a show business immortal.

Intense, his receding hairline arguing with his age, his large nose, large eyes, and protruding ears his most memorable features, Comstock had a talent for turning a little imagination into a lot of money.

He was a native of Buffalo, New York; his first Manhattan venture had been an investment in a play called *The Runaways*. Not exactly a runaway success, it nevertheless brought him to the attention of Charles Frohman, who entrusted him with one of his brightest stars, Edna May, and a vehicle for her called *The School Girl*. It succeeded, and that success brought him to the attention of Morris Gest.

Gest, whose real name was Moisha Gerhonovitch, was one of the most flamboyant figures on Broadway. Dark of hair, eye, and moustache, given to wearing flowing black capes and flaring black hats, he had early in his career established a record of sorts for audacity, individuality, and eccentricity. In 1909, he married David Belasco's daughter Reine, which did nothing to derail his journey toward fame. Father and son-in-law were both exhibitionists with visions, and it was generally acknowledged by those who knew that Gest was going places.

And so, it was an ascending star to which Comstock attached himself. The two, Comstock and Gest, took to each other like crepe hair and spirit gum and established themselves immediately by exploiting Gertrude Hoffman and Her Russian Dancers and Jefferson De Angeles in *The Beauty Spot* (one of the brightest and most successful musical comedies of the 1909–10 season) and taking on the personal management of the two leading black comedians of the time, Bert Williams and George Walker.

Within a few short years, the two producers, still in their early thirties, had acquired the Colonial Theatre in Cleveland, the Auditorium Theatre in Toledo, Hartmanus Bleeker Hall in Albany, the Van Curlor Opera House in Schenectady, and the LaSalle Theatre in Chicago.

But the theatre that interested F. Ray Comstock most was a tiny, 299-seat house at 104 West Thirty-ninth Street called the Princess.

Owned by the Shuberts, William A. Brady, and Arch Selwyn, it was a jewel box that Comstock, as manager, somehow reckoned would make an ideal "Theatre of Thrills." For two seasons, he tried the Grand Guignol formula of gory one-act plays based on trashy thriller novels by unknown writers. And for two seasons, he lost money.

In 1914, a decision had to be made: Sell the theatre or reformulate his vision of it.

Fortunately for Comstock himself, Guy, Jerry, Plum, and the American Musical Theatre, a third figure now loomed on the horizon. And loom Bessie Marbury did. Guy remembered her in later years as a "charming and benign elephant."[1]

Primarily an author and artist's representative, she had gone toe to toe (or, as Plum repictured it, "nose to bosom"[2]) with Comstock over one of his plays called *A Pair of White Gloves.* Bessie complained bitterly that it had been stolen from a play called *Au Rat Mort Cabinet* by one of her clients. The two came out of the confrontation with a healthy respect for each other's judgment and tenacity.

Besides, Bessie had a talent for developing trends. It was she, after all, who had helped to make Vernon and Irene Castle the couple who turned the whole country dance crazy.

Her idea for the salvation of the Princess Theatre was monumental in its simplicity: If the house was small, it was also intimate and ideally suited for interaction between performers and patrons.

Why not, then, construct entertainments specifically for this lovely little bandbox that would enhance its tininess and its charm?

Instead of gore, why not give the audience girls?

And music?

And laughs?

Well, of course, thought Comstock, as long as Bessie's taking on some of the cost.

She did, and the modern American Musical Theatre was born.

Born, but not realized. That would take two years and the hiring of three men. But Bessie's idea and Bessie's plan for saving the Princess would make all of this possible.

Her formula was simple: There would be no more than two sets (the operettas down the street had twelve or thirteen), a chorus of between eight and twelve (operettas employed up to ninety), and an orchestra of eleven (Victor Herbert liked at least forty hard-working musicians to give his scores the richness he and they deserved). The stories would be contemporary, so that costuming would be inexpensive; the performers would be young, so that their agents wouldn't be too obnoxious; and the composers and librettists would be fairly unknown, so that their financial demands wouldn't be too demanding.

Furthermore, Elsie De Wolfe, the famous and talented designer and a sort of Alice B. Toklas figure in Bessie Marbury's life, would design the sets for a friendly fee.

The first production would be budgeted at $7,500, a less than modest sum, even in those days.

This plan meant a search for talent among young and fairly untried composers and librettists. No Victor Herberts, Henry Blossoms, Otto Harbachs, Ivan Carylls, or Harry B. Smiths.

Instead, Bessie turned to—of all people—Paul Rubens. Ten years ago, the very year that Plum and Jerry had met, Rubens had had a moderately successful London run with his comedy *Mr. Popple (of Ippleton)*. Bessie remembered it. It would make a good first property, and Rubens came cheaply.

Comstock agreed, especially with the financial conservatism. But unfortunately, Rubens was also a composer whose star was on a marked decline. Bessie knew this, too, but she had also represented some of the talent in the late and not lamented *Ninety in the Shade.* She knew all about the goings on of that show, and she had a feeling that if Rubens didn't turn out as a composer, she could get a young song writer who was also a veteran interpolater to come in and save it.

In early 1915, she approached Jerome Kern.[3]

# Chapter

# 6

# Reprise: Opening Chorus
## 1915

Jerry was more than routinely intrigued by Bessie Marbury's scheme. There would be no room at the Princess for operetta tricks. His idea of integration in musicals, tried tentatively in the bridges he and Guy had built in *Ninety in the Shade,* had begun to take shape and grow in his mind. With his *tabula rasa,* Guy Bolton, it might be possible to expand what they had begun. The problem was, Guy Bolton was not the librettist for the first Princess show. Paul Rubens was, and Paul Rubens had no more grasp of Jerry's ideas of verisimilitude than Marie Cahill. As rehearsals began, the first Princess musical resembled a shrunken operetta.

A few weeks into rehearsal, Marbury and Comstock became convinced that Rubens had to be replaced, and quickly.

This was the break Jerry had been waiting for.

"I worked with a fellow on *Ninety in the Shade,*" he offered one day in Bessie's office. "He did *The Rule of Three,* too."

"Oh yes," said Bessie. "I know his work. He shows promise."

"And now you're going to promise him shows," stated Jerry, with ingratiating aggressiveness.

71

Or at least that's the way Guy and Plum remembered it later in their book of recollections, *Bring on the Girls*—a work of semifiction that rests some-place between Laurence Sterne's *Tristram Shandy* and Mark Twain's *Auto-biography* as a model of authenticity and veracity.

What *really* happened, according to records of the transactions,[1] was that Bessie gave in to Jerry, but conditionally. She wasn't that much impressed by Guy's work on *Ninety in the Shade,* so she hired him as a *sub*collaborator, without credit. The advance publicity announced that the new Rubens-Kern musical, now titled *Nobody Home,* would open at the Princess during Easter week, April 5, 1915.

The cast was an interesting, interlacing one: Lawrence Grossmith, the brother of one of Jerry's first lyricists and one of Plum's first theatrical mentors, had become one of the most popular British comedians of the time. Adele Rowland was an equally popular singer. They were cast as the leads, and they were the only principals to be hired purely on the strength of their talent.

Marguerite May, the younger sister of Edna May, whom Comstock had to thank for his first success, was cast, as was Coralie Blythe, the sister of Vernon Castle and the wife of Lawrence Grossmith. Add the presence of Elsie De Wolfe, and the only person missing for perfect nepotism was David Belasco.

To augment the clublike atmosphere and to save money, Marbury and Comstock decided to forego an expensive tryout tour and instead scheduled an invitational dress rehearsal for some handpicked friends.

Jerry and Guy observed it from the back of the balcony. Since this balcony contained only two rows, they weren't very far from the source of an evening's misery.

"What do you think?" Jerry whispered to Guy.

Guy thought for a moment, while silence, as of the tomb, rose around them. "I thought these were Bessie's *friends,* " he whispered back.

"There goes another friend," said Jerry, as a man in front of them drew on his coat to the accompaniment of another Rubens melody.

At the desperate conference that followed the fiasco, Kern and Bolton were given roles as show doctors. "Only one thing," said Comstock, menacingly, to cover the absurdity of what he was about to say, "we've got to open this month. And with the same sets and the same costumes."


Quite an assignment. But to the two young men, no demand was too great, no rewriting too insurmountable, no idiotic request of star or producer too preposterous. Klaw and Erlanger and that monster Marie Cahill wouldn't be hanging over them now. Even Bessie and Ray, immobilized by the disaster of that night's performance, would remain at a distance, at least for a while.

So they went to Jerry's again, rolled up their sleeves, tossed out Rubens, and introduced Bolton and Kern.

Eva fed them food, but the real nourishment came from the collaboration, which grew more certain and solidly conceived each day.

Rubens had already come up with a catchy title out of Dickens (Squeers, in *Nicholas Nickleby,* presents Smike to a visitor, smacks him on the head, and notes, "Nobody home"). Guy—perhaps trading on his experience with *The Million*—moved the story out of London and into New York. He honed the dialogue, built up the dance numbers, worked hard and long making the lead-ins to the music smoother and more logical. Now, the boast of the advance publicity, "It is said of 'Nobody Home' that there is a real story and a real plot, which does not get lost during the course of the entertainment . . ."[2] would have a little truth to back it up.

Jerry finally had the free hand he had been seeking. Guy was merely following his instincts with a more experienced collaborator. Neither probably realized that they were making history as well as entertainment, or that the idea of integrating and equalizing music and book would set all of the coming Princess musicals totally apart from the rest of Broadway. That, plus the musicals' intimacy and their two-act form would make them the very first modern musical comedies in America, and the model for *all* musical comedies for the next forty years on Broadway and the next fifty in London.

Large revolutions proceed from tightly expressed ideas. Puzzles begin with a concept. The coming of *Oklahoma!* in 1943 was vividly important to the American musical theatre because it put dance, the last piece of the puzzle, into place. But the *original* concept, the tightly expressed idea of a contemporary, integrated musical theatre, where book and music and lyrics are equal and interdependent, was born in the mind of Jerome Kern, twenty-four years earlier. And it would first come alive, not in 1943, but in 1915, on the stage of the Princess Theatre, when the creative mind of Bessie Marbury and the creative partnership of Jerome Kern and Guy Bolton came together, and produced *Nobody Home.*

Jerry and Guy delivered their rewrite within two weeks. The new version of *Nobody Home,* now credited to Rubens, Bolton, and Kern, but containing no Rubens music and little Rubens book, was subtitled "A Farce Comedy in Two Acts with Music."

Act 1 was set in the Blitz Hotel—a reference to the Ritz-Carlton Hotel, which had opened only eight years earlier in New York and was considered *the* place to stay and be seen.

After the opening chorus, Rolando (Rollo) D'Amorini (Charles Judels) and his overstuffed wife (Maude Odell) arrive at the Blitz to find their daughter Violet (Alice Dovey) has been deflowered since her move to New York. Violet is in love with Vernon Popple (George Anderson), the "pied piper of the dancers."

Rollo, on his first day in New York, immediately establishes himself as a moneyed old man who can't resist grabbing the waist or other extremity of every young girl who passes by. When he meets Tony Miller (Adele Rowland), the famous Winter Garden revue star, he reminisces: "I remember you one year ago at the Winter Garden; oh, what a beautiful costume, I shall never forget that costume." To which Tony tartly replies: "What a memory you have for trifles."

Mrs. D'Amorini will never approve of Violet and Vernon, even if they do alliterate, particularly since Vernon is an old pal of Tony Miller, the revue star. Rollo, to pacify his wife, imitates indignation.

Now, Freddy Popple (Lawrence Grossmith), Vernon's brother, arrives, complete with comic valet. They've made the rocky trip from Ippleton, a one-horse, no-carriage town in the north of England. There's no room at the Blitz, so Tony, because she realizes that Freddy is Vernon's brother, loans him her apartment.

End of act 1.

Act 2 is set in Tony's apartment, where everyone, for no good reason except that this is a musical comedy, shows up.

There's a plenitude of running in and out of rooms. Mrs. D'Amorini is locked in the kitchen when the door knob comes off. Freddy goes trout fishing from the window of the apartment and hooks a cabbie but throws him back because he's too small. Freddy falls for Tony, who likes him but informs him—in a production number—that the Winter Garden show is off to San Francisco, and so is she. Violet and Vernon still try to unite. Mrs. D'Amorini disapproves of Vernon to the bitter end, but Rollo, made street smart by New York, gives his blessing on the last page of the script, just in time for a happy ending.

Working closely with Jerry, Guy jettisoned his penchant for proselytizing and learned the value of keeping the action moving, letting people stop talking when they didn't have anything more to say, and start singing and dancing.

Under the prodding of Bessie, Jerry inserted liberal doses of dance music for Helen Clark and Quinton Tod: a military routine, a "new one step," and an "ultra fox trot."

And, in a further nod to Bessie's indirect introduction of the dance craze and the Castles, Guy named his chorus girls Madge Fandango, Marie Maxixe, Tessie Trot, Hilda Hesitation, Dolly Dip, Gertie Gavotte, Trilby Tango, and Polly Polka—the last played by a teen-aged refugee from *Ninety in the Shade* named Marion Davis. Later that same season, with an *e* added to her last name by Florenz Ziegfeld, Marion would figure largely in much more than the Princess's small chorus and Guy Bolton's address book.

The chorus boys got the barber shop/drugstore treatment: Edward Pinaud and Rexall Liggett led them.

The humor reached no great altitudes. Example: A chorus girl sits down to eat with Rollo, says she's not hungry, and then orders: "Two absinthe cocktails. Hors d'ouevres, hot house melon; petite marmite. What is that?" Rollo helps: "It's a small town in Italy. You no want that."

She shrugs and continues: "Sweetbreads aux truffles, roast mallard duck, asparagus, artichokes, peach melba, coffee, and a bottle of wine."

Rollo splutters: "You not hungry. What do you eat when you're hungry, a small pony?"

But the scene and the humor worked. It worked so well, in fact, that eleven years later, Guy would transplant it, word for word, into *The Five O'Clock Girl,* one of a string of hit musicals written with Bert Kalmar and Harry Ruby.

Joking jibes at marriage and courtship abounded. Guy had a notebook and head full of them: Mrs. D'Amorini opined: "No woman trusts her husband. She only trusts herself to watch her husband."

And Freddy defined his approach to women for his valet, Platt: "Just tell her she's the sweetest thing in the world."

PLATT:   Yes, sir.

FREDDY:   And if the other lady calls, tell her she's the sweetest thing in the world.

PLATT:   You do know what to say to the ladies, sir.

Effective enough. But it was in the fastening of line to music that *Nobody Home* excelled, though not always. Bessie and Ray couldn't resist bringing in inter-polaters, including Lawrence Grossmith, C. W. Murphy, Dan Lipton, Worton David, J. P. Long, and Harry B. Smith. After all, they couldn't *absolutely* defy convention the first time around. Still, most of the time, the show flowed forward, unimpeded by operetta shoe-ins. It was in the construction of the show, the smooth transitions and the interdependence of book, music, and lyrics, that the young duo established the pattern that would soon both elevate and signify American musical comedy:

In act 1, Rollo makes an advance to a chorus girl, who counters with, "I think you have made a mistake." Rollo replies, "The only mistake I made was when I brought my wife here," which naturally leads into the Worton David/J. P. Long song, "You Don't Take a Sandwich to a Banquet."

Later, Vernon and Violet talk about secrets:

VERNON:   I'm not very good at keeping secrets. Look how
          easily you have guessed mine.

VIOLET:   I'm not sure. (*Sings*)
          I see it in your eyes,
          I see it in your silence,
          And I hear it in your sighs. . . .

Rollo, about to exit, says to Tony: "I'll see you later."
Tony asks, "Where?"
Rollo answers, as he exits, "Any old place," whereupon Tony launches into the show's hit, "Any old place is a wonderful place/ If you're there with a wonderful girl. . . ."

Beyond this not inconsiderable achievement, the pattern of the Princess shows was established: contemporary talk, lightning pace, two sets and two acts, chorus girls with names instead of numbers, the old man chasing the young girls, the love affair resolved on the last page, the comic older woman, the wisecracking girl who ends up with nothing but her fame, the show's title as the last line of dialogue, and the finale, with Schuyler Greene lyrics, that sends everyone out of the theatre feeling personally contacted:

> Any old show is a wonderful show
> If you're there with a wonderful girl
> As long as the music has plenty of go
> Any old plot will unfurl.
> It may be tragic or comic,
> But what do you care,
> As long as the girl likes to be with you there,
> Any old show is a wonderful show,
> If you're there with a wonderful girl.

And so, *Nobody Home,* the first of the Princess musicals, opened on April 20, 1915, just two weeks later than originally scheduled.

The critics, resisting the blandishments showered upon them in the finale, didn't think it was exactly a wonderful show, but they weren't unkind, either. The *Dramatic Mirror* judged the show ". . . a good musical entertainment with nothing of special sensational interest. . . ." If it failed to pay attention to Jerry and Guy's first sustained attempt at verisimilitude and economy on the musical stage, it did take notice of the realization of Bessie's ideas: "[The show was] peculiarly fitted to the intimate character of the Princess . . . light and pleasing . . . handsomely staged, and admirably played by a small but compact company." The New York *Clipper* called it ". . . one of the most enjoyable musical comedies of the season."

Only the *Times* cavilled, against just about everything that was not the creation of Paul Rubens, possibly because the Shuberts, who still owned the Princess, were engaged in a feud with the *Times* and insisted on including a note in the program that announced, "This theatre does not advertise in the 'New York Times.'" Or possibly it was because the neglected Rubens had had words with their reviewer. Of Jerry's music, the critic wailed,

> . . . a regret that a tunesmith of New York's Tin Pan Alley should have been called in to substitute his raggy-taggy and fox-trotty-rotty refrains for the genuinely melodious and charming music that Mr. Rubens can write and apparently did write for the original libretto. . . . However, the elusive delicacy and refinement of the English school of musical comedy has never stood a chance in competition with the tump-tump, slapdash tunes beloved of the tangoers, hence the employment of Mr. Kern. . . .

Ironically, seven years later, in the *Atlantic Monthly,* Carl Engel, a musicologist to be reckoned with, tapped the genius at work in Jerry. Writing about *Nobody Home*'s "The Magic Melody," he effused: "A young man gifted with musical talent and unusual courage has dared to introduce into his tune a modulation which has nothing extraordinary in itself, but which marked a change, a new regime in American popular music . . . it was a relief, a liberation."

The Princess publicists turned the *Times* tirade into profit, printing in their promotional material: "A Foxy-Trotty Series of Delights, with a Joyous Zip. . . ."

Of Guy's book, the *Times* critic said, "Presumably Mr. Bolton's task was the wrenching of Mr. Rubens' story from its original setting and its transplanting to an American scenario, with embellishments of slang and topical allusions of the vintage of 1915."

With that sort of inside information, one wonders just how much Rubens had to do with the writing of the *Times* review.

Apparently either ignoring or missing the *Times,* audiences came and were delighted. Women swooned at the dresses; Elsie De Wolfe's second-act black-, white-, and-orange set became the model for fall redecorations of the apartments of the smart; and, in general, the Princess style became the rage of 1915.

Ray Comstock soon saw that the nightly receipts from 299 seats wouldn't turn the kind of profit he wanted. Within two months, he moved the show across the street to the larger Maxine Elliott.

*Nobody Home* ran for six months in New York, four in Boston, and three in Chicago, where Fanny Brice and an augmented orchestra of twenty-two decimated its intimate character. There was still a road company playing to full houses in the 1917–18 season.

The two young creators were buoyed by their success, but Ray and Bessie moved cautiously, casting about slowly for the next Princess show.

A little over a week after *Nobody Home* opened, two of Jerry's songs appeared in London at the Gaiety in *Tonight's the Night,* a show with a main score by none other than Paul Rubens.

On May 1, Jerry made plans to take the *Lusitania* to England. Charles Frohman would be aboard, and presumably, there was work to be discussed. And neither Eva nor he had seen her family in over a year. Eva pleaded with Jerry not to go. England and Germany were at war, and U-boat attacks on British vessels had increased with frightening intensity.

Jerry, however, was unmovable, once he'd made plans or set a course, and her entreaties made no difference. At least, this is the story that Jerry told Guy later. Neither history nor Jerry recorded why, if visiting her family was an issue, Eva wasn't booked on the *Lusitania* too.

Be that as it may, according to Jerry's recollection, filtered through Guy's recollection, Jerry spent a large part of the night before the sailing playing cards. It was an addiction with him, as were late hours. It was the policy of those who knew him not to count on seeing Jerome D. Kern before one or two in the afternoon.

The *Lusitania* sailed at noon on May 1. Jerry didn't wake up until 11:30, and by the time he'd careered onto the dock behind a perspiring cab driver, the liner had left.

Six days later, off the coast of Ireland, the *Lusitania* was torpedoed and sunk by a German U-boat. Charles Frohman was drowned, along with a majority of the ship's passengers.

It was a chastening, humbling experience for Jerry, one that Eva swore never happened. And yet Jerry was certain enough of its authenticity to insist that when Guy wrote the screenplay for MGM's pseudo-biography of the composer, *Till the Clouds Roll By,* he include the sequence.[3]

Jerry had two shows in the works in the summer of 1915: *Cousin Lucy,* a show written for female impersonator Julian Eltinge, which wasn't a full-blown musical and lasted only a short time at the Cohan Theatre, and *Miss Information,* truthfully subtitled *A Little Comedy with a Little Music,* which opened and closed hurriedly at the same theatre a month later.

*Miss Information,* which starred the charismatic talents of Elsie Janis and Irene Bordoni, was more famous for what it contained than what it promised: although Jerry was credited with the main score of four songs, one tune was contributed by another young composer just arriving on Broadway, Cole Porter. Both salvaged their songs for better shows and better times.

Meanwhile, Guy, still convincing himself in the face of reality that, although the musical stage was fun, he was really more a playwright than a librettist, met George Middleton at The Players club, shortly after *Nobody Home*'s opening. They ate lightly, but well. Over dessert, Middleton reached into his mental trunk and pulled out a plan. His father, it seemed, had had a friend. He was a gambler and his name was Delacey, and he owned a lot of pool rooms in New York. As Guy later recalled it, the talk focused on Delacey as a subject for a play.

"He was the most colorful character I ever met," said Middleton. "You'd go to the poolroom to see *him* as much as you'd go there to play pool.

"Well," he leaned forward, "Delacey was elected to some important office in the New Jersey State government. But as soon as he entered office, scandal stalked him. The poolrooms became an issue. He had to either give them up or quit his office. So he gave up the pool parlors. But no sooner had he done this than he closed down all of the *race tracks* in New Jersey. He claimed that they were cesspools of immorality, and they had to go."

He paused, studying the reaction on Guy's face. There was none. "Are you with me?"

"Yes. Go on," said Guy, letting the faintest glimmer of interest through.

"Now," continued Middleton, "this action by Delacey was sweet justice by a sweet practitioner of revenge. He made the moralists eat their slogans." He leaned forward. "Suppose we take the character, move him out of New Jersey—"

"I don't like New Jersey, and I don't know anything about race tracks," said Guy. "But I *do* know about Prohibition."

Prohibition was a hot topic in 1915. Nobody was neutral about neutral spirits.

Before the afternoon was over, George Middleton and Guy had evolved a story about a Billy Sunday-type bartender who shut down bars. Its title was appropriate for a story about liquor: *What'll You Have.*

Guy had learned much from Jerry about the balance of song and story line in a musical. Now he would learn something equally valuable from George Middleton. The play that took form between them was a well-made one, populated with well-made, real people—a first for Guy. It would establish a pattern of collaboration that would remain for most of the rest of his life.

It was here that Guy realized his limitations and reached out to a collaborator who could fashion three-dimensional characters. The ability to do this demands a certain involvement in the lives and emotions of other human beings. But Guy had already begun a slow and inexorable retreat from those who might again wound him. Losing his mother before her death, being rejected by his play-mates at Deal, fancying hatred by his father, losing Ivy to a convent, losing Julie to Cosmo Hamilton—all of these events drove him inward and away from the rest of the world.

It wouldn't prevent him from pursuing beautiful women. On the contrary. But even the chorus girls upon whom he lavished attention and jewelery sensed the distance he kept, as if there were something that prevented him from touching them, a curtain of indifference or shyness or incomprehension or *something* that kept this dazzlingly handsome man from ever going beyond their first heady moments into something more profound or committed. It was as if every meeting were the first one, repeated over and over. To all of the women he would meet in his life, except two, the distance he kept was fascinating, frustrating, and puzzling. To Bolton the writer, it was at the least inhibiting and at the most crippling.

So George Middleton, fully equipped with wit and temperance and intelligence and an understanding of human behavior, linked easily with Guy's sense of form. And the combination pushed the playwriting of both of them into prominence and success. If *What'll You Have* was only a prelude, it was a prelude with much promise. The problem was, nobody wanted to produce it. Guy and George were roundly rejected wherever they went.

Finally, in desperation, they turned to one last manager, a friend of Middleton's: George M. Cohan.

Middleton and Cohan had known each other since Cohan's vaudeville days, and Cohan had a healthy respect for Middleton's work. When the young playwright's *The Cavalier* was produced in 1902, Cohan went before the curtain of his own comedy, then playing on the road, and said, "I want you all to go see the play that's opening here Monday — it's written by a pal of mine."[4]

Very few people saw this side of Cohan. He was not noted for his generosity or his accessibility. The feisty little man had a massive ego, and like most egotists, he was haunted by insecurity. He viewed comic playwrights and dance acts largely as threats to himself.

But he liked the obviously serious George Middleton, and if he and his partner Sam Harris had been able to find the right casts, they would have produced his last two plays. At least, that's what they told Middleton.

So, in late July of 1915, George Middleton and Guy Bolton turned up in the Cohan-Harris office, clutching *What'll You Have.* No one in his wildest fantasies could have guessed what would happen that day. Middleton, in his autobiography, *These Things Are Mine,* recalled it: "When I told him our title, he said: 'That's funny — I'm working on a play with the same title. My leading character is a barkeeper. What's yours?'"

The two young playwrights felt identical drowning sensations. "What do you think?" croaked Middleton.

"Well then, that's it, boys," said Cohan, lighting a cigar. "Can't listen to your play. Might steal something from it. Can't do that, now, can I?"

Guy rose to go. That was it, he thought. Another failure. But George Middleton had a flash of an idea.

He leaned toward Cohan. "Just *listen* to it, George. Maybe it's different. Maybe we can rewrite."

Cohan looked at the younger man for a moment. Then he sat down. "I got no appointments." He had listened to Middleton read his plays before, and he had been able to help the younger playwright. It was always flattering to give advice to young men. Cohan liked that role. He settled back in his chair. "Okay," he said. Middleton remembered: "He seldom moved as he listened. He followed and gave no suggestion of sleep. But he was not otherwise responsive. I had seen him listen all through without a smile; but at the end he said, 'That play is full of laughs.'"

The two young playwrights turned to each other, then back to Cohan, waiting for more words of praise. Cohan rose. "Thanks for bringing it to me, boys. When you get some more stuff, bring that, too." He shook hands and commandeered them out.

The next day, they were back at it, banging on doors of steadily decreasing importance. The day after that, George Middleton left for a two-day trip to Albany, and Guy called on Jerry. He'd heard that Bessie and Ray had made up their minds about the next Princess musical.

Meanwhile, back at The Players club, the phone began to ring off the hook. The first volley in a bombardment of calls from George M. Cohan started to arrive.

When Middleton came back from Albany, he phoned immediately. "Where the hell were you?" stormed Cohan. "I been trying to get you for three days!"

"Sorry, George," was all Middleton could mutter. He remembers the next moments this way:

> "Say, George, how much do you want for your play?" [he asked me]. I was flabbergasted. Before I could find speech—and that means something for me—he went on: "I want to combine your bartender story with mine. I can't get beyond the first act; but I see a way to use you boys' idea." I said I should have to ask Guy. He and I both needed money, and so we accepted. Our names were to go on the program as supplying the idea. He gave us $2500 and a percentage.

And so, *What'll You Have* became *Hit the Trail Holliday,* and a smash from the moment it went up at the New Broadway Theatre in Long Branch, New Jersey.

Opening night in New York—September 13, 1915—was one of the hottest and most humid nights of the summer, but it was clear to the young playwrights as they sat in the audience at the Astor Theatre that Cohan had improved their play more than either of them, at that stage of their careers, could.

Cohan's overhaul was major and masterful. He moved the locale, combined characters, performed major surgery on speeches, added energy and scope, confined romance to the last ten minutes of the play, and threw in the American flag for good measure.

The plot was largely the way Guy and George had written it, though not much of the original dialogue was left. Guy laboriously went through his copy of the Cohan script, underlining all that seemed so.[5] He would, two years later, salvage the play's original location, East Gilead, for inclusion in his and Middleton's *Polly with a Past,* and the year after that, it would appear again in the Bolton and Wodehouse and Kern Princess musical, *Oh, Lady! Lady!!.*

Still, to both young men, the transformation of the unsellable *What'll You*

*Have* into the solid hit *Hit the Trail Holliday* was clear and compelling. The sure theatrical sense of Cohan burned through every scene, even the concluding sequence, which consisted of a musical comedy-type finale-wedding ceremony. The play would run a solid 336 performances in New York.


And what had Plum Wodehouse been doing all this time?

Nothing much.

Establishing an enduring reputation by writing almost every word in *Vanity Fair.*

Gaining even more prestige by writing humorous stories for the *Saturday Evening Post,* one of which, "Extricating Young Gussie," contained, for the very first time, the characters of a fumbling man about town named Bertie Wooster and his manservant, named Jeeves.

# Chapter

# 7

# Bring on the Girls
# (and Plum)
## 1915–1916

Not quite a review and not quite a book show, *Watch Your Step* was the runaway musical hit of the 1914–15 season. It boasted, among many riches, an unfailingly melodious score, replete with ragtime waltz, by twenty-six-year-old Irving Berlin; the dazzling dancing of Vernon and Irene Castle; and the commanding presence of a statuesque, seventeen-year-old showgirl named Justine Johnstone.

The daughter of a Norwegian sea captain, Justine Johnstone was tall and regal, with a cascading mane of authentically blonde hair, a deep voice that reminded those who could compare of Ethel Barrymore, and a mind that must have outraced those of most of the other beauties on Broadway. It certainly left the reasoning powers of her best friend, Marion Davies, in the dust—even if it *was* diamond dust.

A few nights and a favorable review after *Watch Your Step* opened, Florenz Ziegfeld noticed what that show's producers had perceived a few months earlier, and what New York's leading photographers had known for years. He hired the imposing teenager for his *Follies* and in the 1915 edition draped her in an American flag and made her the centerpiece of a patriotic display, which also included Olive Thomas as the Dove of Peace and Bert Williams singing a song (obviously not by Irving Berlin) called "I'm Neutral."

It was a sentiment no man who met Justine Johnstone could harbor for long, and Guy was no exception. But then again, few women remained aloof from *his* spell, either. In *Bring on the Girls,* Guy and Plum captured the Bolton fascination thusly:

> ". . . a flick of the finger, a broken heart—that's Guy
> Bolton."
> "Really?"
> "He once kissed a girl on Broadway, and she shot clear
> up to the top of the Woolworth Building."
> "You don't say?"
> "I'm telling you. Just closed her eyes with a little
> moan and floated up and up and up."

Justine Johnstone probably didn't succumb to Guy's charm to that extent. But she *did* express enough interest to become one of the two women who would consume his private life in 1915, and she managed to hold her own for an astonishingly long time, considering the competition.

Marguerite Namara could flick fingers and break hearts in equal cadence with Guy. Within a year, in a sequence of events a thousand times more fascinating than fiction, she would become the second Mrs. Guy Bolton. But in 1915, she was merely Justine Johnstone's rival.

Her name at birth had been Margaret Banks, and she was the daughter of a man who worked for the California Fruit Trust. In 1893, at the age of five, she became the girl on the Sunmaid Raisin box. In 1895, at the age of seven, she made her debut as, in her own words, ". . . that most horrid of creatures, a [piano playing] child prodigy."[1]

She studied voice with her mother, who had been a popular singer in Ohio in earlier times. When she was ten, she composed a march that was published and played in Italy. When she was eighteen, she cut her first cylinder for Thomas Edison and in the same year was accepted by the Milan Conservatory, where she studied for a year. In 1907, at the Teatro Poletziano in Genoa, she sang her first operatic role, Marguerite in *Faust,* and changed her name from Margaret Banks to Marguerite Namara—Marguerite after both her first major role and her grandmother's first name and Namara after her mother's maiden name, MacNamara.

Her career exploded. By 1910, she was touring in concert with Caruso, Amato, and Goldovsky. Henry Russell, the manager of the Boston Opera, dazzled and impressed and eager, threw thousands of dollars into a massive campaign to promote the new American soprano with an Italian name who would open his fall season.

Long-limbed, willowy, fiery, and blue-eyed, Marguerite Namara possessed not only a magnificent voice but a unique, transfixing beauty. In an age when most operatic sopranos resembled stuffed sofas, she was a creature who could enhance a Ziegfeld staircase.

All of this was not lost on Henry Russell. He wasted no time in rolling out his casting couch. But he hadn't reckoned with Marguerite Namara's third and most striking trait: her fierce independence. Proud of her genius and protective of her honor, and not about to have either compromised, she not only rebuffed Henry Russell's advances; she paid him the supreme insult of marrying his assistant manager, Frederick Toye.

Russell fired both soprano and manager in mid-season, but it mattered little to either. Frederick Henry Toye became not only Marguerite's husband but her manager, and he would continue in the latter capacity until he died.

In 1911, he and his new wife went to Europe for a triumphal tour. While they were there, they met Isadora Duncan, who desperately needed a manager and a friend. Frederick became one and Marguerite the other. Together, the three continued to tour Europe, capping their ventures in Russia, where they appeared before Czar Nicholas II.

But the champagne and the accolades and the royal command performances scarcely satisfied Namara, and she persuaded Frederick to take her back to her native state of California to start a family. He did; they had a son, named Frederick, Jr.; and Frederick, Sr. became the first manager of the Los Angeles Symphony.

Within a year of her son's birth, Namara waxed restless again. The three embarked on a transatlantic trip, this time in a ship without lights because of the threat of German U-boats. In Europe during this junket, Marguerite studied with Nellie Melba until the war and her own angst drove her westward once more.

This time, her destination was New York. All of her life she would inspire the great to create for her and royalty to bestow gifts upon her: the king of the Belgians would give her his own royal conveyance. Debussy would plan to write an opera (with a libretto by D'Annunzio) for her, but would die before he could.

Old and mostly blind, Monet would, in his last years, have a piano moved into his studio at Giverny so that he could take time from his work on *The Water Lilies* to hear her play and sing.

Beginning this trend, Franz Lehar wrote an operetta in 1914 titled *Alone at Last,* particularly for Marguerite Namara. An easy conquerer of the concert and operatic worlds, Namara was now eager to try Broadway. In 1915, she came to New York to begin rehearsals for a scheduled fall opening of the Lehar operetta. Her costar would be John Charles Thomas. Her romantic interest would soon become Guy Bolton.[2]

At the Princess Theatre, Ray and Bessie had finally made up their minds. Their second presentation would be a musical treatment of millionaire-playwright Philip Bartholomae's *Over Night.* Over the strenuous objections of Jerry, they'd decided to leave the conversion of the play into a musical book to its original author and to retain *Nobody Home*'s Schuyler Greene as lyricist.

Summer turned to autumn. Retitled *Very Good Eddie,* the Bartholomae farce with music opened on November 9, 1915, in Schenectady, and although the reviews were enthusiastic, the producers weren't. There were major problems with the show, and Bessie and Ray closed it down for repairs right after its Albany run.

The company, minus its leading lady and choreographer, returned to New York. Florence Nash was replaced by Alice Dovey, and David Bennett was called in to overhaul the original dances of Joseph C. Smith. But there was something far more basically wrong with *Very Good Eddie*—its book and lyrics. Schuyler Greene's efforts weren't even up to those he penned for *Nobody Home.* And so Herbert Reynolds, who, under his previous pen name, Michael Rourke, had supplied the lovely lyrics for Jerry's lovely ballad "They Didn't Believe Me" in *The Girl from Utah,* was called in to supplement Greene's lamentable work.

As to the book: Although Bartholomae had the credentials of a musical comedy writer (his *When Dreams Come True* had opened and closed at the Majestic Theatre in Brooklyn in October of 1913, and his *Miss Daisy* had survived for a month at the Shubert in September of 1914), he didn't possess what Bessie liked to refer to as the "Princess touch"—that sense of where to stop the talking and begin the singing and the ability to create effortless, clever, sophisticated *fun* onstage.

"Are you going to call Guy or not?" Jerry asked Bessie.

"I wasn't *that* impressed with him," said Comstock, from behind his massive desk. "Some clever lines. A few good—"

"Shut up, Ray," said Bessie, watching the redness intensify on Jerry's forehead. "Do you think he'll come in?"

"He'll do anything I ask him to do," said Jerry, sitting back for the first time that afternoon.

"Then tell him to come in for free," said Ray, avoiding Bessie's furious glance.

Guy had been out of town with a little disaster of his own called *Her Game,* which Adele Blood, a crusader for New Theatre, produced as part of her New American Playwrights series. It lived and died at the Teck Theatre in Buffalo during the week of June 22. The *Buffalo Enquirer's* critic observed that ". . . dramatically it [was] intense, while there [was] an occasional livening up through exceedingly clever lines."

By now, Guy knew what would and wouldn't work on Broadway. One look at *Her Game,* and he readily agreed with Adele Blood's determination to cut her losses and close the show.

As usual, he had four or five other products in various pockets. In the summer and fall of 1915, he wrote a one-act play that Douglas Wood intended to produce. He roughed out the plot of a new comedy with George Middleton. He escorted Justine Johnstone to various late night suppers. And he pursued a beautiful, married, and unusual opera singer who was currently in rehearsal at the Shubert Theatre.

To add to this full menu, Ray Comstock now called Guy in on the next Princess production, offered him a salary, and gave specific instructions not to ruffle Philip Bartholomae, whose plot and money they needed as much as they did a play doctor.

Guy and Bartholomae got along well. Both had forsaken family engineering careers for the theatre. Guy liked the original book and handled it with care, although he didn't let those notions prevent him from treating it as an original.

He jettisoned bad jokes and substituted better ones, smoothed out the song lead-ins, and added plot complications, including the interchangeable characters of Elsie Lilly and Elsie Darling. He gave Jack Hazzard, the noted comedian, some additional second-act material. He generally used his architectural sense to re-create a structure that would fit on the Princess stage and satisfy the expectations of both patrons and producers.

He continued the practice begun in *Ninety in the Shade* of giving punned names to the chorus. The girls this time were either watery (Chrystal Poole, Lilly

Pond, Flo Tide) or wanton (Miss Always Innit, Miss Funnie Rekkod, Miss Munnie Duzzyt, Miss Gay Ann Giddy, Miss E. Z. Morrels) and the men were mostly bumpkins (Mr. Tayleurs Dummie, Mr. Fullern A. Goat, Mr. Dyer Thurst, Mr. Watt Punkyns).

In a later letter, Guy recalled, ". . . I laid out the music plot with Jerry and discussed the lyrics in relation to the subjects that the action of the play called for. . . ."

And so, once again, the combination of Bolton and Kern worked its magic, and by the middle of November, Ray and Bessie felt confident enough to schedule three openings for their new Princess musical: one on December 22 for the press, one on December 23 for the Fashion 500 (or, rather, 299, since that was the seating capacity of the theatre), and one on December 24 for whatever portion of the public chose to spend Christmas Eve in a theatre.

The title itself, borrowed from *Chin Chin,* the previous season's biggest hit, was a signal to the cognoscenti that this show would not be old-fashioned, but in the same contemporary mode as the first Princess musical: Fred Stone, as a ventriloquist in *Chin Chin,* had complimented his dummy by saying "Very good, Eddie," and by the end of the season, every swain with *savoir faire* was tossing the phrase recklessly around, in hopes of impressing the object of his affections.

The critic for the *Cincinnati Enquirer,* covering the out-of-town opening of the refurbished show on November 28, hardly gave anyone associated with it heart. He questioned ". . . whether 'Very Good Eddie' would be as entertaining as 'Over Night'" and called the Kern score ". . . reminiscent of about every tune he ever wrote for any other piece."

He was partially right on that point. Practicing frugality, Jerry had moved three songs over from *Miss Information,* the Elsie Janis-Irene Bordoni fiasco of the previous summer.

In New York, more tinkering took place, and the show assumed its ultimate form. The story, pared down and tightened, raced forward at breakneck speed along the Hudson River, from the Dayline pier in Albany to Poughkeepsie:

When the curtain rises, two young married couples, Eddie (Ernest Truex) and Georgina Kettle (Helen Raymond) and Percy (John Willard) and Elsie Darling (Alice Dovey) are about to board the Dayliner for their honeymoons. Meanwhile, a boat race between Ivy League colleges is about to be run on the Hudson, and Madame Matroppo (Ada Lewis) and her batch of singing and dancing beauties arrive for a cruise aboard the same Dayliner.

The boat leaves with one husband from one couple and one wife from the other couple, and that about sums up the first act, except for the presence and peregrinations of a handsome and tenacious ("When it comes to sticking, I've got Mr. Postage Stamp licked!") lover named Dick Rivers (Oscar Shaw), who falls in love with Mme. Matroppo's most beautiful beauty, Elsie Lilly (Anna Orr).

Most of the comedy load in the first act falls upon the broad boa of Mme. Matroppo, who remembers names by association and therefore addresses Dick Rivers as "Mr. Fish," "Mr. Stream," "Mr. Lake," etc. Much later, Guy himself penciled in on his private script, partway into act 2, scene 1: "Isn't this constantly repeated joke too much?" It apparently wasn't in 1915.

Act 2, which takes place at the Rip Van Winkle Inn, shifts the comedy load to Al Cleveland, the hotel clerk (Jack Hazzard). Although the jokes creak curiously today ("I used to be a cashier in a police station." "What did you do?" "Counted coppers as they came in."), there's a richness of visual humor that's ageless—mixed orders of roses, mixed hotel rooms, mixed identities—even mixed food.

Example: Eddie Kettle comes down for breakfast and the clerk can't believe that he hasn't had any yet:

> KETTLE: All I had was a sandwich that Mrs.—that my wife left on her plate and it had so much mustard on it, I could hardly eat it.
>
> CLERK: Gosh! That wasn't a sandwich. That was a mustard plaster!
>
> KETTLE: It was? I wondered why I felt so warm inside.

By the act's end, the right lovers have ended up with each other, after equal portions of manipulating from the hotel clerk, Bartholomae, and Bolton.

The plot, then, was not what made this show the Princess's first solid hit and a historically important musical besides. It was the progression from *Nobody Home* of a conscious integration of song and story, accomplished much more smoothly this time by Jerry and Guy. It was the new two-act formula that worked, the new eleven-member orchestra in the pit, the new sixteen-member chorus, the dazzling opulence of Elsie De Wolfe's second act set, the crowd pleasing, fashionable Hickson gowns, and Jerry's lovely, contemporary melodies.

Above all, it was a sense of confidence that allowed Guy to taunt the conventions of operetta. In act 2, Dick Rivers and the clerk observe that there isn't too much romance in the air:

DICK:     When the girlie I've found finds me, we'll both find a
          nest together.

CLERK:    Sounds like a song cue.

DICK:     It is.

CLERK:    Then this is where I go out and strain the milk.

This contrast made the Bolton integration of other songs all the more seamless.

More than in *Nobody Home,* the flow of the evening was relaxed and unstrained. Although each act opened with a rousing chorus that set the scene and allowed latecomers a last sip in the lobby, the plot plunged forward with scarcely a pause. The two couples meet in the first act, shake hands, and dive headlong into the first song:

MRS. DARLING:    Such fun, our sharing our honeymoons like
                 this.

MRS. KETTLE:     Birds of a feather nest together.

MRS. DARLING:    (Sings) This world's all right when someone
                 loves you.
                 'Tis our delight to do as doves do.
                 From morn to night we coo as doves coo,
                 Pidgy woo, pidgy woo, pidgy woo.

Jerry and Guy couldn't be blamed for the deterioration of the lyric.

And finally, there was the intimacy that patrons at the Princess had come to expect. Carrying forward his title as a tag-line device from *Nobody Home,* Guy let Eddie Kettle assert himself in the final moments of the last act. The clerk observed, naturally, "Very Good, Eddie!," whereupon the entire cast launched into the direct-address-to-the-audience-finale-farewell, to the marvelous melody of the show's hit, "Babes in the Woods":

Moonlight is bright,

We'll say good night.

Hope you enjoyed our play.

With song and jest,

We've done our best,

For a while,

To make you smile. . . .

With those youthful faces singing Jerome Kern melodies set to direct address lyrics like that, small wonder a glow settled over the Princess audiences and critics like Channing Pollock were moved to write that ". . . every single person was being reached personally."

That was precisely what Bessie wanted to happen, especially on the night of December 23, when the Fashion 299 were in place. The Vanderbilts, the Havemeyers, the Astors, the Pulitzers, the Baruchs were all there, mixing in with celebrities like Elsie Janis and Irene Bordoni, no doubt wide-eyed in recognition of some of the songs.

Through some of 1914 and all of 1915, much of the American version of that antic and eminent British magazine *Vanity Fair* was written by Pelham Grenville Wodehouse, under various inspired pseudonyms: J. Plum (which joined a *J* to his nickname), P. Brook-Haven (after the township in which Bellport, his then favorite village on Long Island lay), C. P. West (after his then New York City address, 375 Central Park West), Pelham Grenville (an obvious elision), J. William Walker (in celebration of his favorite exercise), and — in his coveted role as drama critic — P. G. Wodehouse.

Plum was not a passionate man. But he did have one abiding, deep, and driving infatuation, and that was the theatre. And his assignment as *Vanity Fair's* man-about-Broadway on December 23, 1915, was the opening of *Very Good Eddie.*

The way that night was recounted in later years by Bolton and Wodehouse in their memoirs and Kern to his friends was this:

Jerry and Guy joined in the general jubilation over their theatre piece from their vantage points at the rear of the orchestra. In that society-studded audience was, they noticed, a diamond in the rough. He was tall and imposing and sandy haired; he wore steel-rimmed glasses and the relative hairlessness of his head allowed it to pick up and reflect back an inordinate amount of light from the stage. In fact, his formidable form loomed like a glistening Mount Aetna on a Sicilian plain.

"Who's that?" inquired Guy.

"Critic from *Vanity Fair.* Wodehouse," answered Jerry.

And that is probably as far as the exchange went, although in their entirely suspect memoir, *Bring on the Girls,* Guy Bolton and Plum Wodehouse spun it on drolly:

"Wodehouse," [Jerry] said [again].

"I suppose it is," said Guy, "but that's only to be expected on an opening night . . ."

"What on earth are you talking about?"

"You said it's a good house."

"I didn't. I said Woodhouse."

(For the benefit of the uninitiated, that is the way it is pronounced.)

"Yes, of course it is," said Guy petulantly, looking at the set. "It's supposed to be a small hotel in the wilds of the Hudson. Brick would be all wrong."

Jerry continued to be patient.

"Look," he said. "Let's keep quite calm and thresh this thing out. You concede that there's a man over there in the tenth row."

"Yes."

"With very large spectacles."

"Very large spectacles."

"Well, the point I am trying to establish is that his name is Woodhouse."

(We will continue to misspell it until you get the thing firmly in mind.)

"Oh, you mean his name is Woodhouse?"

"That's right. Plum Wodehouse."

A gentleman in the last row, down whose neck Jerry was breathing, turned.

"I've no doubt what you two are saying is a lot funnier than what's going on onstage," he said, "but I can't follow two plots at once."

"Sorry," said Guy, cringing. "Actually, what's going on on the stage is very funny indeed."

"Sez you," said the man in the last row morosely.

Most of this is the wonderfully witty (and Wodehousian) invention of two men, who would, from that December night in 1915 until the death of one of them sixty-one years later, become such fast friends that they would come to think of each other as brothers, as *confidants,* as necessary extensions of the other.

That night, the fortuitousness of Plum's appearance at the opening of *Very Good Eddie* wasn't lost on Jerome Kern, who had, in London, in 1906, worked with the tall and taciturn writer on Seymour Hicks's *The Beauty of Bath.* Fortunately for all of them, he immediately introduced Guy and Plum.

They hit it off, as well they might. Plum had many of the qualities of George Middleton.

He was tall. (So was Middleton.)

He was shy. (So was Middleton, though not quite so shy as Plum.)

He was in love with the very idea of theatre. (So was Middleton.)

He was wonderfully talented as a developer of character and plot. (So was Middleton, though not quite so talented as Plum.)

He had very little ability in or knowledge of dramatic construction. (Neither did Middleton.)

But Plum Wodehouse had other qualities that made this meeting more than just the coming together of two writers: He was British, from Surrey (a short distance from Guy's birthplace); he had an enormous wit (which he hid in conversation); he had the ability to praise without fawning; and he seemed only to be abidingly interested in writing and dogs.

Jerry sensed that Plum could do for the Princess musicals what he had done for *The Beauty of Bath* in London ten years before, so he invited Plum to join Guy and him and a great many other theatrical types at the Kerns' apartment at 226 West Seventieth Street after the opening.

It was a gala occasion, if you believe the recollections of Bolton and Wodehouse. The Grossmith brothers, Vernon and Irene Castle, Fay Compton and her husband Lauri de Frece, all wandered in after the final curtain fell on their own hit, *Tonight's the Night.* Jerry played the piano and Eva Kern passed the sandwiches and Bolton and Wodehouse passed the time.

If you believe Bolton and Wodehouse.

The trouble for history is, you can't. You couldn't then, and you couldn't later.

In fact, Gerald Bordman, in his biography of Jerome Kern, points out the fact that *Tonight's the Night* closed fully six months *before Very Good Eddie* opened, and its cast embarked immediately for England. He thus speculates that the Bolton-Wodehouse meeting didn't happen on the opening night of *Very Good Eddie* at all; it really took place earlier, around the time of Guy and Jerry's play for Marie Cahill, *Ninety in the Shade,* and he cites a publicity release by Ray Comstock and Bessie Marbury, the Princess Theatre producers, in November of 1915 about ". . . a new musical comedy called 'Fully That' . . . book and lyrics are by Guy Bolton and P. G. Wodehouse and the music is by Jerome Kern . . ." to bolster his point.

Guy, however, had no recollection of such a show in later years, and there isn't a shred of evidence in his papers that *Fully That* ever existed, except possibly in the imagination of Marbury and Comstock's zealous and inventive publicity staff.

To further fog the events of the meeting, Bolton and Wodehouse, in *Bring on the Girls,* include two diary excerpts in recollection of the genesis of the partnership. Guy's goes this way:

> Eddie opened. Excellent reception. All say hit. Kerns for supper. Talked with P. G. Woodhouse [sic], apparently known as Plum. Never heard of him, but Jerry says he writes lyrics, so, being slightly tight, suggested we team up. W. so overcome couldn't answer for a minute, then grabbed my hand and stammered out his thanks.

And Plum's goes this way:

> Went to opening of *Very Good Eddie.* Enjoyed it in spite of lamentable lyrics. Bolton, evidently conscious of this weakness, offered partnership. Tried to hold back and weigh the suggestion, but his eagerness so pathetic that consented. Mem: Am I too impulsive? Fight against this tendency.

Now. Add to this the fact that the *actual* Bolton diaries consist mainly of one-line, elliptical entries, such as "Lunch with M." or "Did one scene of *Sally,*" mix well with a letter from Plum to Guy in 1951, when they were working on *Bring on The Girls,* in which he suggests that ". . . truth must go to the wall if it interferes with entertainment . . ." and all recollections by these two men, particularly when imparted to strangers, become as suspect as the boasts of a shy teenager.

And yet, that very inventive approach to the truth is central to their enduring charm and challenge. To the end of his life, Guy would be a peerless raconteur, holding forth with glee and glibness and only passing references to reality. What mattered least was accuracy and what mattered most was a good story.

So, the details remain unimportant. What *is* important is that the meeting of these three muses of the musical stage took place. And because it did, the course of theatre history was changed, some time in 1915, at some party or other after the opening of some Kern and Bolton show.[3]

The partnership was based upon mutual visions, obsessions, and work habits. Jerry was a driven man, as was Guy, in a more quiet yet determined way. Plum, the least overtly assertive of the trio, had his own private and obssessive habits. A day would not, could not pass without a several-hour-long session at his desk, working out, in longhand and in pencil, the first draft of something. Anything. From 1934 on, he would add a battered and beaten-up Royal typewriter to the equation; but in 1915, his modus operandi was from pencil to pen, with multiple revisions along the way.

Guy was nearly the same. No day could pass without some work being done. However, to the end of his life, he would neither trust nor use a typewriter.

Jerry was equally disciplined. In his early youth, he had set himself the goal of a song a day, and that dictum would define the minimum requirements of his work schedule throughout his creative life.

And so, these common traits of energy, ambition, purpose, and writing habits formed the glue that would unite the trio.

As personalities, they were gloriously dissimilar, but complementary, and that would work for them, too, for a while. Jerry and Guy were gregarious and comfortable with themselves in public. Plum regarded the simplest social gathering as something as desirable as the extraction of a tooth.

It was Jerry Kern who was the constantly determined genius. Assured of himself from that first night on a velocipede at Newark High School, he set his own standards and his own irrefutable rules. He composed the music first. The lyricist would write to his music. Once the melody had been set, once Jerry had transferred it to paper, and in a final ritual, tested the strength of the melody on its own, without its inner voicings, by playing it pristinely with the eraser end of a pencil on the piano, it was set in stone.

Neither Guy nor Plum had that kind of self-confidence. Perhaps it was the loneliness and disarray of both of their boyhoods, the common thread of adolescent insecurity, the absence of love when they were young and needed it most, that allowed each to let the other into their deepest, most secret selves. Associates, wives, children would never see, much less walk through those inner doors, or tread the precious and particular pathways between Plum and Guy that had their beginnings on the December evening they met in 1915.

Their connection would remain as rock solid as Jerome Kern's self-confidence for the rest of their long, long lives.

It was Jerry who joined them together, and it would be Jerry who would fling them apart. But no one that night, in that location filled with hope and dreams, the energy of youth, and the friction of genius against genius would have thought that they would ever *not* work together.

At any rate, the final third of the equation was now in place. It was goodbye to the baby talk of Schuyler Greene and the necessary, last-minute calls to Herbert Reynolds and Harry B. Smith. It would henceforth be lyrics only by P. G. Wodehouse.

And so, these three muses of the musical stage talked well into the night—which was Jerry's favorite time. During the evening or night or early morning—neither Jerry nor Guy went to bed until long after the notices arrived and Plum was too excited to sleep—the three agreed upon the obvious: they would collaborate, and the musicals they would write would contain a balance, an integration of music and lyrics and book. No operetta tricks. No songs dragged in by their necks, no dances dragged in by their heels.

Now, what about money and what about percentages? Jerry had enough business sense to realize that details like these, not discussed before the first rush of emotion faded and the hard work set in, had a habit of haunting partnerships.

Guy remembered the next moments in a letter to Edward Cazelet in 1979. He turned to Plum and asked: "How does a fifty-fifty split between us sound?"

"Lyrics aren't worth what the play is, you know that," demurred Plum. (All of his life he would vie with Guy for the title of Worst Businessman in the Galaxy.)

"I'll be coming to you for advice about the book."

"Don't know. Doesn't seem fair," said Plum, honestly confused.

Jerry leaned forward. "It *is* fair," he said, looking levelly at the bewildered writer.

Well, why worry, thought Plum. They were both good chaps; he could tell. It felt fine to be around them and to be near the theatre again.

"I've been negotiating the contracts," said Jerry, in a logical and factual way, "and so it's only fair if I get three percent of the gross. You and Guy will get two percent apiece. Is that satisfactory?"

Plum by this time didn't really care. Gross. Percent. What difference did it make so long as they worked together?

He looked at Guy. Guy seemed to like the idea. Plum nodded affirmatively. "We'll make the contract with T. B. Harms," said Jerry.

"Jerry's a partner, with Max Dreyfus and his brother Louie," said Guy. Plum again accepted, and they shook hands. But the agreement wasn't set to paper for two years.

Why not?

Jerry was a good businessman, but he had just consummated a supreme contract, and enough was enough. He was happy to have brought the three of them together. If they succeeded—and even *his* fertile imagination couldn't foresee how gloriously they would succeed—there'd be time enough to draw up a written contract.

As for Plum: all of his life, he would regard the money he made with amazement and would wonder at the justice that would allow him to do what he loved and make a fortune at it.

And as for Guy: at the time, he was a little less naive but a little more carefree about signed contracts and money matters than he would later become. In 1915 and well into 1916, he was able to live high on his new-found notoriety and increasing royalties without a thought of the future. After all, when you're young and handsome and unattached and the chorus girls and the compliments flowed without cease, why diminish the delirium?

So, with a handshake, the trio was formed and the course of theatre history was changed irrevocably.[4]

## Chapter

# 8

# Bring on the Girls
# Again

## 1916

The next day, Jerry introduced Plum to Bessie Marbury and Ray Comstock as an irremovable partner. Plum's reputation as a humorist was known to the two producers and Jerry's persuasive powers were in full force; several weeks later they agreed that the resident creative staff should be increased by one.

News spread fast—or possibly the Princess's publicity staff got the word out fast. Whatever the source, within the month, both Colonel Savage and Abe Erlanger would contact the trio, through Jerry, with offers.

By the time a few more weeks passed the trio would (1) evolve two musical ideas for the Princess; (2) sign with Colonel Savage to help Anne Caldwell rework a feathery piece called *Pom Pom;* (3) have preliminary contact with Klaw and Erlanger to collaborate with Emmerich Kalman on an operetta tentatively titled *Little Miss Springtime* (Jerry would supply interpolations); and (4) become embroiled in a dispute between Bessie and Ray that would threaten to blow the Princess Theatre apart, almost before it had really come together.

The logistics are fairly staggering: Soon after *Very Good Eddie* opened, Eva and Jerry Kern moved from West Seventieth Street to Sagamore Road in Bronxville, an hour north of Manhattan. Guy stayed in New York, on West Fifty-Eighth Street, close to the stage doors. Plum, who had met Ethel's daughter, Leonora, a few months before and had taken to her as quickly and completely as he had to her mother, looked for and found a bigger bungalow in Bellport for the three of them, when Leonora visited. When she did not, they stayed in New York, at 375 Central Park West.

Neither memories nor records define the details of their collaboration in those days and nights, but the commute must have been formidable for whoever did most of the traveling, and one wonders how any of them had the time or the energy to work at all. But work they did, and well. They were, after all, young, and success had begun to brush each of them, together and apart.

It hardly seemed like a winter that would allow the presence of romance, let alone courtship. But Guy at thirty-one had energy to burn. While Jerry and Plum looked on in something like admiration, he managed a juggling act that would have made W. C. Fields envious.

In September, Justine Johnstone had abandoned her flag in the *Follies* and traded it for the mantle of stardom in *Stop! Look! Listen!,* a new Charles Dillingham show with music by Irving Berlin. It opened at the Globe two nights after *Very Good Eddie*'s December premiere and was a solid success.

During the December rehearsals for that show, she was the recipient of the charms and the gifts of the dashing Guy Bolton. In early January 1916, an item appeared in the *New York Sun,* gushing that "Guy Bolton has given a diamond ring and part of his share of *Very Good Eddie* to Justine Johnstone."

But the story was out of Ray and Bessie's publicity department, working overtime and behind the times. By then, Justine Johnstone's star had begun to fade in Guy's eyes. The brightness was rapidly being taken over by Marguerite Namara, who had opened on October 14, 1915, at the Shubert, in *Alone at Last.* The play received warm but not ecstatic reviews, though Marguerite's "brilliant voice" and "frail, flowerlike variety of beauty" were extolled by the New York press.

The poetry wasn't lost on Guy, nor was the frail and flowerlike beauty, particularly since, as he soon discovered, it was purely a surface frailty. Marguerite was more fire than flower, and beneath the petals she emerged as a tiger lily with the soul of a romantic.

If those who remember her are correct, Marguerite Namara searched for the lovely moment, the rare experience that challenged as much as it fulfilled. She was intrigued by Guy, who excited her sense of adventure.

So, she and Guy became lovers, and in February of 1916, she became pregnant.

It was a development that could not, in that theatrical age, be presented in operetta, nor even on the stage of the renegade Princess.

Guy did the only honorable thing he could in those Edwardian days: He offered to give the child his name. The only problem was that Marguerite was still married to Frederick Toye. So, in a move that would become more and more pervasive as his life spun out, Guy left the unpleasant details to Marguerite and plunged into his work.

Jerry, in addition to the commitments with the Princess and Erlanger and Savage, had contracted to write the score for an untitled musical that the Shuberts and Bessie would be producing, and to supply, at London's Gaiety, some songs for an Ivor Novello show titled *Theodore and Co.*

But, like Guy, he was young and indefatigable, and this commitment didn't prevent him from spearheading one of the fiercest confrontations the trio ever had.

It began with a hairbrained idea of Ray Comstock's. Against the advice of Bessie, he proposed that the new Princess trio look over—and, implicitly, accept—an idea he had of turning Charles Hoyt's 1894 hit, *A Milk White Flag*, into a musical.

The three were summoned and presented with the original script. They retreated to Bronxville. What they read they hated and what they hated they made known to Ray the next day.

"It's all about a funeral, and a mock corpse. Do you think Elsie can design a funeral parlor set?" Guy recalled asking. (He loved to tell and retell this story in later years.)

"Of course she can," answered Comstock. "And that's not important. The corpse has two daughters, and they have beaux. What more do you want?"

"It's not what *we* want. It's what the audience wants that counts," said Jerry. "Besides, where do the songs come in? The daughters think their father is lying dead on ice in the next room. They'll scarcely be in the mood to sing."

"That's up to you," answered Ray, his dander rising. "I'm not writing the show."

And the interview was over.

"All right," asked Guy of Jerry, as they left Comstock's office, "what do we do?"

"We don't do *that* show," answered Jerry, his face set. "We've brought *charm* to the Princess. We're not going to put it on ice. We'll give him some *better* ideas."

"Righto," said Plum cheerily, speaking for the first time that morning.[1]

Within a week, they were back in Comstock's office with two musical synopses—one, a patriotic piece about a girl who dreams of trading her dishwashing job for fame and stardom (working title: *The Little Thing*), and another about a young man who marries despite the protestations of his rich Quaker aunt (working title: *Oh, Boy!*).

Bessie had seen both, and she accompanied the trio to the meeting, ready to help them convince Ray that he was wrong about his funeral musical.

Comstock listened to the synopses and, then, over the unanimous pro-testations of Bessie Marbury and Bolton, Wodehouse, and Kern, established some sort of theatrical record by rejecting, in one day, *two* immortal, if nascent, musicals. One, four years later—as *Sally*—would become the long-est running musical in the American theatre up to that time. The other, with its working title intact, would become the longest running Princess musical by far.

But that morning in 1916, Comstock was adamant. For reasons known only to him, it was *A Milk White Flag* or nothing.

Shock enveloped the room. Jerry broke the fragile silence.

"Then you do it without us," he answered, slamming his hat on his head and leading the trio's exit.

"And without me," added Bessie, lumbering after them.

It was the end of the Marbury-Comstock company at the Princess, and very nearly the end of the Princess itself. In fact, if Ray Comstock had been right—if *A Milk White Flag* had been a success—the history of the American musical might have been different.

Ignoring the reaction of his fellow founders of the Princess, Comstock brought in John Golden and Anne Caldwell and enlisted the aid of Jack Hazzard—when he wasn't onstage with *Very Good Eddie*—to turn the Hoyt hit into his hit.

It was one of his more disastrous decisions. Retitled *Go to It, A Milk White Flag* went nowhere. It opened at the Princess in October, lasted for three weeks, and then took to the road, where it *really* died.

But Ray Comstock, like any producer, was a survivor. He extended the hand of monetary friendship to Jerry by using two of his interpolated melodies in *Go to*

*It*. He agreed to read and then produce *A Happy Thought,* a comedy that Guy and George Middleton had been working on for the past year. And he furthermore agreed to take a second look at the two musical comedy scenarios that Bolton and Wodehouse and Kern had submitted to him some months earlier.

But the trio's momentum had been broken. Whatever work he wanted from them would have to wait. They'd already committed themselves not only to Klaw and Erlanger's *Little Miss Springtime* but to the emancipated Bessie Marbury and a third musical scenario they had developed about infidelity in a department store (working title: *Have a Heart*).

Furthermore, Guy was in trouble. Some of the balls he'd been juggling were beginning to fall on his head. The first draft of *A Happy Thought* rested at the bottom of a pile of papers in his apartment. Despite increasingly pointed telephone calls and fruitless visits from George Middleton, Guy was neglecting the play in favor of musicals and fun and romance.

Now, goaded by an ultimatum from George and the reality of Ray Comstock's agreement to produce it, he returned to the comedy. He wrote a second draft and sent it back to Middleton, who, within a few weeks, came up with the third draft. By March, they were laboring together in Middleton's apartment in Greenwich Village, and by the end of the month, they had a finished script which Guy brought to Comstock.

Ray liked it enough to put it into rehearsal in the early spring. Guy returned to *Little Miss Springtime* and an ill-fated production by Douglas Wood of his one-act play *Children* at the Bandbox.


Artlessness imitated life that spring. In those salad days and nights, the trio could not only savor the sweet life, they could make a living from it. They had experienced enough phenomenal coincidences and fortuitous introductions to convince Plum and Guy that, given the opportunity, life would behave like a musical comedy plot.

Of course, there were dragons to be fought, in the form of producers. Even with a little success behind them, they still quaked in the presence of most of them. At least, Guy and Plum did. Take the case of Abraham Lincoln Erlanger, *Little Miss Springtime*'s producer: small of stature and large of ego, he breathed impressive amounts of fire. "Tell me about Erlanger," asks P. G. Wodehouse of Guy Bolton in their theatrical memoir. "He really exists, does he? You've actually seen him? What's he like? To look at, I mean."

Guy considered.

"He's rather like a toad," he said at length. "It is as though Nature had said to itself 'I'll make a toad,' and then halfway through had changed its mind and said, 'No, by golly, I won't. I'll make a czar of the American theatre.'"

Erlanger surrounded himself with bigness. His office was monumental, containing, besides a desk as large as a pool table, a punching bag, a barber chair, and a wall bookcase that contained a small library of books about Napoleon.

"He has a Napoleon complex," says Guy, again in the Wodehouse-Bolton theatre memoir. "He not only admires Napoleon, he thinks he *is* Napoleon."

Later, Plum would capture—nay, skewer—Erlanger in a Kern song called "Napoleon":

> Napoleon was a little guy:
> They used to call him Shorty.
> He only stood about so high,
> His chest was under forty.
> But when folks started talking mean,
> His pride it didn't injure:
> "My Queen," he'd say to Josephine,
> "The thing that counts is ginger."
>
> He got too fat. We all know that
> From portraits in the galleries.
> He never seemed to learn the knack
> Of laying off the calories.
> But though his waist was large, he faced
> And overcame all foemen.
> He knew quite well it's brains that tell
> And not a guy's abdomen.

But that was later, in *Have a Heart,* a show *not* produced by Erlanger. In the summer of 1916, both Bolton and Wodehouse approached the Dragon of Forty-Second Street with considerably more respect and restraint.

Erlanger immediately demanded that they change the title, *Little Miss Springtime.* "We don't have nothing little at the New Amsterdam Theatre," he said, and the show henceforth and throughout its successful run would be known as *Miss Springtime.* [2]

Erlanger represented more than Napoleonic power: he stood for the Big League on Broadway, and Abe Erlanger and *Miss Springtime* would be to Guy and Plum what Charles Frohman and *The Girl from Utah* had been to Jerry. Not only would they be introduced to the ruthless and redoubtable Klaw-Erlanger Syndicate but to Julian Mitchell, Broadway's leading choreographer, and Joseph Urban, the legendary set designer who dressed the *Follies* as lavishly and imaginatively as Ziegfeld undressed its showgirls.

Life imitated art in Joe Urban, too. He was, if the memories of those with whom he worked are correct, fairly baroque in personality. "In those days," reminisced Guy and Plum later, "people collected Urbanisms as they later collected the quaint sayings of Samuel Goldwyn."

Austrian by extraction, Urban ignored his native tongue in favor of a constructed language: He drank no milk because it cuddled his stomach. He liked the air of Atlantic City because it was so embracing. He always promised producers that he would have his scene sketches ready at the drop of a bucket. Guy and Plum recalled that when they met him and told him they worked at the Princess, he asked them cautiously, "This *Goes to It* — you boys did not write it?" They said not, enthusiastically, whereupon he relaxed. "I am so glad" (they said he said). "For me it is a very bad smell. It should be taken away by the grubbage collector to the city dumpings."[3]

This reconstruction, incidentally, blithely ignores chronology. *Go to It* opened after *Miss Springtime.*

Guy and Plum settled down to their work on *Miss Springtime* immediately. As in *Very Good Eddie,* Guy did little to the basic book. In its framework and its devices of mistaken identity, it smacked of operetta. But Bolton the architect did for it what he had done for the first two Princess musicals: he spiced up the dialogue, replaced old jokes with new ones, smoothed out some of the absurdities and satirized others, and generally greased the ways so that dialogue slid easily into song and song slid serenely into dialogue.

He even managed to steal from himself. The two comic highlights of the evening, carried by Jack Hazzard, whom Erlanger had lured away from *Very Good Eddie* with a very good salary, were a takeoff on old fashioned melodrama ("Fair but Faithless, or The Poisoned Nut Sundae"), and a scene in which molasses candy in the mouth prevents a character from spilling a secret. The last device was, of course, not too subtly out of Guy's 1914 play *The Rule of Three.*

The plot of *Miss Springtime* involves a talented girl from a rundown town in Hungary. The girl—played by Hungarian coloratura Sari Petrass—is smitten by an opera singer who comes home to their shared and simple village to appear in a festival. But the opera singer who shows up turns out to be bogus. The young girl, informed of this, will have nothing to do with an apparent liar. She decides to go to Budapest and find the *real* opera singer to assess her talent. But True to the spirit of operetta, the imposter turns out to be not an imposter at all but the *real* opera star, and he introduces her to the rigors of the artistic life. One glimpse, and she decides to return to her home and her sincere, simple, and abandoned village love.

Guy's refurbishing of this nineteenth-century edifice took the form of chic observations, mostly supplied by the comic couple, Michael Robin (Jack Hazzard) and Maimie Stone (Georgia O'Ramey). Michael gazes into the "plate glass depths" of Maimie's eyes and refers to the imposter as "a baritone with the soul of a tenor." Maimie weeps over an old man's death, telling Michael that "they tell me he dropped dead as he was coming out of the café," to which Michael replies, "No. No! Just as he was going *in*. That was the sad part."

In the second act, Maimie leaves Michael for somebody new, and her excuse is that she only partially returned his affection. Michael agrees. "Yes," he says, "you returned my letters, but you kept the diamond ring." Maimie has an explanation. "Well, my love for you had died," she chirps, "but my feelings hadn't changed toward the ring."

When he tells her she'll be sorry for leaving him, she huffs, "You can't hold a candle to what *he's* making now." "No?" asks Michael. "No," she answers. "He's making ammunition." "I hope his business starts booming," replies Michael.

Jerry interpolated two songs, one of which, "Castle in the Air," became the show's hit. Each is pleasant but perfunctory. Plum's lyrics, however, particularly in "Saturday Night," the other Kern song, sparkle:

> She was a very good girl on Sunday,
> Not quite so good on Monday,
> On Tuesday, she was even worse,
> On Wedn'sday and Thursday, goodnight Nurse!
> She seemed to lose by Friday
> All sense of what was right.
> She started out quite mild and meek,
> But her virtue seemed to spring a leak,
> She kept getting worse all thro' the week,
> And oh you Saturday night!

Clever, never losing their charm, Plum's words added a literate dimension and a gentle touch of satire. Before the show was three minutes old, he had suspended a satirical counterpoint above the opening number, Kalman's popular "Throw Me a Rose." As the lover warbled warmly, the comic counterattacked with:

> Quit your doze—
> Getting out of bed's a task.
> Still it's not so much to ask,
> Just to sling a man one rose. . . .

And in the mock melodrama, he turned positively Gilbertian:

> He was not a pleasant persing
> With his plotting and his cursing,
> But we liked him just because he wanted blood.
> . . .
> You wrong me Lord Chalmondelay
> Although I hugged you fondelay
> Your wife is far more purer than you think. . . .

*Miss Springtime* opened on September 25 at the New Amsterdam to ecstatic reviews. The *Mirror* chanted: "It is a long while since New York has had such an unmistakable combination of gay, tuneful music, witty lines and intelligent lyrics," and *Theatre* later repeated the refrain: "It is good all through, vernal and fresh and blithesome; as good as anything of its kind and better than anything done for years. . . ."

It was a solid hit, the first for the triumvirate of Bolton and Wodehouse and Kern, even though Kern was serving as an interpolater.

But Guy, at the moment, was unable to react to this success. Marguerite had finally outgrown the soft leather costume she loved so much and wore so well on her papier-mâché alp in *Alone at Last*. In early September, she left the show, taking the costume with her for future, slimmer times. She told Frederick Toye she was going home to spend some time with her mother. He offered to accompany her. She refused.

Jerry and Plum were privy to the affair and its impending consequence. "If he's born on the fifteenth, we'll name him Pelham," said Guy to Plum, "in honor of you and your birthday."

Plum beamed uncertainly. Marguerite silently reserved decision. She had met with Isadora Duncan and decided to go back to California with Guy to have the baby; Guy, fascinated and flabbergasted and ultimately rendered speechless by these two determined women, agreed.

Shortly after *Miss Springtime* settled in for the first week of its 224-performance run, Guy and Marguerite climbed aboard the Twentieth Century Limited.

The two unweds found their way to their first class compartment. What occurred next very nearly brought on the birth of a baby in Grand Central Station. Suspecting something more than a trip home, a distraught Frederick Toye, brandishing a revolver, boarded the train, and found his way to the compartment. At least, Guy swore in later years that he had a revolver. He also swore that Toye chased him through the train, and he had to leap for his life.

It was a good story, but totally out of character for Frederick Toye.[4]

Still, whatever happened that afternoon finally and absolutely ended the marriage of Marguerite Namara and Frederick Toye. It was a sad moment. Toye was an honorable man, and although he had never been a match for his unusual wife, he felt that no other man ever would be, either. At least at that moment.

That he was right did nothing to diminish his understandable outrage at the way Marguerite had chosen to leave him. And Marguerite, though an unregenerate rule breaker, had never dreamed of hurting anyone, and particularly not Frederick, who had been and would always be nothing but caring and kind to her. She refused a reconciliation and asked for nothing from him.

Two weeks later, in the San Francisco home of her friend Cobina Wright, attended by her mother, Cobina, and a doctor who was both skilled and silent, Marguerite Namara gave birth to a baby girl.

"It's the fifteenth," said Guy, as he sat on the bed.

"I know," answered Marguerite sleepily.

"Can't be Pelham," he ventured, thoughtfully.

"No," she answered.

"Could be Pamela," he suggested.

"It should be Marguerite," said Marguerite, "after my grandmother. And me."

"How about Margaret?" Guy asked.

"Margaret's good," answered Marguerite, drifting off to exhausted sleep.

And so on October 15, 1916, Margaret Nolan was born to Guy and Marguerite Nolan. (Their names on the birth certificate matched the initials on Marguerite's luggage, which stood in a corner of the bedroom.)

Plum was only mildly put off by the news. "Can't predict such things," he said on the phone, "but I *can* predict this: When you get back to New York, there'll be enough work for you."

He was right. Life had moved out of second gear for the trio.

Jerry and Harry B. Smith were hard at work on the Shubert show, which was having identity problems. First named *Strike the Lyre,* then *For Love of Mike,* then *Girls Will Be Girls,* and finally, *Love O' Mike,* it was slated for a November opening in Philadelphia.

Comstock had moved *Very Good Eddie* from the 299 seat Princess to the 1200 seat Lyceum, where a seventeen-year-old, aspiring composer named Richard Rodgers would sit through it six times. ". . . It pointed the way I wanted to be led," he later wrote.[5]

*Miss Springtime* continued to be a solid sellout. On the strength of its success, Bessie Marbury had convinced Colonel Henry Savage that he should produce their department store show, *Have a Heart*—which would be Bolton and Wodehouse and Kern, from beginning to end.

And Ray Comstock, for the next to last time, rejected *The Little Thing* but decided that he wanted the trio to ready *Oh, Boy!* for an early winter opening at the Princess. In a break with Comstock tradition, he agreed to sign a contract *before* they delivered a script and gave them carte blanche on the casting.

"Those were the days," Plum and Guy would recall exuberantly in their memoirs. Plum, his fondest fantasies of life in the theatre now realized, wrote in *Vanity Fair* under the pseudonym of P. Brooke-Haven:

> . . . The public has at last awakened to the fact that it is possible for the book of a musical comedy to be coherent, sensible, and legitimately amusing, and now it demands these qualities before it consents to allow the boxoffice man to withdraw the two dollar bill from its grasp.
>
> The man who is responsible for this state of affairs, who has revolutionized musical comedy to such an extent that all the other authors will either have to improve their stuff or go back to box stenciling, is Guy Bolton, author of "Miss Springtime." . . . the solid rock on which its success is founded is Guy Bolton's book. It is sane and sincere, and the humor with which it is crammed is distributed evenly instead of being laid on in isolated chunks. . . . His construction is perfect. . . .[6]

Not a mention of Jerry or of Plum himself. But that was Plum's way. His loyalty knew neither logic nor deviation.

• • •

Once Namara had safely delivered their daughter, Guy left her in the care of her mother, Isadora Duncan, and Cobina Wright, and rushed back to New York for rehearsals of *Have a Heart.*

There was trouble. The show was weak in comedy and female leads. Considerably more disconcerting, Bessie Marbury, whose first and most comfortable home was her agency, allowed her interest in the show to be bought out by Colonel Henry Savage.

Colonel Savage drove hard bargains. Although Bessie really had neither the heart nor the hide to be a producer and had probably always wanted to return to agenting, her primary profession, her departure was also prompted by Colonel Savage's noting, in the fine print of their contract, that if she stayed, *he* would have the exclusive use of Kern, Bolton, and Wodehouse for three shows. Bessie's loyalty was as large as she was, and she was not about to sell her clients and discoveries into Savage slavery. She left, taking the contract with her.

Bessie had been their mentor, their goad, and their security blanket during their apprenticeship. Now they would have to face the jungle of Broadway alone.

And if Erlanger was forbidding, Colonel Savage was foreboding. Perhaps he felt compelled to live up to his last name. Guy had only seen him from a distance in 1910. In closeup, the Colonel was regarded by his fellow producers and those who worked for him with a mixture of awe, fear, and resentment. In his mid-fifties in 1916, he was tall and thin and benevolent looking—a sort of Jeff to Abe Erlanger's Mutt. He sported a handsome shank of gray hair and walked with a slight limp—possibly brought on, according to Plum and Guy's reminiscences, by having ". . . been shot in the foot by some indignant author."

When Guy and Plum faced the colonel in his office with the suggestion that they bring in vaudevillian Billy B. Van for the part of Henry the elevator boy (who boasted that he'd told more women where to get off than any other man in New York), Colonel Savage is purported to have agreed to the replacement. But only if Guy and Plum would pay half of Van's expensive salary for the first three months.

The arrangement isn't beyond belief. Although the success of *Miss Springtime* had brought in a flood of offers from producers, the rest of the world was still fairly unaware of Bolton and Wodehouse and Kern. In the next year, the threesome would burst upon the public consciousness like an artillery barrage, but next year was still two months away.

They agreed. They were making more money than any of them had in their lives. And besides, they had the next Princess show to occupy their time and their talent.

# 9

# Here Come the Stars

## 1917

In his sixties and beyond, Guy would boast that they wrote *Oh, Boy!* in six days.

The script that was handed to Ray Comstock in November of 1916[1] may well have taken only six days to complete. But it, like *The Little Thing,* was one that the three had been working up ever since they met.

They toiled, that autumn, mostly at Jerry's home in Bronxville, spending long hours there out of desire and practicality. The trains ran infrequently to Bellport. Guy's apartment on West Fifty-eighth Street or Plum's on Central Park West would have been logical halfway houses, but neither contained a piano. Jerry had a car, but one traumatic ride to and from Bellport with him at the wheel was enough for Guy.

So, they rolled up their collective sleeves and went to work in Bronxville. Guy prepared a rough script, which they tore apart to fit the Kern tunes, then put back together. As usual, Guy liked to work forward and backward from the songs, timing the intervals between them. Three years later, he would tell an interviewer from the *New York Sun:* "Anybody who thinks that writing a musical comedy is easy and is torn off in the hours of rest, meditation, and prayer must think again. A drama is easier to write than a musical comedy. Ibsen didn't have to count his pages back to the last number or count the minutes since the girls were last on when he was doing his bit!"

It was one way of putting it, but not the only way, and although Guy did count pages, by his own admission, his skill was considerably more than mathematical.

Plum liked to work from completed melodies, and Jerry liked that idea almost as much as integrating his music into the plot.

Later, Plum would tell David Jasen, ". . . when you have the melody, you can see which are the musical high spots in it and can fit the high spots of the lyric to them. Anyway, that's how I like working, and to hell with anyone who says I oughtn't to."

As they toiled, their spirits levitated. *Oh, Boy!* began to write itself. The plot fit the songs and the songs fit the plot so easily, it was eerie. Once the show went into rehearsal, the only major book change from their original concept would be a geographical one: originally set in an upstate New York town near a college, it was moved on the road to Southampton, Long Island, near a country club—a location that would be more recognizable and personal to members of the Fashion 500 that would fill most of the 299 seats of the Princess on opening night and at benefits.

On November 3, 1916, the trio delivered a rough script and score to Comstock and his director Bob Milton. One reading, one hearing of the music convinced Ray that what the three had told him on the phone from Bronxville had been no mere boast.

Nothing was spared in pulling a cast together that would make the opening a gala occasion, and Comstock's casting coup of the century would involve two faces from Guy's recent past.

"I've just done something that'll make every other producer on Broadway hate me," said Ray, facing the triumvirate a week into casting.

They refused to pick up on the straight line he'd just thrown them and regarded him with expectant silence. "I've just lured Marion Davies and Justine Johnstone away from Ziegfeld," he added, dramatically.

"What do you mean, *lured?*" huffed Jerry. "Marion was in the chorus of *Nobody Home* before Ziegfeld added an *e* to her name. She's just circling back. And, as for Justine—" His eyes roamed to Guy, who was busily picking lint from his coat sleeve.

"Wait a minute. The script's set," said Guy, lying and leaving his lint.

"So are the songs," added Jerry.

Plum retained an eloquent silence.

"You know nothing's set," said Comstock, regarding their very rough draft. "And anyway, they won't have *starring* parts. Just lines. You know," finished Ray, waving his arms. "Lines."

"Marion stutters," said Guy.

"Stammers. She stammers," rejoined Ray. "And she attracts backers with lots of money."

And that was the end of *that* interview. [2]

The addition to the cast of two of Ziegfeld's most glamorous beauties, one of whom had lately been seen in public on the arm of a middle-aged baron of journalism, certainly added dazzle to the Princess's royal image.

The trio was there for the signing of the contracts. As Plum and Guy later described it:

> There were two town cars parked at the curb before the Princess with a pair of uniformed chauffeurs standing by them. The Delage bore no identifying insignia, but on the door of the Pierce Arrow were two J's intertwined back to back, like the double L's emblazoned on the royal coach of the Sun Monarch.
>
> "It must be the girls!" said Guy.
>
> They went up the stair and found the outer office in a state of flutter.
>
> A ripple of laughter greeted them as they entered Ray's office. . . .
>
> The girls were quite breathtakingly lovely. Marion was eighteen and Justine a year and a half older. Both wore mink coats that even a masculine eye could see were the best that the mink family had to offer. Both wore a spray of orchids as if orchids were an everyday affair—which for them they were. Diamonds sparkled at their wrists and glistened more discreetly through the sheer black silk stocking that covered Marion's slender ankle.
>
> Bob Milton, a mature and serious man, sat on the sofa beside Marion, gazing at her as Bernard Berenson would gaze on a Botticelli Venus.
>
> "Don't waste your time with them," he said, as Guy and Plum were presented. "They're only writers. I'm the man that's going to make you into an actress."
>
> "Yes, b-but they'll have to write the w-words I'm to say," [s-said Marion]. . . .
>
> Justine Johnstone was, if anything, even more likely than her friend to provoke the long low whistle. . . .
>
> "The girls are ready to sign up with us," said Ray . . . "as long as they get parts."
>
> Guy assured them they would have parts.

"And names," said Justine. "Not just 'first girl' and 'second girl.'

"Of course you have names. Yours is Polly Andrews."

"Is that a play on polyandrous?"

Guy later remembered that that flash of Justine Johnstone acumen drove him to the nearest telephone to assure Marguerite long distance that, although Justine Johnstone might be Polly Andrews, he was definitely *not* polygamous.

In June, Comstock opened Guy and George Middleton's comedy *A Happy Thought* at the Colonial Theatre in Cleveland. A week of dismal notices convinced him that the Bolton/Middleton opus about a girl named Polly would never make it to Broadway.

But, sitting in the audience one of the nights that week was David Belasco, who saw what Comstock failed to see in the play. Within a month, he had bought out Comstock's contract with the playwrights.

"Belasco's ready to go ahead with *A Happy Thought*," enthused George Middleton over the phone the day he received the news. "He's going to lure Ina Claire away from Ziegfeld."

"Another lure? I'll never work for Ziegfeld now," mused Guy.

"What do you mean?"

"Never mind."

"When can we get to the rewrites?"

"Soon. After *Have a Heart*. And before we do the final rewrites on *Oh, Boy!*"

"Oh boy," muttered Middleton.

"Don't worry about it, George," said Guy. "We're young. When you're young you always have time."

Middleton was not reassured.[3]

So, with three balls in the air and more to follow, the trio entrained for Atlantic City for the out-of-town opening night of *Have a Heart*.

One look at Grace Field in the pivotal role of Dolly Barbazon and Jerry suggested Louise Dresser, with whom he had worked as a pianist, as a replacement. Dresser had the voice and presence that Field lacked, and Jerry knew that with her in the role his melodies would be sung as he wanted them to be sung. Savage agreed, and when the show opened again, on the cold and snowy evening of December 28, 1916, in Reading, Pennsylvania, Louise Dresser had replaced the not-so-amazing Grace.

That much done, Jerry went back to an ailing *Love O' Mike* and left Plum and Guy to work on *Have a Heart* before its January opening at the Liberty.

His absence shows. *Have a Heart* contains one of Jerry's second echelon scores, although his notes in the prompt script indicate that there was some fairly sophisticated underscoring in the show—a device he would refine still further in *Oh, Boy!*.

Guy missed Marguerite enough to use her name for his romantic lead and for Plum to insert a message into one of the lyrics:

> Oh, the sad time I've had,
> Peggy dear, away
> From you.

It would be the first and last such public display of private emotion from Guy. In fact, Plum, still a newlywed, at least in spirit, probably orchestrated the poignancy for him.

Set in a department store (act 1) and a seaside hotel (act 2) *Have a Heart* was a Princess show epitomized. Ruddy Schoonmaker (Thurston Hall) owns a unique department store, where the well being of the salesgirls outweighs the well being of the customers. As Ruddy observes, via Plum:

> Why pick on some poor little thing
> Who's been out all night tangoing,
> Because she gets to work at one o'clock instead of nine?
> . . . I'm making it my mission
> To improve her sad condition,
> And like Heaven, I'll protect the working girl.
> . . .
> It costs but little to supply
> Dill pickles and martinis dry
> Which put her in a mood to face the labors of the day. . . ."

Ruddy is being sued for divorce by Margaret (Ellen Van Bien) because she thinks he's in love with Dolly Barbazon (Louise Dresser), a present silver screen queen who once worked for Ruddy at the ". . . glassware, rubber plants, goldfish, dog collars, recent fiction and statuettes of Charles Chaplin counter." Ruddy is no workhorse. He explains his relaxed demeanor by admitting airily, "I work so hard, I'm always through."

Comic couple Ted Sheldon (Donald MacDonald) and Lizzie O'Brian (Marjorie Gateson) add to the general atmosphere of abandon, and Henry, the elevator boy (Billy B. Van), decimates determination at every step. Told by Ted that the only way to start anything is to begin at the bottom, he counters with: "That so? How about learning to swim?"

Ruddy and Peggy decide to try to save their marriage by spending a night anonymously at the Ocean View Hotel in Blueport, R.I. (an obvious renaming of Plum's place in Bellport, L.I.). They get away, but not clean, because — shades of *Nobody Home* and *Very Good Eddie* — everybody who was in the department store in act 1 somehow turns up at the hotel in act 2.

There's a running sequence with a confidence man who passes phony twenty-dollar bills and pins it on Ruddy so that *he* can marry Peggy, and an innocent tryst between Ruddy and Dolly that Peggy misinterprets. And, there's a pasting together, at the last minute, of all the mixups and mysteries by Dolly and Henry, so that Ruddy can, on the last line of the show, put his manacled arms around Peggy and declare blissfully, "I want my life sentence."

Along the way, there's merriment and cleverness. Although the entire play is a paean to married life, it's still leavened by the now-to-be-expected Bolton barbs: The confidence man says to Ruddy, "I've met the ideal girl," to which Ruddy replies, "Let her stay ideal. Don't marry her." Peggy's uncle cautions anyone who will listen: "Don't say 'I will.' Those words are associated with the greatest mistake of my life." And his wife chimes in dissonantly with: "Husband and liar — I don't know why the language is cluttered with two words that mean exactly the same thing."

But that's only balance, something to prevent the pervasive sweetness from turning sticky. And although some of the humor is of the gasp and groan variety ("I've got money to burn." "Well, you've met your match."), there's enough true, creative, sophisticated wit to justify Guy's instant elevation in the press to the prime ministership of clever lines in clever musical comedies — a position he would hold for the next two decades.

He once again gave smart swains smart remarks: Owen, the confidence man, is Dolly's cousin, ". . . twice removed — to Sing Sing." Henry calls Dolly a real pal, and she counters with, "I know all about that pal thing. The men tell me you're the nicest little girl under the sun, but it's always some little cuddler who's the nicest girl under the moon." And when Henry effuses to her, "Woman — your beauty maddens me like wine!" she replies, in perfect counterpoint, "Thank you for those few kind words."

*Have a Heart* was a pivotal show not only for Bolton and Wodehouse and Kern but for the American musical theatre in general. What had once been tentatively revolutionary was now undeniably realized. The effortless transition from dialogue into song that Jerry and Guy had begun in *Nobody Home* and developed in *Very Good Eddie* was given, for the first time, the literate dimension of Plum's lyrics.

In act 1, Ted tells Lizzie: "I wish you didn't have to bother with business." He kisses her and follows this with, "Lizzie! Marry me. I hate to have you working in a store!" Lizzie answers, "I'd rather have a job without a husband than a husband without a job," and slides into song:

> I've always said that the man I would wed
> Must be one who would work all the time,
> One with ambition
> Who'd make it his mission
> To win a position sublime. . . .

Later, Henry tries to induce Dolly to go off to the Ocean View Hotel with him. She resists in dialogue, but, as her resistence diminishes, her urge to sing increases, and the interchange continues, to music:

HENRY:    I tell you I'll look like something—I don't know what—but something.

DOLLY:    Well, I'm used to taking desperate chances. All right, Henry, I'll go. How I love to go out to some live spot . . . (*Sings*) . . . where there's light and an orchestra plays—

HENRY:    Where you hand the head-waiter a five spot
             Or you don't get a table for days.

DOLLY:    Where the dresses are all up to the minute
             And where everything's lovely and gay—

HENRY:    And the night's gone before you begin it;
             So you finish things up through the day.

Beyond this, the trio developed a sense of form and balance that would be imitated for years to come. In the case of *Have a Heart,* this balance would be initiated by Guy and Plum—only, probably, because Jerry was busy elsewhere.

Jerry and Colonel Savage were convinced that Ruddy and Peggy's love duet "And I Am All Alone" would be the show's hit and wanted it reprised and positioned with that in mind. But while the Colonel was counting his receipts and Jerry was away with *Love O' Mike,* Guy and Plum were watching the show from the back of the Academy of Music in Reading, Pennsylvania. It was apparent to them that Billy B. Van's rendition of "Napoleon" was the hands-on show stopper. Plum added multiple verses and Guy convinced Jerry and the Colonel that it should be moved to the next to closing spot.

It wasn't an easy transfer. Jerry had been more difficult to convince than the colonel, and an edge of testiness had begun to creep into the exchanges between Guy and him. The *Vanity Fair* article, giving most of the credit for *Miss Springtime*'s success to Guy's book, and the Reading critic's self-contradicting observation that his *Have a Heart* score was "not whistleable" and yet derivative of various other melodies, including the "Merry Widow Waltz," did nothing to improve Jerry's temper.

Riding back with Plum on the train to New York, Jerry confessed to a weariness at Plum's constant extolling of Guy's sense of form, and probably with very good reason. Hadn't he been Guy's first teacher? And hadn't he been the one to originate the idea of musical integration?

Plum's method of mediating disputes was to either ignore them or redirect them. "Don't suppose we should put something patriotic into *Oh, Boy!,* do you?" he asked, sending the conversation off at an insane angle.

"Why?" asked Jerry.

"War raging over there," said Plum, running out of the spoken word. "Everyone's getting caught up in it here now."

"Are you?" asked Jerry.

"What?"

"Caught up in it."

"Bad eyes. Besides. Never get caught up in anything," answered Plum. "Leave that for the active chaps."

Jerry smiled. They understood each other. Still, life wasn't as simple and wonderful as it had been a short year ago. The tiny rift that had begun between Guy and him certainly hadn't been helped by Plum's words and writings. But how the hell could anyone be mad at this benign genius?

Jerry sighed and went to sleep. Let it rest for the time being. Their differences were small. Their successes so far seemed to be big and getting bigger.[4]

• • •

It was snowing again on the night of January 11, 1917, when *Have a Heart* opened. Guy and Plum and Jerry shared the applause, but only Plum and Guy stayed for the reviews. Jerry had spent the day in Schenectady with *Oh, Boy!,* and had arrived, a little breathless and disheveled, at the Liberty Theatre just before curtain time. Now, he was heading for Penn Station to catch an overnight sleeper to rejoin *Love O' Mike* in Pittsburgh.

Guy and Plum, left to themselves, must have been glad they waited up for the notices. The critics were mostly friendly. The *Sun* called *Have a Heart* the "jolliest musical in town," the *Telegram* joined in and pronounced it ". . . a breezy, jolly, care-free musical . . . comparatively unimportant so far as pretense goes."

The *Times* critic, a young man named George S. Kaufman, was fairly grumpy, noting that ". . . the authors have shown considerable skill in distributing the dullness . . . Guy Bolton has such a knack for turning a clever line that it is a distinct disappointment to find him seeking inspiration for librettos in lingerie shops and midnight amours."

But his was the only truly negative reaction. Burns Mantle, in the *Mail,* cheered Guy and Plum enormously: "It is a pleasant entertainment," the dean of critics reported, "concerning the favored domestic topics of Broadway—the various experiences of those who are divorced or would be divorced, the married, the remarried. . . . The plot of it will disappoint no one, unless it be the other librettists who expected to use it this year."

The *Dramatic Mirror*'s judgment was positive enough to let all three of them take heart. "*Have a Heart* [it said] has a plot upon which Mr. Kern's music always has a direct bearing."

*That* was what they wanted to hear.

What they *didn't* need to read was a clumsy error by the *Brooklyn Eagle* critic. The review caught up to Guy and Plum in Schenectady, where they were with *Oh, Boy!* and where the Comstock office forwarded both good and bad news:

> Standing in the front rank of their professions, Guy Bolton, the writer of the book, and P. G. Wodehouse, the author of the lyrics, have woven many clever lines and bright sayings into their latest work, and *Joseph Kern* [italics added], who has written many a tuneful score, has contributed some tinkling music that falls very pleasantly on the ear."

On Monday, January 15, 1917, four nights after *Have a Heart*'s premiere, *Love O' Mike* opened at the Shubert, four blocks away.

The critics were polite and generous about the show itself and fairly churlish about the lack of voices—a criticism that had also been leveled at *Have a Heart*'s leads. ". . . A 'comedy with music,'" sniffed *Theatre* magazine, "it has both in reasonable quantities; but if it weren't for the orchestra, you'd never know about the music." Heywood Broun, in the *Tribune,* lamented, "A smart little show in spots . . . with several captivating little tunes—if only there were somebody to sing them."

Jerry at the time was apparently more interested in orchestrations than singers; he worked carefully with Donald Saddler, his orchestrator, going against the brassy grain of the time by muting the trumpets, lushing up the strings, inserting his favorite mandolin effects and, with more room in the pit than he had at the Princess, cramming two harps into the Liberty for *Have a Heart* and two pianos into the Shubert for *Love O' Mike.*

Ironically enough, although *Have a Heart* and *Love O' Mike* both left the starting gate fairly even, the former show finished strong and the latter came up lame. It all had to do with the strength of the road.

New York audiences liked *Love O' Mike* more and kept it thriving in New York for 192 performances. *Have a Heart* stayed for a mere 76.

In those days, however, New York wasn't everything, and the road had a mind of its own. On more than one occasion, shows written by one or more of the trio fizzled in New York and flourished on the road. Out-of-towners evidently took its title literally, and *Have a Heart* bounced from town to town until April 1919, before being withdrawn. *Love O' Mike,* on the other hand, died on the road, barely making it through the 1917–18 season.

Jerry had little time to think about statistics. In 1917, he and Plum and Guy barely had time to think at all. It was a year of frantic successes, and the biggest of them all opened on February 20 at the Princess.

*Oh, Boy!* had lived up to its promise and its title throughout its tryout tour. Tom Powers took over the male lead in Buffalo; Hal Forde was brought in for the comedy lead in Cleveland. But that was about it, and the show tooled merrily along, with hardly a hitch until the middle of the Cleveland engagement. There, the social schism between the two Ziegfeld beauties and the rest of the cast turned momentarily cavernous—or at least Guy and Plum remembered that it did.

The contretemps involved Jefferson Perry, the company manager. By the time the show reached Cleveland in early February, it was in good enough shape to allow various wives to reunite with various husbands. Ethel joined Plum, Eva joined Jerry, and Mrs. Jefferson Perry arrived to join her husband and her mother, who was a kind of *grande dame* of Cleveland society.

The confrontation, according to Guy, took place in the dining room of the Hollendon Hotel, where the company was staying. Mrs. Perry and her mother were dining with the Kerns; Marion Davies and Justine Johnstone were dining with Ethel, Guy, and Plum. As the two writers told it in print later (and swore to it in person, perhaps a little too vigorously):

> Their meal was the first finished and they filed out, passing the Kern-Perry . . . table. A pause was indicated.

> "You don't know Miss Davies and Miss Johnstone, do you, Mrs. Perry?" said Guy.

> "No, and I don't care to," said Mrs. Perry.

In *Bring on the Girls,* Plum and Guy go on to embellish the story by talking of the contretemps it produced in the cast, some taking sides with the girls, some taking sides with Mrs. Perry, and everyone taking sides against Eva Kern.

Ethel, according to Plum and Guy, saved the day by proposing a peace-producing party—which is believable. Ethel's solution for everything was a party.

But Mrs. Perry, in the Guy/Plum semifiction, lost her way and turned up at a spectacular soiree thrown by Marion Davies, instead of at Ethel's more modest gathering. Properly chastened by Miss Davies's taste in Bollinger and caviar, she lowered her nose and raised her opinions, and tranquility settled like snow on a company, that, from the very first curtain calls before the very first audience, had smelled success and tasted triumph.

Out-of-town critics raved over *Oh, Boy!;* the trades joined in the general jubilation, and by the time the show arrived in New York, anticipation had become feverish.

The Fashion 299, attending the invitational preview on February 19, *really* had something to buzz about this time. There had never, they had been told by out-of-town scouts, been a show so chic, so up to date, so unfailingly tuneful, so unflaggingly funny, and so deliciously clever as this.

Following the opening the next night, both public and critics threw their collective hats in the air. It was the biggest hit the Princess would ever have, and in retrospect and reality, it was the supreme Princess show. Nothing Guy and Jerry had written for the Princess before matched it; nothing they would write for the Princess after would equal its success. It was their watershed. And so, it became a watershed for the American musical theatre.

The story is bright and slight and breezy; the settings classy. There are surreptitious goings and comings through a rich playboy's opulent apartment and at a country club after a polo match; mixed identities, a wife who says she isn't and a comedienne who says she's a maiden aunt. But for all of its sophisticated setting and clandestine goings on, it's still good, clean fun — another trademark that the departed Bessie Marbury had demanded and got from Ray Comstock. You could bring your family from Duluth to any Princess production, and they might be titillated, but they would never be outraged.

*Oh, Boys!*'s goings on center around the just accomplished but not to be consummated marriage of George Budd (Tom Powers) and Lou Ellen (Marie Carroll). Trembling with passion, George is constrained from its consummation because he hasn't broken the nuptial news to his Quaker Aunt Penelope (Edna May Oliver). Aunt Penelope, it seems, is leaving him her considerable fortune and thinks he's merely engaged and waiting for her to approve of his fiancée.

While George and Lou Ellen are in the bedroom packing her things so that she can spend her wedding night elsewhere, George's polo playing pal, Jim Marvin (Hal Forde), accompanied by an entire chorus, enters George's apartment. They're intent upon having a party.

Jim, it seems, once saved George's life and so feels free to conduct midnight revels and just about any other disturbance of the peace in his home in the name of loyalty. This time, Jim has just won the Country Club Polo Trophy and feels a dire need for a little champagne and a lot of debutantes.

Enter, in the middle of the revels, Jacky (Anna Wheaton), a young lady who has just socked an old gent named Tootles, who made a pass at her and took her purse. In the melee, she also hit the constable, who is consequently on a womanhunt.

Tootles turns out to be Lou Ellen's father, Jacky turns out to be the former love of Jim's life, and the landlord just wants to turn George and his revelers out of his apartment house.

Act 2, in which everybody in act 1 turns up at the country club (shades of *Nobody Home*, etc.) is an act of solution: Tootles is unmasked, Jacky is unhunted, Aunt Penelope enters, gets drunk, and forgives all.

The Princess glamour was given body early: the first act entrances of Marion Davies, as Jane Packard, in a ball gown of silver lace and blue tulle, and Justine Johnstone, as Polly Andrews, in a gold dress, stopped the show cold, but that was the only pause in an otherwise headlong, high spirited plunge toward the finale.

The low comedy and slapstick of *Nobody Home* and *Have a Heart* were jettisoned in favor of high comedy and high jinks, mostly personified by Jim Marvin, smiling winningly through thin and thin, and charming audiences and chorus girls with his peculiar, contagious way with words. Asked to go away and leave George alone, Jim replies, "Oh, don't be redic. Come and join the party and be our little ray of sunsh." Asked by Jacky, "Why do you always abbreviate your words?" Jim answers jauntily, "Oh, just a hab."

Again, Guy and the Princess started a trend. Within weeks, theatre-going swains in cafe society were dropping syllables to impress their dates.

Even the puns are of a high order. George notes to the constable that Jacky, the woman parading as his wife in act 2, wouldn't lie. The constable rejoins, "No?" George nods. "She has too much honor." The constable sniffs. "Too much on her? If she had much less on her she'd be pinched."

Prevented by Colonel Savage from punning the names of their chorus girls and boys in *Have a Heart,* Guy and Plum reveled in Ray's more permissive sensibilities—at least about this—and named the girls of the chorus Rhoda Byke, Sheila Ryve, Inna Ford, Wanda Farr, Billie Dew, Annie Old-Knight, and Miss B. Ava Little. And—oh, yes—Polly Andrews.

The men emerged as Olaf Lauder, Ivan L. Ovanerve, Phil Ossify, Phelan Fyne, and Hugo Chaseit.

Even that ages-old, traditional, mysterious theatrical walk-on made the chorus twice: George and Georgina Spelvin rounded out the ranks.

The Princess plot traditions were kept intact: The title tag line came at the end of the whirlwind windup of the plot—in exactly three pages of script—as Lou Ellen, turning to George, threatens softly, "I see, George, I'll have to be a little firm with you." George rejoins, "A little firm? Good. Let's incorporate right now." He kisses her. Jacky turns to the audience and joyously observes, "Oh, boy!" whereupon the cast slides gracefully into a warm and melodic goodbye, a la *Nobody Home* and *Very Good Eddie.*

Plum's presence was felt, gloriously. Before Plum and *Have a Heart,* Guy and Jerry had been traveling through their theatrical careers in conveyances with rusty wheels. Plum added a dimension beyond cleverness. Now, there was a unique sort of felicity and balance, a drollness, a sweetness which never dipped into stickiness. Plum prospered, too. Perhaps the real trouble he had had in writing love scenes had been the absence of Jerry's music.

In *Have a Heart,* the trio showed promise. In *Oh, Boy!,* it was fulfilled. The love song, that sacrosanct interlude, was given a deftness that carried the leads into a love affair in a human way, parrying and thrusting, yet committing themselves, too:

HE:    I never knew about you, dear
And you never knew about me . . .
I'd have let you feed my rabbit
Till the thing became a habit
But I never knew about you. . . .

SHE:    I was often kissed neath the mistletoe
By small boys excited by tea,
If I knew that you existed,
I'd have scratched them and resisted,
But I never knew about you
And you never knew about me. . . .

It was a triumph of effortless balance and understated warmth. To add to the freshness of it, the song was given to the comic leads, not the romantic ones. In another turnabout that worked, Guy and Plum and Jerry gave the lovely and melodious finale to the hero and the *comedienne*, because the story demanded it.

Further, in *Oh, Boy!,* as in no musical before it, songs naturally grew, flowering from the soil of the dialogue, occurring only when, as Oscar Hammerstein would ritualize fifty years later in his advice to young Stephen Sondheim, ". . . the emotions [became] so intense that words [were] inadequate to convey the proper feeling."[5]

The show was of a piece, a created world of its own, and if the world that Guy and Plum and Jerry created onstage was also naive and bright and people didn't really either talk or behave that way in reality, it mattered not at all. In the first place, many theatregoers both craved and loved simple escape. In the second, everybody within the world of that show behaved in the same way. There was a verisimilitude within it that didn't disturb the flow. No bone rattling stops for songs to begin. No artillery barrages of song cues.

True, there were the set pieces that Princess audiences had come to expect, bright satires on the larger productions by bigger producers up the street. Plum had another go at operetta conventions with "Nesting Time in Flatbush," but its verse acted as a believable bridge to the increasingly crazy dialogue that had bounced back and forth between Jacky and Jim:

JIM:    Let us flee from this scene of degradation to some happier sunnier clime—to some peaceful land.

JACKY: Oh, Jim, stop—stop! Remember I have a romantic nature and you are carrying me away.

JIM: To Capri—where the olive trees are decked in bloom. There upon the hillside we will lie and watch the evening star rising above the Felosic—

JACKY: And the petals from the orange groves—ah, tell me about the petals from the orange groves—

JIM: Yes, Cleopat.

*(She shoves him.)*

JACKY: Tell me about the petals from the orange blossoms—

JIM: What's the idea? We're not married yet. Between us—

JACKY: Yay—us—ah!

JIM: Between us—

JACKY: Yay—us—ah!

JIM: What do you mean by "Yay—us—ah"! Between us would lie the greensward.

JACKY: Oh Jim, why do you want a sword between us?

JIM: Jacky!

JACKY: The young bride dreams of resting on the scented slopes of Italy and wakes up to find herself hitting the hay in Flatbush.

JIM: Yay—us—no!

*(Sings):*
I've always liked the sort of songs
   You hear most every day.
Called when its something or other time
   In some place far away.
Oh "Tulip Time in Holland"
   A pleasant time must be—

JACKY: But some are strong for
"Apple Blossom Time in Normandy"!

JIM: But there's another time and place
   That makes a hit with me—

BOTH: When it's nesting time in Flatbush
   We will take a little flat,

JACKY: With welcome on the mat

JIM: Where there's room to swing a cat.
   I'll hang up my hat, I'll hang up my hat
   Life will be so sweet with you,

BOTH: When it's nestingtime in Flatbush,
   In Flatbush Avenue.

Jacky can poke fun at conventions; she's a naughty, but not too naughty, liberated, but not too liberated 1917 American Girl. Told by Jim that when he goes with a girl, he wants to be the star, not just come on in the mob scenes, she shakes her head in disbelief, and turns to the girls.

JACKY: Isn't it funny? Give a man one smile and he thinks it
   hands him the right to scowl at every other male creature on your visiting list.

   *(Sings):*
   Though men think it strange
   Girls should need a change
    From their manly fascinations;
   The fact is, this act is
   A thing we're driven to.
   You don't have much fun
   If you stick to one
    Men have all such limitations
   Look around you, I'm bound you—
   Will find that this is true.
   At the op'ra
   I like to be with Robert;
    To a musical show
    I go
     With Joe.
   I like to dance with Ted,

And go with Dick or Ned
  And at the races
  And other lively places
    Sam and Eddie are fun.
But I'm pining
Till there comes in my direction,
One combining
Every masculine perfection;
Who'll be Eddie
And Joe, and Dick and Sam and Freddie
  And Neddie and Teddie,
    Rolled into one.

All good fun, and in character for Jacky. But when George Budd and Jacky have a duet together, the music and the words turn more serious, even touching, and the words to the song further the scene smoothly.

It's raining outside. Jacky will be staying in George's room, and he'll take the opportunity to leave his houseful of carousers.


JACKY (*Sings*):    It's so sad to think that I have had to
Drive you from your home so coolly

GEORGE:    I'll be gaining nothing by remaining
What would Mrs. Grundy say?
Her conventions, kindly recollect them!
We must please respect them duly.

JACKY:    My intrusion needs explaining;
I feel my courage waning—

GEORGE:    Please, I beg, don't mention it.
I would not mind a bit,
But it has started raining.

BOTH:    Oh, the rain comes a-pitter-patter
And I'd like to be safe in bed.
Skies are weeping
  While the world is sleeping,
Troubles heaping
  On (my, your) head.

> It is vain, to remain and chatter,
> And to wait for a clearer sky.
> Helter-skelter,
>     You (I) must fly for shelter
> Till the clouds roll by!

JACKY:     What bad luck, it's coming down in buckets.
           Have you an umbrella handy?

GEORGE:    I've a warm coat—waterproof—a storm coat
           I shall be all right, I know.
           Later on, too, I will ward the grippe off
           With a little nip of brandy.

JACKY:     Or a glass of toddy draining
           Will you find that more sustaining?
                . . . etc.


Like the balcony scene ten years later in Jerry's *Show Boat,* the song was the scene. Primitive today, it was revolutionary in its time.

When the finale finally came, it was as much a part of the plot as the songs it was reprising.

Instead of Schuyler Greene's serviceable

> Any old show is a wonderful show
> If you're there with a wonderful girl. . . .

or Herbert Reynolds and Jerry's more serviceable

> Hope you enjoyed our play.
> With song and jest
> We've done our best
> For a while
> To make you smile . . .

there was a communication to the audience that had its origin in the story and that occurred entirely within the context of the plot and the characters. Matching Jerry's melody perfectly, Plum created considerably more than a finale-goodbye:

It is vain to remain and chatter,
And to wait for a clearer sky,
Helter skelter, we must run for shelter,
Till the clouds roll by.

The effect was nothing short of miraculous, and the opening night applause segued smoothly into a chorus of critical encomiums.

"If there be such things as masterpieces of musical comedy, one reached the Princess last night," crowed the critic of the *Sun,* and the *Times* echoed, "You might call this a musical comedy that is as good as they make them if it were not palpably so much better."

Marie Carroll was loved as ". . . about 95 pounds of good looks," and the *Telegram* took note of the two girls: "Justine Johnstone spoke her few lines like a real graduate actress," [it said,] "and Miss Davies flickered a pair of remarkable blue eyes almost naughtily [in 'A Little Bit of Ribbon']."

But the highest praise was reserved for the trio, who now, without doubt, had been elevated into the company of the reigning royalty of the musical theatre.

That attendant charge of excitement, that rampant rush of romance and discovery and delirious energy had paid off. Young and relatively untried in the theatre, they had not been afraid to attempt the impossible.

Within a week, the little Princess was sold out, and stayed that way for months. Tickets were being scalped for fifty dollars apiece—a precedent-establishing amount in those days. Within a month, Ray Comstock raised his ticket prices from $2.00 to $3.50, and the box office cash register didn't skip a beat. Six months later, he moved the show to the 1500 seat Casino, and *that* was filled, too. *Oh, Boy!* ran for two years and broke all box-office records up to that time, wherever it played.

By the following fall, five companies toured in *Oh, Boy!,* garnering such notices as that of the *Atlantic City Record*: ". . . not since 'Floradora' has any musical comedy attracted such enormous crowds." There would still be a company on tour in 1922.

It was standard practice in those days for supper clubs to reel on in theatre lounges after the final curtain had fallen. Justine Johnstone had an elite and envied one at the Forty-fourth Street Theatre, and the Winter Garden Roof was a continuing hot ticket.

Two weeks after *Oh, Boy!* opened, Marion Davies, who was now receiving orchids every night from William Randolph Hearst, opened Marion Davies Petite Souper Club in the lounge of the Princess. Designed to accommodate

100 members at $100 apiece, it was considered a joke by the New York press.

If it was, it was a rich one. In its first week, it took in $3,100 over its membership fees.

Justine Johnstone left the show after four months, Marion Davies after six, but it would run very well without them. *Oh, Boy!* had what a show needed for a long run, and what that show needed Guy and Plum and Jerry had provided. They were beginning a long, winning roll.

Offers avalanched in. From Ziegfeld, Erlanger, the Shuberts. And from Ray Comstock, who wanted the trio to get busy immediately on the next Princess musical, an adaptation of George Ade's *A College Widow.* And all on the strength of a little show that cost $29,000 to produce.

There was hardly room or time to breathe, much less busy oneself with personal matters.

But Guy had to; Marguerite was still in San Francisco and growing increasingly impatient.

*Chapter*

# 10

# Trio

## 1917

Letters from Marguerite to Guy that year were bristling with orders and barely concealed fury. She had contacted Frederick Toye and they had drawn up two legal contracts—one, their divorce agreement, and the other, the touching and somehow inevitable understanding that Frederick Toye would continue to represent her in matters artistic.

He had relinquished his position as manager of the Los Angeles Symphony and had taken up the same position with the Boston Symphony. He had already arranged for a concert tour for Marguerite and Caruso and was negotiating with the managers of the Chicago Opera for a guest contract.

These appearances were in the future, no matter how near, and Marguerite wasn't one to sit when she could run. Her method had always been and would always be to meet the moment, not wait for it. She had conquered opera and the concert stage and subdued Broadway. What remained?

Well, among other worlds, that of motion pictures.

Gathering the infant Peggy, she quit San Francisco for Los Angeles, where her mother lived.

At almost the same moment, a young Italian immigrant decided to leave the ailing theatre company in which he was appearing in San Francisco, journey south, and try his luck in the still infant and therefore indiscriminately receptive movie industry.

In one of those collisions of fortune that only real life can provide, Marguerite launched her motion picture career by making a melodrama called *Stolen Moments.* Her beauty and her name entitled her to top billing and a small part for her infant daughter. Costarring with her, and billed below her, was a villainously mustachioed Latin type appearing for the very first time on any screen. His name was Rudolph Valentino.

Marguerite's friendship with Valentino lasted longer than the film. She spoke Italian resonably well, certainly better than Valentino spoke English. He rapidly became privy to her private life and was immediately outraged, to the turrets of his Roman Catholic soul, at the fact that the adorable child who had been featured in their film was not only illegitimate, but unbaptized. When Marguerite refused to correct these two liturgical lapses, he and her mother took matters and Peggy into their own hands, kidnapped the child, and had her baptized Catholic.

The baptism didn't ruffle Marguerite, but the kidnapping infuriated her, and she said as much in letters to Guy, in which she also wondered, more insistently, when on earth he was going to prepare a proper place for their return.

Thus, reality crashed in on Guy Bolton, and reality was a state with which he had some trouble. It was clearly past the time for him to legalize a liason and legitimate his daughter. Besides, he knew and loved this lady with a mind and genius of her own, and he was not about to leave her in Hollywood, especially in the vicinity of her increasingly popular and debonair costar-kidnapper. [1]

What to do?

The apartment on West Fifty-eighth Street had been delightful for dallying; it was scarcely big enough for three. Besides, if *Oh, Boy!* was going to be the solid hit it was threatening to become and if *A Happy Thought,* now renamed *Polly with a Past,* developed as it seemed to be developing, and if the five other shows that had been promised to Bolton and Wodehouse and Kern by various producers turned from promise to production, Guy would *have* to move into more prestigious quarters, for the sake of pride if nothing else.

Perhaps, concluded Guy, reality wasn't all that bad. In fact, it could be downright dazzling. An architect who only dabbled in drama a mere six years ago, he was becoming a theatrical legend at the not altogether tender age of thirty-two. So, encouraged by Jerry and Eva, he searched for quality quarters in Bronxville and found it too far from Plum.

He tried Bellport and found it too far from Jerry and Broadway.

He settled on Great Neck, in 1917 an hour's exhilarating drive (when Jerry wasn't driving) from Manhattan. Lush and luxurious, the Kensington section of that small community on the north shore of Long Island had already become a gathering place for the literati and the theatrically successful.

The Lardner family of literary note was building a home on East Shore Drive, the Heinz family of fifty-nine varieties had one already; Sam Harris, George M. Cohan's producing partner (Cohan was in nearby Manhasset, as was Ziegfeld), Jack Hazzard, Mae Murray and Buck Leonard, Bessie Love, Joe Santner, Gene Buck, Richard Barthelmess, W. C. Fields—all were there. Ed Wynn had a home on Arley Road. In a few months, Scott and Zelda Fitzgerald would loom, in lovely disarray, on its landscape.

And by March of 1918, Plum and Ethel would abandon Bellport for the outskirts of Great Neck, some three miles down the road from the Fitzgeralds.

Guy found a large house that resembled a French chateau at 12 Beverly Drive. It had a long parenthesis of a driveway that swooped past its porticoed front door and disappeared among lilacs and loveliness. There were columns by the windows, a latticed path to the servants' quarters, high hedges for sculpted privacy.

Nothing that Jerry or Plum had inhabited so far matched it for elegance—or company. Behind it was a constantly surprising garden that abutted on the garden of Ed Wynn. Four years later, five-year-old Keenan Wynn would wander through a hole in the hedge separating the two gardens, and five-year-old Peggy Bolton would whack him on the head with her favorite red truck, thus christening a lifetime friendship.[2]

Certainly enough, it was a home befitting the vista-filled future of Guy and Marguerite, and Guy had no trouble at all convincing her that the house on Beverly Drive should become their home.

The problem was the sizable down payment. He had to come up with a large sum of money to put down on the large house, and the only plausible source for this was Reginald.

It was no easy task for him to ask his father for the money. Eventually, he did, and it must have been a disturbing meeting for both men. There was still little warmth between father and son, and Ethelind did nothing to change this. Nor had Guy's meteoric success as a writer drawn the two closer. Reginald fancied *himself* the writer of the family, and if a talent for writing can be inherited, he was convinced that it was his that Guy had received.

Furthermore, Reginald approved of neither his son's divorce from Julie nor his sexual odysseys afterward. Despite his own slight drift from matrimony to Ethelind, he looked with tight-lipped dismay upon what he regarded as the unbuttoned gamboling of the Broadway crowd, the intimations of many midnight amours related by his son's friends, and the Broadway columnists who shadowed them.

So, Guy knew, as he wended his way northward that bitter February evening, that he would have to, for his father's consumption, modify the reality that he was house hunting for himself, his mistress, and their illegitimate child. Reginald had traveled so easily from merely withholding his approval of his son's success to expressing downright disapproval of his personal habits that Guy would have to appeal to his father's family sense. It was the only link the two had or would ever have. Guy knew, as any child knows, where the wall surrounding his parent was the weakest.

His presentation to his father focused on the fact that he was doing the right thing. He was giving the child a name, giving his daughter the sort of surroundings she should need to grow well and whole and healthy. He would have a governess for her and playmates for her and time for her, so that he could regulate and enrich that childhood, as Reginald had for Ivy and him at Deal.

It was effective, probably because it was sincere. In February of 1917, Guy believed what he dreamed.

Reginald regarded him with a mixture of awe and sadness. Perhaps he wished for less pride and more love in each of them; possibly he regretted, for one revealing moment, the loss forever of that simple and authentic communication between father and children that had existed only in the days at Deal in the Downs Art Club.

But he said nothing. His silence was thunderous as he wrote out a check and handed it to his son. And Guy, emulating the father he hardly knew and scarcely loved, buried his own emotions in silence.[3]


Two months later, an equally sad and significant money problem and meeting of unlike minds occurred at the Princess.

It happened after a matinee performance.

Since *Oh, Boy!* had become the sensational, runaway hit it had, it was only appropriate for Guy to approach Jerry and in turn suggest that Jerry approach Ray for more money — ten percent for each of them would be appropriate, Guy thought.

According to Guy's later recollections, Jerry demurred, stating that the

Comstock company couldn't afford that much. Guy was ready to accept his opinion when an odd and revealing incident occurred. From out of the depths of the deserted theatre, the company manager appeared and handed Jerry a slip of paper.

Guy wondered what it was.

"Last night's returns," said the manager.

"Why didn't we get a copy?" asked Guy.

The manager's answer was simple and infuriating. "Mr. Kern has ten per cent of the show," he said. "You don't."

It was a thunderbolt whose echoes would never quite be quieted, and its effect upon the trio of musical fame would be fatal. A small rip in the fabric of their partnership, it would widen until it would eventually rend the entire relationship apart. In later years, for various reasons, Guy would threaten and then demolish other collaborations over sometimes minute money problems. This was the first of them and possibly the model for those to come.[4]

Guy never forgave Jerry for that afternoon's inadvertent revelation. Speaking to Michael Freedlander, one of Jerry's biographers, and to others later in his life, he remembered, "At first I felt that it wasn't the money; it was the fact that a friend could do this to me. Of course," he admitted later, "It *was* the money."

Later, Jerry tried to smooth Guy's ruffled feathers, but it was an odd sort of smoothing: "Tell you what," he said, "I'll give you half of what I get." It was better than nothing.

According to Guy, they shook hands. Jerry smiled. Guy did not.

Even Plum, when he was told of the incident, realized that Jerry had had them. "The bastard has cheated us again," Guy remembered Plum saying. "He's still got twice as much as we have."[5]

Whether or not they entered into further negotiations isn't known. What *is* known is that they weren't quite the seamless trio they had once been. Still, seamless or not, they set out to meet the demands of their new-found notoriety.

First, there was a plan that Klaw and Erlanger had put forth before *Oh Boy!* was more than a week old: Why not, the two producers said, reunite the production and creative staff of *Miss Springtime?* If success worked once, it could work again, they reasoned, with the same blindness that had led legions of producers into countless disasters.

Joseph Urban (sets), Julian Mitchell (ensemble direction), Charles Previn (musical direction), Plum and Guy (lyrics and book), Emmerich Kalman (music), and Jerry (genius and cocomposer) were all recruited. The process was even duplicated: Kalman once again reached into his Viennese-Hungarian trunk for another operetta involving exotic locales, mistaken identity, and rejected royalty. This time, it was *Czardasfuerstin,* yet again a tale that transported its characters and audiences from Vienna to Budapest and back again.

That was their operetta offer. Beyond that, there was Jerry's agreement to interpolate a number into the 1917 Ziegfeld *Follies,* and a contract signed with Colonel Savage to provide a full score for a musical called *Houp-La.*

At the Princess, Ray Comstock was backing and filling in his usual inimitable fashion, but by April he would lock up the rights to George Ade's 1903 campus comedy *The College Widow.* Long before that, he gave it to Guy and Plum and Jerry to read. They liked it considerably more than *A Milk White Flag* and waited impatiently for Ade's assignment of the rights.

Meanwhile, George Middleton snared Guy into rewrites of *Polly with a Past,* which Belasco was busily casting.

And meanwhile, Charles Dillingham and Ziegfeld were growing concerned that, although Victor Herbert was certain to provide part of the score of *Miss 1917,* the second revue to inhabit their new, opulent, uptown Century Theatre, Irving Berlin, whom they had hoped would provide the other part, was busying himself elsewhere.

So, Jerry was invited to replace Berlin, and Guy and Plum were invited to supply some of the sketches.

Finally and simultaneously, the house in Great Neck was nearing readiness for the return of Marguerite and Peggy.

Plants by not only Comstock's fevered publicity department but those of Klaw and Erlanger and Dillingham and Ziegfeld kept the trio's names in the columns and on the minds of playgoers while the writing that justified the attention kept them momentarily closeted. For other novices who had been relatively unknown a mere six years earlier, this might have been the publicity that paralyzes. But to Bolton and Wodehouse and Kern, it was the applause that refreshes.

As Guy and Plum would remember it in their memoir: ". . . it left Bolton and Wodehouse — the latter now better known as the Sweet-Singing Thrush of Thirty-ninth Street — sitting on top of the world and loving it."

Sometime late that winter or early spring, Guy took time off to retrieve Marguerite and Peggy from California, where Marguerite had completed a recital tour. She and Frederick Toye had divorced; somewhere along the way, possibly in Cleveland, which was Marguerite's birthplace, but more likely in Los Angeles, where her mother and grandmother lived, she and Guy were married.

It would be the end of June before the *New York Sun* would break the story of the nuptials—time enough for Marguerite to settle into Great Neck and Guy to have settled far enough into his upstairs study to qualify it as a refuge from reporters.

In early April, the first draft of *Leave It to Jane,* Plum and Jerry and Guy's adaptation of the George Ade farce, was delivered to the Princess's present producers, Ray Comstock, Morrie Gest, and Bill Elliott. Ray was qualifiedly enthusiastic.

Back Guy and Plum raced to the New Amsterdam to finish the overhaul of *Czardasfuerstin* before Abe Erlanger's Napoleanic nervousness overtook them. Guy had already moved the action out of Budapest and Vienna and onto the French Riviera, which made for some interesting settings for Kalman's czardas. Jerry and Guy had completed a perfect, geographically insane interpolation, titled "Bungalow in Quogue."

So, two of the three musical projects were reasonably under control. But now, testy letters began to flow between Guy and George Middleton. Left to deal with Belasco alone, George was finding Guy's unavailability exasperating.

"Are you, or are you not interested in this project?" Middleton wrote to Guy late in April.

"I am. I always was interested in our collaboration," Guy replied.[6] After all, he was the one who had approached George in the first place.

But now the third musical project began to consume Guy. The demands of the two benign giants of the stage, Dillingham and Ziegfeld, were considerable. More and more work was given to Guy and Plum, until they were supplying the largest part of the sketch material for *Miss 1917.* It was their plan to insert some plot structure into an otherwise loosely assembled venture, and they had not yet convinced the powers that had already conceived *The Century Girl,* not to mention the *Follies,* that something more than a succession of laughs and legs was a necessary avenue to success.

Now, Guy's project with George Middleton reached a stage that could no longer be ignored. In early June, *Polly with a Past* opened in Atlantic City. Ina Claire, who had been known only as a lovely on a Ziegfeld staircase, proved to be an enchanting comedienne. Audiences and the authors loved the show. Belasco didn't.

"Atlantic City isn't New York," he told them after the first performance. "We have work to do."

George accepted it; Guy had conferences in New York. He disappeared, leaving George and Belasco and anyone else who cared, to reshape the play. On June 19, George's wife, Fola, wrote to her sister, "George Arliss was down in Atlantic City. He saw the play three times and we had a long talk with him afterward. He made some helpful suggestions, and he feels that everything looks most propitious."7

For a while, Guy extended the parameters of his commute from Bronxville to Bellport to Great Neck to New York to Atlantic City.

And then, he disappeared again.

It took a letter from David Belasco himself to snare Guy and put him back to work on *Polly with a Past.* Guy replied and apparently assuaged the concerned producer by pleading ill health, overwork, and a nervous stomach. On June 28, Belasco wrote to George Middleton. The letter is a masterpiece of controlled fuming:

> My dear George Middleton:
> I have just received a letter from Guy Bolton, saying that he is going to French Lick to get his digestion into shape again, and will be back in ten days, when he will communicate with me at once. Please bear this in mind, as I am very anxious to have the 'script ready, particularly Uncle John's scene, as I want to know as soon as possible whether we are to keep John Cope for the part, or get another man. This is very important. [Apparently, Guy and George solved the problem by writing the character out. There is no Uncle John in the final ms.]
> . . . I am doing all sorts of things with our scenes. I am also sending a woman to Paris to get the latest models from Caillot for Miss Claire's third act costume, and Caillot's dresses, you know, cost over five hundred dollars a piece [sic].
> I want you and Mr. Bolton to do as much for your comedy as I am trying to do, and there are certainly some final touches to be made if we hope to carry off the comedy honors of the season, so as soon as Mr. Bolton gets back, come to me with both your coats off.
>
> > Best wishes,
> > Faithfully,
> > David Belasco8

George forwarded the letter, with the entire last paragraph underlined, to Guy. Guy got the message. *Leave It to Jane* could be left to Jerry and Plum, at least for the time being.

Between last rewrites for the Princess musical, he got down to doing what he did best: tightening and tucking up scenes so that they worked before audiences. George Middleton relaxed. This, after all, was Guy's role in the collaboration, and at last he was playing it.

This rush of responsibility cross-pollinated Guy and Plum and Jerry's musical life, too. Casting about for a thread of a libretto for *Miss 1917* that would be thin enough to allow the specialists their specialties and Ziegfeld his way, Guy found it in his play with George Middleton.

"Polly," he said to Plum as they were walking to the Dillingham office one afternoon in early July.

"Plum's the name," replied Plum. "Are you sure it's your stomach that's gone bad?"

"Polly. A girl with a past who wants a future. On the way, she meets farmers —"

"And farmerettes?"

"And farmerettes. And Lew Fields —"

"And Irene Castle — and — Righto!" Plum brought his hands together appreciatively. By the time they reached the office, they had enough of an idea to convince the powers at the Century that their loose libretto would work.[9]

Later that July, the following item, probably planted by Ziegfeld and Dillingham, appeared in the *New York Times:*

> The indefatigable combination of Guy Bolton and P. G. Wodehouse has been commissioned to write the new Century revue, which means that the second Dillingham-Ziegfeld offering . . . will differ radically from the first in that it will have a real libretto instead of being a jumble of specialties. . . .

The piece goes on to boost the fortunes of the two, and by implication and association, Jerry: "Messrs. Bolton and Wodehouse are writing so many of next season's librettos and plays that Burns Mantle quotes E. D. Price as pointing with pride to a new piece to be produced by Henry W. Savage with book and lyrics not by these collaborators. . . ."

The newspaper piece was pleasant puff and reached its subjects long distance. The trio was already out of town again, in Atlantic City, where, on July 30, the hottest night of the past three summers, *Leave It to Jane* opened at that city's Apollo Theatre.

Local papers and the patrons loved it; Comstock and the trio were less sanguine. There was still too much of Ade's somewhat sticky scenario; the book would have to be given more bite to satisfy New York's more demanding critics.

Furthermore, Jerry was unhappy about the reception of some of his songs, despite Louis Cline's ecstatic encomium that ". . . the inexhaustible supply of Jerome Kern's music was never more pronounced. . . ."

So, during the next month, extensive overhauling took place. The sturdy Princess ending with its direct goodbye to the audience was modified into a more standard love duet ending, in which hero forgives heroine for deceiving him and both convey the harmony of their coming lives together musically. Various windups were tried. Guy and Plum liked the "in" idea of the hero, Billy *Bolton,* going off at the end to Paris to study *architecture* (chuckle, chuckle), but Comstock thought it would be better if he went West instead, to work in a factory for thirty dollars a week.

This was proper Edwardian atonement for disobeying and deceiving a parent, and it remained in the version of 1917. Guy and Plum restored the going-to-Paris ending for the London production, and when *Leave It to Jane* was revived at the Princess in 1927, they jettisoned both windups in favor of a reprise of the show's loveliest ballad, "Wait Till Tomorrow." When *Leave It to Jane* was revived again, for a wildly successful Off-Broadway run of two full years in 1959–61, the 1927 version was used, with much tinkering from everyone but Jerry, who was dead by this time. Had he been alive, he almost certainly would have busily composed some interpolations.

In 1917, true to form, Jerry threw out five songs and added two: "Why?" and the show's set-piece hit, "Cleopatterer."

The result was a strong, though not necessarily cohesive show, which bounced into town at the end of August. *Oh, Boy!* was still packing the Princess, so Ray booked *Jane* into the Longacre, three times the size of the Princess.

Only the second major musical production of the 1917–18 season (the first had been Romberg's *Maytime*), *Leave It to Jane* was greeted with cheers. The *Times* gave George Ade his due: "The unmusical plays of George Ade had always a leaning toward musical comedy [it said] . . . and now the best of them, having leaned a long time, has fallen. Or rather, Guy Bolton and P. G. Wodehouse have pushed it over, to music by Jerome Kern"; the *Dramatic Mirror* felt that the original had been of no help. "Ade's sticky romantic scenes [wrote the critic] Messrs. Kern and Wodehouse have made . . . pleasing and reasonable with the aid of tinkly tunes and chirping crickets," while the *Journal of Commerce* assisted the digestion of audiences by noting that "Guy Bolton, P. G. Wodehouse and Jerome D. Kern, the three chefs . . . who seldom fail to please the public palate with their dishes have done it again. . . ."

Authenticity was not the note of the night: the college campus the trio had put onstage at the Longacre was more camp than campus, but it masked its hokum by bubbling with youth and high spirits, expressed ecstatically and succinctly in one of Plum's more facile lyrics: "I don't know who the fellow was who first invented life,/ But he started a darn good thing."

The plot dealt with such cosmic matters as the rivalry between Atwater and Bingham colleges (one Lutheran and the other Baptist), football mania, campus romance, paternal interference, and undergraduate pranks.

Billy Bolton (Charles Trowbridge) has gained notoriety and an all-American status by playing football for Minnesota. His father Hiram (Will W. Crimans), an alumnus of tiny Bingham College, uproots Billy and sends him east to Bingham, so that his alma mater can bury its archrival, Atwater—and coincidentally win a large bet for Hiram.

But on his first day on campus, Billy meets Jane Witherspoon (Edith Hallor, fresh from the *Ziegfeld Follies*), the lovely and imaginative daughter of Atwater's president (Frederich Graham). He's instantly smitten.

But he isn't alone. Everyone wants to spoon with Miss Witherspoon, including "Stub" Talmadge (Oscar Shaw), who manages, among other feats, a leap over five chorus girls in the second act—which may be an eloquent comment on the state of Broadway choreography in 1917.

Jane isn't impressed. She picks Billy and manages to make him stay with her and play football for, not Bingham, but Atwater. With Billy aboard, Atwater beats Bingham in the big game, and Billy wins Jane after she confesses—in the last three minutes of the show—that she at first wanted Billy to stay at Atwater only to win the game. But his staying won her heart as well.

Mistaken identity gets its due as Billy parades as a visiting botanist. Low comedy enters in the person of Bub Hicks (Olin Howland), a hick freshman who learns fast and teaches his father all the tricks by Thanksgiving.

One of the tricks Bub learns is how to become engaged and then disengaged to Flora Wiggins, played by comedienne Georgia O'Ramey, who had done right with Jerry and Plum's interpolations in *Miss Springtime*, and who did even better in this production with the show-stopping "Cleopatterer."

The wedding of wit to cleverness and construction savvy carried Guy and Plum's collaboration another notch forward. They swiped cheerfully at cafe society: "Just take a tip from me, son," says Bub's dad, "and keep away from Society. You'll meet enough fools during business hours without hunting up the main herd after dark." Bub, however, doesn't seem destined for the snappy world of Society. Asked about Bub's age, Flora answers, "Eighteen," to which Stub replies tartly, "Around the chest or in the shoes?"

Later, Bub comes in for constant kidding about the signs of vacancy in his mind. Flora notes, "The guy who said there was plenty of room at the top was thinking of that boy's head." Later, however, after she's fallen in love with him, she feels called upon to defend another assessment of his intelligence by a fellow classmate: "T'isn't a head at all" [he notes, surveying Bub's cranium], "it's just a button to keep his spine from unravelling."

Fun, but Guy and Plum saved their sharpest satirical swipes for the act 2 football game that takes place offstage while the casualties stagger onstage.

American football was—and remained—mysterious mayhem to these two English gentlemen. Back in *Oh, Boy!*, Jacky had reduced the rules of the game to two: "Use no hooks and bury your own dead." In *Leave It to Jane*, the duo simplified it: "All you have to do is to go into the game with two ears and try to come out with three."

In his lyrics, joined to Jerry's unfailingly lovely and original melodies, Plum shone as brilliantly as he had in *Oh, Boy!* In later years, Gilbert Seldes would characterize Plum's lyrics succinctly: ". . . they had the great virtue which Gilbert's lyrics have and which, I am told, the comic verses of Molière and Aristophanes also have: they say things as simply as you would say them in common speech, yet they sing perfectly."[10]

But Seldes missed most of the point. Plum, in his lyrics and his writings, was *deceptively* simple, and his lyrics for *Leave It to Jane* exemplify this perfectly. Throwaway interior rhymes, alluring alliterations, and fiendishly clever end couplings abound.

In the verse to "The Siren's Song" (an interesting punctuation change all in itself), he noted, in featherlight alliteration, that on an island ". . . Sat wicked sirens all day long/Singing their sweet deceitful song." Later, he allowed Flo to dazzlingly opine, "Gee, a girl sure plucked a lemon in/Being born so weak and feminine! . . . She can never be a quarterback,/Wearing corsets to support her back!"

Simple to observe; not so simple to construct.


Again, integration and verisimilitude were the names of the games in *Leave It to Jane,* and Jerry helped them enormously with a larger portion of underscoring than he had ever used, even in *Have a Heart.* He was joined by the other two-thirds of the trio in managing even smoother lead-ins to the songs, enough to allow Oscar Shaw, in a lecture delivered in Philadelphia during the run of the show, to declaim that, ". . . audiences will no longer accept inconceivable, incredible and absolutely impossible situations . . . what they like is a real story. . . ."[11]

They also liked real characters, and the Princess style of sophistication which was possibly brought to its apotheosis in the lovely linking of words to music in Jane's opening number, "Wait Till Tomorrow." Over a melody that seemed to melt from one note to the next, Plum floated a lyric that absolutely refused to stand for stickiness, and at the same time, etched Jane's character as solidly as if she'd been given a half hour of exposition:

> Wait—wait—wait till tomorrow,
> And, should it chance that tomorrow
>   My love's no stronger
>   Then—just wait a little longer.
> Please, oh please do not hurry;
> You know there's really no hurry:
>   So cheer up—you'll hear from me
>   Tomorrow—maybe.

In "Cleopatterer," Plum and Jerry's set piece, Plum again gleefully rewrote history, the second, after "Napoleon," of many such rewritings:

> At dancing, Cleopatterer
> Was always on the spot.
> She gave those poor Egyptian ginks
> Something else to watch besides the sphinx.
> Marc Antony admitted
> That what first made him skid
> Was the wibbly, wobbly, wiggly dance
> That Cleopatterer did.

And, with even more subtlety than in *Oh, Boy!,* Jerry and Plum sent audiences out into the night with a characteristic Princess sendoff:

> The breeze in the trees brings a scent of orange blossom
> And the skies turn soft and blue,
> When there's no one 'round except the one you love,
> And the one you love loves you.

*Leave It to Jane* sold out the large Longacre for a time. But, even though it was forced to leave after 167 performances because of a booking jam, and although Ray sent out three road companies in the season of 1918–19, it never came close to matching *Oh, Boy!*'s rampant popularity.

With *Jane* successfully launched and *Polly with a Past* in comfortable enough shape to open in two weeks, with the Kalman operetta (now titled *The Riviera Girl*) in rehearsal, and *Miss 1917* partially written, Guy and Morris Gest convinced Plum that he really had time on his hands and should come in on a musicalization of Belasco's ancient comedy *Sweet Kitty Bellairs.* A young and upcoming composer named Rudolph Friml would provide the music, Morrie and Belasco would provide the money, and Plum and Guy would provide the energy.

*Sweet Kitty Bellairs,* however, resisted musicalizing almost as relentlessly as had *A Milk White Flag.* Retitled *Kitty Darlin'*, it refused to endear itself to either audiences or authors. Writing to Ira Gershwin in 1946, Plum recalled:

> "[I think of the time] I helped to write *Kitty Darlin'* the ghost of which rises before my eyes whenever people mention period pieces. *Sweet Kitty Bellairs,* on which the musical was based, was supposed to be the theatre's biggest cinch. Morrie Gest had been holding it for years till he could find someone worthy of having an easy fortune bestowed on them. He practically patted Guy's and my heads when he informed us that owing to our good work on *Oh, Boy!*, etc., he had decided to let us do it. Of all the turkeys!"

*Kitty Darlin'* expired in Baltimore, before the duo's reputations could be too badly besmirched or their time too seriously consumed.

Now, while Plum and Jerry worked on the songs for *Miss 1917*, Guy returned to George Middleton and David Belasco.

On Thursday, September 6, nine days after *Leave It to Jane*'s premiere at the Longacre, *Polly with a Past* opened at the nearby Belasco and secured the comedic reputation of the team of Middleton and Bolton.

"*Polly with a Past* is as light as a meringue and quite as refreshing," quipped the *Dramatic Mirror.* The *Tribune* called it a "well groomed comedy," the *Herald* opined that it ". . . seem[ed] sure of a bright future," and the *Clipper* noted that ". . . Middleton and Bolton have succeeded in writing one of the daintiest comedies our stage has seen in many a day. The dialogue is bright and crisp, the characters are well fashioned and distinctive."

"So, the combination without which Guy could not apparently succeed had succeeded. To his "bright and crisp" dialogue, Middleton had added characters that were "well fashioned and distinctive."

Belasco's painstaking mounting and seasoned hand in the development of the piece certainly couldn't be discounted, and the charismatic presence of Ina Claire in a role that was made for her completed the circle of success.

Both characters and plot had their sources in not only *A Happy Thought* but in *What'll You Have.* Like Ruth Trowbridge, Polly (Ina Claire) is a minister's daughter; like Ruth, she is from East Gilead, Ohio; like Ruth, she's bright and witty and wonderful; unlike Ruth, her French mother and soul-saving father are both dead.

Polly works as a maid for Clay Collum (George Stuart Christie) and Harry Richardson (Cyril Scott). Meanwhile, Clay's pal, Rex Van Zile, (Herbert Yost) is wildly in love with Myrtle Davis (Anne Meredith), who cares more for salvaging souls than saving Rex.

Polly—no ordinary maid but a modern woman bent upon making enough money to go to Paris to further her singing career (Marguerite must have seen the similarity)—suggests that Rex assume the role of a soul in need of saving. "We women are all alike. We love to forgive," she chirps knowingly.

To carry this charade further and to add the dimension of jealousy, Polly winningly impersonates Paulette Daty, a French siren who has caused the suicide of a famous musician and may very well destroy Rex, too, if Myrtle doesn't come to the rescue.

Unsurprisingly but satisfyingly, Myrtle sends in the rescue squad—but too late. Rex and Polly have already decided to save each other by marrying, after weathering a multitude of farcical complications.

The construction is seamless; Guy brought his sure sense of scene endings and bright interplay to the piece; George Middleton was responsible for depth of character and an uncluttered plotline.

The humor is of a consistently high level. Suggesting how Polly, a minister's daughter, can research her role as a fallen woman, Clay suggests, "You could read up on the lives of the dead sirens, and we'll take you around to the theatre and show you a few live ones."

Polly, describing her rescue from drowning by Rex, does it in perfectly rounded form: "And 'e sweem to me. Just as 'e reach me, a great wave sweep ovair 'im—'E sink—I sink—down—down—down through ze green watair!"

Mrs. Van Zile: "And did your sins all rush through your mind like they describe in books?"

Polly: "My sins? Mon Dieu—'ow many *hours* do you zink I am down zaire?"

What a gem of a role it was for Ina Claire. Despite the grumbling of George Kaufman in the *Times,* who called her a "Jitney Jezebel" and Burns Mantle's later opinion that "[It] . . . gives Miss Claire a beautiful chance to devote . . . two acts to her imitation of Gaby Deslys. . . ." Ina Claire became the darling of the dailies, the focus of fan magazines. She was photographed, featured, lionized. Her second-act costumes and her bird of paradise hat—which the *World* reported breathlessly ". . . cost (honestly) $150," was copied and worn by the women who flocked to the theatre.

*Polly with a Past* bubbled on at the Belasco for 315 performances, after which Ina Claire took it on the road for a full two years.

In 1921 she appeared in the film version for Metro, and that same year a smash London production opened with Edna Best, Noel Coward, and C. Aubrey Smith in the leading roles.

It was the beginning of Ina Claire's career as a comedienne, the playing out of a role she loved to the end of her life, and with which she forever identified. On Christmas Day, 1917, two identical photographs of her in costume arrived at the homes of George Middleton and Guy Bolton with the identical inscription: "A merry Christmas to our Author, (signed) Polly Claire."

Meanwhile, back at the Century, chaos reigned. Plagued by a plenitude of talent and an excess of producers, *Miss 1917*'s growing pains were demanding barrels of aspirin.

At the very first rehearsal, Jerry sowed the seeds of a nose-to-nose, knock-down shouting match with none other than the master himself, Victor Herbert—ironically enough, the man who had confided to friends that Jerry would be the one to "inherit his mantle."

It all had to do with the first act finale, a pastiche of impersonations and/ or reprises of star performers singing their famous numbers. Bessie McCoy was to sing "The Yama Yama Man" for the 325th time; Marion Davies was to play Edna May, warbling "Follow On" from the 1897 operetta *The Belle of New York,* etc.

Eighteen-year-old Vivienne Segal, fresh from her debut at sixteen in *The Blue Paradise,* was caught in the middle of a theatrical identity crisis, not to mention two elephantine egos.

"She *is* Fritzi Scheff," opined Herbert. "'Kiss Me Again' is the song for—"

"Nonsense," said Jerry, unruffled by or perhaps for the moment blinded to the prestige of his fellow composer. "Julia Sanderson. So much Julia Sanderson that when she sings 'They Didn't Believe Me—'"

The imposing Herbert quivered, but controlled himself. "Take both of the songs home," he said to Miss Segal. "Come back tomorrow and decide."

Jerry, certain that the decision would go in his favor, agreed.

Vivienne Segal took several days to make up her mind, and then, when she did, she fortified her decision by breaking it in on Charles Dillingham.

"What if Mr. Kern doesn't like it?" she asked.

The courtly Dillingham calmed her with his celebrated coolness. "Stick by your guns," he said, "and I'll stick by you."

The next day, the long scene unfolded without incident until Vivienne Segal walked onstage and began to sing "Kiss Me Again," Fritzi Scheff's signature song from Herbert's *Mademoiselle Modiste.*

Jerry's voice barreled out of the darkness of the auditorium.

"Wait a minute! You're not singing that song!" he shouted, rushing toward the stage. "You're singing *my* song!"

The music stopped, and a petrified Vivienne Segal stepped to the stage apron. "It's more in my range, Mr. Kern," she said, trying to best the butterflies in her stomach.

"What do you know?" Jerry shouted. "You're just a kid. You're just a singer!"

"Mr. Dillingham—" Miss Segal brought on the reserves early.

"He's a *producer!* All producers have tin ears!"

"She's singing 'Kiss Me Again.'" The rumble of Victor Herbert's voice, as the huge man lumbered down the aisle from the back of the auditorium, caromed off the theatre's walls. "And who are *you* to shout in the middle of—"

"Jerome David Kern," answered Jerry, his feistiness challenged, his battery charged.

"Who's that?" thundered Herbert.

And so it went, until Dillingham arrived and drew Jerry aside.

"Think about this," he whispered, "you're not just using an old song in this number. You're writing the music that frames it. And you're writing the music for a major dance number, too."

"Herbert has two songs besides this in the finale."

"Old songs."

"Classics!" shouted Jerry. "'March of the Toys'!"

Dillingham studied Jerry. The young composer's brown eyes snapped back and forth between the stage and Dillingham, to Herbert, to Vivienne Segal, back to Dillingham. He was plainly in a fury. And Jerry in a fury could no sooner be reasoned with than a tiger with a needle in its paw.

The producer stopped whispering, drew himself up to his considerable height and announced in clear, measured tones, "Miss Segal will sing 'Kiss Me Again.'"

"Then I'm out! And my music is out! All of it!" Jerry wheeled, slammed up the aisle, and exited to the street.

Dillingham watched his retreating silhouette. He knew he would be back. Perhaps not tomorrow, but the day after that. A little while in Bronxville and it would all seem unseemly to Jerry. His mercurial moods were simply a part of who he was and a measure of the width and depth of his talent.

As he turned to calm the dumbfounded Victor Herbert and the now tearful Vivienne Segal, Dillingham caught the eye of the slender, intense, nineteen-year-old rehearsal pianist, a young man named George Gershwin.

Gershwin was being treated, in one afternoon, to both the travails and the genius that produced a major musical production.[12]

# Chapter

# 11

# Trio: Second Chorus

## 1917–1918

Fräulein Alt certainly didn't come from the same nannary that had produced Guy's beloved but not very Germanic German governess. She was the perfect picture of Nordic-ness, housing a no-nonsense approach to children that Guy and Marguerite immediately trusted.

It was, in fact, fortunate that she was among the many applicants who answered the Boltons' advertisement for a governess for Peggy. If Guy were to be ceaselessly locked in his upstairs study with a pad and pencil, and Marguerite were to be either on a concert tour or preparing for one, then a responsive and responsible governess was not merely a social grace, she was a necessity.

In later years, Peggy would remember seeing her parents together rarely, though they certainly did meet in moments of repose from their careers, and most certainly on Sundays, when theatres and rehearsal halls, opera houses and concert halls were dark.

On Sundays, in those hectic but halcyon days of the Princess triumphs, Eva and Jerry journeyed down from Bronxville, and Plum and Ethel first endured the Long Island Railroad in from Bellport, then sauntered down the road to the road to join, at play, Guy and Marguerite and a changing cast of fascinating feature players that read like a who's who of the cultural world.

Marguerite, lovely, bright, aristocratic, and charismatic, was the central dynamo that lit the gatherings. But she had formidable competition. Heading a rainbow entourage, Isadora Duncan would frequently arrive and instantly gather in, like a colorful guru, people and ideas that were intriguing to her. Giving off lightning sparks of opinion and challenge and insight, she was for years the toast of Bohemian Paris, beginning with that first grand tour with the Toyes. But in 1917, there was a tragic, fading elegance about Isadora. Her Parisian world had been darkened and then destroyed, first by the horrible automobile accident on the Seine in 1913 that had killed her two children and then by the coming of the war. Ever sensitive and receptive, Marguerite had mourned the deaths of the children almost as much as Isadora had. She had become, from that time forward, not only her friend but her constant comforter.[1]

But on Sundays, tragedies were tucked away. Ed Wynn would drop in at the home in Great Neck, sometimes with his own house guests, out to spend a Sunday with their fellow *Follies* fool.

George M. Cohan, especially when George and Fola Middleton were there, would sit at Marguerite's piano and entertain until someone like Jerry replaced him bodily.

Valentino would appear, in brooding silence, looking for Peggy, and only brightening when she appeared.[2]

Caruso, a charismatic clown on his Sundays off, would take over the kitchen, cooking the inevitable mountain of spaghetti that would cap each Sunday gathering, and patiently explaining his recipe for pasta sauce to Marguerite until she finally got it—and never forgot it. To the end of her life, she would admit that the only edible dish she could cook was spaghetti with Caruso's sauce.[3]

They were full days, reflecting the best times of the trio. In Europe, war raged, laying waste to an Edwardian age that had nurtured both Bolton and Wodehouse. But on Long Island, the war was a world away.

It was here in Great Neck that Jerry finally forgot his feud with Victor Herbert, his rage at Charles Dillingham, and, refreshed, renewed by the bounteous, bucolic offerings of a Sunday at the Boltons, returned to the Century and the messy maelstrom of *Miss 1917*.

And it was here that Plum exhibited a rare and overt—if tentative—taste for socializing. These Sunday soirees were in fact just about the only parties that Plum would ever like, even moderately. Of course, even then, he neither believed in nor practiced overexposure to this type of gathering. While Guy rambled through the winter-gutted gardens with the girls from *Leave It to Jane,* and Ethel gathered the boys from *Oh, Boy!* around her, Plum settled into Guy's study with a good book or his own pen and pad.

During the week, *Miss 1917* pursued its chaotic course, frequently without most of its creators. Plum and Guy and Jerry were with Joseph Urban at the New Amsterdam, tucking up *The Riviera Girl,* which was about to open.

It was well that they were. Louis Sherwin's opening night review would list the merits of the show as he saw them:

1—Joseph Urban's scenery and lighting
2—Wilda Bennett
3—The costumes
4—Wilda Bennett
5—Sam Hardy
6—Wilda Bennett
7—Carl Gantvoort
8—Marjorie Bentley
9—The conductor
10—Juliette Day
11—The song "Our Little Bungalow at Quogue" [sic]
12—The libretto
13—The fat girl in the chorus
14—The other girls in the chorus
15—The music

Besides Joseph Urban's contributions, two of the only other saving graces of *The Riviera Girl* could be traced, at least obliquely, to Jerry: (1) "Bungalow in Quogue"—his and Plum's irreverant comedy number for Juliette Day and Sam Hardy, and Jerry's only interpolation—and (2) the plurally praised Wilda Bennett. Discovered by Henry Savage when she was eighteen, she was first given and then deprived of the part of Sonja in Savage's landmark *Merry Widow* and ultimately saved from obscurity by Jerry and his *Love O'Mike.*

When *The Riviera Girl* finally opened at the New Amsterdam on September 24, 1917 (making it the fifth show in two months written all or in part by the trio), most of the other critics praised it.

The *Journal* called it ". . . winsome, sprightly, vivacious, songful . . ." and the *Sun* thought it better than *Miss Springtime.* "It has better music, plot, scenery

. . . it is Messrs. Klaw and Erlanger's crowning achievement in the field of musical comedy," the critic gurgled on.

But Guy and Plum knew that it really wasn't and accepted stoically Sherwin's reasoning for placing the libretto so low on his list of merits:

> . . . there is no blinking the fact that 'The Riviera Girl' is by no means as funny as 'Oh, Boy!' and other shows written by the venerable Chickens Wodehouse and the coruscating Guy Bolton [he wrote]. Every laugh carries with it the unfortunate suggestion of an oasis. Perhaps that is the fault of the audience. Perhaps we go to shows written by the v. C. Wodehouse and the c. G. Bolton expecting too much. They are being judged by their own standards. . . .

Burns Mantle zeroed in most accurately in the *Mail,* by lamenting and at the same time prophesying that ". . . the time will come, and sooner, I think, than managers suspect, when this flimsy sort of song and clothes rack will no longer be acceptable. It is the very type of musical comedy plot that is dying fast."

Apparently trying to play it both safe and new, Guy hadn't done enough to disguise the millennia-old operetta tale about a vaudeville singer loved by the young son of a count who, in order to avoid disinheritance, arranges a marriage of convenience to an inpecunious nobleman who is really a prince in disguise.

Not even Sam Springer of Fishburg, Illinois (Sam Hardy), his wife Birdie Springer (Juliette Day), and the interpolated Kern song could save the show from the twin preponderances of the Kalman source and score. *The Riviera Girl* packed up and left the New Amsterdam after seventy-eight performances, along with its attention-arousing interpolation, "A Bungalow in Quogue," with its chronicling of stops on the Babylon branch of the Long Island Railroad ("We'll build a little bungalow in Quogue/In Yaphank, or in Hicksville or Patchogue . . .") and its capturing of a 1917 bucolic Long Island:

> One day, if you will show me how,
> I'll go and milk Clarice the cow,
> Or for asparagus we'll dig.
> Or slaughter Percival the pig.
> And if we find a snail or slug
> Or weevil or potato bug,

I'll track them down and wring their necks,
Regardless of their age or sex.
    . . .
Where Hilda, our resourceful hen
Will lay us omelettes now and then,
As easily as falling off a log.
The cheerful chirp of Frederick the frog,
Will greet our ears from some adjacent bog,
When we are sitting up at nights,
Comparing our mosquito bites,
Down in our little bungalow in Quogue."

The trio hardly had time to notice their selective good notices. *Miss 1917* was occupying most of their time and energy and nightmares. Trying to fit this gargantuan creation into the Century was a little like coaxing an elephant through the eye of a needle. Too big to be taken on the road, the show would have to open cold on November 5, two months *after* its announced premiere.

The last two weeks of rehearsal made Jerry's scene with Victor Herbert seem like parlor conversation. Ten days before opening night *Miss 1917* ran almost five hours, not including times out for temperamental chorus girls, jammed turntables and a rain scene that threatened to become the Johnstown flood.

In that last week scenes and lines flew in and out like spitballs in a classroom. A heavily notated script of Guy's dated October 29, 1917 (seven days before opening night), bears testament to the turmoil. The penciled revisions weigh considerably more than the typed script.[4]

One of the casualties of the October 29 version was a draft of a tune by Jerry and Plum called "Peaches." Its lyrics, never destined to be included in a collection of Wodehouse's More Immortal Verses, were, in their dummy form, unsingable:

Mother sat at home preserving peaches ev'ry day;
Father said he'd like to help, if he could find the way.
Mother sent him out to pick some peaches on the spot;
And he picked an awful lot. . . .
Mother caught him picking them one Summer afternoon
Mother's gone to Reno, and the case will come on soon.
Lots of alimony poor Papa will have to pay
When the Judge hears mother say:

REFRAIN

Papa would persist in picking peaches
Perhaps procuring peaches puffed his pate
Papa would persist in picking peaches
Platonic pride the prune presumed to prate
Prematurely pickled when he plucked them
Presenting pretty platinum pins for luck
They pinched his poke
Now poor Pa's broke
Because of the pickled peaches Papa plucked.[5]

Its exile was short-lived. Xed out in mighty pencil strokes, it found its way *back* into the show in a singable form and with the punch line moved to its proper place:

Mother sat at home preserving peaches every day,
Father said he'd like to help if he could find the way
Mother sent him out to pick some peaches on the spot;
And he picked an awful lot.

REFRAIN

Father started picking peaches,
And he never seemed to really rest.
Every day he wandered in the orchard,
Though the work was hard he never kicked.
He picked each peach that came in reach,
And here are a few of the peaches father picked.

PARADE OF THE SHOW GIRLS

Mother caught him picking one summer afternoon;
Mother's going to Reno; the case will come up soon.
Lots of alimony poor Papa will have to pay,
When the judge hears Mama say:

REFRAIN

A fascinating fact is unearthed in Guy's script: the restoration of "Peaches" apparently forced the omission from the first-act finale of Jerry's peripatetic duet, "You're Here and I'm Here," slated to be sung by Vivienne Segal and Andrew Toombs. The inclusion of the song (first performed in a Charles Frohman flop called *The Laughing Husband* in 1914 and later interpolated into five more London shows) seems to have been the carrot that Dillingham dangled before Jerry to woo him back after his altercation with Victor Herbert. Placed immediately after "Kiss Me Again," it might have given Jerry satisfaction. If it had stayed.

Plum had a chance to return to the subject matter of his very first theatrical venture, for 1904's *Sergeant Brue*, "Put Me in My Little Cell." The success of Cecil Lean and Harry Kelly's rendition of "Crooks" would lead Jerry and him to write more underworld songs for the Princess:

We're crooks,
Crooks like you read about in books,
We collar everything in which we lay our hooks,
And our crimes at times are things to shudder at.
We've never been in Congress, for we draw the line at that.

We're crooks,
Crooks like you read about in books.
We're strong on intellect though maybe not on looks.
All your silver spoons and jewels we collect,
But we've never worked on Wall Street, for we've got some self-respect.

We're crooks,
Crooks like you read about in books.
If you leave your door unlocked we come inside,
But we've never been lawyers; we've got some proper pride.[6]

So, with rewrites and removals and moves taking place almost until curtain time, *Miss 1917* opened on November 5, 1917, and ran a full four hours, from 8:15 P.M. to 12:15 A.M.

Despite the production's length, the critics loved it. "The company has more stars than most service flags and more pretty women than most cities boast of," noted the *Herald* the next day. "If there are to be revues, let them be like the new one at the Century Theatre . . ." trumpeted the *Tribune,* while the *Sun* shone on Dillingham and Ziegfeld by calling the production a ". . . most beautiful spectacle."

Bessie McCoy (The "Yama Yama" Girl) received raves and a warm welcome from the audience, as did most of the army of entertainers, which numbered in its swollen ranks Lew Fields, Harry Kelly, Elizabeth Brice, Charles King, George White (a dancer for Ziegfeld before he became his prime Broadway rival), Ann Pennington, Gus Van, Joe Schenck, Irene Castle, and Marion Davies.

The work of the trio received passing—and in the case of Jerry—cool notices. "The lightest possible thread of plot holds the several parts of the Century show together, so light, indeed, that it would quite run without it," opined the *Tribune.*

Light it had to be. Guy and Plum were treading in very large footsteps, in territory that was not only unfamiliar but intimidating. That these two enthusiastic youngsters were able to convince Ziegfeld that any plot at all was necessary was a monumental accomplishment.

Their plot line, or web, centered around Hiram Askem (Lew Fields), a raiser of pickles and the stepfather of Polly-with-a-Past (Vivienne Segal). Polly, it seems, was found by Hiram in the middle of the road in a basket, but this seems to have aroused no sense of loyalty in her. She waits until Hiram is offstage giving the cows their coffee and then slips off with a movie crew that just happens to be passing through the farm.

Joe, the prodigal son (Andrew Toombs), arrives and Hiram hopes he will settle down and help him save the farm, but unfortunately, Joe has just graduated from Sing Sing and has come home only to borrow money.

Bad luck for Hiram. And for Joe. He hasn't even the prospect of a handout until the landlord of the pickle trust (Arthur Cunningham) arrives, allowing that Polly is his lost daughter and worth a $300,000 reward for her return. Eureka. Hiram goes to New York in search of her—and incidentally to open a saloon with an attached cabaret, which accommodates a multitude of specialty numbers, culminating, at the end of act 1, in a spectacle that would leave the opening night audience on its feet and cheering.

Following Bessie McCoy's "Moon Song," which featured Miss McCoy suspended from the flies, singing a patriotic ballad from a Joseph Urban moon, the tabs close in to disclose an old stage door with cobwebs radiating upward from it. A doorkeeper with a long beard (Cunningham) is discovered crooning "After the Ball."

Elizabeth Brice and Charles King enter, discussing a movie they've just seen. "Wasn't that a good picture?" asks Brice.

"I don't know," laments King. "I'm tired of the movies."

They listen to the stage doorman for a moment, and then, they commence the lead-in to the ghostly act 1 finale, a number that could have been the basis for Michael Bennett's approach, fifty years later, to *Follies:*

KING:              It's a long time since I heard that song.

CUNNINGHAM:    It was sung in this very theater. . . . In those days there was no cobweb across the door and every night all the young fellows would gather here and wait for the girl that sang it to come out.

KING:              It's a pity that all those fine old songs had to die.

BRICE:            Perhaps they aren't dead, Charlie. Perhaps there's a Paradise where the good ones go when we forget them.

CUNNINGHAM:    *(Music starts):* I think you're right, Miss. For sometimes at night on that dark empty stage I seem to hear the ghosts of the old songs that were born there sounding all about me.

Brice and King now launch into arguably the best Kern song in the score, "The Land Where the Good Songs Go." Beautiful beyond its place in the show, it was a throwaway, a framework for the rush of nostalgia that was to follow.

"On the other side of the moon/Ever so far./Beyond the last little star,/There's a land I know where the good songs go," sing Brice and King, and when they finish, Marion Davies enters from the stage door, singing *The Belle of New York's* "Follow On!," after which Cleo Mayfield and a chorus appear and launch into "In the Good Old Summertime." Cecil Lean, Emma Haig, and Yvonne Shelton follow with "Dinah," Van and Schenck do a turn with "Under the Bamboo Tree," Bessie McCoy and twelve girls bring down the house with her "Yama Yama"; a swan curtain descends and Harry Kelly sings "Sammy," Vivienne Segal enters stage center and sings "Kiss Me Again," and then, in the space occupied only a week ago by Jerry's "You're Here and I'm Here," Brice and King return for "Baby Bumblebee," after which the curtains part on the famed and inevitable Ziegfeld staircase. All of the principals and several score dancers march upstairs and downstairs to Herbert's "March of the Toys" and Jerry's "Toy Clog

Dance," and eventually, wondrously disappear upward into theatrical heaven, while the act curtain falls and the audience goes wild.

A sure hit?

Not at all.

Again, as in the case of *The Riviera Girl,* the thunderous applause on opening night, echoed by the critics in the early editions of the next day's papers, failed to sustain *Miss 1917.* Even though the Ziegfeld publicity machine ground away with quotes aplenty from the critics, and efforts continued to shorten and liven the show during the first week of its run—Adolf Bolm's "Falling Leaves" ballet was cut entirely, and a program promise was made that Mme. Tortola Valencia would "be presented at special matinees at the Century, when she can give her complete repertoire"—audiences didn't come.

Perhaps it was the stratospherically high three-dollar top on tickets, or the location of the Century, uptown between Sixty-second and Sixty-third Streets. Or perhaps it was just one of those twists of fate that makes everyone connected with the theatre dedicatedly superstitious. For whatever reason, *Miss 1917* became an instant, expensive wallflower.

Within a few weeks, defections in the large array of stars began to take place. Irene Castle was the first to leave. Possibly because all of the New York papers gave first raves to Bessie McCoy, and the *New York Clipper* greeted Mrs. Castle's singing debut with less than warm praise ("Mrs. Castle . . . also sang a song, displaying a type of voice usually associated with dancers," the paper said) or perhaps just because she recognized a sinking ship when she was on it, Irene Castle became a mere memory before the end of November.

Finally, after forty-eight unique and varied performances, the show closed, throwing an army of entertainers out of work, and the producing team of Dillingham and Ziegfeld into bankruptcy.

The trio emerged well paid, but not unscarred. Guy and Plum's effort to introduce a plot and a sense of the contemporary into the spectacle/revue went virtually unnoticed, and Jerry's music was ignored. Unmentioned by every paper but the *Tribune,* he received negative notices by omission. And he could have done well without the *Tribune's* evaluation, which noted, at the end of a rave review, "Only the music for 'Miss 1917' seems lacking in spots, but the spots are not those of Victor Herbert's making."

So, *Miss 1917* joined *The Riviera Girl* as an early show the trio would choose to forget.

As would the rehearsal pianist, George Gershwin, who left *Miss 1917* even before it closed to take a new job as a composer at T. B. Harms—Jerry's company. Like the seventeen-year-old Richard Rodgers the year before, nineteen-year-old George Gershwin revered Jerry's genius for creating seemingly perfect and unhackneyed melodies. The difference was that Gershwin was in the pit and not the audience and thus close enough to be recognized by his idol—who never, then or later, let anger, disappointment, or bad reviews diminish his dedication, drive, faith in himself, or recognition of talent in others.

Now, in the waning days of 1917, it was time for the trio to go back to the Princess. Of course, they had never really left. In their minds, they were still the crusaders for verisimiltude. At the end of *Miss 1917*, in a Palm Beach scene, Guy and Plum had had fun at the willing expense of Ziegfeld: Joe, after a long separation, finally rejoins Polly and says, breathlessly, "I've followed you through two acts and an intermission. Where have you been?"

"I've been in the movies," chirps Polly.

"I should think from what I've seen of this show," answers Joe, "that you've been in vaudeville."

"You really followed me through all that maze of dancers and specialty people?" asks Polly, going into his arms. "Oh Joe!"

"Polly!" murmers Joe, and they launch into a final duet, joined by— according to the script—twenty-four Bathing Beauties and eight One-Piece Bathing Suit Girls, after which Guy and Plum merrily added:

> The Plot having threaded its way through the maze of specialties and dancing acts, emerges triumphantly. The happy ending is almost spoiled by a rain storm.

FINALE[7]

But now, back at their theatrical birthplace, it was time to stop satirizing and move forward. Again, tapping into a wellspring of seemingly inexhaustible energy, the trio had already established contact with a predictably hysterical Ray Comstock. While the three had been at work for Klaw, Erlanger, Dillingham, and Ziegfeld, and Jerry had been off with Colonel Savage and *Toot Toot,* which was an adaptation of a Rupert Hughes farce, *Oh, Boy!* had steamed to the end of its appointed run at the Princess and moved into the Casino, leaving the little theatre on Thirty-ninth Street momentarily dark.

It was time for the fifth Princess musical, and again the trio journeyed to Bronxville, even though Jerry and Eva were in the midst of looking for a new site for a new house.

Jerry, aided by Plum and Guy, tried to bring *The Little Thing* into the Princess again, but Comstock would have none of it.

An afternoon of arguing failed to move the prospering producer, and so, ultimately convinced that their clout with Comstock had not been increased by their skyrocketing success, they went back and began to write *Say When,* their next—and what sadly proved to be their last—Princess musical.

Time was of the essence and formulas save time. Possessing a collective trunk filled by two years of collaboration, and given a specific directive by their producer, the trio borrowed from itself. The show's first act, like the first act of *Oh, Boy!* was set on Long Island, except that, now that Guy was familiar with that island's North Shore, it was moved to Hempstead, a short distance from Great Neck. The act 2 party scene of *Oh, Boy!* was transferred from a country club to Greenwich Village. The Jim Marvin character from *Oh, Boy!* became a wise-cracking, hero's sidekick named Hale Underwood.

The general plot also involved a variation on *Oh, Boy!*: two young people want to marry (in *Oh, Boy!*, they want to *stay* married) and the mother of the bride interferes. A pal of the groom tries to save the situation but only complicates it, and two sets of lovers weather it all to win happiness and each other, three minutes before the finale.

Some of the more successful songs, either consciously or unconsciously, were shamelessly borrowed—notably "Our Little Nest," which was a relocated "Nesting Time in Flatbush," and "Before I Met You," which was a cleverly reconstructed "I Never Knew About You," down to its rhythm pattern and lyrics (instead of singing about past swains, the two lovers confess that they were smitten by Lillian Russell and John Drew):

WILLOUGHBY: Prepare yourself to hear the worst.
I'm sorry, but you're not the first.
My heart to claim,
I own with shame.
I'm thankful that I have confessed:
My conscience now will be at rest:
You may forgive me and love me just the same.
To force myself to say so,

Has been an awful tussle,
Still the fact I can't conceal;
I once loved Lillian Russell.
But that was before I met you, dear.
That was before I met you.
Her image I've banished. All passion has
vanished.
I think you're a million times sweeter than
Lillian.
Don't scold me. You told me to tell you the
truth;
Just count it as one of the follies of youth.
I thought her a queen
When I was fourteen—
But that was before I met you.

And she counters with:

MOLLY:   . . . In days gone by, dear, I idolized John Drew.
I used to hope that some day
We might become acquainted;
And when I got his autograph
I thought I should have fainted.
But that was before I met you, dear,
That was before I met you.
His wonderful profile made all girls, you know, feel
That nothing could cheer them if he wasn't near them.
Romances my fancies would weave about John;
But love seemed to wane as the long years went on;
I thought him divine;
But then I was nine.
And that was before I met you.

Three years after they had joined together and three years into their collective
fame, the patterns of the trio's creations were firmly established. The meddling
mother of *Say When* was more than a complication for the young lovers; she was a
mouthpiece for the veritable barrage of clever aphorisms about marriage that had
made *The Rule of Three* and its fledgling author such a sophisticated, quoted success.

Once more the little books of sayings in Guy's library were hauled out. Barely three lines after the opening chorus, one of the singers observes that a man they just saw on the train must be the groom, since "he'd got that set look in his face that always means a bridegroom or a suicide." Molly, the bride, croons dreamily, "Love is the greatest force in the world." Her mother corrects her, "The greatest farce in the world, you mean." Three pages of script later, Mother notes that "marriage is a lottery, and alimony's a gambling debt," and cautions her daughter to "be careful of that wedding gown darling; remember you may need it again some day."

In the second act, while the bride's mother is offstage refueling, other characters take up the chorus. "Love is a wonderful dream," says one, and the other completes the quote, ". . . and matrimony is a wonderful alarm clock." "Bachelors have consciences, married men have wives," observes another. "One doesn't know what real happiness is till after one's married," rhapsodizes still another, to which his companion observes, "No, and then it's too late."

But it's all meant in good, clean fun, and despite its antimarriage fixation, it was the sort of sophisticated bantering that Princess audiences had come to expect.

What they had yet to expect from Plum and Guy was the pervasive, predictable presence of musical comedy crooks. In *Miss 1917*, to accommodate the talents of the team of Van and Schenck, the two writers had created a couple of gangsters who did Charlie Chaplin and Douglas Fairbanks impressions and sang about the joy of their profession. Audiences loved them, and so did Plum and Guy.

And so, from that point onward, until they entered their eighties, Guy and Plum would include in as many shows as they could their own vision of gangster characters.

Their use of crooks for comic relief wasn't theatrically unique. George M. Cohan had employed this device full time for years. But the facts of the trio's *Miss 1917* success and the current newspaper coverage of Warden Lawes's celebrated prison reform program at Sing Sing led them to introduce the characters of Fainting Fanny and Spike Hudgins into *Say When*.

Work continued in Bronxville at a fever pitch, while Jerry and Eva made plans to move into their new home in the Cedar Knolls section. More and more, *Say When* seemed to be an appropriate choice of title for the new venture. Scheduled to begin rehearsals at the end of November, it ran into casting and other problems immediately—which was perhaps just as well. For one thing, the delay allowed Vivienne Segal, now at liberty after the abrupt closing of *Miss 1917*, to join the cast as Molly Farringdon, the young bride. The delay also allowed the trio to change the title from *Say When* to *Oh, Lady! Lady!!*—words and punctuation considerably more appropriate for the Princess. A blackface vaudeville act called the Kemps had introduced the phrase that season, and it had already entered the vocabulary of the young and informed.

Shortly after New Year's in 1918, the show and its mentors entrained for Albany, and Comstock's first purchased playhouse, Harmanus Bleecker Hall. *Oh, Lady! Lady!!* opened on January 7, 1918, to qualified reviews. It was clearly not going to have the smooth sailing tryout that had made *Oh, Boy!* a breeze.

The Albany critics pointed out rightfully that the show was book heavy. And they also noted that ". . . Jerome Kern's delightful music is pretty and appealing, but not especially lingering."

Coming hard on the heels of his bad reviews by omission in *Miss 1917*, this comment must have irritated Jerry in a particularly painful way. For, while Guy and Plum were apparently acquiescing to Ray's demands for formula following and actually seemed to enjoy it, Jerry was striking out in his melodies in new directions. "Moon Song," the second-act opening, unnerved the chorus with its changes in meter. His unexpected pauses in "You Found Me and I Found You" threw Plum off.

The one unusual song upon which both composer and lyricist agreed was the most daring and exquisite creation in the score. Breaking no rules because it made its own, it allowed Plum a freedom and sensitivity he had not yet used, and Jerry an opportunity to explore a unique succession of harmonies and melodic invention. The song not only broke but expanded the standard AABA form of the popular ballad.

"Jerome Kern wrote me a lovely song for the first act," Vivienne Segal recalled, in 1981.[8] "I liked it, and he did, too. But it didn't work, and when something doesn't work in a show, it comes out and that's that."

The song was "Bill," and it would indeed become a casualty of the expedient but generally wise decisions of producers and directors on the road. Ironically, it apparently almost made it to the New York opening. The fact that a quotation still remained in the first act finale on opening night indicates that its omission was a last-minute decision. So, the song was lost to *Oh, Lady! Lady!!* and most of the world until its reappearance in *Show Boat* nine years later.

In mid-January of 1918, the troop traveled on to Cleveland, where, whittled down and spruced up, the show did better business. Guy, in an interview printed in the local papers,[9] acknowledged that "the company missed the best laughing situation in the first act, Monday night, and passed up another in the second act. They were all tired, and hungry," he went on, "for the trains were late, and there was hurry all around. . . . We're making quite a few cuts in lines, tightening up on situations generally, and trying to make the whole performance more compact."

Translation: Hysteria, which was also conveyed in code in Ray's quotations in the same article: " 'Oh Lady! Lady!!' [sic] looks to be the best of our lot," he said. "It's clean, and fast, and altogether proper. . . . We've aimed to give it tone . . . but you'll notice there's precious little monotone."

By the time the production limped into New York, preparing for a January 31 invitational premiere, nerves were frayed but not exposed. Vivienne Segal re-membered, more than anything, the properness of the entire operation. "They [the director and creators] were always so genteel. So *gentlemanly,*" she recalled, probably remembering it in contrast to the mad altercations of *Miss 1917.* "Everyone was so courtly—except for Jerome Kern." Miss Segal paused, "He was a little difficult. And Bob Milton [Comstock's director] would get up into the gallery and shout down 'I can't hear you,' but that's the only raised voice I remember."

The problems that had forced the Cleveland detour were evidently brought under control by the end of January, and *Oh, Lady! Lady!!,* with punctuation intact and good spirits in place, opened to the traditional invited premiere on Thursday, January 31, 1918.

Plum and Guy's final story spun around the impending marriage of Molly Farringdon (Vivienne Segal) and Willoughby Finch (Carl Randall).

As the curtain rises, Molly and the girls, gathered around the grand piano in the living room of her mother's estate at Hempstead, buzz busily about the important day, while Molly's mother (Margaret Dale), who has been ship-wrecked on the rocks of her own matrimony, tries to discourage the whole idea.

Willoughby arrives and, in a lovely duet in which Plum prefigured Irving Caesar's lyrics for "Tea for Two," bride and bridegroom warble their impatience:

> When this weary waiting's ended,
> We start our honeymoon!
> None near us, to see or hear us,
> The whole wide world we will forget!
> Oh, what a joy to stay in your arms all day—
> But—not yet—not yet—not yet!

Hale Underwood (Harry C. Browne), the Jim Marvin transplant from *Oh, Boy!*, arrives and recognizes Willoughby Finch's valet as none other than Spike Hudgins (Edward Abeles), an ex-con from Sing Sing.

Willoughby accepts his valet's credentials graciously, concluding that an ex-convict is an ideal guard for the groaning table of valuable wedding presents on the premises. He doesn't count on the entrance of Fainting Fanny Welch (Florence Shirley), a combination pickpocket and Spike's fiancée. ("I'm a gentleman's gentleman," Spike announces to her, proudly. Fanny fixes him with a beagle eye. "And I'm what they call a man's woman," she counters.)

Further complications arrive in a telegram from Willoughby's ex-fiancée, May Barber (Carroll McComas), due to arrive from their hometown, East Gilead, Ohio.

Is May a typically sheltered small-town girl? "I should say she is," answers Willoughby. "She told me she used to turn my photograph to the wall while she was getting undressed."

Well then, suggests Hale, they'll scare her off by having Fanny parade as a woman wronged by Willoughby. That should send her screaming back to East Gilead.

May arrives, and she's anything but sheltered and everything but shy. And she's not looking for Willoughby at all. She's been to Paris, is a designer's representative, and remembers Willoughby as the epitome of naivité. "That boy was so innocent," she confides to Molly's maid, "he'd have made Little Eva feel like Sappho."

All is explained, after Hale recognizes her as a girl he fell in love with at first sight that afternoon on the Long Island Railroad (shades of Plum and Ethel) and impulsively spills the plan. But it's too late to call off May, who makes a grand entrance and does her thing well enough in front of the wrong fiancée to bring the wrath of Mrs. Farringdon down on Willoughby and the first act curtain down on two separated lovers and one mixed up comedienne.

Act 2 opens on the twin apartments of Willoughby and Hale, which give onto a Greenwich Village rooftop that is "sown with wild oats."

Complications by the carload arrive right after the opening chorus. Chorus girls and criminals are chased in and out of bed- and other rooms by Cyril Twombley (Reginald Mason), an unlikely detective with a heavy British accent, and Mother Farringdon appears at the precise moment that Molly is energetically making up with Willoughby. May and Hale fall in love—which, in 1918, meant marriage—Spike and Fanny fork over the necklace that Fanny stole in Act 1 and resume *their* marriage plans, and Molly and Bill convince Mrs. Farringdon that their marriage ceremony should proceed, just before the title as tag line arrives:

CYRIL:   Three weddings in one day. Oh, lady, lady!

This time, Guy and Plum merrily monickered their chorus girls as residents of shelves in foodstores: Lettice Romayne, Lotta Pommery, Della Catessen, Hallie Butt, Sal Munn, Marie Schino, Mollie Getawney, Marion Etta Herring, Clarette Cupp, May Anne Ayes, Cassie Roll, and Virginia Hamm. The men fared the same: Artie C. Hoke, B. Russell Sprout, C. Ollie Flower, H. Ash-Brown, and Con Kearney.

*Oh, Lady! Lady!!* was Plum's favorite of all the Princess shows, and it would remain so for the rest of his long life.[10] And there was good reason for his preference. It contained some of his best—and worst—lyrics to date.

The worst belong to an act 2 number called "Little Ships Come Sailing Home," which may not have been entirely Plum's doing. In a letter Guy wrote to producer Ethel Watt during the planning stages of a 1975 revival of the show, he throws some dim light upon its history: "'Little Ships' is the worst lyric in the show," he notes. "It was written by Mike Rorke [sic] [a.k.a. Herbert Reynolds], Jerry's tame lyrist. . . . Plum polished it up a bit but when I asked him what it meant he said he couldn't make out. Apparently there were a group of people whose hearts were represented as ships—the singer having only one heart—and they'd been having a tough time but were back safe and sound in their beds."[11]

It wasn't unusual for Jerry to throw in a trunk tune, complete with lyrics, considering the troubles the show had had on the road, and for Plum to be given the task of performing carpentry on a collapsible structure. A few lines reveal that even if the song's major metaphor was a heart, Plum's heart wasn't in the writing of it:

> Life's an ocean grim
>    That has no charts;
> And the ships that swim
>    On it are hearts;
> O'er that lonely sea
>    Far, far they roam;
> But they've love at the helm, and he
>    Will bring them home.

What was worse than the imagery to Guy in later years was the fact that the song's sentiments warred against the very philosophy that underlay their crusade for verisimilitude. "The words certainly fitted no situation and no character. . . ," Guy continued in his letter to Ethel Watt, and when the opportunity came to revise the show for its stock run, they set it into a "sing along" opening chorus.

What an irony that the song became one of the show's most popular tunes. And what a tragedy that it remained, and "Bill" didn't.

Plum's best lyrics, on the other hand, epitomize the integration of song and lyric to book that had changed the face of musical comedy forever.

In a first-act trio that in other contemporary hands might have been just another interlude, Willoughby, Hale, and Spike deepen and define their characters. The lyrics of each amount to miniature character sketches:

BILL:    Oh, when I fell in love,
           My spirit sort of yearned.
           I wished that I could do, in fact,
           Some great, self-sacrificing act.

HALE:    While all that I can wish
           Is that some wretched, hard-up fish
           Would suddenly arrive
           And touch me for a five.

SPIKE:    Love makes me feel so strong and grand,
           At nothing I would stop;
           I'd like to fill a bag with sand
           And swing it on a cop.

The ultimate apotheosis of character definition came in the excised "Bill," sung by Molly to her bridesmaids early in act 1, before Bill's entrance:

I used to dream that I would discover
The perfect lover
   Some day:
I knew I'd recognize him if ever
He came round my way:
I always used to fancy then
   He'd be one of the godlike kind of men,
With a giant brain and a noble head

Like the heroes bold
In the books I read.
But along came Bill,
Who's quite the opposite of all the men
In story books.
In grace and looks
I know that Appolo
Would beat him all hollow,
And I can't explain . . .
It's surely not his brain
That makes me thrill:
I love him because he's wonderful . . .
Because he's just my Bill.

A quick scan of the lyrics will reveal that the melody is a shade simpler than it was when the song finally reached *Show Boat,* and the lyrics, under Plum's light and graceful hand, are much lighter than that serious operetta would allow, particularly in the second chorus, which never made the trip to the Mississippi and immortality.

He's just my Bill
He has no gifts at all:
A motor car
He cannot steer;
And it seems clear
Whenever he dances,
His partner takes chances,
Oh I can't explain
It's surely not his brain
That makes me thrill
I love him
Because he's—I don't know—
Because he's just my Bill.

Fitted lovingly to Jerry's melody, the song completes Bill's thought in the previously sung trio and says all that need be said about the reasons for the love affair of Molly and Bill.

In wacky contrast, "Our Little Nest," Spike and Molly's joyful act 1 duet, builds upon "Nesting Time in Flatbush," but always in the context of the aspirations of two not quite ex-crooks:

HUGGINS:  Our home will look so bright and cheery,
That you will bless your burglar-boy
I got some nifty silver, dearie,
When I cracked that crib at Troy;
I lifted stuff enough in Yonkers
To fill a fairly good-sized chest;
And, at a house in Mineola,
I got away with their victrola;
So we'll have music in the evenings
When we are in our little nest.

FANNY:  Our home will look so bright and cheery
With all the chintz I sneaked from Stern's
And with all the knick-knacks from McCrary [sic]
And the silk I pinched from Hearn's.
And we'll have stacks—from Saks and Macy's
Of all the things that you'll like best;
And, when at night we're roasting peanuts
Upon the stove I swiped from Greenhuts
Although it's humble, you won't grumble
You'll love our cozy little nest.

And even when Jerry wrote a marginally sticky—though complex for the times—melody for the "Moon Song" that opens act 2, Plum saved it from the saccharine hall of fame by his urbane treatment of an operetta cliché:

Oh Silvery Shivery Moon that I see shining above
I've something to tell you between you and me
    I'm in love.
Yes, there's no concealing old friend
I'm nearly knocked flat
How, how in the world is it going to end,
    Tell me that.

His cleverness continued to abound in a second act trio by Bill, Spike, and Fanny about a Greenwich Village that probably, even in 1918, only existed in the minds of those who had never been there ("Some day somebody will put the *real* Greenwich Village on the stage . . . ," wailed *Theatre*'s critic in his review):

> For in bad MacDougal Alley
> You'll discover gener*ally*
> Life's a wicked and a desperate affair.
>> When you live in dear old Greenwich
>> Your behavior gets quite Fren-nich
> It's a sort of kind of something in the air.

And finally, in Cyril and Hale's lament that "It's a Hard, Hard, Hard World for a Man," his fresh rhyme schemes positively glowed:

> We do our best as we have said
> The straight and narrow path to tread
> Ignoring all temptations fate may send
> But of snares the world has plenty meant
> To trap the man of sentiment
> And one is sure to get us in the end.

Jerry's melodies were mostly new, always fresh, and constantly appealing. His first-act finale was a musical scene all in itself, with dialogue leading into song which led into dialogue which culminated in song, and all of it underscored with far more felicity and imagination than the Princess—or most of American musical comedy—had seen thus far.

So, for all of its trouble on the road, *Oh, Lady! Lady!!* became a large, positive, popular step forward for the trio.

The opening night audience loved the show, and their affection was echoed in print by critics the next day. "The fun is almost incessant," said the *Sun*. "Dainty and fresh," chirped the *Herald*. "A hit," was the judgment of the *Tribune*, and the *Clipper*, appearing on February 6, prophesied that ". . . it promises to be one of the big successes of the season."

To the trio, the interiors of the reviews meant more than the quotable capsules of enthusiasm.

"Listen to the tenor of the *Times*," said Guy, when the trio gathered the next day in Ray's office. "'The book by Bolton and Wodehouse has a measurably novel plot that actually sustains interest for itself alone. The lines are bright and the lyrics well written. The music by Jerome Kern is in his familiar vein of easy gayety tinged at times with reverie and sentiment.'"

"Or the *tessitura* of the *Tribune,*" added Plum. "'For such a sweet, aqua-tinted bit of musical comedy it was surprisingly full of varied charms, and all the elements were in harmony. The lines were a characteristic product of the authors, sprinkled with capital quips;' Ah! Listen to this: 'There was actually a good working plot, and the music was tuneful and pleasing.' Altogether capital, what?"

"At least that," said Guy, folding back the *Telegram* to its reviews. "'There was a pleasant surprise in "Oh, Lady! Lady!!" when one began to realize that the book had almost a plot, at least quite enough of it to supply material for the development of genuinely funny situations and for lines that were truly clever.'"

He turned to Jerry, who had been oddly quiet, for Jerry.

"'Dainty, *tuneful,* brightly humorous and altogether pleasing from first to last,'" he quoted, hopefully, in the composer's direction.

It failed to lift the cloud that had recently positioned itself directly over Jerry's head. Too much tacit acceptance had begun to dull his enthusiasm. He was restless. His work and his ideas, which had launched both the Princess and the trio, were getting only minimal notice. It was time to move forward into new, more noticeable territory.

He glanced around the room. Could the trip be made with Plum and Guy? Maybe. With Ray?

Comstock was reading now. "'The gowns,'" Ray intoned, "'are in admirable taste, with no touch of the sensational or bizarre.'"

No, thought Jerry. Not with Ray. Definitely not with Ray.


The accolades ascended in the weeklies. "Bolton, Wodehouse, Kern" had been the subhead of the *Times* review, and that was all that theatregoers had needed to know, as—according to Guy in later years—George S. Kaufman, the young and then anonymous *Times* critic expanded poetically in a later piece:

> This is the trio of musical fame,
>     Bolton and Wodehouse and Kern:
> Better than anyone else you can name,
>     Bolton and Wodehouse and Kern.
> Nobody knows what on earth they've been bitten by;
> All I can say is I mean to get lit an' buy
> Orchestra seats for the next one that's written by
>     Bolton and Wodehouse and Kern.[12]

And Dorothy Parker, Kaufman's compatriot at the Algonquin Roundtable, wrote, in *Vanity Fair:*

> Well, Bolton and Wodehouse and Kern have done it again. Every time these three gather together, the Princess Theatre is sold out for months in advance. You can get a seat for "Oh, Lady! Lady!!" somewhere around the middle of August for just about the price of one on the Stock Exchange. Only moving picture artists and food profiteers will be able to attend for the first six months. After that, owners of ammunition plants may be able to get a couple of standing rooms.
>
> If you ask me, I will look you fearlessly in the eye and tell you in low, throbbing tones that it has it over any other musical comedy in town. I was completely sold on it . . . but then Bolton and Wodehouse and Kern are my favorite indoor sport, anyway. I like the way they go about a musical comedy. I like the way the action slides casually into the songs. I like the deft rhyming of the song that is always sung in the last act by two comedians and a comedienne. And oh, how I do like Jerome Kern's music. . . .

Personality pieces on the trio began to pepper the pages of other smart magazines. The *Musical Courier* printed an "at home" portrait of Guy and Marguerite, which, according to Namara in later years had been taken more than a year earlier, when she had been pregnant with Peggy, and she pointed to the undone laces at the side of her dress to support her claim.

Plum, in one of his many guises at *Vanity Fair,* later wrote a brilliant and revealing piece called "Our Merciless Musical Comedy Trust," in which he offered encapsulated, embroidered biographies of each of them. Of Guy, he wrote:

> He began his working career as an architect, and to this day indefatigable clients of his dead past call him up just when he is tired out from a long morning of clipping coupons to ask him to design a kennel for their fish-hound . . . he has averaged a success a week. He has the best head of hair of any living dramatist. He lives mostly on vegetables. He has never told a funny story. His shirts are reported to be specially designed by Urban. His socks are the most passionate in New York. . . . He is polite both before breakfast and after a long train journey. . . . He works with a pad and pencil, very slowly and carefully. . . . He never opens letters. He is supernaturally honest.

In a wild mixture of characteristic modesty and mock puffery, he sketched himself:

. . . [He] is the worst-dressed man in New York. He has his shoes shined
when he thinks of it, but never thinks of it. He started his literary career at the
age of nineteen as the conductor of a humorous column on the London *Globe*—
a job which involved the writing of a set of humorous verses between the hours
of nine and half-past ten in the morning for eight years. . . . He does all his
work at a typewriter. He is getting balder every day, though even now he has a
sneaking hope that it doesn't really show. His ideal in life would be to live in
the country and keep a hundred dogs. He smokes too much. . . . He hates
telephoning. He has done more than any living man to raise the level of lyric
writing in America. . . .

And perhaps in an effort to ameliorate the effect of his *Miss Springtime* piece
about Guy, or more likely because of an honest, heartfelt adulation, he wrote
glowingly about Jerry:

. . . He is the only composer who can sing his songs without breaking up the
party. He can drive a car. [The trio and their wives must have gotten an
enormous kick out of that.] He has a dog named Henry, more intelligent than
any theatrical manager in America, except one. . . . He has a bald spot
coming at the top of his head. He has the best luck of any man in New York.
He is a regular attendant at auctions, buying so many pictures that this year he
has had to have a new house built round them. He writes the best "dummies"
for his lyrists of any composer in the business—so good that at one time the
lyrists are said to have copied them out and sent them back as the finished
article. He is the champion pinochle-lizard of Bronxville. . . . Once he
jumped into the Bronx River to save his dog—who rescued him with
difficulty.

Ray was delighted with the reviews and the publicity. In an unprecedented
move, he decided to form a Chicago company of the show immediately and
install it for a week at the Casino. After all, *Oh, Boy!* had played at both theatres
to sellout audiences, and this show would easily outrun *Oh, Boy!*

Now it was time for the next Princess show, and he summoned Bolton and
Wodehouse to his office for a conference. Guy suggested *The Little Thing*. It was
fortunate that Jerry was in Philadelphia with *Toot-Toot!*. Ray's reaction was just
the kind that would have sent the composer into another of his famous rages.

Guy returned to Great Neck to regather his forces. Marguerite had gone to
California to appear with the Minneapolis Symphony. Plum and Ethel had
settled into the comfortable certainty of living down the road from Guy.

And then, without warning or logic, an odd, unexplainable and fatal change
took place at the Princess. The critical and public attitude toward *Oh, Lady!*

*Lady!!* cooled. The monthly and weekly publications failed to share the euphoria of the dailies. *Theatre* magazine rightfully and perceptively called the show "a 1918 edition of 'Oh, Boy!'", and while it generally praised the cast, noted that "Harry C. Browne sings atrociously and dances like a baby elephant." And it saw through the Greenwich Village counterfeit as easily as an X-ray: "Why, oh why," lamented the magazine, "locate a scene in Greenwich Village, with 'every man, woman, and poet there' attending an early morning studio roof party, and then have everybody look, dress, act, and talk like a Mineola weekend?"

But its most mortal thrusts were saved for the trio, and particularly for Jerry: "What was so well worth doing once the Messrs. Bolton and Wodehouse and Kern have naturally thought worth doing again," the magazine noted. "The book, in fact, of the second piece, is quite superior to that of the first. The songs, though delightful, scarcely equal those of the original comedy."

And it was, in a way, true. Not one of *Oh, Lady! Lady!!*'s songs would survive as a Jerome Kern standard. Perhaps, in a giant try for verisimilitude, he had subordinated his songs to the show itself. Perhaps it was just fate that the show's one standard was cut before it opened.

Within a few weeks, attendance started to decline. Two more weeks and it was clear to everyone that the fifth Princess show was not going to run as long as the third or fourth ones.

"We're going to need a new show sooner than I thought," said Ray to two-thirds of the trio.

Guy and Plum exchanged glances. Jerry was already in the middle of a new show for the Selwyns, with a book by Edgar Allan Woolf, the librettist of *Toot-Toot!,* and lyrics by Herbert Reynolds.

He had not even suggested that Guy and Plum join him. In fact, the first they had known of the new show was when they had read a newspaper story appearing three days after the opening of *Oh, Lady! Lady!!.*

It was all very disconcerting, and even ominous.

# THE
# NEAR PAST

"One never knows when a truck is coming before it hits one, does one?" asks *Plum* of *Guy*.

There is a long pause, as their steps echo each other on the rough macadam of the Remsenburg lane.

"Hardly," answers *Guy*. "Or the end of an affair, or a marriage. Or a partnership."

"It was awfully good while it lasted. First rate. But then, one wouldn't want to wear waistcoats in the twentieth century, would one?"

"The theatre is a fickle woman," says *Guy*, who should know. "Gathers you in, plies you with praise, leaves you when she tires of you."

"Jerry was scarcely a fickle woman, chap," remonstrates Plum, in the name of fairness. "But he was theatre. Down to his fingertips, caressing the keys."

"Oh, don't get sentimental, Plum," sniffs Guy. "It's unbecoming."

"Yes," obliges Plum, without rancor. "We called him a bastard at the time, and we had a reason. Still one hates endings, even if they are only act endings."

Guy agrees, silently. He remembers. The end of 1918 was only a pause, perhaps, but it was a pause that would change much for all of them, forever. [1]

Chapter

# 12

# Finaletto

## 1918

In 1918, there was little need for the Comstock-Gest apparatus to crank out prepared stories about the escapades of Bolton and Wodehouse and Kern for the New York press. The local newspapers sought out the trio of musical fame that year; they were the trendsetters, the vanguard, the standard bearers. They had set their Princess musicals on Long Island; Al Jolson's *Sinbad,* which opened on February 14, 1918, was located on Long Island, as was Harry Carroll's *Oh, Look!* —which also borrowed the telltale Princess punctuation. The imitation worked for *Sinbad* (which probably didn't need the help anyway) but didn't for *Oh, Look!* It expired quickly, as did *Biff! Bang!,* another exclamation-pointed musical which was largely a vaudeville starring Lew Fields's son Joe.

Early in the year, Guy obliged the interviewer for the New York *American* by expounding at length about the trio's methods and Jerry's dream. "Our musical comedies," he said, "depend as much upon plot and the development of their characters for success as upon their music, and because they deal with subjects and people near to the audiences. . . . Every line, funny or serious, is supposed to help the plot continue to hold. . . . If the songs are going to

177

count at all in any plot, the plot has to build more or less around, or at least, with them."

That was the guiding principle with which they had begun their Princess odyssey, and with which Jerry had trouble elsewhere. On Christmas night of 1917, his venture with Colonel Savage, *Toot-Toot!* opened in Wilmington, Delaware, to mixed reviews, then stumbled on to Baltimore and Washington, where the Colonel closed it long enough to fire most of the cast. Jerry, busy with *Oh, Lady! Lady!!* didn't participate in the overhaul of the ailing show, although he did manage to add two new numbers to its score.

In the middle of January 1918, a week before *Oh, Lady! Lady!!*'s opening at the Princess, Colonel Savage, with a new cast, took the revised show to Philadelphia, where he announced that he was, patriotically and magnanimously, dropping ticket prices, as "a war measure," to pre-1914 levels. *Toot-Toot!* opened on February 4 to generally negative reviews, which meant another round of rewrites, this time involving Jerry.

The show, with a negligible book adapted from Rupert Hughes's farce, *Excuse Me*—updated to make the hero a lieutenant—and lyrics by Berton Braley, was not destined for the Kern canon, and the fact that the reviewer for the *Philadelphia Evening Bulletin* spent a goodly portion of his review extolling "One Last Long Mile," a marching song with words and music by Lieutenant Emil Breitenfeld, 153 Depot Brigade, Camp Dix, N. J., couldn't have set well with Jerry. Even though his career had been launched with interpolations, Jerry hated to let other interpolaters in on his own main scores. But in this case, he was overruled. Colonel Savage admitted not only Lieutenant Breitenfeld but Anatol Friedland for a second act military ensemble number called "Cute Soldier Boy."

Even all of this interpolated patriotism couldn't save the show. It opened in New York at the George M. Cohan Theatre on March 11 and closed five weeks later. The Colonel kept it on the road into the next season, and Jerry moved on to another venture that didn't include Guy and Plum, a musical adaptation of Margaret Mayo's farce, *Baby Mine,* book to be supplied by *Toot-Toot!*'s Edgar Allan Woolf and lyrics to come from good old reliable Herbert Reynolds.

This time, it may well be that Jerry longed for Guy's libretto-making skill, if not his argumentativeness over financial matters.[1] The show, now named *Rock-a-Bye Baby,* had book trouble from the onset of labor. The reviewers in both New Haven and Atlantic City were delighted with Jerry's music and roundly critical of Woolf's book. The Selwyns, again producing and announcing— erroneously, it turned out—that *Rock-a-Bye Baby* would open the Selwyn, their new theatre on Forty-second Street, sent out a distress call for Margaret Mayo, who came to Atlantic City for rewrites.

For all the show's troubles on the road, it seems that Jerry had a good time with the writing and staging of *Rock-a-Bye Baby.* By all accounts, his professional relationship with the young George Gershwin was continuing; Gershwin was again serving as his rehearsal pianist, and in turn, Jerry was advising him about the fine points of breaking into the Broadway composing racket.[2]

For years afterward, Jerry would insist that *Rock-a-Bye Baby* was his favorite score. In this case, favorite didn't necessarily mean best. Absolutely none of its songs survived the brief, eighty-five-performance run of the show.

Its failure was a bitter disappointment for Jerry. Not only did he have personal affection for the score; he'd stolen Dorothy Dickson from the cast of *Oh, Boy!,* which was still running strong, to bolster the sagging book. Miss Dickson was as magical as ever, as was Louise Dresser, but, although some of the New York critics praised the score, most of them pronounced the show humdrum, and so did early audiences.

So, it was not a very cheery spring for Jerome Kern. Deep in construction of a new home, he could ill afford too many flops, and money must have been a concern of his in early 1918. His chagrin over Guy's challenges to his financial arrangements with managements wasn't mollifed by two failures.

Meanwhile, Plum and Ethel were undergoing their own move. In early March, they left Manhattan and relocated themselves near Guy and Marguerite in Great Neck. Ethel, with her sure instinct for the right spot at the right time, found them a large place on a large tract of land owned by the Grace family, who were presently making multimillions with their worldwide shipping interests. On Arrandale Avenue, on the way to King's Point, it was still in the thick of the Broadway-literati enclave. "Scott Fitzgerald and his crowd lived about three miles from us," Plum told David Jasen in the 1970s. "There were an awful lot of actors there. Ed Wynn was there and so were Roy Barnes, Donald Brain and Ernest Truex. I used to play golf with them at the Sound View Golf Club. . . ."[3]

Shortly after the move, Guy and Plum were approached by producer Al Woods to participate in their own gamble away from Jerry. Their task was to turn the turn-of-the-century farce *The Girl from Rector's* into a musical, with music by Jean Schwartz, the very same Jean Schwartz who had worked with Jerry in Wanamaker's music department in 1904.

The surviving evidence in the Bolton library indicates that, although Guy and Plum were drawing closer to each other, they missed Jerry and hoped that the trio would be able, somehow, to reunite for this venture. But no such reunion occurred.

However, even without Jerry, Guy and Plum carried on the Princess tradition and most of its formula. *See You Later* had three acts, but its first and third acts were set in an estate called The Chateau, on the North Shore of Long Island. Its chorus girls were named Grace Fall, Bee Haive, Ann May, June White, April Folly, Iva Paine, Wanda Holme, Pearl Lea, Ella Trick, and Knight Leigh. It contained a very *Oh Boy!*-ish sounding lyric by Plum that was so reminiscent of Jim Marvin's "ray of sunsh" and "it's a hab" abbreviations that it could be construed as self-plagiarizing. The song, "Our Little Paradise," a duet for Dick and Betty (T. Roy Barnes and Winona Winter), extols, a la "Bungalow in Quogue," the joys of country living:

DICK:   How nice 'twould be to go and dwell
        In some far state—say, Nev. or Del.
        I've heard folks say, who ought to know,
        It's jolly in the state of Mo.

BOTH:   Let us build a home in Mo.
            Way out there, you know,
        Life is never slow:

DICK:       I was told so long ago
            By my aunt in Cleveland, O.
        And you don't need lots of dough:

BOTH:   For in dear old Mo.
        There's no fuss and show:

DICK:   And I've got a hunch
        I'd be a perfect ray of sunsh

BOTH:   In our little Paradise in Mo.

DICK:   Or would it not be more judish
        If we our life began
        In some desirable posish
            Near Kansas City, Kan.
        To Oklahoma let us roam
        And build a little oklahome;

> Why yes! I've heard a lot of folk
> Speak very well of life in Ok.

BOTH: Let us build a home in Ok.
>     Where we needn't choke
>     In the city smoke.

DICK: Ev'ry morn, when I awoke,
>     The old furnace I would stoke:
>     I would shovel on the coke!

BOTH: For to folk in Ok
>     Heavy work's a joke—

DICK: And though short of cash,
>     We'd love each other with a pash.

BOTH: In our little Paradise in Ok.

The lyric goes on to warble about how the couple will coo and bill in Chicago, Ill., and concludes that they would ". . . both endeav/To keep away from Reno, Nev. . . ."

The only extant script of the book of the show is a heavily penciled and revised act 1, and this, too, is rife with Princessisms. Directly out of *Nobody Home* is a scene with a menu. Sam, the waiter (Jules Epailly), offers Lord Glenochtie (George Graham), the bill of fare:

SAM: Here you are, sir. Here's the food scenario. Dishes marked "ready" only take half-an-hour.

LORD G: We'll have two portions of Barcarolle Venetienne.

SAM: Turn it over. You're looking at the music program.

Guy even borrowed, dangerously, from his curtain line from *Oh, Boy!*:

BETTY: . . . Dick's been so naughty, I see I shall have to be a little firm with him.

DICK: You bet you will. Here's the little firm—(Puts arm about Betty) and I'm the silent partner.

There are the customary pairs of lovers, complicated with very operettaish characters who aren't always who they appear to be. "Commodore Walker"

(Victor Moore) is in reality a more prosaic Mr. Greene; Jo-Jo Romaine, the Broadway Bombshell (Frances Cameron) is really Mrs. George Potter of Utica, president of the Young Man's Rescue League and Anti-Cabaret Society.

For all its trappings of mistaken identity, the show is up to date in the Princess fashion. At the opening curtain, everyone is recovering from a wild party the night before; the leading man doesn't remember proposing to someone he doesn't intend to marry; a lady from the hinterlands, entering this smart, Long Island chateau remarks that ". . . orgies are in the very air . . ." and Jo-Jo decides at one point that she had better go to the country "to tell my husband I'm engaged."

In one exchange, Lord Glenochtie entreats Dick to defend the lord's character and tell his fiancée's mother that he's pure.

DICK:    Pure? Pure as the driven snow, but, oh, how that snow was driven!

LORD G:  Be a good friend and tell her all my good qualities.

DICK:    Your good qualities? You don't want a friend — you want an inventor.

There is a typical Wodehousian love song that cautions lovers that, though they were told when they were young to keep out of the sun, ". . . it's in the moon that danger really lies," and an antipastoral ditty for Jo-Jo and the Girls, in which she confesses that ". . . quite the nicest thing in the country/Is the train that leaves for town."

But, from the appearance of the surviving script, the show was clearly in disarray when it opened at the Academy of Music in Baltimore, Maryland, on April 15, 1918. Another composer, Joseph Szulc, was called in to bolster Jean Schwartz's music, but it probably would have taken Jerry, the man who set the Princess style, to really do the job. In fact, a semicryptic, penciled addendum in Guy's handwriting to Plum's lyrics for "The Train That Leaves for Town" indicates that Jerry might have been approached or at least consulted with them. It also indicates that he might have agreed to return for what would become the next Princess show, *Oh! My Dear!* "Note for Kern," it says, then adds, cryptically: "Of course in abandon[ing] this lyric with the music it was attached to — in fact this is being used in 'Oh My Dear.'"

It remained in the program for opening night in Baltimore and so wasn't abandoned; but the show was. The surviving script has massive rewrites of the first third of the first act, with a total change of meeting and relationship for the two lovers and notes for further extensive reconstruction.[4]

But apparently, at this point, the producers decided to cut their losses and close the show. And that was that for *See You Later.*

Meanwhile, in the late spring, Jerry's fortunes turned slightly better. Colonel Savage's production of *Houp-La,* for which he had written a score in 1917, had undergone a change of title. Now called *Head over Heels,* it was slated for a May 25 opening at the Tremont Theatre in Boston.

The show, with book and lyrics again by Edgar Allan Woolf and some lyrics by Jerry himself, starred the colonel's favorite, a diminutive soprano named Mitzi, who was noted, among other things, for her acrobatics.

As *Houp-La,* it had enjoyed a closed-end tryout with the Hartford (Connecticut) Opera Players, and, according to Jerry's biographer, Gerald Bordman, there was little rewriting to do. *Head over Heels* opened to enthusiastic notices. It would remain in Boston, gathering laurels and royalties, for the rest of the spring and most of the summer.

At about this time, news from abroad reached the trio, and it was less than encouraging, particularly for Jerry. In May, a London production of *Very Good Eddie* opened. But it was hardly recognizable, and the father of verisimilitude in the musical theatre was dealt a particularly cruel blow by the British producers. Only five of his songs survived them, and four other composers were brought in to flesh out the score. Interestingly enough, one of these was Cole Porter. His one contribution was a ballad, "Alone with You," for which he shared both music and lyric credit with Melville Gideon.

The production was a disaster and lasted only forty-six nights, yet another failure to tack to the wall for Bolton and Wodehouse and Kern, either together or separately, in 1918.

Small wonder then, that biographers of Kern and Wodehouse mark late 1917 and early 1918 as the time of the breakup of the trio of musical fame. It was a time of mutual and individual disarray.

But 1918 was not the year of their parting. True, they were working apart. But they had not yet *come* apart. Despite the cracks in the solidarity of their collaboration begun with the *Oh, Boy!* confrontation, they were still a team, and still ready to continue beyond the sad demise of *Oh, Lady! Lady!!* at the Princess.

The proof is tangible. First, there were the notes penciled in the margin of *See You Later,* indicating that Jerry was at least in touch with Plum and Guy on a show that would eventually become *Oh! My Dear!*

Second, it was in the spring of 1918 that they signed the contract, drawn up during *Oh, Boy!,* that would give Jerry 3 percent of the profits and Guy and Plum 2 percent each, a raise of 0.5 percent for the librettist and lyricist. Signing a contract is hardly the action of a team that intends to break up.

Third, and most important, the trio decided in June of 1918 to update *The Little Thing* and submit it, for the third time, to Ray Comstock as their next Princess musical. In a 1921 letter to George Middleton, Guy lined out their progress and their purpose: "In June," he wrote, "a scenario was drawn up of a new type of musical show, to wit a 'Barriesque' piece with character drawing of a far more subtle order than obtains in the usual musical comedy and with a patriotic theme, whimsically treated."

That, in and of itself, was a giant step forward for the American musical theatre, particularly in 1918, when practically every musical on Broadway rushed to include a fiercely flag-waving number. It was the year of *Yip, Yip, Yaphank,* and Irving Berlin, the inheritor of George M. Cohan's mantle of super patriotism onstage, was setting the standard.

Satirizing war in 1918 was definitely out of the mainstream, and the idea couldn't have failed to excite Jerry. If the Princess was the scene of the first attempts at verisimilitude and modernity, it would, with *The Little Thing,* become the scene of the first full-scale, truly contemporary antiwar satire in the American musical theatre.

It was risky, but so is all experimentation. It was like the old days, four years ago, when Bessie Marbury was still at the Princess, and they were all breaking new ground. The trio plunged into their new project with gusto.

"In July," continued Guy, "this piece was written and rewritten until the last phrase was polished and everyone agreed that there need be no more than one week of rewrites, as it was a case of sink or swim, for *The Little Thing . . .* being an idea play, there was no further room for tinkering. . . ."

They delivered it to a still skeptical Ray Comstock. Success had bred conservatism, and he hadn't liked the first two versions of the script; on the other hand, they were as famous as he now. "Ray was a little dubious," Guy continues, "so was Bob [Milton, Comstock's director] but the enthusiasm of the authors and particularly of Jerome D. Kern swept them along." The balance, the trio felt, was in their favor, and they left the manuscript with Comstock and Milton and turned their attention to other projects:

Jerry was concerned with both moving into his new home in Bronxville and his old venture with Colonel Savage, *Head over Heels,* which was presently out of town and pointed toward Broadway.

Guy was heavily into the second act of *Adam and Eva,* his second collaboration with, again, an agitated and ignored George Middleton.

Plum was busy on a series of short stories he was preparing for publication in the *Saturday Evening Post.*

And Plum and Guy were under way on the turning of *The Girl from Rector's* into a musical for Al Woods.

None of these projects meant nearly so much to the trio as *The Little Thing,* nor was anything more important to the sustenance of their delicately balanced relationship. If Ray finally accepted it, they all felt that their futures in the American musical theatre would spiral upwards. If not —

They received a call from the Comstock office. "Ray decided," Guy concludes to George Middleton, "it wouldn't do for the Princess. That was that."[5]

And so, *The Little Thing* was rejected for the third time.

In all fairness, it would have been a risk for Comstock, given the revolutionary nature of its book. Only the second act survives, and that was nearly lost. It was discovered in 1981, tucked into a corner of the basement of the Bolton home in Remsenburg, as were so many of Guy's papers. Nearly overlooked, as it was in July of 1918, it deserves retelling for the sheer audacity of it and for its pivotal role in the saga of the trio of musical fame.

Guy called it "Barriesque," and this is hardly evident, unless, by some stretch of the imagination, all fantasy can be called Barriesque. Act 1 apparently ends with a dream sequence, which spills over into the opening of act 2.

As the curtain rises, Sally, the leading character, is dreaming of perfect solutions for the problems of all of the cast members. Three spies — two of them German and one of them a mysterious Gypsy woman named Mareska — skulk around in search of a secret formula for explosives which is controlled by Jack, the hero. Mareska swindles the secret out of Jack by stealing a blotter upon which he has written it and then reading the backward writing in her pocket mirror.

In the midst of this, Sherlock Holmes wanders through, chatting with Sally, and giving himself a fix. Sally relieves him of his needle, admonishing him not to lose *all* touch with reality.

Sally and Sherlock then saunter off; Mareska sneaks back with the formula, tattoo paraphernalia, and Heinrich, one of the German spies. She tattoos the formula on Heinrich's back and then goes off in search of the chemical that will render the tattoo invisible. While she's gone, Sally climbs in through a window, injects Heinrich with the rest of Holmes's morphine, stacks him in a corner, corners the rest of the spies, saves the world, and, in a huge production number, receives her reward from President Wilson.

When she wakes up, all of the characters of the dream appear in her reality. The scene is England. World War I is raging. Hero Jack—who really has invented a new explosive—realizes that he can't save the world with it because it won't explode. But Sally persuades him to look for the silver lining; he can't, after all, always busy himself with big accomplishments. He should be satisfied with "little things" like enlisting and fighting and marrying his love, Claire.

This Jack does, while a captain arrives and announces that he's casting a camp show and needs a small part filled. He offers it to a soldier named Barnes, who turns it down huffily, harrumphing that he's played leading roles with the great Mansfield, among them—you guessed it—Sherlock Holmes.

Sally again saves the day and the show by convincing the actor that doing a seemingly "little thing" like entertaining the troops would be playing the greatest role of his career. He acquiesces grumpily.

And now, near the finale, it's Sally's turn. She does a dance and at its end is offered a job as a dishwasher, because it will be doing a "little thing" for the war effort. She gulps and accepts, and the curtain falls to the strains of "Over There," while Jack and Claire take center stage in wedding regalia.

Except for the patriotic interpolation, it's clearly a Princess show. Even though it ends with a wedding, the groom lightens it by observing that all men are created equal except those who decide to get married.

And a baby-talking chorus girl named Pickles (probably based on a real life chorus girl named Pickles St. Clair, who worked for Charles Dillingham) manages to leaven the war by flattening its stuffy commanders.

"Haven't we any wum?" she asks Tot, another chorus girl who—in name at least—was serving double duty in 1918 in both *The Little Thing* and *See You Later*. "Lord Hawington always dwinks wum."

"He'll get scotch and like it," answers Tot.

"But," notes Pickles, "he says wum's the only thing that clears the cobwebs out of his bwain."

"Offer him a vacuum cleaner," suggests Tot.

"Nonsense," rejoins Pickles, "Lord Hawington is a ver'wy deep thinker."

"He must be," replies Tot. "I notice his thoughts never get to the surface."

Some of this, slightly altered, found its way into later shows by Plum and Guy. What did not were Plum's lyrics or Jerry's music. All but two of the songs have either disappeared or been anonymously absorbed into other shows. As for the rest, only the lyrics remain, and they ache for forgotten melodies. For instance, the historical set piece:

The Emporer Nero lived, you know,
    In the palmy days of Rome;
And things were never, never slow
    When *he* was round the home:
The widow and the orphan, too,
    He persecuted always;
And by degrees had 'em climbing trees
    And ducking into hall-ways.

And one wonders what deliciously melting melody of Jerry's Plum fit to the following gentleness:

I'll put your slippers on for you and light your cigar, pet;
And let you drop the ashes on the parlor carpet. . . .

The world would never know. In one fell swoop, Ray Comstock swept *The Little Thing* into oblivion, but not unimportance. Its leading character and some of its plot would be the small patch of paste that would hold the trio together for another two years and bring them once again into the orbit of Florenz Ziegfeld.

In 1918, Jerry went back to *Head over Heels;* Guy went back to *Adam and Eva;* and Plum and Ethel, despite the war, went to London. There, they took up residence at a house Ethel found at 16 Walton Street.[6] But they only stayed a month. Guy, it seemed, had a new project for them.

Klaw and Erlanger had contracted with composer Ivan Caryll to turn *Madam and Her Godson,* a French farce by Maurice Hennequin and Pierre Veber, into a patriotic musical. Caryll, an enormously successful composer for the London musical stage—five of his shows ran over 500 performances—was equally prominent in America. *The Pink Lady,* with its lilting waltz, "My Beautiful Lady," was the sellout of the 1911 season, and *Chin Chin*, the hit of the 1914 season. By 1918, he had twenty-nine musicals to his credit, and both Guy and Plum counted themselves fortunate to be picked by this superannuated and supremely successful theater legend to provide book and lyrics for his newest venture.

They plunged into the project immediately, and *The Girl Behind the Gun* opened on August 26, 1918, in Atlantic City. Julian Mitchell, Ziegfeld's phenomenal stager of musical numbers and the mounter of *The Pink Lady,* directed the ensembles. The cast included Jack Hazzard, the star of Guy's first successful play, *The Rule of Three,* and the comedy star of *Very Good Eddie;* smashing leading man Donald Brian, who had wowed New York audiences in 1909 in *The Merry Widow* (and who had introduced Jerry's classic "They Didn't Believe Me" in *The Girl from Utah*); and the irrepressible Wilda Bennett, who had delivered Guy and Plum's comic words and lyrics and Jerry's interpolations in *The Riviera Girl.*

The show underwent extensive rewrites on the road, which kept both Guy and Plum busy throughout the end of August and the beginning of September, and as late as September 13, *Variety* reported that ". . . despite reports of the brilliant success of the piece out of town, George M. Cohan is doing a lot of work revising the piece." It might well have been true; certainly Cohan would be the one to sharpen up anything patriotic, and the second act finale, "Flags of the Allies," substituted for the original "Hark to the Drums of France," sounds like pure Cohan. What is suspect is the remainder of the *Variety* story, which states that "Cohan and Harris are interested with K[law] and E[rlanger] in the production." No such credit was on the program when *The Girl Behind the Gun* opened at the New Amsterdam Theatre on Monday, September 16, 1918.

The reception for the show was generally enthusiastic. The *Sun* called it a "merry war time show," and the *Evening Star* pronounced it "silkily smooth, pretty, witty, just a bit saucy, [and] thoroughly pleasant musically."

Guy's book did what it could with the ancient and operettic devices of multiple mistaken identities. Set in France during the war, it involved the embarrassment of Pierre Breval (Hazzard) when a certain Mimi ("the littlest woman I ever saw," according to the most-often quoted line by Hazzard) indiscreetly writes to him at his home, where his wife (Ada Meade) intercepts the letter. From then forward, the plot becomes hopelessly byzantine, as the critic from the *Sun* discovered when he tried to synopsize it: "Mme. Breval received the letter, and then a fat cook named Brichoux (John E. Young) bobbed up as Mme. Breval's godson from the trenches, and Robert Lambrissac (Donald Brian) came in with whiskers and took the place of Mme. Breval's godson and kissed Mme. Breval just in time for Colonel Servan (Frank Doane), Mme. Breval's rich old uncle, to see it, thereby resulting in Lambrissac shaving his whiskers and playing Breval and Breval playing the cook until the final curtain."

The critics saved their encomiums for the cast and Plum's lyrics, notably the title song sung by Wilda Bennett, as Lucienne Lambrissac, with its prefeminist statements:

Ev'ry day new tales we read,
Telling of some gallant deed
Wrought by soldiers fighting to defend their native land
But there's someone I could name,
Who, tho' all unknown to Fame,
Ought to be considered just as wonderful and grand . . .
Far away from the battle whirl
There is work to be done
And that's where you will find the girl
Behind the man behind the gun. . . .

They were particularly pleased by Jack Hazzard's delivery of the multiversed, typically Wodehousian "Women Haven't Any Mercy on a Man":

Gosh! Women are the hardest propositions!
You plead with them for hours and they don't care,
They listen to the silv'ry voice of reason
With nothing stirring underneath the hair.
I flirted with the smallest girl in Paris
But now at home we suffer grief and pain
As if I'd been and gone and overdone it
And flirted with a Violet Loraine.
For women haven't any sense of justice
They never make allowances at all;
They never think it makes it any better
If the girl they catch their husband with is small.
When we dined I had to sit her on a cushion!
But my wife is making all the fuss she can.
I could hardly do her homage,
This "petite" piece of fromage;
Women haven't any mercy on a man!

*The Girl Behind the Gun* rollicked along at the New Amsterdam into the early spring of 1919, when a new edition of the *Follies* sent it on the road. Still, a run of 160 performances was eminently respectable in 1918, and when the show, renamed *Kissing Time,* moved to the Winter Garden in London, where audiences were more openly receptive to Ivan Caryll's music and there was no *Follies* to dispossess it, it ran for 430 performances.

The London version, produced by George Grossmith and Edward Laurillard and with Phyllis Dare doing the Wilda Bennett role and Leslie Henson the Jack Hazzard one, was an extravagant affair. Plum and Ethel once more journeyed to London and rented the Walton Street house, while Plum anglicized Guy's American book, and Clifford Grey provided lyrics for some added Caryll songs.

The success of both *The Girl Behind the Gun* and *Kissing Time* was proof that the trio didn't have to depend upon a three-pronged attack on every assignment that came their way. Plum and Guy alone collaborated on four shows; Plum collaborated with others on one other; Guy was working with still others on two straight plays; Jerry worked with Guy and Plum on two shows, and with others on three. In addition to this, Plum continued to churn out short stories for the *Saturday Evening Post* about a gentleman's gentleman named Jeeves.

There scarcely seemed time for personal lives to be waged, and yet they were. Guy and Marguerite continued their lively existence in Great Neck, while their infant daughter, Peggy, grew out of her infancy. Eva was pregnant in 1918 with the Kerns' only daughter, Elizabeth Jane, named after Eva's mother. She was born on December 16, at home in Bronxville. Plum and Ethel never had children of their own. The reasons are cloudy. Plum, being the taciturn fellow he was, never let on, and so all sorts of theories evolved—that he was disinclined, disinterested, or frightened of the opposite sex; that Ethel was too busy for anything but parties and gambling; that he had been rendered impotent by a childhood case of the mumps. The real reason is interred with him, but some insight might come from a story Guy loved to tell. It, like some of the stories he related over long periods of time, developed two endings. But they both rose from a single, believable root.

Sometime, during the Princess Theatre days, while they were on the road with one of their musicals, Guy induced Plum to have a fling with a chorus girl—the sort of activity that occupied Guy much of the time. In a rare moment of adventure, Plum apparently agreed and sowed, as Guy would later refer to it, "his one wild oat."

Edwardian to his toes, Plum then bought the girl of the moment a jeweled bracelet. In one of Guy's versions, he charged it, and Ethel received the bill while he was still out of town. In another variation, Ethel met Guy and Plum at Grand Central Station and accused Plum of having been with another woman. Plum, instead of denying it, asked her, "Who told you?"

The endings may have been apocryphal; the incident wasn't, and it's scarcely a tale about a man made impotent by a childhood disease. According to Guy's daughter Peggy, this very real incident alienated Ethel from Guy, and as the years lengthened and the two writers became closer, its importance and Ethel's festering dislike for Guy increased, until Plum was forced to slip Guy his share of the royalties from their musicals in cash, away from Ethel's scrutiny.[7]

But in 1918, life rollicked on at the Bolton estate in Great Neck. Sunday afternoons continued to be gathering times for the casts of the latest musical comedies on Broadway. Caruso, when he was in town, continued to spend late Sunday afternoons cooking spaghetti, until one spring day when Marguerite decided that both Caruso and Guy were too fat. She decreed finger sandwiches and banished the parties for two weeks while the two suffered her good intentions. Neither menu nor intentions lasted, and the parties resumed as soon as Caruso left town.[8]

But there was little time for too much frolicking in 1918 for any of the trio. Their creativity, popularity, and earning power were climbing constantly, and that was where they concentrated their energies.

Here, in the late summer and early fall of 1918, is where the trio first publicly suggested a rift and gave rise to a perception of a parting of the ways. Their previous shows were perking along admirably; in October of 1918, George Grossmith arrived from London to negotiate on a West End production of *Oh, Boy!* He left with a contract in hand, and the show, retitled *Oh, Joy!* would open on January 27, 1919, with Beatrice Lillie and Tom Powers in the leads, at the Winter Garden, where it would stay for a respectable but not exactly record-breaking run of 167 performances.

So, the past was intact and still bringing them a livelihood. It was the present and the future that seemed uncertain. Ray Comstock still wanted a new show for the Princess; *Oh, Lady! Lady!!* had closed in August. The fact that the theatre would remain dark for two months indicates some sort of wooing of Jerry. But Jerry, after the rejection of *The Little Thing,* was in no mood to work with Ray. He had, after all, been largely responsible for Ray Comstock's present reputation; the least the producer could do would be to defer to the composer's judgment.

Comstock, however, was not in the practice of deferring to anybody, and so, in one of the more foolish moves in the history of the American musical theatre, he stood his ground. And Jerry left the Princess, never, it was assumed by all parties, to return. For the rest of 1918, he would only contribute two interpolated melodies to Broadway, both to a Charles Dillingham show, *The Canary,* starring Julia Sanderson and Joseph Cawthorn, with a main score by the ubiquitous Ivan Caryll. The first, "Take a Chance," an invitation to the dance with lyrics by Harry B. Smith, remained for the run of the show; the second, a wartime communicate-with-our-doughboys ballad, "Oh Promise Me You'll Write to Him To-day," with lyrics by Harry Clarke, was removed from *The Canary* a week after it opened, when the Armistice made it meaningless.

So, the sustenance of the Princess and its landmark musicals would fall to Guy and Plum, who, although they had their principles, apparently also needed Ray as a producer more than Jerry did. In a frantic rush to fill the darkened Princess, Guy and Plum, minus Jerry, readied *Oh, My Dear!*, the last and least of the Princess musicals.

Plum would, in later years, refer to the show as "our *Ruddigore.*"9 The composer whom Ray hired to replace Jerry was Louis A. Hirsch, a former songwriter in residence for Dockstader's Minstrels, the former staff composer for the Shuberts and a contributor to the 1915, 1916, and 1918 Ziegfeld *Follies*. In 1917, his boisterous and catchy "The Tickle Toe," with lyrics by Otto Harbach, had taken Broadway by storm and was greatly responsible for keeping the curtain up on a show called *Going Up* for 351 performances.

*Oh, My Dear!* was slapped together in a hurry. There are bits and pieces in it from *The Little Thing* and *Miss 1917*, and while cutting and pasting from the past is standard practice on Broadway and especially in the musical theatre, *Oh, My Dear!* carried it to an absurd extreme.

Still, Ray Comstock gave it his best shot. Robert Milton shared the staging credits with Edward "Teddy" Royce, who had given bright life to *Oh, Boy!* and *Leave It to Jane* and who had shared his early, choreographer days with Jerry and Plum and *The Beauty of Bath.* Joseph Santley and his wife, Ivy Sawyer, who had starred in the national tour of *Oh, Boy!*, were also starred, and comedienne Juliette Day, who had helped Guy's book and particularly Jerry and Plum's tunes in 1917's *The Riviera Girl*, was brought in to provide her usual bright moments.

But it was Jerry who had set the tone of the Princess musicals, and his absence was apparent from the first run-through. After a faltering opening night, as *Ask Dad* (a title dropped during the tryout tour) at the Royal Alexander Theatre in Toronto, on September 20, 1918, Jean Schwartz was brought in to interpolate two songs, and Jerry, called in desperation, gave his permission for them to insert "Go, Little Boat," from *Miss 1917*, as the second-act opening. It was a wistful gesture, and ironically, it provided the only tender moment in a truly nonsensical two hours that had their charms and a rewarding sense of verisimilitude, but not the true signature of the trio of musical fame.

In the mold, if not the groove, of the other Princess shows, *Oh, My Dear!* did have its own absurd attractions. Set at the Rockett Health Farm, a bucolic retreat for the moderately insane, someplace in New England, it adhered to the two-act Princess format. Guy and Milton set each act on the grounds of the farm, the first on the porch of the main house, the second on the lawn, presumably to accommodate the larger chorus numbers and dance specialties of that act.

Dr. Rockett (Frederick Graham) is a stock, absent-minded quack who numbers among his patients Broadway Willie Burbank (Roy Atwell), who is there to cure his dypsomania and escape from his estranged but alimony-seeking wife Jenny Wren (Juliette Day). Also on the premises is Bagshott, a comedy mechanic (Joseph Allen), and Bruce Allenby (Joseph Santley), an upright heir of an umbrella cartel who crashes an airplane into the asylum greenhouse and falls in love with Rockett's daughter Hazel (Evelyn Dorn). Shortly after the curtain rises, a bevy of out-of-work chorus girls appears. This time, Guy and Plum named them after New York City telephone exchanges (Miss Lenox, Miss Bryant, Miss Schuyler, Miss Rhinelander, Miss Beekman, Miss Cortlandt, etc.). The men were mere punhandlers: (Jack R. Abbott, Willie Love, Frank Lynn, etc.).

The plot is rife with upheavals, convolutions, and musical comedy crooks: Bruce and Bagshott are fleeing a police charge of attempted murder, since Bagshott bopped a process server with a monkey wrench just before takeoff from Providence, Rhode Island; Doctor Rockett, in order to outwit his witch of a wife parades Bruce as Broadway Willie, which gets Bruce in trouble with Hazel, who of course thinks he's a philandering married man. But, in true Princess form, the last three pages of script contain solutions to mistaken identities and misapprehensions; the right girl finds the right boy and the dirty old man resigns himself to yet another night of nagging from the crone he mistakenly married. Only singing youth marries well in the Princess shows; all married couples who are comics or over forty are miserable.

The pace is breakneck, almost fast enough to hide the borrowings from other sources. There, in all her lisping loveliness, is Pickles, complete with baby talk and fresh from *The Little Thing*. Three chorus girls are described as "busted, disgusted, and can't get trusted," and one of them suggests that Broadway Willie use a vacuum cleaner to clear his head—all dialogue lifted directly out of *Miss 1917*. And then, of course, there was Jerry's gift of "Go Little Boat."

The humor is more on a par with *Nobody Home* than *Oh, Boy!* Pickles notes that Willie is a "vewwy bad egg," to which Willie replies, "And, as generally happens with bad eggs, no one seemed to notice it until I was broke." "Haven't you really any money?" asks a chorus girl. "Sure," answers Willie. "I have a roll that would choke a mosquito."

The antimarriage jokes are multiple and relentless. Asked if his wife keeps him awake at night, Dr. Rockett opines: "Keep me awake? My boy, if I could get a patent on her elbow, the Big Ben Company would never sell another alarm clock." And if Plum couldn't manage to work in a historical lyric, Guy obliged by having Bagshott parade as a lunatic who thinks he's Julius Caesar and misses the debauchery of his Roman past: "Don't you remember the time we used to sit around the old arena?" he asks a chorus girl, "drinking Roman punches an' betting on the old gladiolas?"

That combination of Neanderthal wit and up-to-date references didn't spin out in most of Plum's lyrics, possibly because Hirsch didn't give him the melodic lines in the choruses to work his wily interior rhymes. Only here and there does the old Plum cleverness surface.

In "Phoebe Snow," a specialty for Juliette Day built around the New York Central train of that name between New York and Buffalo, Plum versifies as of old:

> You've heard of Phoebe Snow,
>    Who makes those trips to Buffalo:
> She travels, dressed in white,
>    Upon the Road of Anthracite:
> And somehow, though she looks demure,
>    Though calm and saint-like she be,
> You never know: you can't be sure:
> And I've my doubts of Phoebe. . . .

And his verse to one of the more popular songs from the show, "You Never Know," which was really an excuse for an elaborate Teddy Royce "ribbon dance" is vintage Wodehouse:

> Life is a kind of a gamble:
>    Life is a leap in the dark:
> All things more or less have been in a mess
>    Since Noah came out of the Ark.
> Fate puts a string in our fingers;
>    Says to us "Cheer up." Don't fret!
> So just shut both your eyes and you'll get a
> surprise!
>    And, by jove! That is just what we get.

What is particularly intriguing is the transition from dialogue to song and the extended use of underscoring. It was Jerry who introduced this into the Princess shows and who developed it into a smoothly flowing stream of book and song, and the fact that it survives, even thrives in *Oh, My Dear!* is a testament to his pervasiveness and the loyalty of the surviving two-thirds of the Princess triumvarate.

In the second act, after Bruce has been forced to masquerade as Broadway Willie, and Jennie, intrigued by a change of husband for the better, has gone along enthusiastically, Hilda, his real love, tries to reconcile the two, much to Bruce's discomfort. He, of course, would rather be with Hilda, and so he tries to assure her of the distance between them and their impending divorce:

BRUCE:    I thought you were going back to New York this evening, Mrs. Burbank?

JENNIE:    Oh, I am, a little later, Mr. Burbank.

HILDA:    Aw, you mustn't address each other like this—you
mustn't really.

JENNIE:    Miss Rockett thinks we ought to make it up, don't
you, Miss Rockett?

HILDA:    *(Sings)* I really cannot understand
Why quarrels should occur:

JENNIE:    A loving life as man and wife
Is what I should prefer:

BRUCE:    To me there's nothing half so grand
As true Domestic bliss:

HILDA:    Well, you'd obtain it once again
If you remember this:
Ev'ry morning try to say
Say something sweeter
When you meet her:—

JENNIE:    Say "I love your hair today"
Or, your dimple!
It's so simple.

HILDA:    Praise the hats and rocks she's wearing:
Don't be cross or overbearing:
It's so easy to be happy
If you only know the way.

Jennie kisses Bruce on the cheek, and he tries to wipe it away, as the orchestra underscores dialogue in which Bruce tries to distance himself from Jennie, while Hilda tries to glue them together:

BRUCE:     Say, we're supposed to be divorced, aren't we?

HILDA:     But you haven't any real reason to get a divorce, Mrs. Burbank says so—Oh, I think it's all wrong for people to separate on account of some foolish whim—Now why shouldn't you make it up and start in a second honeymoon tonight.

BRUCE:     What—tonight?

JENNIE:    (*Demurely*) Oh, I doubt if we ought to begin the honeymoon tonight.

HILDA:     Why not? The sooner the better.

BRUCE:     But, really it isn't being done this season. (*Sings*)
            Ev'ry morning I must say
               "Hello dearie" bright and cheery:

JENNIE:    Fix my breakfast on a tray;
               Toast and oolong
               Won't take you too long

HILDA:     Kiss her softly on the forehead;
            Never be unkind or horrid;
               It's so easy to be happy
               If you only know the way.

And the underscoring continues as Hilda exits and Bruce and Jennie begin to find an odd sort of attraction for each other, while Hilda sings pieces of the song offstage at appropriate moments.

When *Oh, My Dear!* opened at the Princess on November 27, 1918, the critics observed the difference, although their criticisms were remarkably gentle. Heywood Broun in the *Tribune* pronounced it ". . . not in the front rank," and the *Times* reviewer opined that it was ". . . several notches below *Oh, Boy!* and *Oh! Lady! Lady!!* It has two exclamation points fewer than the latter," he went on, "and ever so much less comedy. There were moments . . . when it seemed as though the Messrs. Bolton and Wodehouse are beginning to find the going a trifle hard, and are accordingly skimping a trifle in ideas."

Dorothy Parker, in her *Vanity Fair* piece, took Louis Hirsch to task. "His music," she wrote, "is so reminiscent that the score rather resembles a medley of last season's popular songs, but it really doesn't make any difference—Mr. Wodehouse's lyrics would make anything go."

The sad fact was that, for all of Dorothy Parker's blind adoration, Plum's lyrics weren't as good as they had been; he was never better than when he was wedding them to a tune by Jerry, and the *Times* correctly pointed out that "Mr. Wodehouse's lyrics, as always, are workmanlike, although somewhat less intricately rhymed than usual, and accordingly not quite the customary treat."

Still, Plum could perform his Gilbert and Sullivan feats handily, if with a Guy Bolton twist, in a second-act song titled "It Sort of Makes a Fellow Stop and Think." It cheerily demolished marriage and parenthood:

> I've visited this earthly Paradise;
>> But it somehow happens, ev'ry time I come
> Little Percy's having fits upon the hearthrug
>> And little Willie aches inside the tum;
> Then you're told that little Rollo has the measles
>> And little George has drunk up all the ink;
>>> P'raps they're right who say no bliss is
>>> Half so wonderful as this is;
> Still—it sort of makes a fellow stop and think."

The marriage bashing that Guy was so skilled at putting on stage and that contributed to his getting a job at the Princess in the first place drifted out of hand in *Oh, My Dear!*, enough to make the *Times* reviewer observe that "the basis of the comedy, aside from an occasional well-turned phrase, is the familiar theory that there is nothing so funny as a married man, unless it be two of them." Heywood Broun went farther than this, to remark acidly that "possibly the omission of any detailed synopsis of the plot will be pardoned when the explanation is made that it is one of those things in which everybody thinks that Broadway Willie is Bruce Allenby and vice versa."

Neither critics nor public nor creators recognized *Oh, My Dear!* as the sort of Princess show the trio seemed to have patented. It would run for 189 performances, enough to recoup its investment and enough to send out a road company featuring Clarence Rock, Gloria Gray, Wayne Nunn, Del Marie, and

Helen Francis, which would continue through the hinterlands for eighteen months. The company circled back in mid-1919 and played the Shubert Riviera Theater at Broadway and 97th Street and the Montauk Theater in Brooklyn and concluded its travels on May 20, 1920, eighteen months after it had first opened with a different name, at the Royal Alexandra Theatre in Toronto. But that would be it. There would be no calls for revivals, no demand for oleo versions. It would never earn a true place in the roster of the most fully realized Princess shows.

And so an era ended. In four years, there had been six Princess shows — seven, if you count *Have a Heart* — and *Have a Heart* was, in every sense except its production staff, a Princess show. But the little theatre itself would no longer house the most sophisticated and eagerly awaited musical comedies of the season. That would happen elsewhere, for Broadway was developing fast.

And yet, as in all events in real life, the end of the Princess didn't come about dramatically and conclusively. Neat endings only occur on the stage and on the page. Real life is ragged and inconclusive, and the trio wasn't history yet.

# Chapter
# 13
# Duets
## 1919

The reasons for Jerry's lack of visibility on Broadway during the second half of 1918 have been variously described; none of them include a lack of material. The energy of the master is undisputed and staggering. His daughter, Betty, who was born in December of 1918 and so couldn't have been privy to that particular season's habits, was nevertheless a witness to his later, unceasing work schedule. She never remembered a day when her father wasn't at the piano, composing; and that despite an equally unceasing, lifelong, crushing — and inspiring — load of other interests. By the time he and Eva and the infant Betty were firmly in place in the new home in Bronxville, he was already deeply into collecting rare furniture, books, and stamps. And, despite the fact that his income was multiplying like rabbits in the spring, he hired no agents to ferret out his treasures. He had a masterful eye for the real and the fake and where the real was to be found.

Besides this, the Kerns did their share of entertaining — not nearly so much as Guy and Marguerite and considerably more than Plum and Ethel, but abundantly nevertheless. Jerry remained an inveterate card player, favoring poker, but hardly ever turning back a chance for a rubber of bridge or a hand of pinochle. And if there were no cardplayers on the horizon, he would regale guests with a parlor game of his own invention, called "Guggenheim."

The game was a test for anybody's patience, consisting, as it did, of receiving pads printed by Jerry, which contained various categories, such as Cities, Countries, Inventions, Authors, or Producers, then picking a random word from a newspaper or magazine, then jotting down the word, and then coming up with the names of famous people whose last names began with one of the letters of the chosen word. Complex? Of course, and a test by Jerry of a friend's astuteness.

One of those friends, and a regular participant in the Kern soirees, was George Gershwin. The young composer was a quick learner and a bright player, and now, in 1919, he was about to leap from barely credited interpolater to Broadway composer, on the strength of "Swanee," written with Irving Caesar. Caesar had supplied the lyrics for two Gershwin songs sung by Vivienne Segal at the November 18 Sunday soiree held during the run of *Miss 1917*. The two, "There's More to the Kiss Than the X-X-X" and "You—oo Just You," had convinced Jerry that he should introduce Gershwin to Max Dreyfus, lure him away from Remick's, where he was only a song plugger, and put him to work at T. B. Harms, where he would be a song *writer*.

Gershwin and Caesar had placed their music in Jolson's *Capitol Revue* on their own, without the help of either Max Dreyfus or Jerry, and according to both Michael Friedland and Gerald Bordman, Jerry didn't take kindly to this self-propelled launching. He felt betrayed and expressed it to Max. It may be so; Jerry was given to abrupt outbursts which passed as quickly as summer showers.

But Betty Kern Miller had a chance to witness the lifelong admiration and deep affection her father felt for George Gershwin, and was positive that it couldn't have happened. She recalled George Gershwin as a persistent presence in the house during her early childhood and knew that her father loved him as a father loves a son whose talent he's helped to nurture. So, if there was a feeling of betrayal in Jerry over George Gershwin's sudden and meteoric ascendency in 1919, it was an extremely temporary feeling.

On the other hand, Jerry's alienation from Guy and Plum that year was more profound and longer lasting; though again, far from permanent, as was his momentary lack of representation on the musical stage. By February, he was deeply into a new project with Charles Dillingham and on the threshold of a long-term collaboration with a new lyricist, Anne Caldwell.

Anne Caldwell resembled Bessie Marbury in more than girth. She was bright, imaginative, and energetic, and enormously savvy about the theatre and what worked on its stages. She had provided the lyrics for Ivan Caryll's score for *The Canary,* and it's possible that their resolve to collaborate had its genesis there. At any rate, it was Jerry who introduced her to Charles Dillingham, and it was she who would write the libretto and lyrics for the first Jerome Kern show of 1919, *She's a Good Fellow.*

As *A New Girl,* the show opened on April 6 in Washington to largely positive reviews, although the critics were less than ordinarily enthusiastic about Douglas Stevenson and Helen Shipman in the leading roles. And so, that reliable married couple, Joseph Santley and Ivy Sawyer, were brought in to save the proceedings.

This addition, plus the title change, plus the added, last minute presence of the Duncan Sisters, two Southern favorites who sang Jerry's "Bullfrog Patrol" as a stop-the-show specialty, allowed New York critics to follow up the May 5 opening at Dillingham's Globe Theatre with generally positive, though not enthusiastic, reviews. It was enough to allow *She's a Good Fellow* to hang around for 120 performances.

That same spring, Jerry and Guy reunited. First, Jerry interpolated into a notable flop, *The Lady in Red,* a tune from the show that first united Kern and Bolton, *Ninety in the Shade.* "Where Is the Girl for Me?" did nothing to raise that colorful girl's fortunes, and it and the show disappeared after forty-eight performances.

The other collaboration was far more substantive and of the moment. Ray Comstock, with whatever blandishments, managed to talk Jerry and Guy and Plum into rescuing the Princess from the battering it had taken with *Oh, My Dear!* The collaboration would eventually be consummated without Plum, but not because, as the press reported in April and May, a split had occurred between Bolton and Wodehouse.

There was no such rift. There *was* a separation. Plum was busy in London in May, working on the anglicizing of *The Girl Behind the Gun* with Clifford Grey, for its transformation into the long-running *Kissing Time.* He was also spending deserved time with Leonora—his beloved "Snorky"—and beginning an intense creative period. Jerry and Guy and Plum were all on the brink of their most fertile years, but Plum got off to a running start in 1919. During the following ten years, he would provide the lyrics and, at times, a portion of the book for no less than twelve musicals, some produced in New York, some in London; the lyrics for two others that never made it to either city; write or adapt four straight plays; and publish twenty books. In fact, 1919 was the year of the publication in England of *My Man Jeeves,* the first book-length collection of the adventures of

Bertie Wooster's gentleman's gentleman, and the year of the publication in both America and England of *Damsel in Distress.*

The care and tending of this head of steam would cut Plum off from two important projects with Guy and Jerry, and it may be highly possible that his absence was a contributing factor to the eventual breakup of the trio. But this is speculation.

The most important rift in 1919 occurred not between Guy and Plum but between Guy and two close associates—his wife, Marguerite, and his other collaborator, George Middleton.

Barely two years old, the Bolton-Namara marriage was already in trouble. Marguerite had been perfectly willing to assume the role of mother during Peggy's infancy. But a year and a little more had passed, and she was chafing at her removal from the stage. Frederick Toye had negotiated a contract at the Chicago Opera for her, and she was determined to take it. Guy was equally determined that she would not. But he was no match for her iron will. The very qualities of individuality that had made their coming together possible were now nibbling at his insecurities. He had lost one wife to a man of the world. He wasn't happy about the prospect of losing a second to the world itself.

But Marguerite was no Julie, enamored with the idea of glamour. She personified it, she was a diva of divine dimensions, and she was not about to languish at Kensington, their estate in Great Neck. "Daddy loved to be looked after and he loved his home and Mother couldn't boil an egg or look after any man. They looked after her," recalled Peggy years later. "[They] were both stars, both public figures, and that must have been very hard for both of them," she added, ruefully.[1]

That was part of it, but it wasn't the heart of it: there was a continuing withdrawal in Guy that went far beyond concentration on the enormous load of work he had set himself, and it would be a personality trait that set him apart from Jerry and drew him to Plum. Plum was forever docile and withdrawn. Jerry was as comfortable in his own skin as any man could be, or imagine to be. And so was Marguerite. But Guy, as Marguerite would put it in later years, "had a switch in him that he turned off whenever anything got to be too much for him to handle easily." The small boy in Deal, fit into the indentation in the summer hotel and abandoned, had never really left, and possibly, the throwing of the switch was a way never to be touched that deeply again. Had he been charmless, Guy would have probably been intolerable. But he was charming, personable, and in demand, particularly in 1919. So, after long and silent contemplation, he acquiesced, grudgingly, to Marguerite's plans to sing with the Chicago Opera. But in so doing, he moved a notch away from her and from Peggy. He turned his attention to repairing the other rift in his life.

That was with a person of an entirely different temperament. A gentle, sensitive man, George Middleton was nevertheless, in 1919, at the tail end of his exasperation with Guy. After the success of both *What'll You Have* and *Polly with a Past,* he was anxious to continue this successful collaboration. He and Guy had already sketched out the scenarios for two plays. One was a comedy of manners, very much like *Polly,* called *Adam and Eva.* The other was Middleton's idea, a religious drama that would have as its centerpiece the passion play at Oberammergau, which neither of them had attended. Called *The Cross,* it would be largely Middleton's responsibility, while *Adam and Eva,* more in the lighthearted mode that Guy had mastered, would be Guy's charge.

The problem was that George Middleton hadn't heard from Guy in months, not since they had agreed upon a scenario and had worked on the first act. He was unaware that in the interim Guy had interested Ray Comstock and Bob Milton in *Adam and Eva* on the strength of its first act and, without consulting his collaborator, had made production arrangements.

In December of 1918, Marguerite went to Chicago, where she triumphed beyond her wildest expectations. Asked to substitute for an ailing Mary Garden in the title role of *Thais,* her performance received such deafening kudos that Mme. Garden announced publicly, "I shall never sing this role again. I give it gladly to Namara."[2]

Even before the cheering dimmed, Marguerite became deeply ill with the flu. It was the end of the great worldwide flu epidemic, and an alarmed Guy, leaving Peggy in the care of Fräulein Alt for the Christmas holidays, entrained immediately for Chicago to spend Christmas with Marguerite.

Marguerite recovered, and Guy contracted her flu. And whereas he ministered to her, she apparently had no time to see to his needs. She was busy day and night, rehearsing and performing at the Chicago Opera, and also being Marguerite Namara—a full-time occupation. Guy had little company while he recuperated. In a later letter to Middleton, he confessed that ". . . to be shut up in a hotel bedroom . . . with no one to talk to from dawn to dark is an excellent imitation of hell."[3]

By January 26, he had apparently recovered enough to write but not enough to leave the suite at the Congress Hotel. "[It was] a really bad attack that came within an ace of leaving you a job as my literary executor," he wrote Middleton, adding, however, that ". . . the one advantage of this was that in my fever dazed state, I dreamed out a play—a gorgeous idea that I'll tell you of when I get back. Perhaps we can do it this Spring."

He then turned to *Adam and Eva.* "Well, I finished Adam," he announced, "with the last ounce of my strength. If ever a play had heart's blood in it that one has. I rewrote act one, ran acts two and three together and wrote a new act three. It all came out well—very well. Bob [Milton] and Ray [Comstock] are . . . delighted with it. I think we're in for a big success."

Well enough. But then, Guy went on to say that Marguerite had urged him to remind Middleton that they had agreed to change billing with each show they wrote, so that one of them would have first billing every other time. And this was his time to be first.

Middleton shot off an indignant telegram in which he remembered no such arrangement, and Guy fired back a virulent letter in which he accused his partner of trying to welch on a done deal.

Middleton finally applied the brakes to what could have escalated from the ugly to the terminally destructive. He realized that it was a petty problem that, although it made little difference to George Middleton, meant the world to Guy. The argument contained disturbing echoes of the *Oh, Boy!* royalty contretemps with Jerry.

On the 31st of January, Middleton wrote a conciliatory letter to Guy, stating that "it's all too damn foolish for us to act like a couple of children just because we hadn't talked out our ulcers. Let's put away all our rattles and see if we can't get back on a healthy basis after this purge of plain words. . . ."

He went on to remonstrate with Guy for holding up work on *Adam and Eva* for over a year. "I did not mind your doing other things," he continued, referring to the myriad of musicals with which Guy and Plum and Jerry had been involved in 1917 and 1918, "you kept putting me off with promises of getting at it immediately etc. . . . I learned from an outsider . . . that the play was going into rehearsal 'monday' [sic] I learn from somebody else it was booked and from another that cast was engaged. And in all this time not a peep from you or Bob, or the office. Not a request even for me to come to Chicago which would have been the natural thing we used to do. . . ."

The tendency to bull ahead, to change lines and set up contractual arrangements without working with others, the very defiance of collaborative protocol that Guy had seen and decried in Jerry's behavior at *Oh, Boy!* had now become a habit with him and would continue to be a part of his *modus operandi* for the rest of his professional life. Its first manifestation, in early 1919, was with George Middleton.

". . . Your close personal relationship with Bob and Ray has always made me feel like an outsider," Middleton complained,

> only because we four have never once got together for consultation and conference . . . all I ask is that henceforth you will recognize my equal rights with you in settling and discussing all the affairs wherein we are equal partners. [As to the billing] if it means something to you I am glad this war of words has brought it to the surface. So many monsters swim in the deep and the only way to kill them is surface treatment.

He agreed to have Guy's name first on the play and concluded, perceptively,

> Is the slate sufficiently clean? You're a damn irritating person at times and I suspect I am too. Lets [sic] try once more to understand each others [sic] temperament a bit better. Theres [sic] no reason in the world why we cant [sic] continue our profitable work relationship, do things worth while; and if this quarrel results in a better understanding and franker friendship it will not have been in vain. . . .

It was an understandable frustration that never invaded Guy's relationship with Plum. There was something unspoken and indestructible there, and it had much to do with Plum's adoration of and dependence upon Guy for his theatrical acumen. In 1920, Plum confided to boyhood friend William Townend,

> Guy and I clicked from the start like Damon and Pythias. We love working together. Never a harsh word or a dirty look. He is one of the nicest chaps I ever met and the supreme worker of all time. I help him as much as I can with the book end of things, but he really does the whole job and I just do the lyrics, which are easy when one has Jerry to work with.[4]

Notwithstanding the wistful wishing of the last sentence, it's a revelatory letter, as is George Middleton's.

In 1919, Guy was working overtime and a little more. By February 1, he was back in Great Neck, at Kensington, with his own doctor in attendance. "[He] tells me I've got to lie up for several weeks if I don't want to leave a permanent vacancy in the ranks of the playwrights . . . ," he wrote Middleton, as he enclosed the rewritten third act.

*Adam and Eva* opened on February 17 in Detroit, went on to Cleveland, then to the Shubert-Belasco in Washington in mid-March. The cast was a first rate one: Otto Kruger and Ruth Shepley were in the title roles; the remainder of the cast, John Flood, Reginald Mason, Roberta Arnold, and William March were strong and would remain in New York. Guy was unhappy with Jean Shelby, and in a letter from the Royal Poinciana Hotel in Palm Beach, where he'd gone to recuperate, he advised Middleton to prevail with Bob Milton and fire her. "She is utterly out of the picture," he wrote. "I never saw Bob go so far off on a character. . . . Don't let him keep her. She can never be right. Ray thinks so too."

There's a certain mystery about this. On March 17, when the show opened at the Park Square Theatre in Boston, Jean Shelby's name was replaced by Marie Namara. It might have been Marguerite filling in as Guy attempted to replace Miss Shelby. But that's also speculation. When *Adam and Eva* finally reached the Longacre in New York on September 13, Jean Shelby had been restored to her original role.

But back to the beginning of 1919.

From Palm Beach, Guy also suggested to Middleton that they mark *The Cross* for a spring tryout, suggesting that he was filling up his plate, as usual. The plate began to overflow shortly after this, when Ray Comstock and Morris Gest suggested that Guy rescue a foundering but sure-fire commercial script by Frank Mandel, a young and popular playwright who was presently matching Guy in prolificacy. In 1918, he had had two plays (*The Sky Pilot* and *Bosom Friends*) successfully produced; in 1919, the figure would climb to four (*Look Who's Here, Luck, My Lady Friends,* and the script he brought to Comstock and Gest, *The Five Million*).

After being assured that his name would be billed ahead of Mandel's, Guy took on the job of making the play playable. It was, he agreed, a sure-fire formula for commercial success: a comedy with a patriotic theme about returning soldiers.

Having taken on this assignment, Guy took on more, as did Comstock and Gest. Some time in early April, the two approached Guy with a plan to once again revive the Princess shows. The failure of *Oh, My Dear!* was, they felt, the inevitable working of the percentages. The unbroken string of successes of the trio's musicals for the Princess was still strongly in the minds of the theatregoers of 1919; it was worth another try.

Guy, as usual eager to take on more work than the average human being could even imagine and, like Plum and Jerry, entering his most productive and energetic period, accepted and contacted Plum immediately.

Totally embroiled in the anglicizing and transformation of *The Girl Behind the Gun* into *Kissing Time* and in galleys for the plethora of printed works to which he was committed, Plum sadly replied that he simply couldn't take on another lyric writing job.

So, the Comstock and Gest publicity people ground out yet another rumor of a rift between Bolton and Wodehouse. It was apparently a cover, to allow Buddy De Sylva, young and unknown at the time but soon to become the front end of the famous songwriting team of De Sylva, Brown, and Henderson, to assume Plum's place, temporarily.

Guy picked as his source for the new Princess show the 1906 comedy hit by Winchell Smith and Byron Ongley, *Brewster's Millions.* It was the story of a young man who is the recipient of an eccentric will that states that he must spend one million dollars in one month in order to inherit seven million dollars.

Comstock and Gest and presumably Guy now set out to snare Jerry. All of them were perfectly aware that the early demise of *Oh, My Dear!* could be traced to the lack of a score by Jerome Kern, and they were not about to repeat that fatal error.

They picked their time well. There were no immediate projects on the Kern horizon, and Jerry could spend just so much time on collecting books and writing trunk tunes. But just to sweeten the pot, the producers hired Julian Mitchell to fill in for Bob Milton, who was busy with both *Adam and Eva* and *The Five Million.* Marie Carroll, one of the sparks of the *Oh, Boy!* cast was hired, as was Harry Fox, the matinee idol of the moment.

It was more than a composer could resist, and Jerry didn't. Despite the fact that he had just signed on for Dillingham's next musical, he agreed to write the score for *Maid of Money,* as the show was deceivingly called that spring. The trio was at least a duet, headed back to the Princess.

Plum returned from England, after the triumphant opening of *Kissing Time* and the publication of two books, just in time to be talked out of his rational refusal to take on more work. Unfortunately, he was also just in time to become ensnared in the fourth project of Guy, Ray Comstock, and Morris Gest, a musical with music by Armand Vecsey, the chief violinist and conductor of his own society orchestra at the Oval Room of the Ritz-Carlton. Faced with the persuasiveness of Guy and Ray, Plum crumbled and accepted the job of lyricist. In *Bring on the Girls,* he and Guy gave its genesis, and their memories of it, a delicious twist:

"The writing of this blot on the New York theatrical scene was due entirely to too much rich food, too much potent liquor and the heady effect of Oriental music on top of these," they wrote, blithely painting over the fact that neither of them either drank or ate to excess. "The consumers of the food and the liquor," they went merrily on, "were the pair so shortly to become the toast of Cain's Storehouse . . .", Cain Theatrical Scenery Storehouse, that is; the graveyard, in Syracuse, New York, for generations of shows that closed before their time — or at least the time their creators had decreed them.

Vecsey was apparently also a persuasive fellow. "He played superbly," wrote the two, "and when he dished out the Chinese suite he had composed, the brave and the fair curled up like carbon paper and the Messrs. Bolton and Wodehouse, puffing their cigars and taking another beaker of old brandy, told each other emotionally that this was the stuff. Not realizing that practically anything sounds good after a well-lubricated dinner, they agreed that a musical play written around these marvellous melodies could not fail to bring home the gravy. A week later they were writing *The Rose of China.*

"It just shows how overwork can dull the senses. . . ."

There was as much truth as humor in the last line, for this meant that Guy was involved in no less than five projects simultaneously. And yet, in the spring of 1919, he foresaw no trouble, nor did Plum, who had come back to spend the summer relaxing and playing golf in Great Neck. Nor did Ray Comstock, that most ambitious but half-blind of producers. Nor, apparently, did Jerry, who always wrote the music before the lyrics, anyway, and so could set his own pace.

Something had to give, and that something turned out to be *The Cross.* Comstock and Gest agreed to produce it, but not until 1920.

Its removal wasn't enough. Guy's plate was still too full, and the show to which he should have been devoting the bulk of his time — *Maid of Money,* whose title had now been changed to a more logical *Zip Goes a Million* — would be the real casualty. The blame for its failure would land squarely on Guy's shoulders.

The show's trouble wasn't in the music. Jerry wrote an exquisite score, one that showed a marked development, a new richness that "They Didn't Believe Me," "Till the Clouds Roll By," "The Land Where the Good Songs Go" and "Go, Little Boat" prefigured. While the reviewers could justifiably call his scores for the early Princess shows "tinkly" and still used that adjective to describe Hirsch's melodies for *Oh, My Dear!,* Jerry's score for *Zip Goes a Million* was something entirely beyond this. Its melody lines were spun of more delicate stuff; the surprises were more abundant, the variety was continuous, the underscoring more ambitious. Jerry was clearly moving ahead, with constant acceleration and growing depth. And his score, written, according to Gerald Bordman, in one month, but probably consisting of melodies and reworkings of music he had composed during the months without a show at the end of 1918, is an unplayed masterpiece.

However, in the summer and autumn of 1919, it was far from out of sight. Only the librettist of the show was invisible. He was, at that time, out of town with *The Five Million,* readying it for its July opening in New York. Comstock and Gest insisted on the summer premiere, despite the lack of air conditioning on Broadway. Their reason: there were at least six other plays about returning soldiers being readied for the 1919–20 season. The first didn't have to be good, just first.

So, on July 8, 1919, *The Five Million* opened at the Lyric Theatre. Heywood Broun, writing in the *Tribune,* commented drolly that "of course, as skilful [sic] a theatrical technician as Guy Bolton could write such a play with one finger. We rather think that he has, for while one hand was engaged with the typewriter, the other was held firmly upon the public pulse. . . ."

The play certainly was a work written with public taste aforethought. Its tale of a returning war hero finding his true love behaving untruly, his law practice gone, and the shadow of a crime he supposedly committed hanging over his head was pure patriotic formula. Told with some subtlety, it might have become a respectable addition to that particular theatrical genre. It was, instead, a muddy mixture of melodrama and comedy.

The declamations of some of the characters in *The Five Million* were dangerously out of the past, echoing the Guy Bolton of 1912. "It's when I think of them — of all the wonderful fellows I knew who felt that everything they had wasn't too much to give for their country . . . ," said Doug, the war ace who was thought dead but who had returned to find his prewar world devastated.

Turning to Ruth, his fiancée who wore a gold star on her sleeve while she had become engaged to a slacker who stayed behind, he regaled her with, "Yes, you were wearing a gold star on your arm. Even that beautiful symbol which the grief of thousands had made sacred was a lie. Your pretense of joy at my return — each kiss you have given me — everything — lies — "

The anchor to keep this highfalutin' language earthbound was the humor, practiced by Doug's two side kicks, one a veteran who tried to teach his French wife English from the sports pages of the local paper and the other a diminutive friend of Ruth's who referred to herself as "The Little Thing."

The script in the Bolton library is full of bad grammar and misspellings, something that Guy's solo efforts never contained. And so, it's logical to believe that there was more of Mandel in the play than met the casual eye. The future writer of the libretti for *No! No! Nanette!*, *The Desert Song*, and *The New Moon* could possibly have been growing through the same melodramatic shaking-out period that Guy had undergone in the past, and his presence might have flung Guy slightly backward, which in no way excuses the dreadfulness of the play.

The critics were mixed in their reactions. Although lauding the cast, they divided their opinions of *The Five Million*, the *Times* calling it "lightly entertaining . . . a fast moving, workmanlike comedy . . . ," while Charles Darnton in the *World* pronounced it ". . . essentially old fashioned. . . ." The *Mail* hailed it for its "'sure fire formula [which] makes a sure fire hit"; the *Sun* grumbled about the ". . . creations of stage hokum [that] walk through the acts of a bucolic play . . . a bright first act [followed by] a disappointing collapse in the last act, a collapse which becomes ruin. . . ."

On the strength of its timeliness, and the jump it got on the rush of returning-home plays yet to come, *The Five Million* might have struggled through enough of the season to recoup its investment. But on August 7, a thunderbolt hit Broadway. Actors, tired of being manipulated by producers, of working inhuman hours in rehearsal, and being unceremoniously fired out of town without return fare, formed Actors Equity Association and walked out of their plays.

It couldn't have come at a more propitious time for them or a worse time for the producers. The summer of 1919 was a record breaker for Broadway; the professional theatre ranked fourth in the nation's industries that year, and the strike was a crushing blow. Megastars like Eddie Cantor, Lillian Russell, Marie Dressler, Ed Wynn, and Ethel Barrymore joined the ranks against the Producing Managers' Association. On the night of August 7, half the shows on Broadway went dark. Twelve shows, including *The Five Million*, closed for good during the following week.

While chaos reigned on Broadway, out-of-town froze in its tracks. It was unfortunate for *Adam and Eva*; it was ready to come in. On the other hand, *Zip Goes a Million* needed all the time it could muster. Guy had updated the Smith play to the present and made Monty Brewster into yet another returning war hero, who encounters his grandfather's goofy will at a surprise welcoming home party. It all began like a Princess show all right, but Guy was having a hard time compressing its original five acts into the two that Princess audiences expected.

Still, he journeyed to Bronxville and worked with Jerry on several occasions that spring and summer. An interview he gave to the *Sun*, which was published on April 13, 1919, is revealing of not only his working methods but of those the trio utilized to bring the Princess formula to fruition:

"We had carte blanche in . . . 'Oh, Boy'" he told the interviewer,

> and there was nothing irrelevant in it. From start to finish it was straight and consistent comedy with the addition of music. [Jerry must have bristled at that.] The plot was connected and every song and lyric contributed to acceleration of the action. The humor of "Oh, Boy!" was based entirely on situation—not on interjected comedians, and I think I am right when I say that it was the first successful play of its kind to be attempted along these lines. . . .

> In the development of our plot we endeavor to make everything count. Every line, funny or serious, is supposed to help the plot continue to hold. This is true of all drama, but it seems never before to have been applied to musical comedy. This makes the technique of writing musical comedy much more difficult than it would seem, because if the songs are going to count in any plot the plot has to be built more or less around or at least with them. After I have discussed the plot and I have received the songs I have to reconstruct the entire plot, practically working backwards and forwards from the songs, as the case may be, to get the proper intervals of time between them.

> Anybody who thinks that writing a musical comedy is easy and is torn off in the hours of rest, meditation and prayer must think again. A drama is easier to write than a musical comedy. Ibsen didn't have to count his pages back to the last number or count the minutes since the girls were last on when he was doing his bit!

It was obvious that Guy was enjoying himself and was back in the Princess groove with *Zip Goes a Million*. Plum, working down the road from him in Great Neck, must have been sadly envious, regretting his rational, long-distance decision not to become part of the project. If so, he never expressed it on paper, but the prospect of breathing new life into the Princess without him must have made him restless, at least.

Jerry continued to turn out new material to match the changing directions of the book. He had written two lovely ballads for Monty and his childhood sweetheart, Peggy, "The Language of Love" and "Forget-Me-Not," and a delicious satirical send up of contemporary Broadway to be delivered by Trixie, a chorus girl Guy had invented to flesh out the plot. The song satirized the deliveries and demands of Al Jolson and George M. Cohan and culminated with a send up of *Nobody Home* and Jerry's own early style.

But for all its potential riches, the show was on hold, because of the dual problems of Guy's sprawling book and the actors' strike. It could have used more rehearsal time, but its librettist would not stand still.

Guy was a moving target for everyone in 1919. He decided, between jobs, to join with George Middleton in yet another project, the reworking of *Hilda*. The play was one of Middleton's that Cohan and Harris had tried out, unsuccessfully, at Nixon's Apollo Theatre in Atlantic City with Lola Fisher in the lead. Cohan, furious and determined to stand up to Actors Equity, had lost interest in the play entirely and closed it. Guy figured that no opportunity should go untried, and so he added it to his already overstuffed schedule.[5]

In that summer of simmering tempers on Broadway, while the actors and producers were facing off, the playwrights decided that they too should form an organization not only to protect their material, but to give them casting rights. ASCAP, the American Society of Composers, Authors and Publishers, had been around since 1914, watching over composers and lyricists; it was time for the playwrights and librettists to establish their rights, too.

Theatrical histories generally give the credit for organizing the Dramatists Guild to George Middleton. But in a carefully written and rewritten manuscript in Guy's papers, *he* takes the credit.

"I founded 'The Dramatists Guild,'" Guy states unequivocally.

It was at the time of the actors' strike in 1919. . . . Eleven playwrights had plays that had been closed by the strike and I wrote to all of these, pointing out that our properties, which were the basis of the theatrical entertainment business, were being banded [sic] about by the contestants, without our having any say in the matter. I asked them to come to a room I had taken at the Astor to discuss the situation.

The eleven came, most of them, because it was the actors who had brought the strike, directing their animus against them. I was wholeheartedly on the actors' side so, after some arguments and some drinks, we decided to summon the whole complement of playwrights and I hired a secretary, looked up addresses, and sent letters to all the dramatic writers we were able to reach.

I took a larger room, stocked it with bottles and, on the appointed day, found myself greeting a numerous gathering of playwrights and journeymen writers. With them came a glowering, middle-aged character, who introduced himself as actor Henry Dixey, one of the strike leaders, but justifying his presence as author of a play called "Adonis" in which he had starred. He had come, admittedly, as a spy, and was convinced we were planning to line up with the managers.

It was agreed at this meeting that we should form an association, and I

called Joseph P. Bickerton, a theatrical lawyer, who took dips into producing. . . . [He had produced Guy's *The Rule of Three.*]

Our first objective was to help in ending the strike and I was able to combat
a group headed by Sammy Shipman and Max Marcin, who saw future
advantage in lining up with the managements.

The chief intent we had in mind was the establishment of a contract that
would see to it that playwrights, including beginners, were treated fairly and
the play be recognized as being it's [sic] writer's property, with the manager
accorded the position of a lessee.

They named me head of the organization but, after enjoying that honor for a
couple of business meetings, I was too tied up with work . . . and I put
forward my friend . . . George Middleton . . . as being ready to take my
place. . . .

Middleton, and most historians, remember it differently. In his autobiography, *These Things Are Mine,* Middleton talks of its founding as an arm of the
Authors League, and it seems much more logical than Guy's history of those
steamy days of August 1919, at the Astor Hotel.

Guy goes on: "I had paid all expenses for meetings at the Astor, which
included a fair number of bottles and boxes of cigars. . . ."[6] And perhaps that
was the real extent of his involvement. He was not an idealist, as Middleton was,
and his political awareness was only slightly more elevated than Plum's—hardly
to the point of argument and rarely to the point of action.

As August gave way to the cooler, calmer winds of September, the managers
finally gave in, Actors Equity Association became the voice of actors on Broadway, and *Adam and Eva* opened. When the curtain rose at the Longacre on
September 17, its cast was intact. A play about a business man who knows how
to make money but has trouble relating to his family—a fair image of Guy
himself—the play centers around the problem of simultaneously making money
and tending to a family.

It was a good, solid comedy, honed, by all of its travels, to a fine edge. Of all
of the Bolton-Middleton plays, it probably best exemplifies the wedding of
clever lines to believable characters. Each collaborator brought his own quality
to the work, and here, perhaps even more so than in *Polly,* the combination
clicked. "One of those wholesome plays that the whole family can go and see
. . . ," said the critic for the *New York Star,* and the *Clipper* predicted that
". . . when most of the plays of the present season have come and gone and late

Spring tells the story of what ones have succeeded by a glance at the names of those that still remain, 'Adam and Eva' will most likely still be twinkling in electric lights over the entrance of the Longacre Theatre. . . ."

As it turned out, the *Clipper* was right. *Adam and Eva* became a paying tenant of the Longacre for 301 performances, and two road companies kept it alive for two more seasons. It would be the second of the Bolton-Middleton plays to be made into a silent film. The first was *Polly with a Past.* David Belasco negotiated a contract with Metro Pictures for the filming of it with Ina Claire still in the lead, in December of 1919, at a price of $75,000 for the two authors.

A year later, William Randolph Hearst bought *Adam and Eva* for Marion Davies, who was now firmly installed as his primary interest. It would be a notorious failure, following hard on the heels of her 1922 flop *When Knighthood Was in Flower.* What was a simple little family comedy would be turned by Luther Reed's screen adaptation into a Ziegfeldian extravaganza, with a repro-duction of a Venetian carnival designed by Joseph Urban that contained gigantic festival barges and a fleet of gondolas, manned by real gondoliers. Middleton later referred to it as "one of my most acute embarrassments."

In 1919, however, it was a comfortable stage hit, freeing Guy to go back to *Zip Goes a Million, The Cave Girl* (as *Hilda* was now called) and *The Rose of China.* *Zip Goes a Million* had been slated to open in late October at the Princess. At the beginning of September, it was rescheduled for a January 5 premiere to allow more major carpentry. The trouble was, Guy, its master carpenter, was lulled by the delay into devoting his time to his other three projects.

Jerry continued to pour out gorgeous melodies, including a duet for Fox and Carroll, "Whip-Poor-Will," a rouser for Fox to deliver, "You Tell 'Em," a delightful production number, "The Mandolin and the Man," and a touching number in the mode of "Till the Clouds Roll By," "Look for the Silver Lining."

It was all beyond the hearing not only of Guy but of Comstock and Gest, who were readying the imminent entry of two major shows into New York within two nights of each other, each with themes enough alike to have been turned out on the same lathe. Following up on their attempt to cash in on the flush of returning soldier shows that hit Broadway after the Armistice, they tried, in the 1919–20 season, to also cash in on a two-season-long Oriental craze.

As Gest noted for the *New York Times,*

> This season, if the taste inclines in any specific direction, it seems to gravitate toward an Oriental flavor. Thus, we have "East is West" holding over for a second season; "Chu Chin Chow" in its second edition; John Masefield's play,

"The Faithful" produced by the Theatre Guild; Mr. Belasco's spectacle, "The Son-Daughter" with Lenore Ulric; "Aphrodite," and, last but not least, "The Rose of China."

Once again, as in their gamble with *The Five Million,* Comstock and Gest hoped to climb aboard the Oriental bandwagon and ride it to instant success. And, when *The Rose of China* opened in Atlantic City in late October, it seemed that they had chosen the right vehicle. Audiences gasped in wonder at Joseph Urban's first-act Oriental garden and broke into wild applause at his second-act Oriental cottage. The laughs were in the right places, and the cast, headed by Oscar Shaw, Frank McIntyre, Cecil Cunningham, Edna May Oliver, and a charming newcomer named Jane Richardson, was met with approval.

But for all its visual splendor, the show was long and unwieldy, running nearly three hours on opening night. When it followed the revised *Chu Chin Chow* into the Alvin, in Pittsburgh, on November 3, it was still three hours long. Guy, commuting between his multiple projects, would never get around to shaving much more time from it, nor would he ever succeed in paring down *Zip Goes a Million*'s gargantuan girth. Cutting and shaping the two shows simultaneously, while giving George Middleton the time he rightfully demanded for *The Cave Girl* and *The Cross* was a little too much for even the indefatigable Count of Kensington, and all suffered.

By November, Comstock and Gest demanded that Guy direct most of his energies toward *The Rose of China.* This was the one that was going to bring home the box office bacon, and their faith was in it and him. He acquiesced, leaving the two plays to Middleton and *Zip Goes a Million* in the hands of a neophyte director, Oscar Eagle. There would be time, producers and librettist reasoned, to bring Guy, Bob Milton, and Julian Mitchell back to the project after the triumphant opening in New York of *The Rose of China.*

The Pittsburgh run bolstered both their faith and their bravado. Critics and audiences alike were ecstatic, as were those in Washington, the following week. But when *The Rose of China,* in all its bloated grandeur, opened at the Lyric in New York, on November 25, 1919, the Gotham critics were considerably less ebulliant. Only the *Clipper* effused unreservedly. ". . . [J]udging from the applause it received," raved the paper, "[*The Rose of China*] bids well to take its place among that class of theatrical plants which will bloom for many seasons."

The *Times* punningly pronounced it ". . . a triumph of lines over matter," and the critic for the *Sun,* finding it somehow improper for a show to begin its last act at 11:00 p.m., nevertheless applauded the efforts of Armand Vecsey and lauded Plum's lyrics, pronouncing his rhyming of "Los Angeles" and "man jealous" as ". . . probably the greatest single achievement of its kind of the season." But he had few good words for Guy. "The fault," he went on, "appears to lie with Mr. Bolton, who has supplied a highly deliberate Chinese-American romance, which, even if it does require the three acts which Mr. Bolton has given it, certainly should not require until 11:30 in the evening to unravel." Even Guy's comic lines fell flatly for him. "Mr. Bolton has peppered [*The Rose of China*] with some of his characteristic witticisms, but the seasoning was not high," he concluded.

It fell to Burns Mantle to put it into perspective.

> This is certainly China's year in the theatre. She may lose Shantung, but she is sure to gain several hundred American Ming Toys of one kind and another. . . . 'The Rose of China,' the book of which was written by that eminently sane and witty homebred librettist, Guy Bolton; the lyrics by his equally gifted partner, P. G. Wodehouse, and the music by Armand Vecsey, who is [a] considerable composer, is another of those opulent productions that go to show what some producers are doing with their increased profits. . . .

Still, for all his reality, Mantle was charmed by the show's operetta trappings. "One of the best books and one of the most musicianly and melodious scores of the season are sure to find a big public for this attraction," he concluded, and the creators, reading the papers on November 26 certainly must have been cheered by this.

But the public was considerably less sanguine and accepting, and agreed resoundingly with the nay sayers. Whether this public was sated with an overabundance of pseudo-Orientalism on Broadway or whether word-of-mouth spread about the truly claptrap nature of the piece, or whether theatregoers expected something far more spare and sophisticated from Bolton and Wodehouse than what they received, one will never know. They stayed away in droves, and the box office failed to sustain itself, even after a published complaint by J. S. Tow, secretary of the Chinese Consulate, that *East Is West* and *The Rose of China* depicted China and the Chinese in derogatory and inaccurate ways.

The probable reason for its failure was that it was, as Guy and Plum wrote in *Bring on the Girls,* a sorry affair, absolutely anti-Princess in its lack of worldliness and cleverness, in its operetta structure, even in its thirty-five piece orchestra. A mix of *Madame Butterfly, The Mikado,* and *The Ziegfeld Follies, The Rose of China* was no pure blossom, only a wilted counterfeit.

Its main conflict is caused by Tommy Tilford (Oscar Shaw) and his substantial sidekick Wilson Peters (Frank McIntyre) who are two Occidentals accidentally in China. Unaware of its customs, Tommy kisses Ling Tao (Jane Richardson), and that, according to custom, disgraces her in her caste. Besides, Tommy is already engaged to Grace Hobson (Cynthia Pero). Sidekick Wilson, who has answered a lonely hearts ad from a girl named Polly from Vermont (Cecil Cunningham) calls her in to solve the dilemma. She comes up with the operetta device of having Tommy parade as Wilson.

Oriental cunning exposes the trick; Tommy, showing great irresponsibility, marries Ling Tao, thinking he will invalidate the marriage, and, through the grace of Grace, leave China. But a child arrives, a la *Madama Butterfly,* followed closely by a happy ending, in which Tommy falls for Ling Tao, Wilson falls for Polly, and Grace gets offstage just before the final curtain falls.

Guy's research seemed to have consisted of a couple of conversations with David Belasco and three hours at a performance of *East Is West,* where he must have jotted down some of Fay Bainter's pidgin English. The Chinese dialect in *The Rose of China* is indicated by inconsistently transposing some l's and r's, and insinuating many allee samees. "Chelly tree," "Clome down at once," "Allee light. Will you clatch me . . ." are but three of a bushel of examples of these witless, tin-ear translations, which ultimately tangled Ling Tao's otherwise touching farewell (before the happy ending) into laughable tongue twisting: "Less [yes], it's true glood-bye, Tom-me. Here, take little chu-sha-kih flower to m'lember Ling Tao by—and when big lady moon come and look down at you, bling this out and look at it and think of little moth you knew only for one day."

Mixed in with the dialect was a bushel of contemporary witticisms. There were standard anti-Prohibition lines ("An optimist is a man who still keeps a corkscrew in his desk drawer") and antimarriage ones ("I put an ad in the *Herald* personal column," says Wilson. "You know those things: attractive girl with straight hair and curly features would like to meet eligible young man—object alimony"). There were rewards. Guy's knack for a turn of phrase was undiminished. ("They want guard to give you to them so they can knock you on head with clubs," relates a young Chinese man who has been imprisoned. "They want to bring you to a hard wood finish.") And his Princess-style marriage-must-out curtain speeches were warmly in place. ("It's a wonderful feeling," confesses Tommy, "once you've said that fatal wilt thou, and she's wilted in your arms. . . .")

And finally, Plum was as agile as ever with a lyric. Critics and audience alike chuckled as Lee, a Chinese graduate of Yale, reminisced:

Though from fair New Haven
I have had to part,
Have I forgot?
I'll say I've not.
Still that name's engraven
Neatly upon my heart:
Though far away,
Still I am dreaming of it night and day.
After ev'ry meal I
Cheer for dear old Eli:
In my tub, I never fail,
While I scrub, to think of Yale. . . .

But these treasures were minimal in the greater—or lesser—scheme of the entire production, and *The Rose of China* closed eight weeks—forty-seven performances—after it opened. Comstock and Gest took it immediately on the road, where it triumphed, duplicating its pre–Broadway run, and once again, less demanding hinterland audiences handsomely paid back an investment on a wrong-headed venture.

But long before the benevolence of the road recouped their money, the production team had dashed off to other boiling pots: Comstock and Gest sprinted to New York to open *Aphrodite,* a super-spectacular with passing nudity, a plethora of semiclad chorus girls, and to give it class, dances by ballet great Michel Fokine. It would fill the Century for months to come.

And Guy, Bob Milton, Julian Mitchell, and the Princess orchestrator, Donald Saddler, dashed off to various rehearsal halls to minister to *Zip Goes a Million,* a show in a load of trouble.

Patched up, tucked up, and tended to, *Zip Goes a Million* finally opened at the Worcester Theatre, in Worcester, Massachusetts, on December 8, 1919, and was greeted with understandable puzzlement by an audience that was forced to sit through nearly three hours of three long acts containing enough material for three shows. Most critics, as bewildered as the audience, gave it little notice, merely reporting, as the *Evening Gazette* did, that ". . . the performance last night ran considerably over time, but the audience evidently enjoyed every minute of it. . . ."

Guy shuttled back and forth between New England and New York, where *The Cross,* now titled *Through the Ages,* was in rehearsal. Buddy De Sylva, borrowing the chorus girls' names from *Oh, My Dear!,* fashioned "Telephone

Girls," which, as Guy and Plum had a season ago, utilized all of the New York City telephone exchanges. It merely mystified the audiences in Springfield and Providence.

"Look for the Silver Lining" was pulled from the show and went back into Jerry's trunk. But out of that same trunk, from *Oh! Lady! Lady!!* came "Bill," and, in one of the most intriguing transformations in theatrical history, it was now given to Monty to sing. Down on his luck and short at the bank, he sang it not to a person but to a dollar bill. The De Sylva lyrics are gemlike, though the initial pun could only be fully appreciated in an encore, which the song failed to get:

> I found a friend, I want you to meet him.
>> You'll gladly greet him, I know—
> Though he's an old offender, he's *tender,*
>> To friend or to foe—
> To see him coming makes you glad,
>> Then to know he's leaving you makes you sad.
> But great and small his worth proclaim,
>> And you'll know him when I tell his name:
> He's Bill, Old Bill, who sticks to you until
>> You need him most.
> He's willing to
> Keep thrilling you,
> By leaving your track and then
> Hurrying back again.
> In these hard times,
>> He's worth about three dimes, but still—
> I'm sure he can bring me happiness,
>> 'Cause he's my old pal Bill.

Plum, when asked for permission for this transgression, must have flinched, but with a customary burial of his ego, evidently relented.

Even this song failed to cure the ills of *Zip Goes a Million.* By the time it reached Washington, carrying as much book trouble as it had had in Massachusetts, Jerry's patience was at an end. Once more, the possibility of a revived Princess series, with the trio of musical fame back in their accustomed, acclaimed places, was aborted, and this time not only by its producers—who had admittedly given it short shrift—but by Guy himself. With Guy and Jerry and

Buddy De Sylva constantly in final attendance, working tirelessly to pare and shape, as Jerry and Guy and Plum had once so easily done, it might have worked.

But it didn't. Despite a sudden surge in attendance in Washington and a last week gross of a healthy $14,000, Comstock and Gest decided to cut their losses and close the show. They had had a taste of the grandiose in *The Rose of China* and *Aphrodite* and found it sweet. Their interest in reviving the intimate daring and bright pattern-setting of the Princess dimmed, then vanished.

And so, one of Jerry's most delightful scores would go largely unheard. Two songs—"Whip-Poor-Will" and "Look for the Silver Lining"—would be only briefly interred. And "Bill," probably the only participant in *Zip Goes a Million* to profit from its demise, was saved the indignity of appearing in New York cross-dressed.

It was another bitter experience for Jerry, one that had the potential of driving an irrefutable wedge between at least two members of the trio. And yet, even it would not, as the events of the next six months would prove. But for the present, at least, Guy and Jerry parted company unamicably, each to return to New York and disparate projects.


Guy scarcely had time to remove his hat and coat before plunging into last-minute work on *The Light of the World,* as *Through the Ages* was now called. It had come a long way from its opening, in its previous incarnation, on May 16 in Detroit. And that way had not always been paved with the best of intentions.

Detroit had loved it; the *Detroit Free Press* had, in fact, run an editorial that called it ". . . a drama of singular power and beauty, and of striking ethical significance. . . . It is a work of such import that it demands recognition beyond the ordinary critical review."

Moving on to Baltimore, it received even higher praise, and both Guy and George Middleton, feeling that they had another winner in the league of *Adam and Eva,* decided, as they had in that play, to buy into the show.

And then, the overloading of Guy's schedule and the priority list of Comstock and Gest momentarily shelved it. While Guy was out of town with *Zip Goes a Million,* the producers took over its fate.

It was a tragic error; though Comstock and Gest had many qualities that allowed them to succeed as Broadway producers, the one quality they lacked was taste. Ray had proved that from the very beginning of his career; without Bessie Marbury, he wouldn't have had the reputation he enjoyed in 1919; now, in partnership with one of the most flamboyant men on the Great White Way, unfettered by the sanity of Bessie and self-fulfilled by a bulging portfolio of successes, Ray Comstock had become unforgivable.

In the fall of 1919, thinking big and very little else, he and Gest proceeded to inflate *The Light of the World* to elephantine proportions. Music was added. The sets were rebuilt, larger than before. Offstage choirs huddled in the wings, underlining and pumping into pageantry scenes that were, in the spring, merely—and purely—impressive. Then, in an apparent ploy not only to give the play a stature they felt it deserved but to link it to their wildly successful *Aphrodite,* the two producers suggested that the names of Bolton and Middleton might be too linked in the public mind to comedies. Why not, they suggested, invent a French pseudonym for the author? The public was going crazy over French authors. Look at the crowds that continued to stampede *Aphrodite,* which was adapted from Pierre Louys's novel of the same name.

Both authors were resistant. Both had earned the right to billing. The producers persisted. Guy gave in, and then, reluctantly, Middleton did too. He was discouraged. What had been to him a beautiful play was being cheapened and assaulted. He wanted no more of it; he signed over his share to Guy, who had recently lost much of his share of the sale of *Polly* to the movies in the stock market, with the plummeting fortunes of something called Vanadium.[7]

And Middleton was right. *The Light of the World* had in it many warm and valid qualities. It told the allegorical tale of one Anton Rendel—whose mother is named Mary—and his best friend Simon, known elsewhere as Peter, who are preparing to appear in their village's passion play. Anton has been picked to play the Christus, but his other friend Jonas—read Judas—is jealous because he feels he should have received the part. Marna Lynd—Mary Magdalene—has been impregnated by Simon; Anton shields Marna and loses his part because Jonas lies to the town, spreading the word that the child is Anton's. The town tries to burn down Anton's house and drive Marna out, but Anton gently prevails, the truth is told, and the ending is happy.

Three comic characters from the outside world—an American newspaper man, a Dutch art expert, and an English poet—are brought in to provide comic relief and contemporary perspective, and their lines are pure Bolton.

The play has the ring of sincerity about it, and the characters, as in all of the Middleton-Bolton creations, are truthful and believable. However, in production, truth met Broadway, and *The Light of the World* became a casualty of the collision.

As the January 5, 1920, opening at the Lyric Theatre neared, Comstock and

Gest flooded the newspapers with stories of the producers' trip to Germany the year before the war, where they picked up the play, recognized its genius but kept it under wraps for fear of negative public reaction, then discovered it had been written by a Frenchman, and so rushed to have it translated and put into production. "It was a press-agent trick to get a news story when our authorship was revealed," wrote Middleton, in his autobiography. "But what operated more than anything else against the venture was that the same managers, who were exploiting the Christ story at the Lyric, had another play at the Century Theatre called *Aphrodite*. This was based on the lurid, sexy Pierre Louys novel, with a much publicized scene where a naked lady got up from her couch just too fast for the waiting police to focus on her with a summons. The sincerity of the whole set-up was quite naturally questioned. . . ."[8]

And if that wasn't obvious enough, Comstock and Gest scheduled a private opening night on January 5 for New York City clergy and public officials. The public and the press were to be invited the following night. The program contained a further invitation to ascend to the roof of the Century Theatre, where *Morris Gest's Midnight Whirl,* featuring "36 Beauties, music by George Gershwin, scenery by Joseph Urban and Julian Mitchell staging," might balance the dose of religion they'd received at the Lyric.

It was all too tacky to succeed, and it didn't. *Variety* and the *Clipper* liked *The Light of the World.* Alan Dale of the *American* gave it a largely favorable review, albeit framed in faintly qualified phrases: ". . . quaintly set, agreeably told, and perfectly conventional story of what is usually called 'man's perfidy and woman's weakness.' You know. . . . There were times when the lesson sank in wonderfully well; there were others when mere claptrap seemed to exude from the sentiments expressed. But the effect of the play, on the whole, was excellent."

That was about all the good news the producers received. The *World* pronounced it ". . . a curious mixture of religious symbolism, ordinary melodrama, music, choirs, Biblical precept and Broadway hokum . . . ," the *Sun* wondered if it was ". . . intended as an antidote for *Aphrodite*," and Alexander Woollcott, in the *Times,* pronounced it ". . . [an] eye-filling, pretentious, and entirely tasteless theatrical entertainment. . . ."

*The Light of the World* closed after thirty-one performances, never to be seen, either in New York or on the road, again. Middleton had at least had the good judgment to withdraw his money from the play; Guy lost everything but his faith in it.

In an ironic postscript, he gave a copy of the play to Armand Vecsey, apparently a man with many contacts and little responsibility. Vecsey, on one of his junkets to Europe, then gave it to Fritz Wreede, Germany's leading play agent. Wreede in turn gave it to the great Max Reinhardt, who loved it and handed it on to composer Richard Strauss, who likewise became excited about turning it into an opera, and interested his librettist, Hofmannsthal, in it. Elated, Wreede wrote to Vecsey in America, entreating him to cable him immediately.

But the letter didn't reach Guy and Middleton until 1936! Somehow, Vecsey had overlooked it and forwarded it, without comment, to Middleton fifteen years after it had been sent, and Wreede, Reinhardt, and Hofmannsthal had all died. Small wonder that both playwrights forever regarded the play as jinxed.[9]

Meanwhile, back at the American Musical Theatre, life was considerably more relaxed. Jerry was once again working with Anne Caldwell on Charles Dillingham's latest project, *The Night Boat,* a delightful romp with some distant echoes of *Very Good Eddie* in both its plot and its casting.

It was all about a fellow, played by *Very Good Eddie*'s durable comedian Jack Hazzard, who poses as the captain of an Albany night boat to escape for an extramarital romp, and it contained some lovely experiments and Kern melodies. Miss Caldwell hit upon the idea of having six chorus girls, dubbed "Plot Demonstrators," capsulize the "story so far" during the first half-hour of the show to accommodate latecomers and to run it through rapidly in the last half-hour for those who had to catch an early train.

*The Night Boat* opened at Baltimore's Academy of Music on December 29, 1919, where its production was hailed. Its book was not. The show was, in fact, little more than a series of specialty acts that included some expected interpolations for Marie Cahill, as Hazzard's crone of a mother-in-law.

But the local papers loved Jerry's melodies, more of which were fitted out with longer melodic lines, the sort that had graced *Zip Goes a Million,* and one, "The Left All Alone Again Blues," satirized the blues and employed a counterpointed rendering of "The Bluebells of Scotland." This and "Whose Baby Are You?," an uptempo early dance number for Louise Groody and Hal Skelly were later recorded by Victor Herbert, and no doubt helped to establish the show's long run.

*The Night Boat* wove its way through Rochester and Philadelphia, arriving at the Liberty in New York on February 2, 1920, to ecstatic reviews. It would be touted as the "hottest ticket in town," and Dillingham would install a boat above the Liberty's canopy with a revolving light that swept 42nd Street every few seconds. It would remain safely moored in New York for 313 performances, then tour for the following three seasons.

Jerry was comfortable with Anne Caldwell and his old mentor, Charles Dillingham. There was no need to return to the mad, bad taste of Comstock and Gest, nor the annoyances of Guy's chaotic planning. And he probably would have adopted Miss Caldwell as his sole lyricist of the time if an imperious telegram had not arrived during the last weeks of preparation for *The Night Boat*'s New York opening. It was from Palm Beach, and it summoned him to meet with Guy, Plum, and the most important summoner in the American musical theatre, Florenz Ziegfeld.

# THE
# NEAR PAST

"What was that story they told about Flo and his formality?" asks Plum, as he and Guy round a turn in Remsenburg.

"Don't remember," answers Guy.

"Come now, chap. You used to tell it all the time."

Guy thinks a moment. "You mean the rehearsal story?"

"Yes." Plum's eyes light.

"The one Ed Wynn told?"

"Precisely."

"Not a very reliable source for the truth."

"Who in our racket is, old boy?"

"Well," Guy prepares to resume his role as The Great Raconteur. He knows that, next to his pekes, Plum is his most appreciative audience. "Flo used to come down and have his own dress parade. Always did that. Liked to see the girls in their diaphanous costumes. And he was always so correct. Pomaded hair. Shined shoes. Pressed suit. That was his hallmark. Formality. Nobody called him anything but Mr. Ziegfeld. Never. And one day, he was sitting in the orchestra of the New Amsterdam, stock center, where he always sat, and the girl he was bedding at the moment—"

"Who was she?"

"Ed said Lillian Lorraine, but you know how reliable Ed was."

"Right. Oh, right."

"Anyway, she was complaining a blue streak. 'Ziggy,' she'd say. 'I can't wear this. Oh, Ziggy, this zipper is all wrong. Ziggy, this is impossible.' On and on like that for a minute or so, and then this stentorian voice rose like a wraith from the darkness: 'Mr. Ziegfeld in the theatre,' it said. 'Ziggy in bed.'"[1]

*Chapter*

# 14

# Production Number

## 1920–1921

The *Ziegfeld Follies* of 1919 was a monumental, seminal success, even more opulent and more breathtaking than the 1918 edition. In 1918 Broadway audiences had not only seen the expected elegance of Joseph Urban's fertile imagination, the talents of Eddie Cantor, W. C. Fields, Ann Pennington, and Will Rogers but the introduction of a teenage singing and dancing wonder, Marilynn Miller.[1]

For the 1919 edition, Irving Berlin, fresh from the army, was brought in to supply his usual full menu of comedy, sentiment, and production number underpinnings. He outdid himself, giving Eddie Cantor "You'd Be Surprised," comedian Bert Williams a rousing statement of indignation to the framers of the Volsted Act, "You Cannot Make Your Shimmy Shake on Tea," and to the world for far longer than the 1919–20 season, "A Pretty Girl Is Like a Melody."

But as marvelous as the Berlin score was, as funny as Cantor and Williams and Van & Schenck were, the public came to cheer its adopted darling, Marilynn Miller. John Mason Brown, in his memoir, *Dramatis Personnae,* could not shake his memory of the gracefully dancing and slightly singing *Follies* star. "For me Miss Miller has never stopped dancing," he

227

wrote. "She haunts me as a vision of spangles and sunshine, beautiful of body, empty of face, and supreme in grace, eternally pirouetting as Broadway's Pavlova."

Ziegfeld had stolen her, literally, from his theatrical enemies, the Shuberts, and put her in a sweet-sixteen number in the 1918 *Follies*. The Shuberts thought they had a five-year contract with her for their Winter Garden shows, but Ziegfeld pointed out that she had been a minor when she signed the contract, fresh out of her vaudeville days with *The Five Columbians*.

It was one of the best investments of the Great Glorifier's career, although there would be plenty of times when he would regret it. Notorious for employing not only a casting couch but requiring repeated sexual favors from the girls he glorified, he met his match in Marilynn Miller. Sweet onstage, she was a driven, calculating climber off. She was the world's hardest worker, but that energy drove her to acts of random cruelty and the making of mountainous demands. She apparently dispensed her favors to Florenz Ziegfeld, but made him aware that he was to repay them in kind and give her her way with costumes, billing, and constantly renewable creature comforts.

Then, during the rehearsals of the 1919 *Follies,* she paid Ziegfeld the supreme insult; she fell in love with another cast member, a man twelve years her senior at that. Frank Carter, a former acrobat turned singer and dancer, was a charming, intelligent man who took a genuine interest in the teenage Miss Miller without threatening her freedom. It was more than a young girl could resist, and Marilynn Miller didn't.

Ziegfeld was furious, first trying to consume all of her time in trumped up rehearsals and conferences, then forbidding the engagement, then taking away Carter's one solo, a last-gasp patriotic number called "I'm Goin' to Pin a Medal on the Girl I Left Behind." When all else failed, he fired him.

It was just the sort of challenge Marilynn Miller loved. In May, she and Frank Carter eloped and were married. Faced with a purely business decision—he knew a dancing gold mine when he hired one—Ziegfeld capitulated and gave them his grudging blessing. But he never ceased to believe that if he could continue to help Marilynn Miller's career to ascend, she would soon tire of her adolescent crush and gratefully resume her role as his Galatea.

In February of 1920, with the 1919 *Follies* on the road, and his pockets bulging from the New York receipts, he took himself to Palm Beach. There, he booked a suite at the Breakers and chartered Leopold Replogle's impressive and aptly titled yacht, *The Wench*. All the while, plans for the following season danced in his head, and one of those ideas involved a show written particularly for the person and talents of Marilynn Miller.

Utilizing his special contract with Western Union, which allowed him to send three million words a year at a reduced rate, he fired off three wires to Jerry, Guy, and Plum, inviting them to Palm Beach as his guests. Object: a show.

It was the sort of summons that promised enough to make friends of enemies. No matter what the differences were among the trio, they would have been the world's supreme fools to entertain, even for a moment, thoughts of refusing the invitation.

Jerry caught a train immediately. Plum, back in Great Neck for a short stay before returning to the England he found ideal and peaceful and conducive to writing, joined Guy on a buying spree in New York. "They bought straw hats and pongee sticks," Guy and Plum recalled in *Bring on the Girls*. They bought bathing suits. They bought tickets to Palm Beach."

Once there, Jerry and Guy made a fortuitous decision that filled Plum with terror. Once more, they would propose *The Little Thing*.

"But Ray—" Plum remonstrated.

The other two proceeded to remind him that the defining quality that would forever separate Ray Comstock from Florenz Ziegfeld was taste. Had Plum forgotten *A Milk White Flag? Aphrodite? The Rose of China? The Light of—*

Plum agreed, and when, the next day, the three settled into three soft wicker chairs aboard *The Wench,* preparatory to a sail along the Indian River, they were united in their projected reply to Ziegfeld.

The cast of characters aboard the yacht was wide and varied: automotive czar Walter Chrysler, novelist Arthur Somers Roche and his wife, singer Ethel Pettit, producer Messmore Kendall, newspaper executive Paul Block, and Ziegfeld beauty and favorite Olive Thomas joined the Great Glorifier to appreciate the Florida sun, shimmeringly reflected in the barely mobile surface of the Indian River.

Ziegfeld wasted no time in getting down to business. His need was for a vehicle for Miss Miller. But his plan was to give her something that was her own, tailored to her wistful, spun-glass look, and her skills at ballet, tap, and lighting up a stage.

Once more, for the fourth and last time, Bolton and Wodehouse and Kern offered up *The Little Thing,* with its story of Sally, a waif who wants to be a ballerina, who has the last name of Rhinelander because she was found in a telephone booth, and who, in loving memory, places flowers on it every Mother's Day.[2]

Soft-pedaling its now outdated war scenes and flag waving, Guy recited the plot to Ziegfeld, who sat impassively in his royal wicker chair. When Guy had finished, Jerry went to the piano with which the yacht was outfitted and in his own, faintly flowery style played two of the songs the trio had written for *The Little Thing*—a comedy, pseudohistoric number called "Joan of Arc," and the expected Princess finale, "The Church 'Round the Corner." Then, as an offhand offertory to the gentle, sincere nature of Marilynn Miller, he rippled into "Bill," the musical orphan from *Oh! Lady! Lady!!* and *Zip Goes a Million*.

The trio was offering something profound and important that winter day on the Indian River: it had been the first product of their first time together, and like some mystical *leitmotif*, it had run through the entirety of their collaboration. At some of the most auspicious moments of that frequently turbulent time, *The Little Thing* had surfaced, bound them together, then disappeared, signaling separation. And yet it had remained, like some invisible bond, or connective tissue, binding them to each other through good times and ill.

Ziegfeld nodded. He liked the idea. He liked it very much. He could see possibilities for it, *if* they dropped the depressing and not very funny character of Esmeralda and *if* Sally's realized dream was not to become a ballerina, but to dance in the *Follies*.

The trio looked at each other in stunned relief. Finally, *The Little Thing* had found a home, and with Ziegfeld as her landlord. They agreed, without hesitation. Jubilant, armed with an agreement, they headed northward with visions of *The Little Thing* dancing—literally—in their heads. It was proof beyond challenge that their taste and imagination had only to find a producer who had the vision of a Ziegfeld to bring it to life.

But life, even around the stage, proved once again to be more complicated than Guy's plots. Within a few weeks, a notice in *Variety* crowed that Florenz Ziegfeld had finally found the ideal vehicle in which to feature his superstar, Marilynn Miller: a musicalization of the Ethel Barrymore triumph *Captain Jinks of the Horse Marines*.

A quick call to the Ziegfeld office revealed that it was only a publicity plant, but that Mr. Ziegfeld, as usual, was interviewing other composers, librettists, and lyricists, too, and all were hard at work turning out a new book show for Marilynn Miller.

The three had been around Broadway long enough to accept it philosophically. And anyway, Ziegfeld was having problems of his own with the mercurial

Miss Miller. She was anxious to return from the road and rejoin her husband, Frank Carter, at the Idaho Apartments at 162 West Forty-fifth Street. And when Marilynn Miller dug in her heels, she dug in her heels.

The trio buried their disappointment in work. Guy returned to *The Cave Girl*. Plum went back to Great Neck for a while, to block out a book—*The Adventures of Sally*—that was, like the book he was preparing for publication—*The Little Warrior*—a story of a chorus girl. In the interstices, he developed several short stories for the *Strand, Cosmopolitan,* and *McClure's.*

All was not peaceful in Great Neck. Guy and Marguerite's marriage was obviously in trouble. Marguerite's career was once again up to speed. She was making movies at the Astor Studios in New York. She was singing at the Chicago Opera. There was some talk of her doing Gilbert and Sullivan for the Shuberts. A contract with the Saint Louis Symphony for a Western tour was in the offing. She had been extended an invitation to sing at Paris's Opéra Comique. Still, she had time to spend with their daughter, Peggy.

Guy, apparently, did not. Marriages, for good or ill, have been saved by a mutual love of the children of the marriage. And, while Plum adored Leonora, though she was his stepdaughter, and garnered every moment he could to be with her, and Jerry worshipped his daughter, Betty, and for the rest of his life would carve out meaningful moments to be spent with her, discussing the world, mankind, and their mysterious ways, counseling her on her life and its problems; Guy spent very little time with Peggy. "I never remember my parents together in Great Neck," Peggy would later say, and it was indicative of his behavior throughout all of his four marriages.

It was not that Guy disliked children; he simply couldn't understand them and felt uncomfortable around them. His efforts to raise Joanie and Dickie ended in failure; from all accounts, he hardly tried to raise Peggy. It would only be later in life, when grandchildren began to appear, that he would allow glimmers of affection through.[3]

So, by early spring of 1920, Plum and Ethel, sensing that all was not well at Kensington nor likely to get much better, determined to sell their Great Neck house and spend more time in England, near Leonora and Plum's London publishers.

Jerry, meanwhile, struck up a lasting friendship with Irving Berlin. He was beginning to acquire the reputation that would later be articulated by George Gershwin, Richard Rodgers, and Berlin, as the melodic mentor of all of them. Berlin, no easy dispenser of compliments or adoration, would, decades later, confess to Abel Green, the editor of *Variety,* his admiration for Jerry. "I think,"

Green said in an interview with musical historian Max Wilk in later years, "if Irving ever had a hero, it was Jerome Kern."[4]

Jerry wouldn't wait that long to praise Irving Berlin. In 1924, he would write to Alexander Woollcott, who was preparing a biography of Berlin, a recollection of a dinner he attended in London in 1921. "I was asked what, in my opinion, were the chief characteristics of the American nation," he told Woollcott. "I replied that the average United States citizen was perfectly epitomized in Irving Berlin's music. He doesn't attempt to stuff the public's ears with pseudo-original ultra-modernism, but he honestly absorbs the vibrations emanating from the people, manners and life of his time, and in turn, gives these impressions back to the world—simplified, clarified, glorified. In short, what I really want to say, my dear Woollcott, is that Irving Berlin has *no* place in American music, HE IS AMERICAN MUSIC."[5]

There was another reason for the solidifying friendship between the two men. Alexander Woollcott once described Harpo Marx as a "genius . . . with a fine sense of double-entry bookkeeping." The same could be said for both Jerry and Irving Berlin. Both were prolific geniuses; Berlin was awesome in his management of himself; Jerry, under Max Dreyfus's careful tutelage, had come a long way from the day he was talked into buying two hundred pianos for his father's furniture store.

On a bustling Broadway, at the entrance to a decade in which an average of 225 shows opened every season, Berlin and Kern were industries unto themselves, and Guy, for one, tried to emulate that special and unique way of life. He would never quite reach either end of the equation, but that would never keep him from trying. In the 1918 contract the trio signed, a clause gave him not only royalties for the book but fifty percent of the royalties of the lyricist, too. It was an agreement that Plum acquiesced to easily. "Lyrics aren't worth nearly as much as the book," he would repeat, over and over, to Guy.[6] But other lyricists wouldn't be nearly so sanguine about the arrangement in future years, and the Bolton library is overstuffed with indignant letters in reply to persistent urgings from Guy, referring to enclosed checks for $6, $3, $12. One letter from the normally mild-mannered Ira Gershwin talks of enclosing stamps as a final payment.

Still, they weren't paying for work withheld. In 1920, both Guy and Jerry were masters of prolificacy. In the early spring, however, Jerry's energies produced little that was either tangible or memorable. Bob Milton collaborated with the famed novelist Alice Duer Miller on a comedy called *The Charm School,* and Jerry contributed a song to it, with lyrics by the novelist. And he once more united with Anne Caldwell on a modest revue, *Hitchy-Koo 1920*, starring Raymond Hitchcock and Julia Sanderson.

Meanwhile, back in the Ziegfeld orbit, high drama and authentic tragedy were unfolding. In April, the *Follies* wound down its national tour in Philadelphia. Frank Carter and Marilynn Miller were idyllically in love and had bought a spanking new Packard with their initials monogrammed on each door. On May 9, Carter left to drive to Virginia, where he was slated to produce a soldiers' and sailors' show. He never arrived. In Grantsville, Maryland, on the Maryland National Pike, he collided with another car and was killed instantly.

Ziegfeld left for Philadelphia as soon as the news reached him. And, although Marilynn Miller voiced determination to continue in the show, he convinced her to take a sea voyage with her mother and spend the summer mending herself.

It was necessary for him to devise a vehicle for his widowed star immediately, not only to trade on the nonstop international media attention that was being paid to her but to cement her further and possibly closer association with him. By the middle of May, he had made up his mind. It would be Jerry and Guy and Plum's script that would bring Marilynn Miller to Broadway in her first book musical. Once more, he fired off three telegrams, this time assuring a contract.

Plum had already taken the *Adriatic* to London and had, since the end of April, been back in residence at Walton Street, churning out stories and novels. "I now write stories at a terrific speed," he wrote to William Townend that month. "As a rule I like to start work in the mornings, knock off for a breather, and then do a bit more before dinner. I never work after dinner. Yet in the old days that was my best time. Odd. Plots: they've been coming along fine of late."[7]

Still, despite his fierce work schedule, Plum was delighted that all three of them would once again be working together. It would be an easier than usual task; the lyrics for *The Little Thing* were already written. If any changes were needed, he could return when the show went on the road. Meanwhile, there were cables and the mails, and he wouldn't have to break the rhythm of his writing in England. He wired his acceptance and then joined Ethel at Quinton Farm, Felixstowe, near Leonora's school.

But Ziegfeld, receiving Plum's cable, had no such pastoral thoughts. He wanted his creative staffs constantly near and always at his bidding. Guy and Jerry succeeded in mollifying him, for the present, and Guy set to work in bringing *The Little Thing* into the up-to-date world of 1920, while at the same time—in keeping with his usual schedule—working on *The Cave Girl* with George Middleton.

The play was about a child of nature who convinces a millionaire and his family, burned out of their cabin in the Maine woods, that back to nature is best. It was in not much better shape than it had been when Cohan and Harris had dropped it. Still, to their credit, Comstock and Gest stuck with Guy and George Middleton, when their June 21 opening at the Shubert-Belasco Theatre in Washington, D. C. was met with a less than lukewarm reception.

As usual, Middleton provided the characters that mattered and the theme, which examined not only freedom in nature but the nature of freedom. Guy changed the leading lady's name from Hilda to Margot and proceeded to jazz up the proceedings with witty lines and interpolated comedy situations. The cast, with Grace Valentine replacing Lola Fisher as the cave girl, was a willing one, absorbing the multiple rewrites that Guy and Middleton constantly threw at them during July.

It was certainly not among the collaborators' best work, possibly because Guy's main mission in the summer of 1920 was keeping Florenz Ziegfeld semisatisfied. *The Cave Girl* limped into the Longacre Theatre on Wednesday, August 18, trailing tales of road problems.

The worst proved to be true. Even their old friend, the *Clipper,* called it a "dull play, saved by good acting," and Alexander Woollcott's brief notice in the *New York Times* reflected the general attitude by critics and public alike. "Through all this comedy of the wilderness," he wrote, "there runs a curiously discordant note of Broadway. It is in the speech of the players, of course, and particularly in that of the little Down East heroine, whose accent suggests forcibly that her habitat is about as far down east as East Forty-Second Street."

*The Cave Girl* lurched along for a few weeks and then ended not only its run but the partnership of Guy Bolton and George Middleton. It was a mutual parting of the ways, with no recriminations, merely the realization by Middleton that his sanity and his expectations could best be sustained away from the high-powered, Broadway tempo upon which Guy seemed to thrive.[8]

And with *Sally of the Alley,* or *Sally in the Alley,* the two alternating titles of the transformed *Little Thing,* that tempo was increasing. It was not like the Princess days, where the trio was left pretty much to itself and had a decisive role in the casting of the show. Ziegfeld was Ziegfeld, and that meant that he was present in every phase of the production at any moment.

Still, Guy sent the first draft of the script to Plum, and the two gave it a Princess feeling—again, as in *Oh, My Dear!* and, by lyrical extension, *Zip Goes a Million*—naming the chorus girls after New York telephone exchanges: Miss Rhinelander, Miss Vanderbilt, Miss Worth, etc.

The remainder of the story strayed far from *The Little Thing* in everything but its beginning, ending, and main character. Reset in Greenwich Village, it was now a standard Cinderella story, a literal rags to riches tale of an orphan who begins as a dishwasher at the Elm Tree Alley Inn (actually a chic nightclub) and, through a series of chance meetings with theatrical agents and displaced royalty, finds love, loses it, and finds it again, as she's signed to dance in the *Ziegfeld Follies*.

The original songs written for *The Little Thing,* divorced from their original libretto context, gradually disappeared, leaving only two: "Joan of Arc" and "The Church 'Round the Corner"—Plum's favorite of all, because it was about the Little Church Around the Corner at which Plum and Ethel were married. It was time to introduce new material, and Plum was, alas, not exactly around the corner.

Nevertheless, he wrote two new lyrics and sent them off. They were apparently never used. Meanwhile, Ziegfeld kept his fine hand in, hiring first Walter Catlett, a tall comedian who, among other accomplishments, invented the saying "Hot diggedy dog!"; then, closer to the beginning of rehearsals than either Jerry or Guy would wish, Leon Errol to costar with Marilynn Miller.

Guy wrote in the part of the exiled Duke Constantine of Czechogovinia to suit the particular talents and audience expectations of Errol—a not unusual task in the musical theatre of the teens and twenties. He went about it with few complaints, for, as he noted in *Bring on the Girls,* "Ziegfeld authors might wind up sticking straws in their hair and cutting out paper dolls, but they could afford expensive nursing homes in which to do it."

Jerry, pressed by the imminent opening of *Hitchy-Koo 1920*, a show which would flop miserably, reached into his trunk and pulled out two songs from *Zip Goes a Million*, "Whip-Poor-Will" and "Look for the Silver Lining," but alas, not "Bill." There was no place in *Sally of* (or *in*) *the Alley* for dear old "Bill," nor was Marilynn Miller particularly happy with the song, so once again, "Bill" was put away.

Now there were two lyricists—Plum and Buddy De Sylva—each with two songs apiece and some new songs by Jerry that were, for the moment, wordless. Plum, from his vantage point across the ocean, couldn't see his way clear to return; his publishers were demanding too much of him, and removed from the madness of a Ziegfeld show in preparation, he remained sanguine about the whole operation.

Ziegfeld acted, and while Jerry once more dipped into his trunk and came up with "The Lorelei," which he had written with Anne Caldwell, and "Catamarang," from 1910's *The King of Caldonia,* he hired Clifford Grey, a British lyricist whose words, wed to the music of Nat D. Ayer, had produced "If You Were the Only Girl in the World" in his first show, 1916's *The Bing Boys Are Here.*

Informed of this, Plum went into a fit of uncharacteristic pique, and fired off an angry cable to Ziegfeld, withdrawing his lyrics from the show. Jerry was in a state of high stress himself. He was undoubtedly smarting under the failure of *Hitchy-Koo 1920,* and the critics' universal passing over of his music for that show, plus Ziegfeld's decision to bring in Victor Herbert to compose the music for the "Butterfly Ballet," Marilynn Miller's penultimate *Follies* number in *Sally of the Alley.* He fired back, more resonantly, and with more ammunition.

In a later letter to Leonora, Plum, considerably calmer by then, recalled the long-distance fight:

> You remember I sent my lyrics over, and then read in *Variety* that some other cove was doing the lyrics and wrote to everybody in New York to retrieve my lyrics. Then that cable came asking me if I would let them have "Joan of Arc" and "Church Round the Corner," which, after a family council, I answered in the affir. Well, just after I had cabled saying all right, I got a furious cable from Jerry—the sort of cable the Kaiser might have sent to an underling— saying my letter withdrawing the lyrics was "extremely offensive" and ending "You have offended me for the last time!" upon which, the manly spirit of the Wodehouses (descended from the sister of Anne Boleyn) boiled in my veins— when you get back I'll show you the very veins it boiled in—and I cabled over "Cancel permission to use lyrics." I now hear that Jerry is bringing an action against me for royalties on *Miss Springtime* and *Riviera Girl,* to which he contributed tunes. The loony seems to think that a lyricist is responsible for the composer's royalties. Of course, he hasn't an earthly, and I don't suppose the action will ever come to anything, but doesn't it show how blighted some blighters can be when they decide to be blighters?[9]

The action never came to anything, nor did Plum's rescinding of permission to use his lyrics stand. Guy, once again taking credit for more than he rightfully deserved, wrote, in 1922 to John Rumsey, one of his agents, "*Sally* was written without a lyric writer. I took two lyrics written by Buddy De Sylva for ZIP GOES A MILLION one by Ann [sic] Caldwell and four by P. G. W. and fitted them in. . . . After this was done Clifford Grey wrote the seven that remained including openings and finales."[10]

Finally, in mid-October, the show went into rehearsal, after more last minute casting dictates by Ziegfeld, who vetoed all of Guy's suggestions for the part of Mrs. Ten Broek, the society matron who eventually marries "Connie," the Leon

Errol character, and cast the Amazonian beauty from his *Follies* tableaux, Dolores. The unlikely combination worked, to the delight of audiences.

Guy did win two decisions, however. First, he managed to sneak Pickles and Tot in from *The Little Thing*. And, in a more meaningful showdown with the producer, who demanded a star entrance for Marilynn Miller, he enlisted the diminutive but determined lady's help in devising one of the most effective and famous and understated of all star entrances: no sweeping violins, no staircase, no parting of the waves of chorus people, but a simple, in-context entrance of a bunch of grubby orphans. Dialogue, dialogue, and then discovery: of the fabulous but shabby Miss Miller at the end of the line of orphans. A natural directorial decision today, it was revolutionary then — stars demanded and received staircase entrances. The opening moments, thanks to Guy's persistence and Marilynn Miller's help, became the talk of Broadway.

But then, so did the remainder of the show. From its first opening at the Academy of Music in Baltimore, on November 29, 1920, still as *Sally of the Alley,* word began to spread that something special and exciting was headed to New York. Interviewed by Baltimore reporters, the eighteen-year-old Miss Miller struck her most demure and grateful pose: "I have always dreamed of some day being a star," she said, after crying a little, "but it has been like a fairy tale, and I never expected to realize my ambition until I was about 35 — really old, you know. . . . Mr. Ziegfeld gave me my great chance when he offered me the part of Sally. It was all so hurried — only three weeks to rehearse in — and now we are all about dead."[11]

The show moved on to Nixon's Apollo Theatre in Atlantic City on December 6, then to the Broad Street Theatre in Newark, where it achieved its final identity as *Sally* and where the local papers crowed that ". . . an epochal entertainment is headed toward Broadway."

By opening night, December 21, 1920, at Ziegfeld's New Amsterdam Theatre, interest had climbed to a fever pitch. Hundreds were turned away. Word of mouth, passed on by ecstatic explorers who had journeyed to New Jersey, prepared the first nighters for an unforgettable evening. And that was just what they experienced. "*Sally* cast a charmed spell over first nighters until nearly midnight," reported the *Sun* the following day. Charles Darnton, in the *World,* pronounced it ". . . nothing less than idealized musical comedy," and Alexander Woollcott, in the *Times,* confided that

> . . . it bears witness to the fact that the annual production of the "Follies" does not exhaust the energy and talent of a producer who knows a little more than

any of his competitors the secret of bringing beauty to his stage. . . . as you rush for the subway at ten minutes to midnight. . . . you think of Mr. Ziegfeld. He is that kind of producer. There are not many of them in the world.

Jerry's music received universally favorable, though not very perceptive, notices. The *World* accepted it, admitting that it "had the pleasing cadence of the period," and Heywood Broun in the *Tribune* noted, condescendingly, "Jerome Kern seems to have set his heart on popularizing a tinkling tune called 'Look For the Silver Lining' which is ingratiating enough in its own mushy way to fulfill this purpose admirably, but our favorite is another more comical ditty called 'The Schnitza Komisski.' . . ." So much for tin ears.

Guy's book received scant notice, except to be called to task for its "vulgarisms." It's perhaps a comment on the theatrical taste of the age that audiences and critics alike were most impressed by the tacked-on third act, devoted almost entirely to Victor Herbert's ballet. "Although it was uncomfortably late when Victor Herbert sidled down an aisle and climbed into the orchestra pit to raise his baton," said Charles Darnton, "we had something more than his hunch of the shoulders that the best was yet to come—and we had the right hunch!"

The ballet, with its setting of night-dark blue shot through with silver birches and its hordes of beauties focusing upon a frail and ethereal Marilynn Miller, caused audiences to gasp in delight for 570 performances. *Sally* would establish a record of longevity, running longer than any musical to that time.

And yet for all the exhalations of wonder, the ballet was really penultimate, not ultimate. Audiences would leave the theatre with a lingering last image and echo not of it but of a Joseph Urban-ized wedding scene for three couples—a Princess knot-splicing, in other words. And it would all be to Jerry's lilting waltz and Plum's highly personalized lyrics written four years before, when the trio, in the bright heat of a suddenly realized partnership, had finished *The Little Thing:*

> There's a church 'round the corner that's waiting for us:
> It's just above Madison Square.
> I'll borrow a dollar and buy a clean collar,
> And then I'll be meeting you there.
> There'll be crowds in the pews and excitement and fuss,
> For I mean to be married in style,
> And the girls will go dizzy and whisper "Who is he?"
> When I start to step up the aisle.

Dear little, dear little Church 'Round the Corner,
    Where so many lives have begun,
Where folks without money see nothing that's funny
    In two living cheaper than one.
Our hearts to each other we've trusted:
    We're busted, but what do we care?
        For a moderate price
        You can start dodging rice
            At the Church 'Round the Corner,
            It's just 'round the corner,
            The corner of Madison Square.

For Jerry and Guy, the transformation of *The Little Thing* into *Sally* had been anything but a happy experience. There had been too much turmoil during its production, too many recriminations, too much ignoring of *them*. Writing to George Middleton on January 9, 1921, Guy would say, "I had a lot of trouble and unpleasantness to cope with in writing it, but I guess it was worth it."[12]

Jerry would be even more negative about his memories of *Sally*. He would never say precisely why, but he would, years later, tell producer Edwin Lester that it was the only one of his hits that he actually hated.

Perhaps it was the fact that once again, faced with the formidable presence of Victor Herbert, he had been minimized, even after writing that most exquisite of all Kern classics, "Look for the Silver Lining." Perhaps it was the argument with Plum, an explosion of hostility that both must have regretted deeply.

Probably, it was the whole turgid atmosphere that surrounded any venture with Ziegfeld and Marilynn Miller in the same theatre. Patricia, Ziegfeld's daughter, wrote in her memoirs, *The Ziegfelds' Girl,* about her night at *Sally,* which was also her first night at a Broadway show, and her first introduction to Miss Miller.

"Hello you lousy son-of-a-bitch," was Marilynn's greeting for Ziegfeld, when he brought the child backstage to meet her.

"You've heard me talk about Patricia, haven't you?" he asked the star, pushing his daughter forward for an expected hug.

"Yes, to the point of nausea," Marilynn snarled and then launched into a tirade about her costume. "This piece of crap you call a costume," she went on. "It weighs a ton, and as far as I'm concerned, you can take it and shove it!"

Ziegfeld tried to shush her in front of the child, but she would have none of it.

"What the hell are you being so goddamned quaint about?" she shouted. "You sound like Daddy Longlegs."

Patricia remembered the sound of a glass ashtray shattering against the wall as they closed the door behind them.

Still, the outward look of *Sally* breathed nothing but serene success. Ziegfeld had a new costume provided for Marilynn Miller every night of the run and brought in Sloan Farley to redecorate her dressing room in satin with velvet trimmings. He even staged a concert dedicated to the memory of Frank Carter in June of 1921. In return, she married Jack Pickford, despite Ziegfeld's repeated telegrams forbidding it.

And yet, Marilynn Miller missed only one short spate of performances, when she was ill, and Mary Eaton momentarily—very momentarily—replaced her. The remainder of the cast, with the exception of Mary Hay, stayed with the show throughout its entire four-year run. On December 21, 1921, Jerry, Guy, Victor Herbert, and Clifford Grey occupied a box with Ziegfeld, who made a speech on the first anniversary of its opening. After its final Saturday night, he threw a giant farewell party for the cast on the New Amsterdam roof. Walter Catlett lightened the proceedings with a satire of the show, after which Ziegfeld retired, presumably to count the five million dollars in profit he made on its New York run alone.

But by this time, both Jerry and Guy were into separate ventures that would carry them far afield. Both found themselves universally and continually courted at the beginning of 1921. Dillingham and Anne Caldwell had a new project, *Good Morning Dearie,* waiting for Jerry; Guy was approached by two new, potential collaborators, bearing projects.

The first was his former partner from *Very Good Eddie,* Philip Bartholomae. Bartholomae was working with the composer-lyricist team of Monte Carlo and Alma Sanders on *Tangerine,* a South-Sea Island musical tailored to the twin talents of Frank Crummit and Julia Sanderson. The story, involving a trio of men jailed for nonpayment of alimony who end up on an island where the women do all the work and pay all the alimony, was custom-made for Guy, and he took on the project gladly.

The fact that his own marriage was in serious trouble may or may not have accounted for such lines as:

KING [King Home-Brew of Tangerine, a part that would be
               played by Jack Hazzard]: All night I dreamed
               I was talking to my first wife.

CLARENCE: Oh no, your majesty—for hours and hours you didn't utter a sound.

KING: That's the time she was talking to me.

Or:

FRED: There was a man who stayed home with his wife every evening for twenty years.

KATE: That was love.

FRED: No it wasn't. It was paralysis.

Or:

KING: Wives spoil naturally—like milk.

Or:

KING: The gimmies—the American woman's national game.

With song titles like "It's Great to Be Married and Lead a Single Life" and "The Woman Is Part of Creation (But the Man Is Lord of It All)," the audience was left with no doubt about the show's apparently misogynistic attitude, carried through an act and a half, until the women finally revolted, in time for a happy, Princess-style ending.

It was a tired businessman's show, impure and simple, in which the chorus girl-islanders were costumed in outfits that the King colorfully described as "shredded wheat dresses . . . tough for the moths and great for the mosquitoes."

Guy and Bartholomae worked on *Tangerine* through the early spring of 1921, and it opened on August 9 at the Casino to generally favorable reviews. The New York critics pronounced it a trifle dated but nevertheless liked its brightness, its speed, its chorus girls, and its stars, Frank Crummit, Julia Sanderson, Jack Hazzard, and a vaudevillian named Fred Allen. It would run through the season.

The second, nonmusical play presented to Guy immediately after *Sally's* opening was from writer-producer Max Marcin, who had lately teamed with various partners, among them, Charles Guernon, Louis K. Anspacher, and Edward Locke, to churn out popular mystery melodramas. Marcin, coming freshly off his first successful producing venture, that of *Three Live Ghosts,* approached Guy in early 1921 with the idea of turning a melodramatic script he had written into a comedy-melodrama. It was turn-of-the-century shlock, with shadows cast upon walls, murder, suicide, and even a weird invention, purportedly imported from Australia: a crossing of a .38 automatic with a penlight that allowed murder in the dark.

From all evidence, it seems that Guy served as comic interpolater and construction supervisor. His hand was heavily evident in the insertion of the character of Jerry Hammond, played by John Daly Murphy, a detective who spouts antimarriage comedy, such as remarks that the coroner should have been a woman because he asks so many questions, etc.

Produced by Marcin, *The Night Cap* opened at the Thirty-ninth Street Theatre on August 15, 1921, to favorable reviews. The *Clipper* summed up opening night reaction: "'The Night Cap' starts out as though it were going to be a perfectly good melodrama with real murdering done and all that," it commented. "But the author's funny bone evidently got the upper hand, and as the play stands now it is one of the best comedies in town. . . ." It stayed in for a healthy run, but its most important contribution to the future of Broadway was the casting of a young British actor named Ronald Coleman in the role of the sinister butler, Charles.

For all its success, the days of *The Night Cap* and its genre were numbered. That year, 1921, was one of the last during which audiences would sit still for this sort of melodrama, even with a comic icing. Eugene O'Neil's *Beyond the Horizon* had already made the trip up from downtown, and his *Anna Christie* was slated to open that season. And that very summer, a young British playwright named Noel Coward would arrive in New York with seventy-five dollars in his pocket and a world of ideas in his head.

The same summer was a time for Jerry and Guy to steam in the other direction across the Atlantic. The London company of *Sally,* under the tutelage of George Grossmith, was scheduled to open in September, and the casting and rehearsal of the show was their eventual target. But it was also to be a time of separate but equal vacations for Jerry and Guy, now drawing even in affluence and international fame with their third member, Plum.

Jerry sailed with Eva and Betty at the end of April. But his vacation ended early. All three checked into a hotel in Paris, to spend the gentlest season of the year in the loveliest city on earth. But Jerry was not his usual energetic self. A doctor was finally called, and he diagnosed Jerry's malaise as measles. And so, while Paris romped in springtime splendor beyond the drawn curtains of Jerry's hotel room, he spent the next ten days in darkness and disuse. On August 9, after a vacation the like of which even he hadn't imagined, he returned, alone, on the *Olympic* to deliver his score for *Good Morning Dearie* to Dillingham and Caldwell.

On the very next eastward voyage of the *Olympic,* Guy and Marguerite embarked for Europe. It was, in many respects, a desperation move, an attempt to rescue, through a deferred honeymoon, their crumbling marriage. Marguerite had returned from a Western tour with the Saint Louis Symphony, and Frederick Toye had already concluded preliminary discussions with the Opéra Comique for a long-term contract.

She and Guy had spent precious little time together during the past year. She had been on the road and was a practicing free soul; she strongly suspected that Guy was up to his old habits with the chorus girls from *Sally* and *Tangerine.* Still, there was a profound mutual admiration, and the physical attraction that had drawn them to each other and blasted apart her previous marriage was still palpably present. The chance of some time away together to mend what was merely broken and not yet destroyed was enough of an inducement to allow Guy to miss the back-to-back openings of both *Tangerine* and *The Night Cap.*

Aboard that particular crossing of the *Olympic* was Charles Chaplin, traveling alone. As handsome and debonair as Guy, he was smitten, as hundreds of men were, by Marguerite's exotic and individual beauty. Although he had once been a guest at Kensington in Great Neck and had met both of the Boltons previously, he related later in his slim volume of travel memoirs, *My Trip Abroad,* that he was first struck by her from across the ship's dining room, and wasted no time whatsoever in insinuating himself into the company of the Boltons.

The three dwellers at the summit of success spent most of the remainder of the voyage together, and although Guy was aware that Chaplin was more interested in the conversation and the presence of Marguerite than him, he flipped the internal switch to which Marguerite later referred and refused to see a steadily heightening attraction that grew each day between his wife and the international film star. Or, if he did, he breathed a sigh of relief when they finally reached Southampton, and he went to oversee the debarking formalities, leaving Marguerite to attend to the steward's transfer of their baggage.

When he returned to the cabin, both Marguerite and her luggage had vanished. And so had Charles Chaplin. The two had gone off together to spend three weeks growing close enough for Chaplin to decorate the covers and binding of *My Trip Abroad* with small pictures of Marguerite and himself.

When she returned to Guy without apologies, Marguerite made light of a situation that the still-Edwardian Guy couldn't comprehend. In step with the times, he could comfortably explain a man inhabiting the beds of women other than his wife's, but was scandalized by the opposite arrangement. Trying to soothe Guy, she told him that Chaplin had offered her a million dollars if she would give him a baby as beautiful as the one she had given Guy. Chaplin, she said, with a light laugh, remembered Peggy from Great Neck.

It soothed him somewhat, but not enough to extinguish the fire and doom and incompletion in the air when Marguerite left London for conferences in Paris and Guy turned to the Winter Garden Theatre, where casting problems had already arisen. [13]

The recollections of those involved lend a *Rashomon* quality to the summer events surrounding another unpleasant experience for Jerry and Guy. According to George Grossmith, Jerry was adamantly opposed to the casting of Dorothy Dickson, the dancing star of *Oh, Boy!*, as Sally. First of all, he had recent memories of Marilynn Miller's minimal voice doing injustice to his melodies. Secondly, he may have shared Noel Coward's later evaluation of the popular dancer's mental capacities, "Don't be vague; be Dorothy Dickson."

For whatever reason, Grossmith recalled that Jerry "put a definite embargo on her," [14] and convinced Ziegfeld, who still retained a financial interest in the show, to side with him in forbidding the casting of Miss Dickson.

Guy, on the other hand—and again, the master raconteur may have been at work—remembered Jerry giving him permission to audition Dorothy Dickson in London. This recollection does seem logical, considering Jerry's enthusiasm in 1919 for the star—an enthusiasm that had caused him to appropriate her from the road company of *Oh, Boy!* for his own *Rock-a-Bye Baby.*

Guy auditioned Miss Dickson at the Winter Garden without her knowledge, he said, secreting himself in the darkened theatre while she sang for a stage manager. Then, acting upon Bolton's recommendation, Grossmith took her to lunch—Miss Dickson remembered that part of it, but not the audition—and hired her, against the firm prohibition of both Jerry and Ziegfeld.

It doesn't ring true, considering the personalities involved, but it does make for good theatrical legend. And it may well be that the reason that Jerry, when he arrived back in London at the end of August, didn't raise the theatre's roof over the casting of Dorothy Dickson in the lead was a preoccupation with two tragic occurrences in his personal life. First, Donald Saddler, his close and respected orchestrator, died at the end of March. Then, he received the news, upon arriving in London, that Lauri de Frece, the best man at his wedding to Eva and one of his closest and oldest friends, was dying of stomach cancer. While *Sally* was in rehearsal, de Frece passed away on August 25, at the age of forty-one.

Small wonder, then, that Jerry took little part in rehearsals, preferring to remain at the back of the darkened auditorium. And when, on opening night, he appeared backstage at Miss Dickson's dressing room, at the end of the second act of a show he hated with tears on his face, it was touching proof of both his precarious emotional state and the effectiveness of the star. [15]

The British production, headed by Dorothy Dickson and joined by George Grossmith in the Walter Catlett role, Leslie Henson in the Leon Erroll role, and Heather Thatcher as Rosalind the manicurist, a part that Guy expanded for her, might also have been partially responsible for Jerry's reaction to the second-act curtain. Those who saw both productions agreed that the London one discovered a warmth and humanity in *Sally* that Ziegfeld's fast-paced and royally glitzy one did not.

Once again, *Sally* would win over huge audiences, running for 387 performances at the Winter Garden and spawning three companies in the hinterlands. It was the beginning of the trio's decade of fame, one that would bring them all international recognition and the final severing of their professional relationship.

*Chapter*

# 15

# First Act Finale

## 1921–1924

Nineteen twenty-one was the year of the horses for Plum and Jerry. Still in the vanguard of collecting, Jerry had added, to his antiques, books, and stamps, horses. There was room for them to roam in Bronxville, and Betty would become an expert rider before she left her teens.

In London, meanwhile, Plum bought Ethel her heart's desire of the moment, a racehorse named Front Line. In October, writing from their new digs at 4 Onslow Square, Plum erupted to Leonora: "The Wodehouse home is *en gete* and considerably above itself this P.M. Deep-throated cheers ring out in Flat 43, and every now and then I have to go out on the balcony to address the seething crowds in St. James Street. And why? I'll tell you. This afternoon at Hurst Park dear jolly old Front Line romped home in the Hurdle Handicap in spite of having to carry about three tons weight. . . . With what Mummie (the well-known gambler) got on at six to one, we clear five hundred quid on the afternoon." [1]

Ethel was indeed an inveterate gambler and would remain so for most of her married life. Plum, becoming increasingly wealthy, dispensed her stakes without question or regard. Money, like most material necessities of the world, remained, and would remain, a mystery to him; and gambling, after all, was at the heart of every theatrical venture.

Back in New York, Jerry's score and Anne Caldwell's lyrics again graced Broadway with the November 1 opening, at the Globe, of *Good Morning Dearie*. A standard Cinderella story, very much like *Sally*, except that it also included a spate of musical comedy crooks, it starred Oscar Shaw as—what else?—a high society Lothario, who, while engaged to a society girl (Peggy Kurton), falls for a couturier's assistant (Louise Groody).

In a season that would produce little over which they could honestly cheer, *Good Morning Dearie* charmed critics and public alike, and Jerry's score, rather than being overlooked, was praised warmly. "It would make a pup wiggle his ears with joy," cheered the *Herald,* and the *Times* agreed, joining the *Herald*'s opinion that "Blue Danube Blues" and the title song were destined for immortality.

The real survivor from the score was, however, passed over by most critics, though audiences gave it much applause during every one of its 347 performances. The song was "Ka-lu-a" (listed as "Kailua" in early programs), a melodious, ersatz Hawaiian, let's-get-away-from-it-all ballad. Before the season was out, "Ka-lu-a" would appear in two shows and a courtroom.

The shows were *Good Morning Dearie* and *The Cabaret Girl,* which Jerry would write with George Grossmith and Plum in London later that season; the courtroom would be that of Judge John C. Knox, and later that of Judge Learned Hand. In February of 1922, Fred Fisher, who had collaborated with Jerry back in 1907 on "Right Now" and "I'd Like to Make a Smash Hit 'Mit You," sued Jerry, T. B. Harms, Charles Dillingham, Anne Caldwell, and Teddy Royce for one million dollars in damages. Apparently previous collaboration didn't cut the mustard with the talented but litigious Mr. Fisher, who had already sued seven other composers, charging them with plagiarizing his megahit, "Dardanella." With Jerry, he didn't accuse him of stealing the melody, only the bass line.

The suit was put over for nearly two years, until November 1923. By then, an unconcerned Jerry had made a bundle of royalties on "Ka-lu-a" in both America and England and entered the Woolworth Building courtroom of Justice Knox with a load of confidence and a wide smile.

First of all, he was represented by none other than Fred Fisher's former attorney, Nathan Burkan, who had brought about the first seven suits. Fisher and Burkan had had a falling out, and so Burkan had offered himself to Jerry.

Second, Jerry must have felt securely at home in a courtroom that contained, in addition to its usual decorations and personnel, an eight-piece jazz band, a piano, a Victrola, and Victor Herbert. "DARDANELLA SUIT TURNS COURTROOM INTO 'CAB' [cabaret]" shouted *Variety*'s headline writers the next day, and life was indeed that for the trial's participants.

Burkan, working at a decided advantage, proved that Fisher hadn't really originated "Dardanella," either, but had bought the rights to the music from a songwriting duo named Black and Bernard. Victor Herbert, demonstrating at his cello, proved that even *they* had stolen it from some unrecorded (by the court clerk or newspaper reporters) classic, thus putting it definitely into public domain.

The judge dismissed the case; Fisher's attorney appealed. On January 26, 1924, Judge Learned Hand found for Fred Fisher, thus establishing the fact that an accompanying bass figure as well as a melody can be copyrighted and protected from plagiarism. But Fisher's litigation got him more bad publicity than remuneration. Deciding that it seemed to him ". . . absurd to suggest that [Fisher] has suffered any injury," the judge awarded him the fixed minimum, $250, plus court costs, but not counsel fees.[2]

It was only one of many plagiarism suits that Bolton and Wodehouse and Kern faced—Guy was going through another plagiarism suit at the same time, in fact—but it would be the only one that established a precedent.

In the interim between the charges and the trial, all three worked away at their customary, furious pace. Immediately after *Good Morning Dearie*'s delirious success, Jerry and Anne Caldwell plunged into another musical, which would not share *Good Morning Dearie*'s encomiums and become a grief to both.

First of all, there was the problem of casting. It was to be one of those shows constructed around a star, and the star was to be Ina Claire. The trouble was, ever since Guy had persuaded David Belasco to sign her for his *Polly with a Past,* she'd decided that she was much better suited for comedy than musical comedy. Charles Dillingham finally persuaded her to star in *The Bunch and Judy,* as the show was named, but no sooner had she signed and Jerry and Anne Caldwell had set to work than she was offered a gem of a part in a gem of a straight comedy, *The Awful Truth.* She pleaded for, and got her release from her contract with Dillingham. Jerry and Anne Caldwell continued with the show anyway.

Meanwhile, as Jerry was going through his trials of many varieties in New York, Guy, journeying to Paris to be with Marguerite, met Franz Lehar. Lehar had written the operetta that had brought Marguerite to Broadway and Guy, and before he left Paris, Guy extracted an agreement from Lehar to write an operetta in collaboration with Jerry, Plum and Guy. During the early autumn of 1921, he and Plum managed to outline a stock one called *The Blue Mazurka,* and Plum even managed to write two dummy lyrics, "The Hickey Doo" and "If You've Nothing Else to Do." But that was as far as *The Blue Mazurka* traveled toward a production. For a reason buried in forgetfulness and history, although it acquired Colonel Henry W. Savage as producer, it lived and died in the autumn of 1921.

Perhaps one of the reasons was the work schedule of Plum Wodehouse. Out-Guying Guy, Plum had a more than overflowing platter that season; before leaving for America the previous spring, he had signed on with Fred Thompson and Ivor Novello for an Adelphi show slated to open in October. "I promised Fred Thompson I would work at it on the boat and I didn't touch it," he confessed to Leonora in a late August letter.[3] This project, plus his usual novel writing and short story writing, plus George Grossmith's suggestions that they collaborate on a follow-up show to replace *Sally* when it would, as all good things must, end its run at the Winter Garden, understandably overloaded the Wodehouse desk and mind.

*The Golden Moth,* as the Ivor Novello-Fred Thompson show was eventually called, was a happy experience. The creative team worked smoothly together; Plum had ascended to the level he would maintain for the rest of his career as one of the prime humorists writing in the English language; Ivor Novello was the most popular composer of the English stage—a title kept for the rest of his life, and beyond—and Fred Thompson was as much in demand as a librettist on the West End as Guy had become in New York; Adrian Ross, a journeyman lyricist, turned out journeyman lyrics. *The Golden Moth* opened to positive reviews and ran for a healthy 281 performances.

Plum now turned to the writing of the *Sally* sequel with George Grossmith. The plot was a virtual replay of *Sally*—an indication that Grossmith knew a good formula when he produced one. A rags-to-riches tale that traded its Greenwich Village first act for a Bond Street music publisher, its Long Island estate second act for an estate outside of London, and its Ziegfeld *Follies* third act for the cabaret which would give the show its title (*The Cabaret Girl*), it was a clone if there ever was one.

The similarities bothered Plum not at all; in fact, it was his opportunity to atone for being out of touch with *Sally* in 1920, and he plunged into the project with alacrity, no doubt getting chuckles out of naming the heroine Marilynn Morgan. The device may or may not have led Marilynn Miller to drop the affected, extra *n* in her first name that year.

Grossmith, Plum, and Ethel arrived in New York in March of 1922 with enough of a script to convince Jerry to write the score. Not only would Jerry do it, he would, he decided in a devilish moment, use "Ka-lu-a" to serve as the wordless centerpiece of the third act. Cheated out of that by Ziegfeld's bringing in Victor Herbert's "Butterfly Ballet" in *Sally,* Jerry would have the final note and thumb his nose at Fred Fisher besides.

That spring, Plum and George Grossmith stayed at Jerry and Eva's home in Bronxville, while they readied *The Cabaret Girl* for its late summer opening. They must have worked fast; by June 27, Plum was back in London and writing to William Townend about his current, breakneck schedule: He was beginning another series of stories for the *Strand,* with Ukridge as the chief character, and he was busily tearing apart and putting together *Leave It to Psmith,* whose "MS is all anyhow," he confessed to Townend.

"I have now contracted to finish a novel, six short stories and a musical show with Guy Bolton, by the end of October," he went on. "By the way, am off to Dinard on July 15th. Probably only for a fortnight, or three weeks, as rehearsals of *The Cabaret Girl* . . . begin in August."[4]

It was just the sort of life Plum loved at that moment, he recalled much later. "Popping in and out of managers' offices . . . what fun!"[5]—he wrote to Ira Gershwin when he recalled the 1920s. He loved it almost as much as working and living on Onslow Square, whose only disadvantage was its traffic, which sometimes threatened his ubiquitous pekes. "The puppy was run over by a motor bike the other day and emerged perfectly unhurt but a bit emotional," he wrote to Townend. "We had to chase him half across London before he simmered down. He just started running and kept on running till he felt better."[6]

It was a perfect reflection of the actions of both Jerry and Plum in the summer and fall of 1922. *The Cabaret Girl* went into rehearsal in mid-August, with a stellar staff: George Grossmith directed; Jack Haskell staged the dances; the cast starred Dorothy Dickson, fresh from the just-closed *Sally;* the rest of the list of principals consisted of tall comedienne Heather Thatcher and the rollicking riot from the Gaiety Theatre, Leslie Henson.

Jerry arrived by the first of September, and Grossmith announced the opening for September 14. Energetic, whimsical, his fine eye for detail as sharp as it would ever be, Jerry threw himself into the midst of the action, while Plum retired to the back of the darkened auditorium, proferring selected and softly phrased suggestions now and then. It was a good collaboration, not perhaps as warm as that between Plum and Guy, but considerably smoother, in Jerry's eyes, than it had been when the three of them had worked together. Then again, West End productions were considerably more genteely produced than those on Broadway, and George Grossmith was neither a Ray Comstock nor a Florenz Ziegfeld.

The Winter Garden was akin to the Princess in its sophistication and the glamour of its white-tied, bejeweled and begowned audiences. And it was its practice to open its shows without tryouts. *The Cabaret Girl* broke this tradition only slightly, when, on the morning of opening night, Leslie Henson fell ill and a replacement, Norman Griffin, was rushed in. The rehearsal period was extended for three days, and the show opened on Monday, September 18, to cheers and critical acclaim.

"Honestly, old egg," wrote Plum to Leonora, "you never saw such a first night. The audience were enthusiastic all through the first and second acts, and they never stopped applauding during the cabaret scene in act three—you know, the scene with no dialogue but all music and spectacle. . . . Grossmith was immense, so was Heather Thatcher. As for Dorothy Dickson, she came right out and knocked them cold. . . . Jerry's music was magnificent. Every number went wonderfully, especially 'Dancing Time.'"[7]

It was, then, a solid success, and although Jerry once again used some worked-over numbers from *She's a Good Fellow* and *Good Morning Dearie* ("Ka-lu-a" was performed, probably on legal advice, without the questionably original accompaniment figure), his score was noticed, and the notices were positive, often ecstatic. The show would run for 361 performances at the Winter Garden, just 26 shy of *Sally*'s total, and would spawn a second company for the provinces.

While all of this was unfolding, Guy was busily getting himself into trouble in America. With the collapse of *The Blue Mazurka* and with Marguerite determined to remain in Paris for the foreseeable future, Guy returned to Great Neck to an empty home but a full docket of career possibilities.

Peggy was sent for by Marguerite and would soon join her for the greater part of her childhood and adolescence. It would be a turbulent and glamorous growing-up period for Peggy, populated by the greats of the literary and artistic world. Marguerite would only return to the United States for visits, as would Peggy, for the rest of their lives. From that point forward, both mother and daughter would join an international whirl of world figures including Picasso, Monet, Debussy, D'Annunzio, Hemingway, Fitzgerald, and always and inevitably, Isadora Duncan. It was at this period that the king of the Belgians presented Marguerite with the Roulotte, a kind of rolling, five-room, rosewood-lined trailer, outfitted with, among much fine furniture, scores of satin pillows which were constantly sprayed with perfume by Coty, donated by that house to the lovely diva of the Opéra Comique.

By the beginning of 1923, Marguerite and Harry Lochman, an American painter of great talent and charm, had moved in together at 6 rue de Val de Grasse, near the Luxembourg Gardens, and Peggy would, shortly thereafter, begin a long series of stints at boarding school in Montreux, Switzerland. For all intents and purposes, the marriage was over, although Guy would arrive in Paris from time to time over the next two years, and Marguerite would discreetly hide the fact and person of Harry Lochman as she and Guy spent long and amorous afternoons together in the living room and then the bedroom at 6 rue de Val de Grasse.[8]

For a while, the two would play at marriage again, but gradually they drifted into a respectful friendship, the sort that might have formed the basis of a marriage had the two been other people. But they were not. Each had a need for and a dependence upon the applause and the ministrations of others. And since neither had much knowledge of *giving* applause and ministrations, their relationship became a Mexican standoff.

So, Guy once again flipped his famous internal switch and turned his attention to work and playing the debonair bachelor. The musical to which Plum referred in his letter to Townend was a proposal by Ziegfeld to write another Cinderella musical, again trading on the *Sally* formula, possibly with the trio of musical fame as the creators.

Jerry was busy with both *The Cabaret Girl* and *The Bunch and Judy* and had little appetite to subject himself to another season with Ziegfeld. Plum was busy with at least as much, but, as usual, the prospect of working with Guy outweighed common sense, and he agreed. Ziegfeld brought in young Vincent Youmans, whose *Two Little Girls in Blue* had been one of the larger successes of the 1920–21 season. Critics had agreed that although the composing chores for the show were divided between Vincent Youmans and George Gershwin — with lyrics for all of the songs supplied by Ira Gershwin under the pseudonym Arthur Francis — it was the Youmans music that was best.

The contract was signed, but before work could begin on the Ziegfeld musical, Guy was obliged to finish work on *Daffy Dill,* a Frank Tinney musical with music by Herbert Stothart and lyrics by a tall, soft-spoken, gentle giant named Oscar Hammerstein II.

This future icon of the American musical theatre had made his debut as a lyricist and colibrettist in two shows in the 1920–21 season, *Tickle Me* and *Jimmie.* Both had Herbert Stothart scores; both had lyrics and book by Oscar

Hammerstein II and Otto Harbach; both were produced by Oscar's uncle, Arthur Hammerstein. The first, a vehicle for Frank Tinney, was by far the more successful, chalking up a six-month run, and Arthur Hammerstein and Tinney hoped to repeat that success in the 1921–22 season.

Of course, it would have to be strictly a star vehicle for Frank Tinney, who, along with the other two blackface comedians of the 1920s, Al Jolson and Eddie Cantor, exacted only one stipulation from their librettists: that they allow the book to have huge holes into which each could sink his vaudeville routines. Jolson regularly threw away the book by 10:30; Frank Tinney was noted for doing the same thing in the middle of the first act.

Harbach was busy elsewhere; Arthur Hammerstein, no matter how much he loved his nephew, refused, probably at Frank Tinney's insistence, to trust him with the sole job of creating both libretto and lyrics, and so he hired the more experienced and older Guy Bolton.

The book that Guy and Oscar Hammerstein ground out was pathetic, even for the 1920s. It dealt with a *Sally*-like character named Lucy Brown who runs a lingerie shop which abuts a sports shop run by Daffy Dill-Tinney. The lingerie shop allowed the chorus girls to run around in nothing much; the sports shop allowed Tinney to do his standup and juggling routines with sports paraphernalia and to deliver some very Guy Bolton-ish, antimarriage routines, such as trying to sell a pair of boxing gloves to a prospective bridegroom.

There were enough production numbers, directed by Julian Mitchell, to flesh out a revue; the sets included such diversities as The Old Watering Hole and A Millionaire's Hideaway described in the script as a "Chinese bungalow." Guy utilized a two-page, windup, let's-get-married finale straight from the Princess, as well as Jackie's description of the rules of football from *Oh, Boy!*, "Use no hooks an' bury your own dead."

It hardly mattered; what truly mattered was that he make space for Frank Tinney. And this sometimes reduced the writing to its barest essentials, perhaps to match the costumes of the chorus girls. The entire fourth scene of act 2 in the script reads:

TINNEY AND GIRLS
PIANO SPECIALTY

There really wasn't much for a librettist to do, and Guy did little and grew restless, and that was a sure formula for trouble for him.

On the day of dress rehearsal, Oscar Hammerstein, as trusting and straightforward as Plum, confessed that his wife Myra was afraid of being left alone in the Hammerstein home in Douglaston, Long Island, near Great Neck. Guy confessed that he was sick of the show already, couldn't abide watching another minute of it, was going to skip the dress rehearsal, and would be happy to drop in on Myra and the kids and keep them company until Oscar got home from what looked like an all-nighter.

Oscar agreed; Guy called on Myra; and so began an affair which would, in part, account for the dissolution of the Hammerstein marriage. In all fairness, Guy wasn't Myra's first love outside of wedlock. But Oscar, when he learned of it, was devastated. He was too gentle a man to chase Guy with a revolver, as Frederick Toye had purportedly done, and anyway, Guy was only passing time; Myra was no Marguerite. But the immensely sensitive young lyricist never quite forgave himself for allowing it to happen. In notes he later made for an unrealized autobiography, he wrote, "Great need—False values—my fault as well as hers. I am an idiot but work hard."9

*Daffy Dill* opened on August 22, 1922, at the new Selwyn Apollo, and Alan Dale in the *American* put the critical reaction into a succinct little bundle: "'Daffy Dill' is a Summer show, designed for people with warm weather intellects," he said. "It is an entertainment presided over by Frank Tinney in very BLACK type and Georgia O'Ramey in smaller type. These two come on and do turns of the vaudeville length, and when they are off stage girls gyrate and chirrup; an attenuated and palsied plot befuddles those who try to fathom it, and—well, there you are."

The show lasted nine weeks, which was slightly less than the duration of Guy's affair with Myra. And it would be the one and only collaboration—for very good reason—of Guy and Oscar Hammerstein II.

It had not been an especially joyful autumn for Guy. At the same time that Jerry was being sued for plagiarism by a former collaborator, Guy received a letter from George Middleton, which Guy construed as a charge of plagiarizing the plot of *Polly with a Past* for *Sally.*

The note stated, in the mildest sort of language, that some friends of George's from the Authors League had advised him that there were "to them . . . curious resemblances to Polly. . . . With some reluctance I went to Philadelphia yesterday," he continued. "After seeing Sally I feel you and I had better have a little heart to heart talk about her past. That seems the most sensible thing for two old friends to do first, dont [sic] you think?"10

Sitting down at his desk at Kensington, in a fine dudgeon—which probably

indicated the state of mind in which he had been since his return from Europe—
Guy laboriously laid out the two plots and their premises, side by side.

"If you see any resemblance between these two plots and feel like suing me,
go ahead," Guy wrote, heatedly.

> I had supposed neither our old friendship nor our promise of future collabora-
> tion was to be ended by an unpleasant lawsuit but I can certainly see no hope
> for any other result if you imagine I am the sort of man who would deliberately
> steal anything that in any way belongs to you. The only explanation I can find
> for all this letter of yours lies in the fact that SALLY uses the line about
> Paraguay and Uraguay which I wrote in POLLY after previously using it
> regarding the similar character of the siren, Senorita Estrada, in NINETY IN
> THE SHADE. There is also a scene at the end of Act I in which Sally dresses
> up in Rose's cloak and uses the Russian accent which, of course, resembles the
> one in which Polly is dressed up and uses the French accent. I need scarcely
> remind you that this scene was not original with us and the idea that you
> would write me such a letter on the basis of this one incident is preposterous.
>
> Wodehouse and I are constantly using little scenes and bits of business
> which are from the common store of our collaborations and I cannot under-
> stand a fellow-worker being ungenerous about such a matter. . . .
>
> I trust upon reflection you will see that your accusation is highly offensive
> and will forget your letter as I shall. In that event, I shall be most happy to
> lunch with you as if nothing had happened. If not, my lawyers are Messrs.
> O'Brien, Malevinsky & Driscoll, No. 1482 Broadway, New York.
>
> > Your sincere friend,
> > Guy Bolton

Apparently, Middleton thought better of the whole affair, and four days later
the clouds parted and Guy dashed off a cheery invitation for George and his wife
Fola to come out to Great Neck for lunch. "Sorry I lost my temper but I did
think you might have asked me about SALLY instead of chasing off to Philadelphia like that. However, never mind," Guy wrote, and then perhaps to smooth
it all over, enthused about a project that would not reach fruition for six years:

"I'll tell you what I was thinking," he went on. "Supposing I make a musical
comedy on the POLLY story. I think there's a good one there and God knows I
can place it. That ought to square things up for since I shall get royalty on
writing it, I'll see you get the lion's share for the original. I can't do it
immediately as all my work has come at once but the smoke of battle will be
cleared away by January first."[12]

The smoke to which Guy was referring came from three simultaneous fires: first, there was the Ziegfeld musical with Plum and Vincent Youmans; then, there was a straight play idea that Guy had sold to Winchell Smith, as a starring vehicle for Genevieve Tobin; and finally, there was a musical called *Sitting Pretty* that he and Plum had already turned into outline form. They had done all of this during the late spring or early summer of 1922, while Guy was still in Europe and Marguerite was completing a three-concert series at the Albert Hall in London.

Working feverishly at Plum's Onslow Square flat, they were in a flush of excitement over an unusual prospect: *Sitting Pretty* had been broached by Guy to none other than Irving Berlin's partner, Sam Harris, as a vehicle for the Duncan Sisters, twins who were international vaudeville sensations.

"The Duncan Sisters," Guy and Plum would recall merrily in *Bring on the Girls,* "were two small girls who created the impression of being about twelve years old. Their names were Rosetta and Vivian, though their friends, and their friends were legion, called them Heim and Jake. Their forte was the delivery of numbers like 'The Bull-Frog Patrol' [a song Jerry had written for them three years before in *She's a Good Fellow*] in close harmony, and they were — there is no other word — terrific."

The way the two remembered it, the Duncan Sisters were, in 1922, appearing in *Pins and Needles,* a revue at London's Royalty Theatre, and he and Plum broached the idea of the new show to them backstage at that theatre. "They looked like something left over from a defunct kindergarten," wrote Plum and Guy.

They were anything but. They drove a hard bargain, and the fact that Irving Berlin had consented to write the score apparently convinced them that they'd love to do the show.

Berlin, like so many theatrical giants both then and now, respected Plum's lyrics enormously. He agreed to break precedent and let Plum supply some of the words to his music. It was an exciting prospect.

Now, in the mid-autumn of 1922, wires began to arrive like bullets from a machine gun. Ziegfeld was at it again, and he wanted Guy and Plum in New York, working with Vincent Youmans on his musical. Immediately.

They obliged, boarded a ship for America, and Plum moved in with Guy at Kensington. The two knocked out the script for the Ziegfeld show in short order. And then, as suddenly as they had begun to pile up, the wires from Ziegfeld stopped.

On December 16, Plum wrote, in exasperation, to William Townend,

Life has been one damned bit of work after another ever since I landed here. First, Guy Bolton and I settled down and wrote a musical comedy — tentatively called *Pat,* a rotten title — in two weeks for Flo Ziegfeld. It has been lying in a drawer ever since, Ziegfeld having been busy over another play, and doesn't look like getting put on this year. This, I should mention, is the play Ziegfeld was cabling about with such boyish excitement — the one I came over to do. You never heard anything like the fuss he made when I announced I couldn't make the Wednesday boat but would sail on the Saturday. He gave me to understand that my loitering would ruin everything. [13]

Not to let any moss grow on his northern extremities, Plum plunged into finishing *Leave It to Psmith,* which the *Saturday Evening Post* had agreed to serialize. He told Townend he managed 40,000 words in three weeks, a not unbelievable amount, considering that he and Guy were also working on *Sitting Pretty* and, as Plum continued to Townend, "This is complicated by the fact that Guy's new comedy has just started rehearsals, and he is up to his neck in it."

The new comedy was called *Polly Preferred,* and this time, the Polly of the title is an out-of-work chorus girl made so because one of the backers of the show has a girlfriend who is taking over her two lines. Proud Polly (Genevieve Tobin) quits rather than remain silent. In an Automat, drinking coffee with her pal Jimmie (Beatrice Nichols) she encounters Bob Cooley (William Harrigan), who hits on the idea of selling shares of Polly — common and preferred — to form a movie company whose star will, of course, be Polly.

From there on, it's a fast-paced satire of Hollywood, (one of her first films is *Joan of Arkansas*) with a bathetic love affair thrown in. Constructed like a musical comedy, in seven scenes and two acts, its lines sound like musical comedy dialogue, too. Jimmie, the wise-cracking comedienne, replies, when asked if she was ever in love, "I was in love . . . once — only he would forget and call me by his wife's name!," and when a prospective buyer asks Polly "Miss Pierpont, you're pretty anxious to have this project financed, aren't you?" she chirps, "You mean, 'Does Polly Want a Backer?'"

Directed by Winchell Smith and produced by Ray Comstock and Morris Gest, *Polly Preferred* opened at the Little Theatre on January 11, 1923, and met with high critical approval and large audiences. And a lawsuit — a real one this time, from a man who had no interest in either having lunch with Guy or doing a musical with him.

It seemed that in early 1921, Ossip Dymow, a Russian playwright, submitted a translation of his play *Personality* to Guy, with the understanding that Guy would adapt it for production. Guy held onto the play for several months and then returned it to Dymow, stating that he didn't find it suitable.

And then, *Polly Preferred* appeared, with a plot that was suspiciously parallel to *Personality.* Dymow wrote again to Guy, this time demanding a share of the royalties. Guy wrote back, in a style similar to his indignation over George Middleton's mild inquiry, and Dymow replied with a lawsuit for plagiarism.

In the summer of 1924, the case went into Eastern District Court. Guy was represented by Moses Malevinsky, who paraded a lineup of playwrights including Winchell Smith, Channing Pollock, and Arthur Richman for the defense, but the judge decided in Dymow's favor. Guy, Comstock, and Gest appealed the case, and early in 1925, U. S. District Judge Edwin L. Garvin ruled that the plagiarism was "unconscious." Nevertheless, he awarded Dymow $100,000 in royalties.

Meanwhile, Jerry was having troubles of his own, though his were in the court of public opinion. On November 6, 1922, *The Bunch and Judy* began its out-of-town tryout tour at the Garrick Theatre in Philadelphia. In book trouble from the beginning, it underwent such wholesale libretto overhaul that its tale of a musical comedy star who marries a Scottish lord, is snubbed by his snooty friends, and returns to her true love in the States, was ultimately buried under a barrage of specialty acts and production numbers. A tacked-on third act set in a cabaret was even hauled in, in imitation of *Sally* and *The Cabaret Girl,* but it merely baffled audiences.

Not even the charismatic presence of Adele and Fred Astaire, fresh from their last season triumph in *For Goodness Sake,* in which Teddy Royce originated their trademark circle dance, could rescue the show. It opened in New York at Dillingham's Globe Theatre on November 28, 1922—a one-day postponement to try one last panic job of fixing—to decidedly mixed reviews.

Adele Astaire, playing the Judy of the title, came in for a fair share of plaudits, as did the dance numbers with her dapper and dauntless brother. But Jerry's score received scant attention, and that was, for him, negative. Even Alan Dale, a longtime advocate, noted sadly in the *American* that "although the worst of his music was perhaps better than [that of] many of his colleagues, it was a disappointment. It lacked the original phrases and the quaint mellifluous ideas that this composer used to put forth so agreeably."

Dillingham closed the show after sixty-three performances, and for the rest of that season, Jerry had to be satisfied with a desultory interpolation in *Rose Briar,* a Booth Tarkington comedy starring Billie Burke and produced by Florenz

Ziegfeld. "Love and the Moon" with a lyric by Booth Tarkington was heard far longer than the score for *The Bunch and Judy*.

Later that winter, Jerry almost involved himself in another lawsuit, but cooler heads prevailed before it came to pass. That September, *Sally, Irene and Mary*, a Shubert-produced, deliberate takeoff on a trio of hit shows of the 1920–21 season, rankled the sensibilities of the Vanderbilt Producing Company, the producers of *Irene*. They approached George M. Cohan, who had written *Mary*, and Ziegfeld to join them in a lawsuit against the Shuberts. Neither producer was interested in pursuing it, no doubt seeing beyond the trees of a lawsuit into the forest of good publicity that such an obvious takeoff of their successful productions could bring.

The show, an expansion of Eddie Dowling's act in a prior New York Winter Garden show, did have a lot of *Sally* in it, including Mary's last line. "They're waiting for us at the Little Church Around the Corner." But it was a good-natured spoof, and audiences loved it enough to sustain it for the entire 1922–23 season. Even when Ziegfeld changed his mind and tried to whip Jerry into joining him in reviving the lawsuit, the composer demurred.

And yet, from that point onward, Jerry would harbor an abiding dislike for the Shubert Brothers, who were not among Broadway's best-loved personalities anyway. Marguerite, earlier on, delivered her opinion of J. J. Shubert, when he tried to soft-talk her to his casting couch, with a roundhouse punch that sent him sprawling and a scratch on his face that he would carry for days as a reminder of her standards. But Jerry's aversion to the brothers was more profound and long-lasting. There was something morally reprehensible about the Shuberts, something beyond crass. Jerry was a man who thought and felt deeply about much. He loved and hated, accepted and rejected, forgave and did not forgive with great certainty. He was extremely complex, and it was no secret that the musicals with which he was faced in the early 1920s were much simpler than he was.

His next project again put him in partnership with Plum and George Grossmith, again at the Winter Garden, and again with the same basic rep company that had turned *Sally* and *The Cabaret Girl* into long-playing gold mines.

After a short vacation in Palm Beach, he joined Plum to begin work on the music and lyrics of a show titled *The First Prize*. Plum was still living with Guy in Great Neck, (Ethel was in Paris with Leonora), and he and Jerry worked in the winter of early 1923 at Bronxville, where they could gaze, in their rare moments of repose, across its terraced yard at the placid, frigid hills of Westchester County.

In a piece published in the *Strand* in 1929, Leonora offered some insight into the way the two labored:

> A thing that has always amazed me about Plum is his ability to write lyrics, set them to music, and to carry a tune in his head that he had probably only heard three or four times. He's not a bit interested in music and can't play a note. Tosti's "Good-bye" and "Red-Hot Mamma" would sound exactly alike if hummed by Plummy, and neither of them could be recognized. . . . But in spite of this, at the back of his mind the tune is there; with no knowledge of music he recognizes the rhythm, the short beats and the long beats. . . .

That and his writing of fiction were the easiest parts of Plum's winter in America. Writing to Townend that December from Great Neck, Plum complained,

> We are having the devil of a time over the Duncan Sisters show. All attempts to get hold of Irving Berlin about the music have failed. We went into New York last Monday to keep an appointment with him and found that he had had to rush off to the dentist. He then made a date with me over the phone to lunch with him on Thursday and work all the afternoon. I went in and called at his flat and he was out and had left no message. Heaven knows when the thing will ever be finished![14]

*Sitting Pretty* was put off until October, to allow Berlin and Harris time and space to ready their second *Music Box Revue,* and so Plum poured his considerable energies elsewhere. He, Ethel, and Leonora took a place in East Hampton, considerably further out on Long Island than either Great Neck or Bellport, or even Quogue of "Bungalow" fame. There, Ethel entertained, while Plum and George Grossmith worked on *The First Prize* in other, more private parts of the house.

At the beginning of August, they returned to London, were joined by Jerry, and rehearsals for *The First Prize* got under way at the Winter Garden. Not only were Dorothy Dickson, Leslie Henson, Heather Thatcher, and Grossmith himself in place in the cast, but the vast majority of the chorus girls were there in the worklight-lit cavern of a theatre, bucking and winging it to Julian Mitchell's directions.

By the end of August, the show had been renamed *The Beauty Prize,* and it opened on September 5, 1923, again without a tryout. The show was a success, though the critics either ignored Jerry's score or noted, as the *Daily Mail* correctly did, that it was "below the level of 'The Cabaret Girl.'" Still, they liked the book and the lyrics and were apparently unconscious of the fact that "A Cottage in Kent" was baldfaced self-plagiarism, a transparent transplantation of "Bungalow in Quogue" to the British Isles.

But Plum wasn't waiting around for notices, good or bad. He and Ethel sailed for America the day *The Beauty Prize* opened to rejoin Guy in Great Neck and to finish work on *Sitting Pretty.*

Jerry stayed on for another week, and then he too sailed back to New York, where a Dillingham vehicle for Fred Stone, *Stepping Stones,* with lyrics and book again by Anne Caldwell, was waiting for his return to go into rehearsal.

Plum, meanwhile, found Guy himself working on last-minute revisions on his second straight comedy without George Middleton, *Chicken Feed.* It was one of two plays Guy was bringing into reality, side by side, that summer. The other, in collaboration with Frank Mandel, was *Nobody's Business,* a story about the defense of virtue against male predators and the true artist defending himself against the business school of playwriting.

It never found a stage; the only evidence of it is the August 10, 1923, version, an actless five scenes that is rife with what must have been racing through Guy's mind that not very happy summer. The hero's curtain line could have been almost a confession: "There is no argument that can hold against love or against loyalty," he says. "Sixty years of living has taught me that a damn fool in love or a blockhead who's loyal can lick a wise man who is only sensible."

But the other play, *Chicken Feed,* which was a bucolic version of *Lysistrata,* did find a production under John Golden's aegis and with Winchell Smith again directing. It opened on September 24, 1923, at the Little Theatre, with Roberta Arnold, Marie Day, and Leila Bennett playing the wives who go on strike rather than accede to the unreasonable demands of their husbands. It was a play that, for three-quarters of its length, anyway, would have warmed the hearts of Marguerite Namara, Isadora Duncan, and Fola Middleton. But, in step with the times, Guy, in the final moments of the last act, caused the wives to come down with terminal cases of regret. "I don't want to show I'm clever at business — I don't care anything about that kind of success . . ." says Nell, who began the whole thing. "Romance! Real romance — is worth all the practical ideas in the world." And so, the mares returned to their stalls, with a little assist from the moonlight and the playwright.

The critics and the public accepted it as good-natured hokum; it ran for the rest of the season and was eventually sold to Fox Pictures, which gave it to Frank

Borzage to direct, and it was released in late 1926 as *Wages for Wives,* starring Jacqueline Logan, Creighton Hale, and Zasu Pitts.

While he was waiting for his best friend and best collaborator to circle and land, Plum played some golf, worked on the galleys for *Ukridge* and on turning the collection of more Jeeves stories into what would ultimately become *Carry On, Jeeves,* and took time to ruminate, however fleetingly, on recent news that first informed him that middle age, though not present, was in sight.

"Herbert Jenkins's death was a great shock to me," he wrote to William Townend that summer. Jenkins, who had published all of his British editions since 1917's *Piccadilly Jim* and whose house would continue to publish all of Plum's work for the rest of his life, had died suddenly in June. "I was awfully fond of him," Plum went on, "but I always had an idea that he could not last very long. He simply worked himself to death. . . . One used to wonder how long he could possibly carry on. He shirked his meals and exercise and concentrated entirely on work. You can't do it."[15]

On into his nineties, Plum would never eschew either regular meals or regular exercise, though his work output could have challenged and possibly surpassed that of Jenkins.

Now, while *Chicken Feed* was on its way to Broadway, disaster struck *Sitting Pretty.* The Duncan Sisters, not at all eager to wait around for the anticipated October opening, asked Harris for permission to appear on the West Coast in a little something they had written, called *Topsy and Eva.* The show, described by Plum as "a sort of comic *Uncle Tom's Cabin,*" turned out to be an instant, roaring success, which the two sisters weren't about to abandon. On they went to Chicago, in preparation for a late season entry into New York. *Topsy and Eva* would remain sold out in Chicago for forty-three weeks and open in New York in December of 1924, where it would enjoy a moderate success.

So, Harris lost the Duncan Sisters, and Irving Berlin lost interest in the project. It was a star vehicle, as he saw it, and without that vehicle's twin pilots, couldn't possibly fly.

Plum was inclined to agree with him, but Guy felt otherwise. Jerry had read their script outline in London that summer and had become excited by it, to the point of proposing that should Berlin back out, he would be interested in composing the score. That prospect—of once more uniting the trio of musical fame—was enough to sweep away Plum's doubts and send Guy to see Jerry.

And there in Bronxville, in the spring of 1923, it all came together again. The Princess musicals weren't history after all, as long as its creators were alive and willing to work with each other.

And the natural producers for this property in which Sam Harris was no longer interested? Who else but Comstock and Gest?

The two, not doing very well at the moment, leaped at the opportunity, which would have to wait while *Stepping Stones,* Jerry's current center of creative attention, played out its string. The show was a typical Fred Stone vehicle, in which the title had more to do with its star than the story, an eminently foolish and forgettable retelling in burlesque of the Little Red Riding Hood tale.

*Stepping Stones* would be remembered by audiences primarily for the debut and abrupt rise to stardom, as the opening night performance was being played, of Stone's seventeen-year-old-daughter, Dorothy. The young, arresting, and vibrant girl played Rougette Hood, pursued through two hours of acrobatics and comedy by Oscar Ragland, as Otto De Wolfe. Stone, as plumber Peter Plug, provided out-of-context interludes that demanded specialized music, which most of the public and many of the critics overlooked.

One who didn't was Alexander Woollcott, who pronounced the evening "abrim with sweet melodies by Jerome Kern." His favorite was an exquisite ballad, "Once in a Blue Moon," sung by a quintette that featured Evelyn Herbert, who reportedly possessed one of the purest, most musical voices on Broadway at the time. Unhampered by the vocal limitations of a Marilyn Miller or a Dorothy Dickson, Jerry was thus able to expand still further into the freer, more flowing and extended melodic writing that he would develop in the next three years.

Although Jerry gave his best song to Evelyn Herbert, he was as appreciative of the ascending star of Dorothy Stone as anyone else and presented her with no less than a piano as an opening-night gift. It was that sort of time for each of the members of the trio of musical fame. They were making that kind of money and were that much in demand. The public was, in fact, so familiar with them that, when the advance publicity emerged for *Sitting Pretty,* it contained only the phrase "Bolton and Wodehouse and Kern" as creative credit, and advance sales soared.

In Bronxville and Great Neck, the show now began to take its final shape. The trio worked together as smoothly as ever. In later years, Plum would recall misgivings over trying to cast the two leads with nontwins. Guy wanted the

Dolly Sisters to replace the Duncan Sisters, but they were unavailable. Attention turned toward individual performers.

Gertrude Bryan, called at the height of her career "an unexpected blend of Ethel Barrymore, Maude Adams, and Rebecca West,"[16] had retired early to marry. However, she let it be known along the Main Stem that she was ready to rescind the retirement. Jerry was her chief advocate, and although Comstock and Gest were less than enthusiastic—she didn't come cheap—they acquiesced, provided that Jerry could get her non-show-business husband to sign an agreement not to pull her out of the show for the length of its New York run.

Jerry got the agreement.

For the part of Dixie, the other twin, the trio suggested a round-faced, rising, and sprightly dancer-singer named Queenie Smith. Miss Smith had begun her career as a dancer with the Metropolitan Opera, had debuted on Broadway in 1919 in *Roly Poly Eyes,* and had garnered good reviews in 1923's *Helen of Troy, New York.* Comstock and Gest had no trouble signing her, and she brought the part to life delightfully.

Not so Miss Bryan. As soon as rehearsals began, the production team knew trouble was in the offing. Noted before her retirement for her cooperation, Gertrude Bryan had developed some Marie Cahill-style mannerisms and pro-ceeded to make life miserable for her fellow cast members and directors Fred Latham and Julian Alfred. When the show opened and Queenie Smith walked off with all the good notices, Miss Bryan resigned in a huff, and Eleanor Griffith was brought in to replace her. There were no regrets.

Guy and Plum's plot owes as much to Dickens as did Guy's title for *Nobody Home.* Uncle Jo, a very benevolent Fagin, has, as his private Oliver, a young fellow named Horace. They're principals in a burglary ring that insinuates itself into the hearts and estates of rich men by offering Horace up for adoption.

Just coincidentally, Mr. William Pennington, a very wealthy man, is in the market for a son and a daughter, and Horace fits the son bill precisely. And just coincidentally, the Pennington estate is next door to an orphanage, where two orphaned sisters, Mae and Dixie, have a habit of sitting on the wall between, pining to be Penningtons.

Horace falls for Dixie and hopes that Mr. Pennington will adopt her, but Dixie manages to ruffle Mr. Pennington's feathers and he picks May instead. May, meanwhile, has fallen in love with Bill, Mr. Pennington's disinherited real son.

The action moves in act 2 from an estate in Short Hills, New Jersey, to an estate in Florida. Bill, in the six months since act 1, has become a successful private detective, and Dixie a successful dress designer, who arrives from Paris to design May's party dresses. Uncle Jo still wants to steal the family jewels, but love has lent Horace a conscience, and he foils the plot in time for the final curtain. Even Uncle Jo finds love in a typical Princess finale that includes the signature Princess title in the last line—Bill turns to Mr. Pennington and exults, "Gosh, pop. When it comes to founding families, you're sure sitting pretty."

Guy and Plum plundered *The Rose of China* for some of the best quips of the evening. "Lower your voice," says Horace to Uncle Jo, and Uncle Jo replies: "I can't. I'm a tenor." And later, Horace gushes to Dixie: "You look good enough to eat," to which Dixie quips: "So does a golf ball to a goat."

In fact, it's not difficult to see why Queenie Smith made enough of a hit to drive Gertrude Bryan out of the show. Plum and Guy, realizing her gifts, gave her the best wisecracks of the evening. She cries so much from missing May, she gives herself rheumatism from sleeping in damp beds, and when she arrives at the Pennington mansion in Florida, she confesses that she's "as broke as the ten commandments."

Having written their favorite characters—musical comedy crooks—they set up situations in which the set pieces of the Princess days were given time and space, and Plum's penchant for interior rhymes was never in finer fettle. In "Tulip Time in Sing Sing" Uncle Jo reminisces about the good times he had there, as spring reminds him of his happy days,

> And the birdies every Spring sing:
> Aren't you coming back to Sing Sing
> Where you used to be so happy long ago?
> Oh I'd give a lot to go there
> Life was never dull or slow there
> Every night there was a concert or a hop.
> Or I'd sit discussing Coué
> With my old pal Bat-eared Louie,
> Quite the nicest man that ever slugged a cop.
> We were just a band of brothers,
> Each as good as all the others
> As the humblest sort of sneak thief you might rank,
> But when you'd been there a week, well
> You were treated as an equal
> By the high and mighty swells who'd robbed a bank.

In the other set piece, "Bongo on the Congo," Uncle Jo, Horace, and an old pal, Judson, reminisce about what they've never done. As inspired nonsense as Edward Lear or Lewis Carroll ever wrote, it contains some of Plum's most brilliant lyrics:

| | |
|---|---|
| HORACE: | Beneath the silver Afric moon, |
| | A few miles south of Cameroon, |
| JUDSON: | There lies the haven which you ought to seek. |
| | Where cassowaries take their ease |
| | Up in the Coca-Cola trees |
| | While crocodiles sit crocking in the creek |
| HORACE: | Though on some nearby barren height |
| | The heat's two hundred Fahrenheit, |
| | Down in the valley it is nice and cool. |
| UNCLE JO: | And yet I don't know why it is |
| | The girls of all varieties |
| | Wear little but a freckle as a rule. |
| ALL: | In Bongo! It's on the Congo! |
| | And oh boy, what a spot! |
| | Quite full of things delightful |
| | And few that are not. |
| | Have no misgiving, the cost of living |
| | Isn't cheaper anywhere. |
| JUDSON: | If wifie needs another frock, |
| | You needn't put your watch in hock, |
| | You simply tell a native Chief |
| | To pick a poison ivy leaf. |
| ALL: | In Bongo! It's on the Congo! |
| | And I wish I was there! |

Later in the same song, Plum had at his greatest adversaries:

> When Government assessors call
> To try and sneak your little all,
> You simply hit them with an axe
> That's how you pay your income tax. . . .

But the show went far beyond mere cleverness. Buoyed by the certainty of their shared fame, and at the peak of their powers, the trio was able to realize more fully than before Jerry's concept of verisimilitude. In no other show of theirs was there a greater equality and interdependency of book, lyrics, and music, and in no other show did Jerry put more demands upon Guy and Plum.

The exposition, a normally mechanical device given wholly to the librettist in the 1920s, was instead contained entirely in the opening chorus. The gardeners and Mr. Pennington set the scene:

GARDENERS:   Good morning, sir!
Since the dawn we've been astir!
For honest work
Is a thing we never shirk!

PENNINGTON:   I see my roses have
Been nibbled by greenfly, and I'd
Suggest you go and mix
Some arsenic or cyanide
And squirt it over them
Before the creatures try and hide!

His son Bill enters, and the girls, who know Bill but not his father, ask him:

GIRLS:   Say, tell me, who do you think
Is this forbidding old gink?
Shall we vamp the glum thing
With our smiles that win? . . .

BILL:   Why, Uncle, this is fine!
I hope you're fit!
Come on, girls, form a line
And shake his mitt!
You've often heard me speak
Of Uncle Will
Step up and meet the sheik
And get a thrill!
Why, he shouldn't get sore if I
Start taking a whirl
At trying to glorify
The American girl! . . .

Uncle Will does get sore, of course, and so the plot gets off to a running and dancing start.

In comes Judson, and we know all about him in six sung lines:

JUDSON:   This lovely garden
          Actually has a lake in it!
          My gosh! It's simply just
          An Eden with no snake in it!
          Oh gosh, we shall enjoy
          The cocktails which we shake in it!

Plum's greatest challenge was to accommodate himself to the extended, lusher lines of Jerry's melodies, his eschewing of standard measure counts, his experimentation with changing meters. The results were magical, in such songs as "There Isn't One Girl," in which Bill offers his opinion of himself and his past to the world while May listens in from the top of the wall:

> . . . There were lots of girls around
> But one and all they passed me by.
> Got married to some other guy!
> I'm so lonely, I don't know what to do.
> It's sad but it's true.
> There isn't one girl in the world for me,
> There isn't one parson who needs my fee!
> Oh, every day some lovely belle
> Is packing up to go and dwell
> In the Niagara Falls hotel,
> But not with me, but not with me! . . .
> . . . On every side I see a crush
> Of happy brides who smile and blush,
> And everywhere the ushers ush,
> But not for me, no, not for me!
> I needn't put oil on the old latchkey,
> For no one cares if I get home at three!
> For all the punch that march of Mendelssohn's has
> He might as well have written nothing but jazz,
> There isn't one girl in the world for me!

This is the trio of musical fame. (LEFT TO RIGHT) Guy Bolton, P.G. Wodehouse, and Jerome Kern, during the Princess Theatre years. The photo captures the nature of the partnership. Plum and Guy were inseparable. That the two are looking over photos of showgirls is in character for Guy, alien to Plum, unless the expression on his face is one of confusion. Jerry, on the other hand, was always his own man, a distinct and contemplative genius. It was his vision that shaped the Princess shows, the partnership, and the future of the American Musical Theatre.

(ABOVE, L TO R) Elizabeth Marbury and her close companion, Elsie De Wolfe. It was Bessie Marbury who convinced Ray Comstock to abandon his trashy Grand Guignol format at the Princess Theatre, and turn it into the birthplace of the Modern American Musical Theatre. Elsie De Wolfe gave the Princess productions much of their chic cache. Her second act interior scenes became the models for the redecoration of scores of New York City apartments.

Ethelind and Reginald Bolton, Guy's stepmother and father. For all of their lives, there was a mutual competitiveness, lack of communication and emotional deprivation between father and son.

(ABOVE)
George Middleton and Bolton at the beginning of their collaboration, which produced a spate of bright comedies between 1916 and 1920. The spate might have turned into a flood if Guy hadn't succeeded so well in such Princess musicals as *Very Good Eddie*, during which he met and courted Justine Johnstone (RIGHT) one of Ziegfeld's most unusual beauties. By the time she joined the cast of *Oh Boy!*, Guy was courting elsewhere.

(ABOVE) The Boltons' Great Neck manse, *Kensington*, at 12 Beverly Drive, with an equestrian Peggy Bolton, watched over by her nanny, Fraülein Alt. The gardens were the scenes of Sunday afternoon soirées in 1918, when the Trio of Musical Fame was at its peak. (BELOW) A rare moment of close repose for Marguerite, Peggy and Guy. Peggy rarely remembered her parents together; Guy, working at a pace that he would maintain for most of his 96 years, was usually locked away in his study.

(RIGHT) Marguerite, Peggy and Guy poised by the famous Roulotte, presented to Marguerite by the King of the Belgians, after she opened at the Opéra Comique in Paris. Peggy and Marguerite toured Europe in this elegant trailer, with its rosewood interior, suffused with the aroma of perfume by Coty, sprayed periodically on its cushions by the famous parfumerie. Guy only posed by it; he was rarely invited aboard.

(LEFT) Marguerite and Charlie Chaplin on deck during the action-packed Atlantic crossing of the *Olympic*, in 1920. Chaplin was smitten; Marguerite was flattered; Guy was abandoned.

(RIGHT) An early portrait of Namara when she was appearing with the Chicago Grand Opera Company. A remarkable beauty in any age, her willowy charm was in marked contrast in a time when opera sopranos were customarily of Wagnerian proportions. Small wonder that Caruso preferred her to most of his other divas.

(ABOVE) Peggy and Guy. (LEFT) Namara in her famous floor-length ermine coat and Bird of Paradise Hat. A law was passed in 1919 fining the wearer of a Bird of Paradise Hat $1,000 and allowing the police to remove it bodily. Marguerite of course ignored all of this, and appeared in the hat frequently.

The beach at Juan Les Pins in 1924.
Peggy, Mindret Lord and Namara
stayed with Zelda and Scott Fitzgerald
that summer at the Villa America.
(ABOVE) Peggy is in the foreground,
next to the real Madame Dubonnet,
before Sandy Wilson's *The Boyfriend*;
Mindret Lord and Namara are at the
right; Isadora Duncan leans against an
unidentified lover in the rear center.

(RIGHT) Namara and Isadora
Duncan pose in customary costume.
Shortly after this photo was taken,
Isadora Duncan died tragically and
senselessly on the Grande Corniche.
Namara was devastated.

(ABOVE) Namara with Claude Monet, in his studio in Giverny. Harry Lochman is to the right of Namara, an eminent but unidentified painter is sitting to the left of Monet, and Monet's three daughters are seated. Behind them all is the partially completed "Waterlilies" tryptich. (RIGHT) Plum, accompanied by Leonora (his beloved "Snorky") and Ethel, about to board the boat train at Waterloo Station.

(LEFT) Jerry, Betty, Steven (Betty's son by Artie Shaw), and Eva on the lawn at the Beverly Hills house in the 1930's.

(ABOVE) Betty and Jerry at poolside in Beverly Hills. Jerry was a warm and thoughtful father, constantly counseling, frequently challenging Betty's mind in sessions that invaded the early morning hours. (LEFT) Jerry, sporting one of his Crawford "Liberty" cravats and not looking at all happy about life at the Hotel Del Coronado.

(BELOW) A historic moment. The train that took the Gershwins west for the first time paused in Albuquerque, N.M. Taking time out from the marathon cardgames: Ira Gershwin, Lee Ephraim, Guy Bolton, Leonore Gershwin, Sidney Bernstein (later Lord Sidney) and two local children, coralled for authenticity.

Marion Redford, Guy's third wife and the mother of Guybo. While Marion and Guy battled, Guybo tried to reach both of them, even duplicating Guy's handwriting in a desperate, futile attempt to please his father.

George Gershwin, Guy and Ira Gershwin at the time of *Girl Crazy*.
They weren't quite that close.

Guy and Peggy at
Glyndebourne,
August, 1939,
toward the end of
his triumphant
time in England,
when he could
write no wrong.
Peggy obviously
inherited the
beauty of both of
her parents.

The Trio of Musical Fame in maturity. Their paths and fates crossed constantly. (ABOVE, LEFT) Jerry remained the master melodist of American Song, the visionary who saw beyond European Operetta and into the American Musical Theatre. (ABOVE, RIGHT) Guy remained on the fringe of fame, respected and remembered only by theatre people. Had he been able to capture the tragedy of his own life, he might have become a major playwright. (BELOW) Plum went on to increasing international acclaim, still caring only for solitude, Guy, Ethel, Leonora, his pekes and the time and space to write.

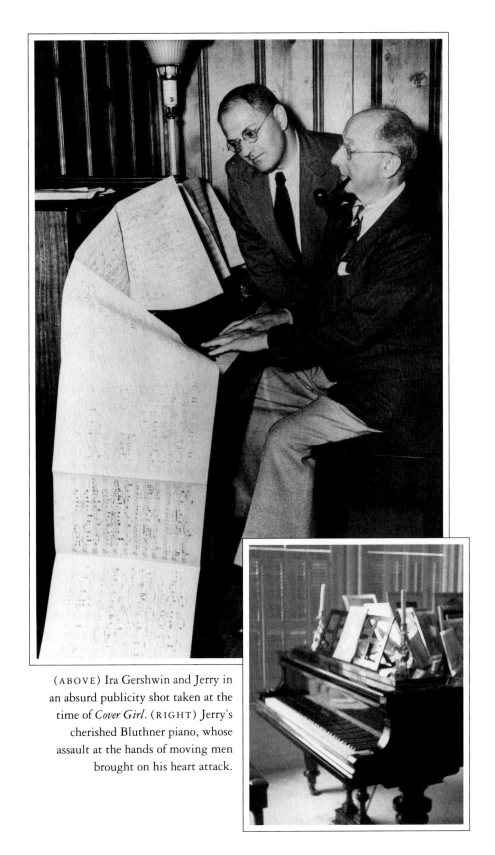

(ABOVE) Ira Gershwin and Jerry in
an absurd publicity shot taken at the
time of *Cover Girl*. (RIGHT) Jerry's
cherished Bluthner piano, whose
assault at the hands of moving men
brought on his heart attack.

It could be well argued that Ethel and Virginia were part of the force that allowed Plum and Guy to live into their nineties. Both loved and received the unquestioning love of these two superannuated gents as they spun out their final years. (ABOVE) Ethel thrived on elegance and an afternoon cocktail on their Remsenburg patio, overlooking her proper English garden. She was glamorous to the end. Virginia, on the other hand, (RIGHT) deteriorated markedly toward the end of her life, and her untimely death left Guy desolate and directionless.

The inseparables. There is no photo that better captures the relationship of Wodehouse and Bolton than the one above, taken by a local photographer in Westhampton when *Bring on the Girls* was published. Writing and dogs were their real first loves, and everyone and everything else had to take second chair for both. Playing rounds of golf, taking their daily walks through the Remsenburg woods accompanied by their pekes, the topic of their conversation was always writing—done, in progress, or coming up. It was a bond stronger than brotherhood.

Guy always thought of himself as a serious playwright who just happened to have a talent for libretti and comedy. In his later years, *A Man and His Wife*, (ABOVE) with Barbara Kinghorm and Emrys Jones and *Anastasia*, (RIGHT) with Viveca Lindors and Eugenie Leontovich consumed him. *A Man and His Wife* failed; *Anastasia*'s recognition scene became the best 17 minutes he ever wrote.

This is followed by an entirely underscored dialogue scene—a practice that Jerry had begun in earnest in *Zip Goes a Million* and which he was utilizing, more and more. Although Victor Herbert had used the device as far back as *Naughty Marietta,* it was Jerry who would extend and deepen its use until he created entire scenes in which dialogue and music and lyrics interwove like the threads in a garment. And *Sitting Pretty* created a particularly smooth weave.

There were echoes of the past, almost reprises of the best that the trio had accomplished. "All You Need Is the Girl" recalled the very first of the Princess shows, with the added P. G. Wodehouse charm:

> All you need is a girl,
> Just one dear little girl,
> Standing near you to cheer you
> When everything seems going wrong . . .

And *Miss 1917*'s "Land Where the Good Songs Go" was reincarnated in "Days Gone By":

> . . . Ghosts stand close at hand all the while,
> And watch with a smile,
> Tap time to the tunes which they too used to know
> Long ago.
> Dear gentle ghosts of bygone ages,
> Come back again from history's pages
> Softly and wistfully calling you seem
> Like a faint melody heard in a dream.
> Hid from our sight you stand and listen
> Watch us tonight with eyes that glisten
> Maybe you laugh at us, maybe you sigh,
> Dear vanished ghosts of days gone by. . . .

And finally, if Plum didn't have the Little Church Around the Corner to remind him of his past, he had a more mobile jogger of memory, the Long Island Railroad, where he had courted Ethel a decade before. While Jerry gave the song a glorious, driving melody, Plum recalled his courting afternoons with romantic reality:

It's quite a humble train you know
And some folks grumble that it's slow
It stops to ponder now and then;
The air inside needs oxygen.
It's not like some trains known to fame
But it's enchanted just the same
No train could be quick enough to suit me
When I'm coming back to you. . . .

Jerry would use the Magic Train concept to fashion an overture that dynamited the musical comedy tradition of stringing together a long medley of the tunes of the show to fill in the gap between early and late arrivals. But that was just the beginning. He experimented in attaching a melody described by conductor John McGlinn as one of "aching sadness" to a lyric of supreme optimism: "Bees in the clover will hum this refrain:/'Winter is over and spring's here again!'"

Even Robert Russell Bennett, the tall and slender and young heir to Frank Saddler's orchestrator's mantle, let informed whimsy have its inventive way, with Jerry's blessings. In the orchestration for "Shufflin' Sam," a high-kicking production number, themes from Dvorak's *New World* Symphony rose, like mountains in the mist, beneath the chorus's joyful singing.

It was arguably Jerry's best score to date, Plum's cleverest and most touching lyrics, and Guy's most finely tuned book. Comstock and Gest's publicity department crowed happily of the coming of "The Seventh of Their Series of the Princess Musical Comedies."

The opening, on March 23, at Detroit's Shubert Theatre, did nothing to dampen the enthusiasm of either creators or producers. The show did run long, and before it finally arrived in New York, it would lose six numbers, mostly to shorten it; but in one case—that of the title song—because of certain limitations of a cast member. Plum had included the phrase,

I want to sit,
Just sit and sit and sit
With you the whole day through. . . .

and concluded:

I want to sit
And hold your little mitt

On chairs that fit just two
For I'd give half the city
If I were sitting pretty,
Sitting pretty, little lady, with you.

Charming wordplay. But unfortunately, Dwight Frye, who, as Horace, would have to sing the song for it to work in the book context, possessed, according to Queenie Smith's recollections, "a slight speech impediment." Somehow, filtered through this, the repeated "sits" emerged as something totally different. And the song was cut.

The Detroit press was enthusiastic the next day, pronouncing Jerry's score "evenly excellent" and, much more to the point, "[music that] fit to the story instead of being dragged in whenever someone decides to break into song."

When the show opened at the Fulton Theatre on April 8, 1924, all the signs pointed toward a huge, Princess-style success. New York critics echoed the encomiums of Detroit. They reminisced about the old Princess shows and pronounced this one at least up to that standard, and possibly a bit better. The *New York Times* crowned Jerry "America's best writer of light music"; Burns Mantle praised Plum's lyrics, noting the joyous cleverness of the comedy songs and noting that "the love lyrics are soft without being mushy." Guy's book was called "workmanlike" and quoted at great length, revealing the fact that it was considerably more than workmanlike.

The box office was strong, but not spectacular. Jerry, in a move that has been interpreted as self-destructive and petulant but was probably neither of these, announced that he would not allow this, his best score to date, to be played in cabarets or recorded. He accompanied his prohibition with a long and somewhat rambling indictment of modern music practices:

None of our music now reaches the public as we wrote it except in the theatre. It is so distorted by jazz orchestras as to be almost unrecognizable. . . . The psychological moment has arrived not only for the revival of the tuneful, melodious and mannerly musical play which had its vogue several years ago with such pieces as "Nobody Home," "Very Good Eddie," "Oh, Boy!", "Oh, Lady! Lady!!" and "Leave It to Jane," but also for a revolt against the manner in which all music, even classic, is currently rendered through the sources which reach the popular ear. The public, through the cabaret and radio broadcasting, is not getting genuine music, only a fraudulent imitation. . . . The trouble with current popular musical rendition is that it runs everything into the same mold. . . .[17]

The fact that he managed to include the titles of all of the Princess shows in his diatribe indicates his real purpose was probably to boost box office sales. The fact that he greatly respected George Gershwin's emerging jazz style and would eventually write convincing jazz tunes himself bolsters this presumption.

But if that was his purpose, it backfired. Without the benefit of the new practice of popularizing a score and publicizing a show through phonograph records and performance by bands thumping away in the city's speakeasies, *Sitting Pretty*'s box office take began to dip dangerously. Within three months, the closing notice went up, and *Sitting Pretty* became a ninety-five performance flop.

It was a tragedy for many reasons and in many ways. At the end of May, shortly before *Sitting Pretty* closed, Jerry was called upon to act as an honorary pall bearer at the funeral of Victor Herbert. It marked the end of an era, the closing of the book on the beginnings of a native American musical theatre. Herbert had originated American operetta, and he publicly passed that mantle on to Jerry, who proceeded to originate something brand new: American musical comedy. He might have done it alone. But he chose to do it with Guy Bolton and P. G. Wodehouse. And as the trio of musical fame, they would all share in that historic founding.

But now the beginnings were at an end, and events and time were beginning to take over. Each of the members of the trio would continue to grow. Some of their greatest work, in fact, lay ahead; and so in 1924, *Sitting Pretty,* and the passing of Victor Herbert constituted more of a pause than a conclusion in each of their careers. But for the partnership that launched the American musical in its truest, purest form, it was the end of an act. The three would never collaborate as a team again, though their lives would intersect constantly in fascinating and fruitful ways. That their parting should be in sadness, with the too brief run of *Sitting Pretty,* was, perhaps, as it should have been written. All first acts in the musical theatre end with the principle players separating, sadly, but necessarily.

*Chapter*

# 16

# Entr'acte

## 1924–1927

For the rest of his life, Guy would complain to anyone who would listen that because of his commitment to *Sitting Pretty,* he was forced to give up an offer to write the book for *No! No! Nanette!* Vincent Youmans wanted him; Teddy Royce, who was directing, wanted him; Otto Harbach, in spite of Guy's peccadillo with Oscar Hammerstein's wife Myra, wanted him. But, after initially accepting the job, he found it impossible to continue and suggested Robert Benchley. Benchley turned it down, and Frank Mandel took it and rode it to a fortune that Guy envied. Or, so he said.

Asked by this author if these were the facts or another delicious raconteur's tale, Irving Caesar, *No! No! Nanette's* lyricist, replied, in 1985, "It's entirely plausible. If anybody wanted a librettist for a musical in the 1920s, the first person they thought of was Guy Bolton."

Guy had no shortage of offers in 1924. As soon as *Sitting Pretty* opened, he joined Plum on a ship for England, taking along the manuscript of a mystery play he had copyrighted in February under the pseudonym of R. B. Trevelyan. As in *The Light of the World,* Guy hoped that by hiding behind a false name, he could maintain his reputation as a writer of light and musical comedy. That same month, he had also bought the rights to a play by the Hungarian playwright Ernst Vajda, which translated roughly into English as *Grounds for Divorce*—just the sort of exercise at which Guy excelled.

But aside from a trip to Paris to spend two weeks with Marguerite, his main reason for sailing for London was to work on a new George Grossmith musical called *Primrose*. It was to be the new Winter Garden show—the first in two years without a score by Jerry. The why of it is buried in history, but responsible speculation might be that Grossmith recognized a rising star when he heard one, and he had been listening lately—as had many knowledgeable theatre men—to the music of George Gershwin.

Gershwin had had a terrible flop in London in 1923, a revue called *Rainbow,* which had, legend goes, been torpedoed on opening night by a vitriolic speech delivered by the comedian, complaining that Americans were taking over the London stage and making it tough for native Britishers to make a living.[1] *Rainbow* closed quickly, but back in New York, in February of 1924, Gershwin premiered his *Rhapsody in Blue,* wrote his first opera—a twenty-minute melodrama called *Blue Monday Blues,* which George White pulled from his 1922 *Scandals* after opening night—and had a success with 1924's *Sweet Little Devil,* book by Frank Mandel and lyrics by Buddy De Sylva.

So, when the 1925 Winter Garden show loomed, Grossmith hired George Gershwin. Desmond Carter was engaged to supply most of the lyrics, but George's brother Ira, finally shedding his *nom de poet,* Arthur Francis, was also brought in to provide the lyrics for seven of the eighteen Gershwin songs.

Despite some—as the papers reported—"booing from up aloft"[2] on opening night, *Primrose* was an enormous success, with its catchy music that included "Boy Wanted," "Naughty Baby," and a delightful duet called "The Mophams," done to an encore-demanding turn by Leslie Henson and Heather Thatcher.

Guy and George Grossmith collaborated on the book, which chronicled the misadventures of Hilary Vane (Percy Heming), a novelist who is loved by Joan (Margery Hicklin), a ward of a ratty neighbor who lives on the houseboat next to him, and of Pinky Peach (Heather Thatcher), a beautician in love with Toby Mopham (Leslie Henson), a playboy whose mother has installed a nightclub in her Park Lane mansion to keep her errant son home at night. The chorus girls, named by Guy Miss Tishy, Miss Toshy, Witch Hazel, Lady Kitty, Lady Katty, etc., were the only remnants of the Princess. It was a posh Winter Garden show, three-acts long and brimming with spectacle, and it ran to full houses through the West End season.

The relationship of Guy and the Gershwins was in for a considerably longer run. In London at the same time that *Primrose* was in rehearsal was the young producing team of Alex Aarons and Vinton Freedley. Aarons was the son of producer Alfred E. Aarons; Freedley was a former actor with a sizable inherited income. Their first and only production had been Cosmo Hamilton's *The New Poor,* and now they wanted the Gershwins and Guy to create a musical for the rising song and dance team of Fred and Adele Astaire. It would be the first Broadway show with all of the music and lyrics entirely by George and Ira Gershwin, and the two brothers leaped at it enthusiastically, as did Guy, who suggested Fred Thompson, Plum's collaborator on 1921's *The Golden Moth,* as his collaborator on the book. Aarons and Freedley agreed, the contract was signed, and once *Primrose* was launched, they all boarded a ship for a working crossing between London and New York.

The partnership appealed to Guy mightily. Fred Thompson and he got along beautifully—and would, for eight more shows. George Gershwin possessed the same kind of creative engine that drove Jerry, as well as the same nocturnal habits. And Ira, who took considerably longer to turn out lyrics than Plum, nevertheless had the same droll sense of humor, fierce talent at complex rhyme schemes, and what was most striking, the same soft and retiring nature as Guy's closest friend. The gentleness cloaked more steel than did Plum's, but it was essentially the same, and when the two met, a year later, they would form an instant bond that would remain for the rest of Plum's life.

On the boat, in September of 1924, the Gershwins and Guy began *Black-Eyed Susan,* as it was then called, while Aarons and Freedley worked the wealthy aboard for backing money. One of those caught in their snare was millionaire industrialist Otto Kahn, who was kindly disposed toward George Gershwin's music anyway, and told Aarons and Freedley that, with the kind of talent they'd already signed—Guy and the Gershwins and the Astaires and Walter Catlett, the hot-diggity-dog man from *Sally*—they didn't need his money.

However, George Gershwin was as persuasive a fund raiser as any producer, and installing himself at one of the ship's pianos, he played a ballad he'd written for the show called "The Man I Love," for Otto Khan.

"If that's going to be in the show, I'll invest in it," Kahn is purported to have said and promptly sat down and wrote out a check for $10,000.[3]

Ironically, "The Man I Love" never made it into the New York opening of *Lady, Be Good!,* as the show eventually became known, nor would it find a home in any Gershwin show. The tale is familiar by now of how it was tried in and discarded from both the 1927 and 1930 versions of *Strike Up the Band* and how at the same time Lady Mountbatten convinced her favorite dance band, the

Berkeley Square Orchestra, to play it regularly, causing it to become the sensation of Britain and the Continent, and how, again ironically, the song would experience its final rejection from a show when Marilyn Miller refused to sing it in *Rosalie*—a vehicle written by Sigmund Romberg, the Gershwins, Guy, and Plum.[4]

*Lady, Be Good!* opened in Philadelphia on November 17, 1924, and was an immediate success. Its story, about Dick and Susan Trevors, a brother and sister dancing team down on their luck and out of rent money, was a little like *Sally* doubled. But the opening scene, with the two tossed out on a Norman Bel Geddes street, surrounded by their belongings, drew immediate applause and delight every time the curtain rose.

The working out of the dilemma—Dick playing up to a rich girl, Susan impersonating a Mexican widow to gather an inheritance—bridged the space between the Gershwin songs in a snappy, crazy fashion that would earn Guy and Fred Thompson critical praise and the respect of George and Ira Gershwin.

The rest and best of the show were the music and the lyrics, from the title song sung by Walter Catlett to a flock of flappers, to "Little Jazz Band" done by Cliff Edwards as Ukelele Ike—a name he would adopt for the rest of a long career—to "Boy Wanted," plaintively sung by Adele Astaire, to "Fascinatin' Rhythm" danced to a high-flying climax, the Astaires' trademark circle dance, in which they whirled in ever-increasing circles until they disappeared offstage.

*Lady, Be Good!* opened on December 1 at the Liberty Theatre and ran for 330 performances, a healthy hit in any season. It would, more than any show so far, define the difference between operetta and contemporary, jazzy musical comedy. Jazz, in fact, came to Broadway to stay with *Lady, Be Good!,* as did the Gershwins.

The show would have a long life and be especially kind to Guy's pocketbook. It would eventually be filmed by MGM, in 1941, four years after George's death, with only three of the original songs — "Fascinatin' Rhythm", "Hang on to Me," and "Oh, Lady, Be Good!" Again, in one of those ironic circlings of fate, the most famous piece of music in that score, and one that would win the Academy Award for Best Song that year, was an interpolation: "The Last Time I Saw Paris," written a year earlier by Jerry and Oscar Hammerstein II. It was the only song Jerry ever wrote in which the lyrics came first and which was written not for a show, but for a city. And since it came about that way, Jerry, with great grace and honesty, refused the Academy Award.[5]

• • •

A day less than two weeks after *Lady, Be Good!* opened in Philadelphia, Jerry's entry in the 1924–25 season opened at the Times Square Theatre in New York. It would not be a show for which he would later be remembered, and yet it was important in a number of ways:

Convinced now that continuing to collaborate with Plum and Guy would be very much like rewriting echoes, he went in search of a new lyricist. His ideas of verisimilitude, he felt, needed a fresh voice to accommodate his constantly increasing demands and assiduously developing melodic moods. The lyricist and librettist would have to be rooted in the present and yet have the ability to interweave word and song in the same seamless way that Jerry heard it. Not only that; he or she would have to accurately reflect the expanded moods conveyed in the constantly more sophisticated music he was beginning to write. Of course the music was, in 1925, still developing, and there would be frustrations along the way to its realization.

During the run of *Sitting Pretty,* producer Philip Goodman approached Jerry. Goodman, a comrade in reputation to Colonel Henry W. Savage, was known to cow lesser personalities. The legend goes that Jerry presented himself in Goodman's office and before the glowering, formidable tyrant could utter a word, said, "Mr. Goodman, I've heard you're a son of a bitch, and you probably aren't; and you've heard I'm a son of a bitch, and I most certainly am!"[6]

Betty Kern Miller, whose recollections of her father are understandably of the most benign variety, dismisses the story as somebody's fiction. Her father wouldn't act that way, she avers. Others say the dialogue, which has undergone many revisions over the years, is plausible; Jerry was a man of many, many moods.

At any rate, the Goodman-Kern relationship began as and remained a tempestuous one, given its character early by Goodman's signing of Edgar Selwyn as librettist. Selwyn had been the coproducer of *Rock-a-Bye Baby,* and that show rattled loose anything but happy memories in Jerry. Selwyn had no previous credits as a librettist, but he had plenty of business pedigrees. The one that interested Goodman most was his ownership, with his brothers, of the Times Square Theatre, a perfect, inexpensive home for the show.

His suggestion of a twenty-eight-year-old journalist and publicist named Howard Dietz as lyricist was met with equal negativity by Jerry, who had somebody else in mind.

Noel Coward had returned to America, a little less broke than he had been the first time and a good deal more famous. *London Calling!* the previous year had given him a West End cachet, and he was in New York with a new play, *The Vortex.* He admired Jerry's work, which he had seen in London, and he became a regular visitor in Bronxville.

During one or more of the visits to Bronxville, Coward wrote two lyrics for two songs Jerry was writing for *Vanity Fair,* as the musical was then called, "My Morganatic Wife" and "Tamaran." They were apparently the only lyrics he would ever write for music not composed by himself, and they were apparently a disappointment to Jerry, who later gave them to Howard Dietz to rewrite. "My Morganatic Wife" never made it to the rehearsal stage; "Tamaran" became "Gypsy Caravan" and survived with Dietz's lyrics for the run of the show.[7]

Dietz himself was overwhelmed at being invited to work with Jerry. He recalled his first day in the Kern library at Bronxville, with its vast walls of rare books and the great Bluthner piano, in detail for Kern biographer Gerald Bordman.

Not given to getting underway before noon and then not ceasing to either compose, play cards, or talk until two or three in the morning, Jerry invited Dietz to catch an 11:22 A.M. train to Bronxville. Taxiing to the white-shingled, black-trimmed Kern home, Dietz was treated to a civilized afternoon with Jerry, who was attired in a brocaded smoking jacket and who confessed right off that he was going to use some old melodies that he had composed for England, but which had never been heard by audiences. Sending him off at 5:00 P.M. with the melodies, Jerry asked Dietz if he could deliver some lyrics in two days. The dazzled young journalist/publicist and now lyricist mumbled that he would.[8]

Bordman suggests that Jerry was bitter about the Gershwins and Guy being selected for that year's London Winter Garden show, and perhaps he was right. Certainly the fact that Jerry was working for Philip Goodman instead of George Grossmith must have rankled, and the stormy trip of *Dear Sir,* which *Vanity Fair* eventually became, from creation to opening night couldn't have comforted him. The shouting matches that took place between Jerry, Goodman, and Selwyn at Philadelphia's Ritz Hotel became so boisterous that eviction warnings were sent up repeatedly from the front desk.

Furthermore, bad omens and tragedy stalked the show from the beginning. A chorus girl broke her back and was crippled from the accident. Jerry arranged a special benefit performance for her of *Stepping Stones,* which was then on the road and slated to play in Philadelphia in January. Goodman refused to hire Jerry's preferred orchestrator, Robert Russell Bennett, and hired instead Allan

Foster, who, in all fairness, did highly praiseworthy work. And finally, at one point, Jerry became so frustrated over musical director Max Bendix's inability to handle the long phrases of his music that he dashed from the theatre and into a side alley, where he burst into tears. The next day, Bendix was replaced by Gus Salzer, who would continue to conduct Jerry's work for years to come.

Despite the turmoil he himself often created, Goodman didn't stint with the cast. Genevieve Tobin, Oscar Shaw, and Walter Catlett headed it (Catlett would join *Lady, Be Good!* after *Dear Sir*'s brief run). But somehow, the show never truly came together. Goodman closed it at the end of its second week and sailed for Europe, leaving behind a landscape littered with unpaid bills and an embittered Jerome Kern, who would treat Goodman with glacial coolness for a great many years.

The critics pronounced the music "beautiful," and some thought the show much in the Princess tradition. And Alexander Woollcott pronounced Dietz ". . . a most capable substitute for P. G. Wodehouse as lyricist in chief to Mr. Kern." But this did little to cheer Jerry that season.


Ethel Wodehouse, meanwhile, had done what any resourceful wife of a proper and successful British writer would do: she bought a fashionable house in Mayfair, at 23 Gilbert Street, facing onto Grosvenor Square. The two moved in, in October of 1924, and Leonora joined them soon afterward.

It was a furiously active winter, and Plum was not all that delighted to be working in the middle of London. Without doubt, Ethel was; it gave her ample opportunity to socialize and throw parties, two activities that Plum despised.

Still, his output was staggering. Along with turning out short stories for the *Saturday Evening Post* and the *Strand,* collecting Jeeves stories for a delightful volume titled *Carry On, Jeeves,* and completing the novel *Sam, the Sudden,* Plum longed for, but did not work in the theatre that year. The one man who could goad him into that was across an ocean, riding the crest of his glittering success with the Gershwins, and having his own troubles with his mystery drama, *The Dark Angel,* written under an assumed name.

The play finally opened at the Longacre on February 10, 1925, with Bob Milton, Guy's old director from the Princess days, directing and producing. Even before the opening, word was leaked, probably by Milton's publicity department, that the real author was Guy. And Alexander Woollcott's review, while largely favorable, confessed that the play was an odd patchwork that contained studied stretches studded with brightness. His conclusion was that it was really a collaboration between Guy and Michael Arlen, the wildly successful author of *The Green Hat*.

There's no evidence of this; it was just Guy allowing the two sides of him through: one, the ambitious playwright anxious to be taken seriously; the other, the comic master, at home and more comfortable writing clever fluff, but feeling, always, just a little bit guilty for doing so. These two shades of Guy would persist throughout the rest of his long life, and the buying of *The Dark Angel* — despite its lamentably short sixty-four performance run — prodded him to continue, Janus-like, leaving him forever fragmented and incurably ambitious.

Meanwhile, back in the Aarons and Freedley office, the two young producers were having growing pains. Seeking to capitalize on the wild success of *Lady, Be Good!*, they put the Gershwins and Fred Thompson back to work immediately. Guy, busy with *The Dark Angel* and a trip to Europe to be with Marguerite, was unavailable for the moment. The two refused to wait, hired William K. Wells to collaborate with Fred Thompson, hired Buddy De Sylva to be the Desmond Carter to Ira, and opened *Tell Me More* at the Gaiety Theatre on April 13, 1925.

It was a show all concerned with would try to forget. George Gershwin turned out not one notable melody; the score boasted such immediately interred numbers as "When the Debbies Go By," "In Sardinia," and "Ukelele Lorelei." All about a heroine who conceals her true, royal identity to parade as a shopgirl, it lasted for thirty-one performances in New York, but shipped to London as a vehicle for Heather Thatcher and Leslie Henson, it succeeded. George Gershwin went with it to supply two more songs, and when he returned at the beginning of the summer he had with him the beginnings of the Concerto in F.

Aarons and Freedley cared little for that side of George Gershwin. But realizing the folly of their haste, they reassembled the *Lady, Be Good!* creative team, with Guy in place and William K. Wells and Buddy De Sylva out, and put them to work on their next hit, *Tip-Toes*.

Their revised judgment was correct. Fred Thompson, like Plum and a long list of other musical libretto collaborators with whom Guy would work, supplied clever situations and lines. Guy did that and more: he was again serving as the architect, the master constructionist.

This time, he and Fred Thompson capitalized on the current Florida land boom, and set most of the musical in Palm Beach. The tale of the Kayes, a trio of vaudevillians headed by Tip-Toes Kaye (Queenie Smith) who are stranded penniless in the land of the outstretched palm, it chronicled their misadventures as they managed to work their merry way into high society. Before the first-act curtain, Tip-Toes was stuck on glue tycoon Steve Brighton and by the end of act 2 had married him.

This time, the Gershwin brothers, minus an extra lyricist, turned out a brilliant score, which included the expositional "These Charming People," the love duet "That Certain Feeling," the love song "Looking for a Boy," and the lovely, lively production number "Sweet and Low-Down," which included, among many marvels, a chorus of kazoos.

For once, Guy encountered somebody with a plate more full than his own. As rapidly and abundantly as Jerry composed, George Gershwin outran and outwrote him—as he did everyone. That December, no fewer than four of his compositions and/or scores were heard in New York concert halls or theatres. On December 3, 1925, his Concerto in F premiered at Carnegie Hall, with Gershwin at the piano and Walter Damrosch conducting the New York Philharmonic (then known as the New York Symphony). On December 28, at Carnegie Hall, Paul Whiteman performed Gershwin's twenty-minute opera from the Scandals, Blue Monday Blues, which was now retitled 135th Street. The next night, December 29, Tip-Toes opened. And the following night, his show with Herbert Stothart, The Song of the Flame opened. Guy was, then, with George Gershwin at the very moment that his energy and creativity were beginning to soar. No wonder Guy would say in future years, with no disrespect meant for Jerry or Plum, that George Gershwin was the one true genius with whom he worked.[9]

Tip-Toes was received with delight. Queenie Smith and Alan Kearnes came in for huge kudos, as did the flamingly redheaded, richly voiced Jeannette MacDonald, who had started on Broadway four years before in the chorus of Jerry and Anne Caldwell's The Night Boat. Since this was the period in which nudity was almost de rigueur in large Broadway musical comedies, every critic spent an inordinate amount of time on the chorus girls. The Times man opined that "'Hamlet in Modern Dress' was interesting because among other reasons, it was new. But 'Tip-Toes' in modern underclothes is fascinating." Still, they managed to notice that Guy and Fred Thompson's book was frothy, spicey, witty, and sophisticated.

The most telling praise came in a letter that Lorenz Hart, who with Richard Rodgers had just burst upon the Broadway scene with The Garrick Gaieties and was building upon Plum's heritage, wrote to Ira Gershwin. "Your lyrics," he wrote to the understated and softspoken Gershwin brother, "gave me as much pleasure as Mr. George Gershwin's music, and the utterly charming performance of Miss Queenie Smith. I have heard none so good this many a day. . . .

It is a great pleasure to live at a time when light amusement in this country is at last losing its brutally cretin aspect. . . ."[10]

That was the sort of praise that Jerry would have appreciated and for which he was now preparing himself. It probably infuriated him to read the glib pronouncements Guy gave to the *American* shortly after *Tip-Toes'* triumphant opening: "You don't derive the scenes from the plot," he said. "You see what good scenes you've got and use the plot as a bright ribbon to wrap them together."

"Has he forgotten everything we ever worked for at the Princess, and that we set so beautifully right in *Sitting Pretty?*" Jerry must have thought. "Is he unlearning what we learned so well?"

That's exactly what Guy was doing. From this point forward, he would be a good, journeyman librettist. Whatever the demands of the show, he would provide them, well and popularly. Jerry, on the other hand, stayed the course the trio had set and moved the American musical theatre forward in a direction that would forever carry his imprint.

By the time *Tip-Toes* opened, Jerry had already discovered the lyricist and librettist with whom he would ultimately enjoy his greatest successes and the fullest realization of his vision for the American musical theatre. Not that 1925 was a year of unalloyed success. He would have two humiliating flops that year — *The City Chap,* which preceded *Tip-Toes* into the Liberty and, in the same month, *Criss Cross.*

But it was the show that preceded them and cast them into a shadow that rendered these stumbles practically invisible and that marked yet another turning point in the career of Jerome D. Kern. That event took place sometime in the spring of 1925, when Otto Harbach, scholarly, reserved, and enormously successful (his first show, *Three Twins,* in 1908, with his lyrics — "Cuddle Up a Little Closer, Baby Mine" — to Karl Hoschna's music, had established him as one of Broadway's brightest lyricists), came to call.

In 1920, Harbach had been brought in by Arthur Hammerstein as the experienced tutor of young Oscar Hammerstein II, and by 1925, the two had collaborated on four shows, the most successful 1924's *Rose-Marie.* Harbach, who at the moment was basking in his considerable contributions to *No! No! Nanette!,* was in great demand. But his major reason for a journey to Bronxville that spring was to introduce his young protégé to Jerry.

It wasn't an overtly fateful convergence; it was once more Jerry at home in the library, greeting still another young lyricist graciously, owlishly sitting down at the piano and trying out a few trial tunes to test the younger man's mettle.

The examination was apparently passed; the three signed with Dillingham to perform a task that Jerry approached without much relish. Marilyn Miller, it seemed, had dropped not only the extra *n* from her first name but her long standing and turbulent relationship with Florenz Ziegfeld. She had offered her talents at making fortunes for producers to Charles Dillingham, and he had instantly accepted, casting her in a production of *Peter Pan,* for which Jerry had written two songs. Audiences, Dillingham reasoned, wouldn't stand for a Marilyn Miller Peter Pan who didn't both dance and sing.

The production hadn't caught on with the public, and Dillingham was desperate. If he didn't come up with a star vehicle for Miss Miller soon, she was ready to return to Ziegfeld. Could the three supply that vehicle, in short order?

They could, and they did, but it was going to cost Dillingham plenty. Acting upon Dillingham's suggestion, given to him by Marilyn Miller and given to her a couple of years earlier by Walter Catlett, he asked them to consider a circus theme, with Miss Miller as a bareback rider.

The two did, and so *Sunny* was born. Its concept delighted the diminutive but volatile superstar. Its myriad of scenes would encompass a circus tent, an ocean liner, a Long Island mansion, a fox hunt. Her costume changes alone would go on nearly forever.

Dillingham spared no expense. He hired Hassard Short and Julian Mitchell to direct, tap dancer Jack Donahue, the eccentric dance team of Clifton Webb and Mary Hay, comedians Joseph Cawthorn, Esther Howard, and Pert Kelton, and Cliff Edwards/Ukelele Ike, fresh from his triumph in *Lady, Be Good!* He budgeted the show at an unprecedented $500,000, which forced him to up the top ticket price from $4 to $5.

September, the month in which he had scheduled *Sunny* to open, would contain formidable competition: *No! No! Nanette!*, *Dearest Enemy,* and *The Vagabond King.* It would have to be special.

Jerry, Otto Harbach, and Oscar Hammerstein II worked together beautifully, with enthusiasm and rewarding results. It was the trio of musical fame raised to a higher, more complex power: Harbach's book, as outlandish as it was forced to be by its prehired stars (Ukelele Ike specified that his specialty was to be performed between 10:00 and 10:15 P.M. only) accommodated Jerry's concept of songs that were scenes in themselves. Oscar Hammerstein's lyrics were brilliant, rivaling Plum in their whimsy but containing the added dimension of realized romance.

Marilyn Miller breezed into New York at the end of the summer, fresh from a vacation in Europe with her husband, Jack Pickford, and a newly smitten lover,

Ben Finney. The legend of her first auditioning of the score, in which she supposedly listened in silence, then asked, "Where do I do my tap specialty?"[11] may or may not be true, though it is in character. What is undeniably factual is that she immediately swelled the production by bringing in both the "Marilyn Miller Cocktails" (eight long-limbed precision dancers trained by British dance-master John Tiller), and her old friend Fred Astaire to stage her tap specialty. The inevitable Miller dancing moment was tacked on to a song called "The Wedding Knell," which made the number a little longer than endless.

When *Sunny* first opened at Philadelphia's Forrest Theatre on September 9, 1925, it was greeted coolly by the local critics, who pronounced it "pretty puny"—a difficult feat, considering the grandioseness of its production, which also sported several live circus animals. Jerry's score, which included two of his immortal standards, the title song and "Who", was said to have "not a single catchy number or even haunting piece of melody throughout."

Either Philadelphia's critics had a bad night, or an enormous amount of work was done in the seventeen days between the Forrest Theatre premiere and opening night at the New Amsterdam in New York. On September 22, 1925, the New York critics and the New York audiences went justifiably crazy. It was Marilyn Miller as they remembered her from *Sally*—adorable, petite, blonde, fragile, magnetic. She'd made audiences gasp at Guy's singular opening for her in *Sally* as a little waif at the end of a line of orphans. Her entrance in *Sunny* brought different kinds of gasps.

This time, she was preceded by a baton-twirling drum major in a blindingly multihued costume, leading a sixty-piece brass band, which ushered on a long parade of clowns, acrobats, and freaks. A few times around the stage for them, and then, the lights dimmed, a fanfare blared, the spotlight hit a wing, and out rode Marilyn Miller, in shimmering spangles, atop a magnificent, prancing white horse. It got the audience into the habit of applauding, and they kept at it for the entire evening.

*Sunny* became the hit of two seasons, running 517 performances—53 less than *Sally,* but because of its higher ticket prices, equaling *Sally's* gross. Marilyn Miller would, as she had in *Sally,* remain for the run of the show. She had no tempestuous scenes with Dillingham; those she reserved for Jack Pickford, who had a few things over which to be angry. At several music rehearsals in Bronxville, Ben Finney showed up, remaining respectfully in a corner of the library, but making his presence nevertheless known. It was reported that Pickford arrived close to opening night gunning for him and that Finney thereupon bought a pair of dueling pistols and had them delivered to Pickford's hotel with the note, "My second, Jefferson Davis, will be around to see you in the morning."[12]

Evidently maturing away from the Great Glorifier, Miss Miller didn't treat Betty Kern as she had little Patricia Ziegfeld when Jerry brought her backstage to see her. Instead, she had copies of her clown costume made for Jerry's entranced daughter.

*Sunny* was, in a way, a watershed for Jerry. The collaboration with Otto Harbach and Oscar Hammerstein made all the difference. From that point forward, everything important that Jerome Kern would do on Broadway would include one or the other or both of these men.

While this was happening and while Plum was preparing *The Heart of a Goof* for publication, meeting his idol Sir Arthur Conan Doyle, and mulling over an offer to turn a Russian light opera into something fit for the West End, Guy was again getting into trouble.

The marriage with Marguerite had long since run its course; Guy's wandering eye had settled on a high-spirited, red-headed dancer named Marion Redford, who was dancing in *Tip-Toes.*

She apparently wasn't the only love of his life at the time. One other woman occupied a large part of it, enough for him to save, for the rest of his life, a cache of her impassioned letters. She was apparently a singer, and a very successful one, who had an apartment at 34 East Fifty-First Street, and who, in January of 1926, traveled to Havana on a private yacht. "It's wonderful to be rich," she luxuriates in one of the letters and talks of winning at bridge and signs it and many more, "Your lonely wife."

Most of the missives center on their intense love affair, on her desire to meet him in Palm Beach, or anywhere at all. She tells him how jealous she is of everyone. "I know you love me but I always think there's a possible chance of your being influenced if you are alone," she goes on. "I'm even jealous of poor little Peg,"—which may indicate that she had met his daughter Peggy at some time.

At one point, she mentions a friend who "intimated that she knew several things about you that *I* didn't know—but would not tell me what they were—not that I would believe her but her manner was very catty and I'm fed up. . . . I will tell you more when I see you. *(I believe my Baby not my eyes!)*"

There are constant imprecations—"Darling—I hope you won't be led astray when you return to New York," she pleads. "You know a flock of wild women

. . . I haven't been told about who will undoubtedly call you some time or another—and if you are lonely you may weaken. . . ." Several times she remonstrates with him for leaving her, and she repeatedly asks him for clues to his past. [13]

It was a classic romance, the sort that Guy would repeat scores of times, as George Middleton would note much later, in a letter of reminiscence. "Well," he would write, "you've made quite a career with your pen and your penis, haven't you?" [14] It was an apt description of Guy in the 1920s, when Middleton was near.

The forty-one-year-old librettist was traveling a great deal then, to Hollywood, where he wrote the screenplay for the Samuel Goldwyn production of *The Dark Angel,* to London to collaborate with H. M. Vernon, Douglas Furber, Irving Caesar, Albert Sirmay, and Harry Rosenthal on *The Bamboula,* and to Paris to be with Plum and Ethel and Marguerite. On one of these trips, in 1923, he caught Gertrude Lawrence in a small review called *Rats,* at the Vaudeville Theatre. She was twenty-four then, brimming with vitality and talent, yet possessed of a wistful quality that gave her energy depth. "She could bring off that sure fire combination of the tear and the laugh with the artistry of a Chaplin," Guy later recalled.

"That night I wrote Gertie a note asking her to come to New York and promising to find her a vehicle . . . as I was convinced she could make a success . . . ," he continued. [15]

In 1926, he convinced Aarons and Freedley that Gertrude Lawrence should be the reason for the next Gershwin musical. She had created a sensation in New York in the 1924 Charlot's revues; they could create a coup by bringing her in for her first book musical. Guy had an idea that would embrace not only a British character, ideal for Gertrude Lawrence, but prohibition, bootlegging, and musical comedy crooks. And the ideal person to collaborate with him on the book of the show would be his old chum from the Princess Theatre days, P. G. Wodehouse. Aarons and Freedley bought this idea, too.

In June of 1926, Guy wired Plum to catch a July 8 sailing to begin work on the new musical in which Gertrude Lawrence had agreed to appear. Ethel wasn't at all keen about going to America; they had been offered the use of Hunstanton Hall, a Blandings Castle lookalike in Norfolk for July and August, and she wasn't about to give up a summer in a castle. She refused to accompany him.

But Plum, having adapted the Russian play, which he renamed *Hearts and Diamonds,* and written a few of the lyrics in collaboration with Graham John to music by one Bruno Granichstaedten, had had his taste for the theatre reawakened.

He packed his bags, prior to leaving for America on July 24. Through the beginning of that month, he made as much use of Hunstanton Hall as he could, floating in a punt in the moat with his typewriter perched on a bedtable, pecking away at an adaptation of Ferenc Molnar's *The Play's the Thing.* Guy had long since convinced him that adaptations were the thing: Find a play by a Hungarian or Serbian or Hindustani, adapt it, give it your own signature, and there you were—a success without the chore of concocting characters or a plot.

Arriving in America, he went straight to Kensington, where he and Guy got down to work on what would eventually become *Oh, Kay!* "The thing I remember most vividly about *Oh, Kay!*" Plum would later write, "is the period of what is known as gestation—that is to say, the summer months during which Guy and I were writing it at his home in Great Neck. The summer of 1926 was considerably hotter than blazes, and it is not too much to say that I played like one of those fountains at Versailles, taking off some fourteen pounds in weight. It seemed for a time as though those lovely willowy curves of mine would be lost to the world forever, but fortunately they came back during rehearsals. . . ."[16]

Not that the writing of *Oh, Kay!,* which at that time was known as *Mayfair,* was all that occupied Guy and Plum's talents that summer. Guy was called in by Philip Goodman to work with the songwriting team of Bert Kalmar and Harry Ruby, to doctor the book of *The Ramblers,* their star vehicle for Bobby Clark, Paul McCullough and Jack Whiting. The partnership was so felicitous that when, in the autumn of 1926, Guy was approached by Jack Hulbert and Paul Murray to write the libretto for a Gaiety musical that would star Hulbert and Cicely Courtneidge, he brought in Kalmar and Ruby as coauthors. The show was to have a score by Richard Rodgers and Lorenz Hart, who, according to Rodgers's recollections in *Musical Stages,* would rather have worked with their usual librettist, Herbert Fields. Still, they signed, and Hulbert and Murray went back to England, leaving the show in Guy's hands.

Plum, meanwhile, was busily preparing *The Play's the Thing* for a fall production. It would have a tryout down the road from Guy's home at the little Great Neck Summer Theater and then go on to the Gilbert Miller, where Charles Frohman would mount the production, starring Holbrook Blinn, Reginald Owen, and Catherine Dale Owen. It would open five nights before *Oh, Kay!*'s premiere and run for 326 performances, and it and the income from *Oh, Kay!* would allow Ethel to buy them a grandiose, sixteen-room house at 17

Norfolk Street, just off Park Lane in the heart of her beloved Mayfair. Stocked with no less than eleven servants and secretaries, it would be the first of many posh domiciles they would occupy in the next decade and a half.

Still, Plum and Guy's chief interest in the summer of 1926 was the musical, which had now evolved into *Miss Mayfair,* then *Cheerio!* and finally, in early autumn, the very Princess-sounding *Oh, Kay!*

Plum had been nervous about his role. He knew that George and Ira Gershwin were a composer-lyricist team. "George being the composer means that Ira Gershwin will write the lyrics, so that I shall simply help Guy with the book as much as I can," he wrote William Townend.[17]

But Plum's assessment of the situation turned out to be slightly inaccurate. He and Ira Gershwin were two brothers in both talent and personality, and their long and respectful friendship began that summer. No lyricist would be held in higher regard by Plum than Ira Gershwin; he would treasure the copy of *Lyrics on Special Occasions* that Ira would later send him and keep it next to his bed, to ruminate on and savor before sleep. And, while respecting Plum and taking to him readily, Ira did compose most of the lyrics for *Oh, Kay!* and would have written all of them, were he not stricken with appendicitis during its tryout tour. Plum would later, with Ira's full blessing, anglicize many of the lyrics for the London production. And, in his papers, there are some handwritten lyrics destined for a "green light mysterioso scene" which was cut before the New York opening. So, Plum minded not at all that his role when the show opened in New York was strictly as colibrettist with Guy.

The story the two ground out ran true to the Princess formula. It updated the team of Spike and Fainting Fanny from *Oh, Lady! Lady!!* to that of sometime butler Shorty McGee and Lady Kay. The duo was turned into a trio to add Kay's duke of a brother, broke and given to rum-running.

Set in Southampton, Long Island, a location that had served well for *Oh, Boy!* and wasn't that far from Great Neck where the story was written, act 1 romped through the mansion of bachelor Jimmy Winter, normally absent, and so unaware that the duke was using his place to stow bootleg booze. Kay was once saved from drowning by Jimmy. So, when she reappears, he naturally falls in love with her, helps the trio escape the revenue agents, renounces his many romances, and marries Kay in time for the final curtain.

Princess-veteran Oscar Shaw was cast opposite Miss Lawrence, and Gerald Oliver Smith was hired as the duke. Plum and Guy were adamant about casting Victor Moore—who had created a hit in *See You Later*—in the part of Shorty McGee, which they had written with him in mind. Aarons and Freedley were less sanguine about the roly-poly comedian, and as the opening in Philadelphia neared, they became more than a little anxious. "They went so far as to say they would pay ten thousand dollars if Moore would withdraw from rehearsal," Plum and Guy recalled later. "And, on the opening night in Philadelphia, they had two comedians watching out front, one of them, Johnny Dooley, having been virtually promised the part."[18]

Victor Moore was a smash and would become a long-term meal ticket for the two producers. "Looking back through a past that bristles with mistakes," preened Plum and Guy in *Bring on the Girls,* "the authors like to recall such occasional triumphs of judgment. The Bolton epitaph: 'He wasn't always as much of a damn fool as he was sometimes,' will owe something of its validity to Victor Moore."

The Philadelphia tryout run, in late October, was one in which legends were born by the bushel. Three of the more truthful ones survived: Ira was stricken with appendicitis, taken to Mount Sinai Hospital in New York, and Howard Dietz was brought in to finish his lyrics, a puzzling decision by George Gershwin, until you consider the decidedly British tone with which Plum's other, unsung lyrics for the show resonate.

Then, there's the legend of George Gershwin passing a toy store, seeing a rag doll in the window, buying it, and giving it to Gertrude Lawrence as a touching prop to which to sing "Someone to Watch Over Me," a song that had met with only moderate audience reaction until then. The understated staging turned the moment memorable.[19]

The third legend is somewhat suspect, but it makes for one of the musical theatre's most delicious stories, and it involves New York Mayor Jimmy Walker's girlfriend Betty Compton, a surpassingly beautiful girl and a moderately talented dancer, who for some explainable reason ended up with speaking parts and special privileges in some of the biggest hit shows that opened during the mayor's tenure in office. One of the backstage taboos she was allowed to break during *Oh, Kay!*'s tryout was the prohibition of pets in dressing rooms.

Guy jotted down the incident, which he and Plum later expanded in *Bring on the Girls.* The shorter version bears retelling in full:

> It was the third night of the show's opening in Philadelphia. Betty Compton, soon to be the wife of Jimmy Walker, had left her dressing room door open and her beloved pooch, Buggsie, strolled out and started to case the joint.
>
> Never was there a more ill-starred moment for a dog to select to make his initial bow on the stage. Long windows stood half open on a moonlit beach;

the door to the bedroom was unclosed, there was also a stair. None of these appealed to Buggsie. He chose instead to make his entrance through the fireplace where a log fire was smouldering realistically. He paid no attention to Gertie or Oscar [who were singing a duet], but walked down to the footlights and stared at the audience from under shaggy brows, like a Scotch elder rebuking sinners from the pulpit.

He then walked over to the proscenium arch, cocked his leg, scuffled with his feet and made his exit — through the fireplace. The two singers fancied the revenue man must be making comic faces behind their backs, they sang manfully on:

> I remember the bliss
> Of that wonderful kiss . . .
> Oh, how I'd adore it
> If you would encore it.

At this point Buggsie made a second appearance, climbing over the logs and coming down wagging his tail.

"Oh, do, do, do, what you done, done, done before, Baby," sang Gertie, and, as if in response, the obliging Buggsie made his way over to the proscenium arch. One frequently hears that some performer 'stopped the show' but I question if anyone ever stopped the show like Buggsie did.[20]

*Oh, Kay!* moved on to New York, where it opened on November 8, 1926, at the Imperial Theatre, to stupendous applause and a multitude of critical encomiums. More Gershwin hits survived from it than from any Gershwin show so far. Besides "Someone to Watch Over Me" and "Do Do Do," there was "Clap You' Hands," "Fidgety Feet," "Maybe," and "Heaven on Earth."

Burns Mantle, in the *Daily News*, effused, "Farseeing are Aarons and Freedley . . . in the employment of the best talent they can buy. The book of *Oh, Kay!* was written by Guy Bolton and P. G. Wodehouse, than whom there are no better librettists writing for our stage." And Brooks Atkinson, in the *Times*, opined, "Usually it is sufficient to credit as sponsors only the authors and the composer. But the distinction of *Oh, Kay!* is its excellent blending of all the creative arts of musical entertainment."

*Oh, Kay!* would run for 256 performances in New York, 213 in London, and continue to be a constantly self-renewing money-maker for all of its creators. And it became the launching pad for the American careers of Gertrude Lawrence and Victor Moore.

Guy and Plum had never been more popular than they were in 1926. Demands for their services poured in. Word of mouth from Philadelphia had convinced the Shuberts that they needed them, and only them, for a musical they planned based upon the life and career of Jenny Lind. They announced their plans to the duo, adding the information that Armand Vecsey had been hired to provide the music. The two agreed, and signed, apparently forgetting *The Rose of China*.

Guy, however, was needed immediately in London, where his absence had convinced the Gaiety management to credit the book of *Lido Lady* to Ronald Jeans. Rodgers and Hart, eager to return to more familiar territory and their customary librettist, Herbert Fields, had already sailed for America and rehearsals of *Peggy-Ann*.

Rodgers would later recall the creation of *Lido Lady* as a thoroughly unpleasant experience. Guy, however, joining the show in Manchester, found it delightful. He did what he could with the script and apparently it was enough. *Lido Lady* opened on December 1, 1926, at the Gaiety and ran for a healthy 259 performances.

Scarcely catching his breath, Guy boarded the next boat for America. When he docked, a familiar, if unwelcome piece of news greeted him: Marion Redford, one of his chorus girl loves, was pregnant.

# Chapter

# 17

# Opening Chorus, Act 2

## 1927–1931

Broadway has never been in better health than it was in 1927. No fewer than 268 shows opened that year. "Its aims were high, its costs were low," wrote John Mason Brown, in the New York *Post,* "and happily its offerings were not condemned to being flops just because they were not hits."

The first musical to open that year was *The Nightingale,* Plum and Guy's biographical musical about Jenny Lind. It was greeted politely and expired after ninety-six performances.

Plum, joined in America by Ethel before *Oh, Kay!* opened, stayed on with an increasingly desperate Guy at Kensington. The last time Guy was in this sort of fix, he was at least unmarried. Now, Marion was threatening to go public and blow his burgeoning career out of the water in the public press. What to do?

Plum was willing to listen but was of no help whatsoever in affairs of the heart, or other parts of the anatomy that responded to the heart. The only one who could possibly understand and give counsel was Marguerite, and Guy wrote to her.

She was understanding, compassionate, and knew Guy. Of course, she would give him a divorce immediately. He could marry Marion, and the rest was up to him.

Guy breathed a sigh of great relief and presented Marion with an out: he would marry her and give the child a name, support the child for his or her entire childhood, and make a sizable financial settlement with her, provided she would divorce him immediately after the birth of the baby. She agreed, provided Guy turned over Kensington to her and his child.

There was a problem. The home in Great Neck had been a wedding present to Marguerite and was in her name. Once more, Guy wrote to her. She answered immediately, giving it to him, and charging him nothing at all. And so another son, Guy, nicknamed Guybo, was born.

It would be the beginning of one of the most tumultuous and ultimately tragic periods in Guy's life. Marion reneged on her promise to divorce Guy, and for the next decade she haunted him, hounded him, and eventually obtained close to two million dollars in various payments from him. She would appear, suddenly, wildly, outside of the windows of his home, in a theatre, on a street, and proceed to scream at him, beat upon him, and generally torment him for one irresponsible moment in 1926. [1]

Guy, having made his peace as he saw it, flipped the hidden switch and lost himself in his work. Others might drink. Work was Guy's shield and his path into forgetfulness, and it was Florenz Ziegfeld who would supply that work, not only to Guy, but to each member of the trio of musical fame.

On October 12, 1926, the opening night of *Criss Cross,* his second disaster of that personally sorry season, Jerry encountered Alexander Woollcott. Woollcott had promised to introduce Jerry to Edna Ferber. Not only a collector of rare books but a reader of many books, Jerry had been struck by her novel *Show Boat* and, seizing upon Woollcott's Algonquin Round Table status, had phoned him for an introduction, which had not been forthcoming.

That October night, as kind fate would have it, Ferber was in the audience. And so, *Show Boat,* the musical that would make all that came after it beholden to it, was born.

Having found in Oscar Hammerstein II quiet intelligence and an expansiveness of emotion, Jerry called him, urged him to buy the book and read it, and come up with a scenario. Meanwhile, he would write his own scenario. In two weeks, they would compare them and either move forward or not.

The scenarios turned out to be remarkably similar, and the two went in search of a producer. Oscar suggested his uncle Arthur, but Jerry, realizing the scope of the piece, felt that Ziegfeld was their best choice. And once more, using the persuasiveness that sometimes moved Ray Comstock and frequently jogged Philip Goodman and always caused Charles Dillingham to take on his work, Jerry convinced Ziegfeld to produce a show that would be, at the very least unique, and not at all in the tradition of the girl-laden spectacles upon which the Great Glorifier had built his reputation.

It was only one of many Ziegfeld projects for 1926 and 1927; two of them involved Plum and two of them involved Guy. And so once again, the trio's paths wound about each other, intersecting in fate's cat's cradle of coincidence.

All through the end of 1926, Ziegfeld was readying his new, signature theatre. The Ziegfeld was a marvel of its time. Joseph Urban's design now spilled from the stage into the entire house. Done in gold, swept clean of boxes and nineteenth-century ornament, it was a modern miracle of spacious elegance. For his inaugural show, Ziegfeld hired Guy and Fred Thompson to provide the book for a spectacle that would feature no fewer than one hundred Ziegfeld girls and allow Urban to provide a multitude of settings and breathtaking variety.

*Rio Rita* was the product of their pens, an operetta squarely in the tradition of *The Desert Song,* which had opened, a roaring success, in November of 1926, at just about the time *Rio Rita* was going into rehearsals. Whether the story of the notorious bandit the Kinkajou—a Spanish cousin of *The Desert Song*'s Red Shadow—came about in a last-minute rewrite at the behest of Ziegfeld, whether Guy and Fred Thompson consciously stole it from Oscar Hammerstein II and Frank Mandel's book while *The Desert Song* was trying out out of town, or whether it was just coincidence will probably never be known.

What emerged was a tale of the half-breed Rio Rita (Ethelind Terry) in love with the Texas Ranger Jim Stewart (J. Harold Murray), who is after her brother, in reality the mysterious outlaw bandit, the Kinkajou. The music by Harry Tierney and the lyrics by Joe McCarthy were traditionally operettaish, with a march for the stalwart, stouthearted Rangers, ready to sing at the drop of a downbeat ("Rootin' pals, tootin' pals, scootin' pals, shootin' pals . . .") and a song title that could have been part of a rule book for writers of operetta: "When You're in Love, You'll Waltz." Even on the prairie.

The song cues ignored fifteen years of verisimilitude and leaped back to the Henry Blossom antiquities of the pre-Princess days. At a party . . .

ESTABAN:   I want you to sing a song for me.

RITA:   Sing for my supper, ees that it?

ESTABAN:   No, no—it ees just that I love to hear your voice.

CHORUS:   Yes, go and sing, Rita! Please sing! Just one song!

Or, in a love scene . . .

JIM:   It's just an old country house with trees like you never see down here, and there's a river that runs along the foot of the garden.

RITA:   What sort of river? Is it nicer than the Rio Grande?

JIM:   No river is nicer than the Rio Grande. Do you know why?

RITA:   Yes. I know why; but I like to hear you tell me again. (*And he sings.*)

The finales began halfway through each act and the last five songs were nothing but reprises, but there was the leavening lightness of humor, provided by Guy and Fred Thompson to Bert Wheeler and Robert Woolsey, making their debut as a team in *Rio Rita*. ("You mustn't—stop!" says a chorus girl to Wheeler. "How is that punctuated?" he replies.)

But the audiences loved it, loved the spectacle, the girls, even the new dance craze, "The Kinkajou." On February 2, 1927, *Rio Rita* launched the new Ziegfeld Theatre in style and remained there for a week less than 500 performances.

Buoyed by this, Ziegfeld immediately rehired Guy to come up with a new operetta plot for Marilyn Miller, who had apparently made up with her first glorifier and was ready to work for him again. Guy immediately hit upon the idea of making over the tale of the October 1926 visit of Queen Marie of Romania to the United States. Fred Thompson was busy with a new Aarons and Freedley show for the Gershwins, so Guy took William Anthony McGuire for a collaborator, and the two wrote the first draft of *Rosalie*.

Ziegfeld's third operetta venture, *The Three Musketeers,* would also involve William Anthony McGuire and add Plum Wodehouse as lyricist to Rudolph Friml's music. Thus the cat's cradle swung, but not before Plum figured in a theatre landmark which combined debut with tragedy.

Again venturing into the realm of adaptation, while working away at a new novel, *The Small Bachelor,* based upon Guy's plot for *Oh! Lady! Lady!!,* Plum was approached by producers Gilbert Miller and Al Woods. They were in trouble with a Valerie Wyngate adaptation of a Jacques Deval French play. *Her Cardboard Lover* was already in tryout, starring Laurette Taylor, and it was simply not working. It required a complete overhaul, and Plum, they assured him, was the man for the job.

Plum accepted and worked on it in February of 1927. When it opened in New York on March 21, Jeanne Eagels had replaced Laurette Taylor. But the talented, temperamental and mercurial star, who had chiseled her mark on Broadway as Sadie Thompson in Somerset Maugham's *Rain,* was to be eclipsed that March night by her costar, making his debut in New York. Young Leslie Howard, given by Plum some of the best lines in the show, stole it handily from Jeanne Eagels (Percy Hammond wrote the next day, "Mr. Leslie Howard, in one of the richest roles of the season, rather kidnapped the play from its rightful proprietor.")

As the final curtain fell, and Miss Eagels, in gold and pink chiffon, stepped forward for her solo bow, the audience chanted "Howard! Howard! Howard!" She ignored them. The curtain rose and fell, rose and fell, and she remained, alone on the stage, until the customers finally gave up and stopped applauding.

From then onward, she would treat Leslie Howard with courtesy offstage but indulge in multiple tricks onstage which brought her up time and again on charges before Equity. Finally, a year later, after a lover's quarrel (not with Howard), she drank herself into oblivion and failed to appear for her first entrance, and the show was cancelled. She never appeared on a legitimate stage again.[2]

"Mr. Wodehouse's fine hand is noticeable in some dialogue, the main ingredients of which are bestowed on Mr. Howard," commented the anonymous critic of The *Times* after *Her Cardboard Lover*'s opening. It could be argued then, that Plum had an unwitting hand in the demise of Jeanne Eagels's career, by giving the best lines in the play to Leslie Howard. Or, that the lady was destined to self-destruct that season anyway.

Plum, being Plum, would never have wished it to end that way. By the time the reviews came in, he was back in London with Ethel, his new home, his eleven servants, a new Pekingese, a new Rolls Royce for his new chauffeur to drive, and the task of anglicizing *Oh, Kay!* for its imminent London opening.

As if that weren't enough, he was writing a new novel, *Money for Nothing,* adapting a play by Ladislaus Fodor, which would eventually become *Good*

*Morning, Bill,* and reading the galleys for the upcoming publication of *Meet Mr. Mulliner,* a collection of previously published *Strand* stories.

And then, in September, another imperious wire arrived from Flo Ziegfeld. Plum later described the telegram and its consequences in a letter to William Townend sent from 14 East Sixtieth Street, the apartment Guy had taken after turning over Kensington to Marion:

> I would have written before this, but ever since I landed I have been in a terrible rush. I came here with George Grossmith to do *The Three Musketeers* for Flo Ziegfeld, and we finished a rough version on the boat. But like all work that is done quickly, it needed a terrible lot of fixing, which was left to me as George went home. I was working gaily on it when a fuse blew out in Ziegfeld's Marilyn Miller show—book by Guy Bolton and Bill McGuire—owing to the lyricist and composer turning up on the day of the start of rehearsals and announcing that they had finished one number and hoped to have another done shortly, though they couldn't guarantee this. Ziegfeld fired them and called in two new composers, Sigmund Romberg and George Gershwin, and asked me to do the lyrics with Ira. I wrote nine in a week and ever since then have been sweating away at the rest. Meanwhile Gilbert Miller wanted a show in a hurry for Irene Bordoni so I started on that, too—fixing the *Musketeers* with my left hand the while. By writing the entire second act in one day I have managed to deliver the Bordoni show in time [it was never produced], and I have now finished the lyrics of the Flo show and the revised version of the *Musketeers,* and all is well—or will be until Flo wants all the lyrics rewritten as he is sure to do. We open the Bolton-McGuire-Ira Gershwin-Wodehouse-George Gershwin-Romberg show in Boston next week. It's called *Rosalie,* and I don't like it much, though it's bound to be a success with Marilyn and Jack Donahue in it. . . .[3]

While Ziegfeld was busy tormenting his creative staffs, Charles Dillingham decided to overshadow a little of the Great Glorifier's glory. In January of 1927, he hired Jerry to compose the score of a show that would open at the New Amsterdam to challenge *Rio Rita*'s unearned success. Jerry's heart and time were both devoted to *Show Boat,* but he acquiesced, probably because Dillingham had been good to him in harder times and possibly because he thought he could fill in with trunk tunes.

Otto Harbach was hired to write the book and lyrics, and he was treated shabbily by all concerned. Jerry supplied the idea for *Lucky,* as the show was called. And so, he demanded, and got from the understated Harbach a large percentage of the librettist's royalty. Then, Harry Ruby and Bert Kalmar were rushed in to supply more music and lyrics. Then, in Philadelphia, Dillingham became seriously ill, and Jerry inexplicably had Harbach barred from the theatre while he, Kalmar, and Ruby went to work fixing a show that had been blasted by the Philadelphia critics.[4]

The whole unhappy mess opened in New York on March 22, 1927, with Mary Eaton, Joseph Santley, Walter Catlett, Ruby Keeler, and the Albertina Rasch Girls featured in stupendous and elaborate production numbers. It closed after seventy-one performances, an expensive failure, the third in two years for Jerry.

It was probably the lowest point in both his private life and professional career. That year, Eva suffered a nervous breakdown. Jerry was devotedly concerned about her; his inhuman schedule probably kept him away from her more than he wished. Nothing seemed to be working for him on Broadway and certainly not the way he envisioned it. The absorbing nature of the task he had set Oscar Hammerstein and himself in creating *Show Boat*—the like of which had never been attempted on Broadway before—certainly must have caused unbearable tension. And, in the midst of this, Flo Ziegfeld decided to be Flo Ziegfeld. Wiring Jerry from Palm Beach four days before *Lucky*'s unlucky Philadelphia premiere, Ziegfeld roiled the waters:

> I feel Hammerstein not keen on my doing Show Boat. I am very keen on doing it on account of your music but Hammerstein book in present shape has not got a chance except with critics but the public no, and I have stopped producing for critics and empty houses. I don't want Bolton or anyone else if Hammerstein can and will do the work. If not, then for all concerned we should have someone help. How about Dorothy Donnelly or anyone you suggest or Hammerstein suggests. I am told Hammerstein never did anything alone. His present lay-out too serious. Not enough comedy. . . ."

And so on for another hundred expensive words.

Knowing this, Kalmar, Ruby, and particularly Otto Harbach forgave Jerry his obstreperous and erratic behavior, and all remained close friends and collaborators for most of the rest of their lives.

Eva recovered slowly, and Jerry and Oscar Hammerstein managed to ignore Ziegfeld's predictable hysteria. Jerry had picked Helen Morgan for the part of Julie months before, and she returned from London at the beginning of September 1927, to begin rehearsals. *Show Boat* would go through an unusually long rehearsal period for the 1920s, matching its long period of writing and rewriting. It was a time marked by the usual barrage of wires from Ziegfeld, demanding a finished product now, and now, and now again.

But Jerry and Oscar resisted. And as the spring of 1927 gave way to summer, Oscar grew as he wrote the book. Various versions indicate that he was casting off easy musical comedy solutions to scenes, developing characters through dialogue and lyrics, keeping to Ferber's book with a remarkable fidelity while compressing and focusing it for the demands of the musical stage. It was as near to perfection as any collaboration can be: Jerry was finally realizing what he had planned and originated; Oscar was growing to meet and fuse with that realization.[5]

The result was revolutionary. The integration of music and book was enormous. Although *Show Boat* would produce a plethora of deathless standards, they were more than songs in the show; they were the centerpieces of scenes, fluently stitched together with thematic underscoring.

The scope of the musical was likewise enormous, spanning a generation in time and ranging in space from a Mississippi show boat and the levee in Natchez to the boat's interior to the Chicago Exposition to a convent to a Chicago boarding house to a Chicago night club to the *Cotton Blossom,* a generation later. That, Joseph Urban was eager to realize. What he didn't have was the luxury of the extensive waits between scenes that often elongated various editions of the *Follies.* And undoubtedly that accounted, in some part, for the four-hour-and-fifteen-minute run of the show on its opening night in Washington.

That Ziegfeld didn't get his way in lightening up the story is a further testament to the dedication and vision of Jerry and Oscar Hammerstein. It remained true to the novel, a tale of miscegenation, drinking, wife desertion, gambling, and bigotry. It demanded intelligence and concentration from its audiences, and a sense of adventure and chance on the part of its producer. And it received both.

When the curtain rose, at 8:30 P.M. on Tuesday, November 15, 1927, at the National Theatre in Washington, D. C., history was made. As musical theatre archivist Miles Krueger wrote, "The history of the American Musical Theatre, quite simply, is divided into two eras: everything before *Show Boat* and everything after *Show Boat.*"[6] That Jerry and Plum and Guy were responsible for the setting of the path toward which *Show Boat* became the ultimate, glorious, and perhaps inevitable end, is why they're integrally important. That it happened, finally, is why Jerry was and will always remain the true father of the American musical.

That night, the first act ended at 10:30, and the last notes of the second-act finale weren't heard until 12:40 in the morning. The audience seemed to love every minute of it, and the next day's reviews were unrelieved raves.

Still, the show was unconscionably long, and those involved with it knew it. During the next month, as it traveled to Cleveland and then Philadelphia, numbers and scenes were trimmed or dropped and others were added. By the time the show arrived in New York at the end of December, an hour of running time had been snipped from *Show Boat*.

Ziegfeld had planned to bring it into the Lyric on Forty-Second Street, but it soon became apparent that the show was far too big for that house. So, he moved *Rio Rita* from the Ziegfeld to the Lyric and scheduled the New York opening of *Show Boat* for Tuesday, December 27, 1927 at his flagship theatre.

It was perhaps poetically appropriate that the premiere of one of the most important shows in history should occur at precisely the peak moment for the Broadway theatre. No week in history until that time or since has equaled Christmas week of 1927 for the number of shows opening in one confined period. No fewer than eighteen premiered in a span of six days. Eleven of them opened on Monday the 26—eleven in one night!

On the 27, only two shows premiered: Philip Barry's *Paris Bound* and *Show Boat*. Most of the first string critics attended the Barry play. And those in the audience on that historic night at the Ziegfeld recall an eerie quiet, a strange absence of applause. It so unnerved Ziegfeld that he moved up to the steps to the balcony, where he sat in silence with his secretary, "Goldie" Stanton. And then, finally, as nothing followed nothing in the audience, he burst into tears.

"The show's a flop. I knew it would be. I never wanted to do it," he sobbed.[7]

In other parts of the house, the other creators, though less demonstrative, were sharing the same confused doubts. They were used to gauging reactions. But how do you measure silence?

They left the theatre puzzled and depressed. There was no feeling of hope or fulfillment after *Show Boat*'s opening, merely bewilderment. And that bewilderment would remain until the following day, when, in a burst of praise, the reviewers told them what their perceptions had been unable to comprehend the night before.

The reason for the strange silence that greeted the show suddenly became clear, stamped in stone by the long lines at the box office. The opening night audience had simply been too stunned, too overwhelmed to applaud. They had never heard something like "Ol' Man River" in a Broadway musical before, nor the musicalized balcony scene with "Make Believe" as its centerpiece, nor a revelation scene about miscegenation with "Can't Help Lovin' Dat Man" as its center pole; never been subjected to a real story in a musical, unfolding, rolling along, and reaching quite so far into their emotions.

*Show Boat* overwhelmed them as it never would again. To another generation of theatregoers, this reaction would be mysterious, because no one since the first run and the 1932 revival of *Show Boat* has really heard *and* seen it as Jerry and Oscar Hammerstein originally realized it. Jerry's overture was a dark and foreboding one, operatic in its structure and its intent. Robert Russell Bennett's orchestrations were spare and sometimes cruel, employing a tuba and a banjo to give the music a hard edge.

It would only remain that way on Broadway until 1932, when it had its last pure revival. In 1946, when *Show Boat* was again revived, Bennett substituted a standard, medley-style overture, removed the tuba and banjo, and added a lusher string section and more orthodox brass voicings. It did much to remove the bite and the darkness from the show and turn it, like its 1936 movie version, romantic and gentle.

Nor would later audiences have the privilege of seeing a cast that was more stellar by any standards, including Ziegfeld's: Helen Morgan (Julie), Norma Terris (Magnolia), Howard Marsh (Gaylord Ravenal), Charles Winninger (Cap'n Andy), Edna May Oliver (Parthy), Jules Bledsoe (Joe), Tess "Aunt Jemima" Gardella (Queenie), and a ninety-six-voice chorus, part of it white, part of it black.

*Show Boat* audiences were treated to one final treasure: Jerry and Plum's peripatetic song from *Oh, Lady! Lady!!*, "Bill." After a long journey, the song finally found a home and the right singer. Helen Morgan would be identified with "Bill" from then to the end of her tragic life. Oscar Hammerstein rewrote a small portion of the chorus, to deanglicize some of Plum's more British sounding phrases, and this occasioned a change for the better in the melody. But Oscar, being who he was and, as all lyricists in the American musical theatre, respecting and loving Plum and his lyrics, gave full credit to the originator of the song. "Lyrics by P. G. Wodehouse" would appear, by contract, in every program of every production of *Show Boat* from that moment on.

All through 1927, Ziegfeld drove hard on *Rosalie*. He knew his mercurial Miss Miller and was anxious to see that there was a show for her when she was ready. Guy, however, taking advantage of the Great Glorifier's preoccupation with *Show Boat,* took on not only another project but a partnership with Harry Ruby and Bert Kalmar. The three formed a producing company.

Their first venture was *The Five O'Clock Girl,* for which Guy teamed with Fred Thompson. About a Sally-type shop girl who leaves her job at the Snow Flake

Cleaners every day at five to call a young man whose telephone number she has accidentally found, it went on to chronicle the love affair between Sally and her mysterious man, who just happened to be a millionaire, thus making the development of their relationship predictable and painless.

It opened on October 10 at the Forty-Fourth Street Theatre, with Mary Eaton and Oscar Shaw as the shop girl and the millionaire. Critics liked it. They took particular note of the Kalmar and Ruby music and lyrics, which were largely responsible for keeping the show alive for a healthy 280 performances.

Meanwhile, back at *Rosalie,* the enormous mix of librettists, lyricists, and composers was managing to pull off a minor miracle. The show became a solid success, in the tried but not necessarily true Marilyn Miller tradition. The *New York World* described her entrance ecstatically and minutely:

> Fifty beautiful girls in simple peasant costumes of satin and chiffon rush pellmell onto the stage, all squealing simple peasant outcries of "Here she comes!" Fifty hussars in a fatigue uniform of ivory white and tomato bisque march on in a column of fours and kneel to express an emotion too strong for words. The lights swing to the gateway at the back and settle there. The house holds its breath. And on walks Marilyn Miller.

Guy and Fred Thompson had mixed operetta cornball and Princess porridge with up-to-the-minute Lindbergh imitations (her American football hero flies the Atlantic alone to be with her), and although Romberg failed to come up with a memorable melody, Plum and the Gershwins provided two standards, "Oh Gee! Oh Joy!," and "Say So!," a pleasant production number, "New York Serenade," and some discards: from *Funny Face,* the Gershwins' recent Aarons and Freedley hit, "How Long Has This Been Going On"; from *Oh, Kay!* "Show Me the Town"; from *Primrose,* "Wait a Bit Susie" (newly titled "Beautiful Gypsy"); and from *Strike Up the Band,* a landmark musical that had failed out of town but which was to reemerge in 1930, "Yankee Doodle Rhythm." The song that didn't make it into the show because Marilyn Miller hated it was "The Man I Love."

*Rosalie* opened at the New Amsterdam on January 1, 1928, five days after *Show Boat*'s premiere, and it would remain there for 335 performances.

But neither Guy nor Plum were on hand for it. Nor would Guy be around for the premiere of a Beatrice Lillie-Clifton Webb-Jack Whiting-Irene Dunne disaster that was first called *The Love Champion* and then *She's My Baby.* Guy had originated the book with Kalmar and Ruby to a Rodgers and Hart score, but had bailed out when the pressures of *Rosalie* piled too high. In December he left for London to work with Graham John on a new musical for a young producer, Lee Ephraim. It was to be a vehicle for Evelyn Laye, the twenty-eight-year-old star of Daly's Theatre, where she had scored a triumph as Sonya in a 1923 production of *The Merry Widow.* Depressed over the dissolution of her marriage to Sonnie Hale, who would go on to marry — and divorce — Jesse Matthews, she was not overly interested in working, but Ephraim convinced her that salvation lies in work, particularly in a vehicle fashioned for her by him. Besides, it would be a major occasion. The show would be the opening attraction of the brand new Piccadilly Theatre, then only partially completed.

On January 13, 1928, shortly after *Show Boat* began its record-establishing 575-performance run in New York, Jerry, Eva, and Oscar Hammerstein boarded the *Majestic* for England. The London production of *Show Boat* was already in preparation, with Paul Robeson, Jerry's first choice for the part of Joe, signed. His other major reason was to provide the score for the new Ephraim and Laye vehicle scheduled to open the new Piccadilly Theatre.

Plum and Ethel were, by one of those coincidences that make a mockery out of reality, also aboard the *Majestic,* thus completing the temporary and geographic reuniting of the trio of musical fame. Plum was not headed for the Piccadilly Theatre; he was on his way back to work on a novel that had been rummaging around in his head for a month, called *Summer Lightning,* to bask in the success of *Good Morning, Bill,* which, starring Ernest Truex and Laurence Grossmith was presently packing them in at the Duke of York's Theatre, and to work, later that summer, with Ian Hay on the dramatization of *A Damsel in Distress.* He was leaving *The Three Musketeers* up to the machinations of fate and Florenz Ziegfeld. The show would open at the Lyric on March 13, 1928, starring Dennis King, and run for a respectable 335 performances. Nothing that Plum Wodehouse touched in the 1920s seemed to be less than uproariously successful.

Not so the last collaboration of Jerry and Guy. *Blue Eyes,* as the Evelyn Laye show was called, was more than a step backward; it was a miles-long leap. Jerry manfully turned out more beautiful melodies, continuing to invent and sustain vocal lines the like of which he had never produced before. But the demands of the ponderous, operetta-style book by Guy and Graham John left no room for the sort of musical scenes Jerry and Oscar had fashioned for *Show Boat.*

Even by pre-Princess standards, the book and lyrics creaked deafeningly; Guy, apparently dazzled by *Rio Rita*'s roaring success, was determined to become the throwback librettist of the musical theatre, at least for the moment.

Graham John was no help. He had left the London stock exchange and become involved in the production of *Adam and Eva* in New York years ago and since then had contributed to various Hulbert Revues in London. Guy was relying upon him to know what London audiences wanted, and in that capacity he succeeded.

The company, with a still distraught Evelyn Laye (she would remain that way through the first week of the London run) opened the show on Easter weekend at the Kings Theatre, Southsea, Portsmouth, and the local critics were delighted, both by the fact that a major musical was being tried out in Portsmouth and that they liked it. [8]

But apparently those involved with *Blue Eyes* were less sanguine. Jerry left the settling in of *Show Boat* to Oscar Hammerstein; he and orchestrator Robert Russell Bennett stayed on in Portsmouth to minister to *Blue Eyes.*

Meanwhile, workmen were racing to ready the Piccadilly Theatre. Situated at the corner of Denman and Sherwood streets, across the way from the Regent Palace Hotel, it was a marvel of modern architecture. Its green and gold decor, its walnut interior, its 1400 seats, its 30 dressing rooms all bespoke elegance and comfort.

But when the company arrived, shortly before the scheduled April 27 opening, the backstage area was hardly ready for habitation, much less production. Rigging was still being hung; floors had yet to be finished; doors were in place, but opened the wrong way. Singers inhaled the dust that carpenters left hanging in the air after their departure the afternoon of opening night; recalcitrant hinges threatened scene and costume changes.

But audiences seemed to love the show, and critics were at least polite. "The book is in the manner of a Waverly Novel," noted the *Times.* "Alas that the tale is to be taken so seriously! It is quite prettily contrived—and adorned here and there by shrewd, laughing comments on the sentiments of the century—but— . . . even the sentimental songs are weighted by the general solemnity."

Jerry's score produced three lovely melodies, the title song, "Back to the Heather," and the most durable of them all, "Do I Do Wrong?" The last was apparently inserted after the show opened—the creators did as much after opening night at the Piccadilly as the carpenters—and would surface again, with a new Otto Harbach lyric and a new title—"You're Devastating"—five years later, in *Roberta.*

And so, with *Blue Eyes* Jerry left not only the pre-Princess days behind but his two collaborators. He would never again work with either of them. Guy had ceased to grow. Jerry was convinced of that from the misery of *Blue Eyes.* And he was right. Perhaps it was the gloom of Guy's personal problems in 1928. More likely it was the price of success. Everybody wanted Guy in 1928. But everybody hadn't yet realized the thunderous impact that *Show Boat* had had upon the musical theatre. And sadly enough, neither Guy nor Plum would fully realize, for the rest of their lives, that *their* musical theatre, for all intents and purposes, died in 1928.

It was, however, not to a magically transformed Broadway that Guy returned late that summer. *Show Boat,* with Edith Day, Paul Robeson, Cedric Hardwicke, and Marie Burke, was a sensation at the Drury Lane in London, while sailing along serenely in New York at the Ziegfeld. But Guy, ignoring its lessons, immediately plunged into the project he had promised George Middleton during their argument over *Sally* and *Polly.* True to his word, he sold the idea of turning *Polly with a Past* into a musical to Oscar Hammerstein's uncle Arthur.

In January of 1928, Arthur Hammerstein suggested that Guy work with Isabel Leighton on the libretto. She had adapted Edwin Justus Mayer's steamy 1924 play *The Firebrand*, about Benvenuto Cellini, into *The Dagger and the Rose,* which never made New York. Nevertheless, Arthur Hammerstein strongly endorsed her, and Guy, who was always more eager to collaborate than work alone, agreed, turning over three-quarters of his two percent and cajoling Middleton into turning over a half percent to Miss Leighton.

By May, Guy, recovering from *Blue Eyes,* wrote Middleton from the May Fair Hotel on Berkeley Square in London, noting that Rodgers and Hart, who had apparently been signed by Arthur Hammerstein, were either busy elsewhere or cooling on the idea of *Polly,* and Guy was all for bringing in Kalmar and Ruby.[9] That plan apparently either fell through or was rejected by Hammerstein. The composer-lyricist team of Phil Charig and Irving Caesar, responsible for *Yes, Yes, Yvette* in 1927, was eventually hired.

By all accounts—and there were many of them—there was chaos from the very beginning. Middleton didn't participate in the rewrite but came to the New York rehearsals and used the material he got there for a long article for the *Elks Magazine* about the bedlam that is a show in rehearsal:

> While the director of the book is working with the principals in some nearby lodge room, the dance and music directors peel their coats for action. The lyricist now comes into the picture to distribute the printed sheets on which the words of his songs are typed. Most audiences never understand

what the chorus is singing anyhow; but the girls must have to have something
to learn. . . .

What is more interesting is Middleton's observation that "nowadays we are
finding more and more plays like *The Show Boat* [sic], built upon a dramatic
story; but I'm speaking here of the type of entertainment so recurrent each year."
Even if his nephew was taking part in a musical theatre revolution, Arthur
Hammerstein was interested in turning out a commercial success, what they
called in the twenties "a leg show."

And finally, what is most interesting about Middleton's article are his
comments on comedy writing: "Of course," he writes, "no author supplies all
the 'gags' and 'nifties' in such a piece. Here is where the comedians get in their
fine lines; for many not only roll their own but write them. . . ."

The musical rehearsed its four weeks in New York and then went to
Philadelphia, where its troubles really began. It would remain there for a month
while it was totally overhauled. First of all, since the British musical star June
was featured, Polly's birthplace was changed from Ohio to Ottawa; then, Isabel
Leighton was fired; then, Leon Errol, probably, next to Jolson and Cantor, the
most in-demand comedian in the musical theatre in the 1920s, was hired,
which demanded still another complete rewrite.

From the Ritz-Carlton in Philadelphia, Guy wrote of his frustration to
Middleton in New York. "The show closes on Saturday and is to be entirely
rewritten for Leon Errol to star in with June featured!" he exclaimed. "He is to
play her father (a drunken Bob Eccles) and she is to be a cabaret girl instead of a
maid. I'm afraid our good old 'Polly' will about disappear but it's this way or
close altogether. Arthur is determined that it is 'too polite' for the audiences of
1928."

Guy goes on to give Middleton the job of not only telling Isabel Leighton that
she's out but to try to get his half percent back. "I don't feel disposed to do all
this new work and cancel my job with Plum as I shall have to for nothing. I
would sooner bow out than let someone else tackle it. But I do feel a sense of
obligation to you, . . ." he goes on.

Guy did go off to Atlantic City with Leon Errol to rewrite. "I've already
written the play over completely twice since making the original version," he
wrote again to Middleton. "This means buckling to and doing it once more for
the most cross-grained difficult comedian that ever drew breath. . . . I'm
damned tired. Errol talked with me until 5. Then Arthur came to see me at 9!
What a business to be in!"[10]

The Atlantic City weekend produced a mound of material apparently supplied by Leon Errol, which Guy managed to squeeze into the script. But then,
Clifford Grey, phoned by Errol, was brought in to rewrite it.

The new material was tried out; it failed, and Errol left the show.

In an even finer dudgeon, Guy set down a recap for Middleton which offers
some insight into the preparation of musical comedies of the time:

> I sailed at Arthur's behest Aug. 6th from England. This means four months
> solid work out of my year! It seems incredible. . . . Here is a list of rewritings
> (to date)
>
> 1–1st version.
>
> 2–2nd version when part of Sue had to be built for Inez Courteney. [She left
> the show shortly thereafter.]
>
> 3rd version. When Arthur was persuaded Fred Alan [sic] wasn't right for
> Harry and I wrote in the reporter character suppressed Sue and built Jennie. A
> complete reconstruction.
>
> 4th version—changes all through Act I to make Polly in love with Rex from
> start and other changes made prior to Philly closing.
>
> 5th version. Complete rewriting making Errol's new character of "Dad" the
> biggest thing in show and starting with cabaret girl and Broadway night club
> atmosphere.
>
> 6th version. Cutting Errol part down and shifting numbers to Harry part,
> building Harry again into biggest comedy part and making Dad a character
> comedy role. . . .[11]

The prolonged residence in Philadelphia of *Polly* did little to improve the
show. It opened at the Lyric on January 8, 1929, without Leon Errol but with
the glamorous and charismatic June as the star, and the young, rising comedian
Fred Allen as a reporter for the Sag Harbor *Bee*. Set mostly in Southampton,
Long Island, the location of *Oh, Boy!,* it apparently carried neither the charm of
that hit show or that of its Belasco-inspired original, the play that changed Ina
Claire's career. Lambasted by the critics, it closed after a scant fifteen
performances.

The four months of *Polly*'s alterations in Philadelphia did produce something
considerably longer lasting, however. June and Guy began a love affair that
would continue, in many forms, for the rest of their lives. It was as profound as
most of the rest of Guy's life at the time was not, a rich and intense relationship
that would weather time, husbands, and wives.

From the very first, June would write scores of poems and letters to Guy, which he preserved. In Philadelphia, in December of 1928, she sent him this capsule of their affair, written on Ritz Carlton stationery:

> Some hours have passed since you were here
> Yet still among the shadows hangs your smoke
> And still within my loving mind there stay
> Your gestures and each simple word you spoke.
> And there's the indentation that your brown head made
> Upon the broidered pillow in the chair
> And where you for a moment laid your hand
> The silver cover of my bed is crumpled, there
> Rendering the precious proofs of your dear presence
> Close beside me in the twilight gloom.
> But these will pass and I shall wonder if I dreamed
> You were beside me in my quiet room. [12]

They spent Christmas together and the two-week run of the play, and then it became a mostly epistolary romance. Like the heroine of some seventeenth-century novel or the lead in an operetta, June would return to England in January of 1929 and marry her fiancé, Lord Alan Inverclyde, a Scottish nobleman.

Nobility was less than June anticipated and more than she could stand. A few months, and she fled from Castle Wemyss in Renfrewshire to various international cities and filed for an annulment in 1930, after a series of stormy confrontations with her alcoholic but powerful husband. At the end of 1929, she went to Hollywood, where Guy was at the time, and there they might have made something lasting and public of their romance, had Guy not been married to Marion.

June went back to England, where her career in the theatre flourished and where Lord Inverclyde won a divorce, accusing June of adultery with Lothar Mendes, a Hollywood director. In 1937, she married Edward Hillman, an American, and lived a contented life, writing an autobiography, *The Glass Ladder,* from whose pages Guy is conspicuously absent.

Jerry took a year off in the 1929–30 season. He had found the lyricist with whom he best liked to work; he had found the voice he had been seeking since the Princess; he was making a great deal of money.

Some of that money went into maintaining the unique, sartorial splendor of Jerry. Like Ziegfeld and Guy, Jerry had become noted for his elegance in dressing and particularly for the wide scarves from Crawford's of London, which he transformed into grand cravats, knotting them neatly around his neck in lieu of more ordinary ties.

Then, much of the money he made went into fine books for his collection. But in 1929, a large chunk of it was used to purchase a seventy-two-foot yacht, which Jerry logically christened, with Edna Ferber in attendance, *Show Boat.* It was spacious, though fairly narrow, with two decks, comfortable accommodations, and a grand piano built into its grand salon. Not as booklined or cosy as the library in Bronxville, perhaps, but a reasonable approximation, it allowed Jerry to maintain his creative schedule no matter where it sailed.

One favored location from 1929 onward was Palm Beach, where Flo Ziegfeld had summoned the trio years before. The captain and crew took Jerry, Eva, Betty, and some card-playing friends down the Inland Waterway on several occasions, the first of which turned out to be an unexpectedly elongated one. Unfamiliar with the yacht's drawing capabilities, the captain managed to run her aground, and there she remained, with her passengers aboard, for nearly a week.

*Show Boat* also served as a workplace for Jerry and Oscar Hammerstein to create their next show. It was an exercise in nostalgia, its story the result of a dream Jerry had about people on old-fashioned bicycles. First called *Just the Other Day,* it eventually matured into *Sweet Adeline,* and although it was undeniably a star vehicle for Helen Morgan, it retained some of the song-scene structure realized in *Show Boat.* The melodic lines, written for Morgan's plaintive voice, were longer than ever, resulting in one of Jerry's loveliest and most enduring songs, "Why Was I Born?" (Later, Jerry would confess to Betty that he thought it was the most depressing song he ever wrote.)

This time, Jerry and Oscar Hammerstein went to Uncle Arthur, who, after *Polly,* needed a hit. *Sweet Adeline,* which opened at Hammerstein's Theatre on September 3, 1929, was a moderate one, tempered by two circumstances:

First, Arthur Hammerstein may have been able to convince Guy a year before that *Polly* was "too polite for 1928 audiences,"[13] but he was apparently either unable or unwilling to advise Jerry and his nephew that Jazz Age audiences preferred jazz. Percy Hammond's review, which stated that it was "one of the politest frolics of the new year," did nothing to boost box office sales.

Second, October brought the stock market crash. Though its first two months were sellouts, *Sweet Adeline* succumbed to the steadily disappearing audiences that the Depression caused on Broadway and closed after 234 respectable performances. But by that time, Jerry was on his way westward, to California. Sound had arrived in Hollywood, and the movies needed composers.

Guy shed few tears for *Polly's* early demise. Ernst Vajda, whose play he had used as the basis for 1924's *Grounds for Divorce,* had been engaged by fellow Hungarian Ernst Lubitsch to write the script for the great director's first talkie. It was to be a musical, and Vajda sent for Guy. If musicals were to be made in Hollywood, librettists were needed. And Guy was still the musical theatre's most famous and in-demand librettist.

Plum, all along, had been inordinately busy in London. First, there was the dramatization of *A Damsel in Distress,* which he and Ian Hay accomplished in record time. "I liked collaborating with Ian because it's like collaborating with Guy," Plum wrote to William Townend. "He liked doing all the stuff himself. I was just to contribute the book. We talked it all over and got our scenario and the characters and everything and then he wrote it."[14] The show opened at the New Theatre on August 13, 1928, and ran for a solid—for London—242 performances.

The next week, the London production of *Her Cardboard Lover* with Tallulah Bankhead and Leslie Howard opened at the Lyric, and it, too, was a success.

Happy with Ian Hay and anxious to keep his love of the theatre requited, Plum again collaborated with Hay on the dramatization of one of Hay's short stories, *Baa Baa Black Sheep.* It opened at the New Theatre on April 22, 1929, and ran for 115 performances, thus freeing Plum to again rent Hunstanton Hall for the summer.

On May 27, he received news that his father had died at the age of eighty-three, in Sussex. His mother chose to move in with Plum's brother Armine and Armine's wife, Nella. Ethel and Plum lived on peacefully in the country until the end of August, when yet another imperious wire arrived from Florenz Ziegfeld. This time, he wanted Plum immediately, to write the lyrics for a musical version of *East Is West,* with a libretto by William Anthony McGuire and music by Vincent Youmans, ". . . if he ever gets around to doing any," Plum later wrote to Townend:

> I am collaborating on the lyrics with a very pleasant lad named Billy Rose, who broke into the Hall of Fame with a song entitled "Does the Chewing-Gum

Lose Its Flavour on the Bedpost Overnight?" As far as I can make out, Billy and I are the only members of the gang who are doing a stroke of work. I go around to his hotel every morning and we hammer out a lyric together and turn it in to Youmans, after which nothing more is heard of it. [15]

That sort of schedule allowed Plum to take on a rewrite of a Graham John adaptation of a Siegfried Geyer play called *Candlelight*. Gilbert Miller wanted Plum to sharpen Graham's work—which had already had a successful London run—for a New York production to feature Gertrude Lawrence in her first nonsinging role, Reginald Owen, and Leslie Howard.

Plum took to it delightedly, whipped it up, watched it enter rehearsals and then, without uttering a word to either Miller or Ziegfeld or anyone concerned with either of the shows upon which he was working, took a train west for Hollywood. Guy was there, and with talking pictures coming in, who knew who might need a lyricist?

———◆———

# THE
# NEAR PAST

"Elsie Janis's house? Norma Shearer's? Who did own your first digs in Hollywood?" asks Guy of Plum as they round yet another curve.

"Ethel," replies Plum, removing his golf cap, shining the expanse of unblemished skin at the top of his head, and restoring the cap. "Ethel made it all her own, bless her. She always does that. Makes and remakes the world. Lonely without her. And without you."

"Never heard of anyone being lonely in Hollywood," remarks Guy, tossing a stick for Squeaky, who careers madly after it.

"That's you, old chap," chuckles Plum.

"It's just that they don't let you alone."

"Who?"

"The studios."

"Oh." Plum pauses for a moment. "I thought you meant, well, you know—June."

"Yes," smiles Guy. "Heard from her again, only yesterday. Another lovely letter. They never stop, bless her."

"And Virginia."

"The Little Thing."

"Your Five O'Clock Girl."

"My girl for all seasons."

"Well," admits Plum, after a pause, "I do suppose there were our countrymen there—"

"*Your* countrymen," corrects Guy.

"Come, chap. Did you plunk yourself into that house next to Edgar—" He stops, recalling a sunset evening in Beverly Hills. "There was a woman in Hollywood who was next to him. Didn't live there, like you, but—"

"But what?"

"Ethel gave a party—" he begins.

"One party?"

"One of several hundred. And there was this elderly woman sitting next to me at dinner, and she turned to me and said, 'This is a great moment for me. I can't tell you how proud I am. I think I've read everything you've ever written. In fact, we all love your books. My eldest son reads nothing else—'"

"Really?"

"Yes. I was speechless with joy, of course. And she went on. 'My eldest son reads you and no one else. And so do my grandsons. We all love your books. The table in their room is piled high with them. And when I go home tonight and tell them that I have actually been sitting at dinner next to Edgar Wallace, I don't know what they'll say.'" [1]

Chapter

# 18

# Hollywood Scene
## 1929–1933

It would be Guy who would lead the way to Hollywood for the disassembled trio and score the first success there. The script he and Ernst Vajda wrote for Lubitsch was pure *Rosalie,* all about a princess and her thwarted love affair with a dashing cavalier. Given the sophisticated, satirical "Lubitsch touch," *The Love Parade,* starring Maurice Chevalier and Jeannette MacDonald, with music by Victor Schertzinger and lyrics by Clifford Grey, was the first truly successful screen musical, and it established Guy's credentials in Hollywood early. It would also, coincidentally, make him such an astronomical amount of money all at once that he was able to face Marion's lawyers with confidence.

Plum and Jerry had longer to travel toward acceptance. Plum's 1929 trip to visit Guy convinced him that California would be a pleasant place in which to work, but it did nothing for either his pocketbook or his ego. "The only person I knew really well out there was Marion Davies, who was in the show *Oh, Boy,* which Guy Bolton, Jerry Kern and I did for the Princess Theatre," he wrote Townend. "She took me out to her house in Santa Monica and worked me into a big lunch at the Metro-Goldwyn which they were giving for Winston Churchill. . . .

"I have reluctantly come to the conclusion that I must have one of those meaningless faces which make no impression whatever on the beholder. This was—I think—the seventh time I had been introduced to Churchill, and I could see that I came upon him as a complete surprise once more. . . ."[1]

Another surprise was occurring three thousand miles away, in New York. The *Candlelight* company suddenly discovered that Plum was missing. And so when, after a few days in the California sun, he strolled back into the Lyric Theatre, he was, by his account, greeted with a glacial welcome by Gertrude Lawrence. Fortunately, the glacier thawed under the heat of good notices.

Plum oversaw the last minute changes that helped to bring these about and then headed back to England. Not so Ethel. She was determined that if Guy was going to make all that money, Plum should, too. Besides, she couldn't have failed to read about the multitude of parties given in Hollywood. It would be fertile ground for her social imagination, and so Ethel traveled in the opposite direction, to Hollywood, where she would negotiate an MGM contract for Plum that would pay him $2,000 a week for six months, with an option to renew.

Guy, meanwhile, rushed back to New York for four new projects and to London for one: First, there was an up-to-date musical with Bert Kalmar and Harry Ruby, titled *Top Speed.* The book that Guy fashioned was twenties hokum salted by stock market, prohibition, and border guard jokes, all of it ending in a speedboat race. "It does not attain, probably, the top of all possible speeds," wrote critic Richard Lockridge in the *Sun,* "yet it never lags too obviously. It has, almost always, a clean hard surface and it does not bog down unduly in the soft spots of sentiment."

That was exactly what the producing team of Bolton, Kalmar, and Ruby planned, and so the hard surface, some bright Kalmar and Ruby tunes, and the debut of a seventeen-year-old fireball named Ginger Rogers sustained the show for a little more than thirteen weeks.

At the same time that he was writing *Top Speed,* Guy received a distress call from Fred Thompson, who was working on *Sons O' Guns,* a vehicle for singer/dancer Jack Donahue. There was dire book trouble, and Guy's construction skills were needed. He came in as an uncredited collaborator and in the busy autumn of 1929, also had time to enter into a brief but brightly burning affair with Merielle Perry, an eighteen-year-old Parisian singer, who was understudying Lily Damita in *Sons O' Guns* and who would take over the role the following year in the London production.

"Guy showed me New York," Miss Perry told this author, "and especially the doors of famous buildings. He told me about his architecture background, and how you could tell the character of a building by the attention paid to its doors. He was charming. Such a charming, handsome man."

The third of Guy's simultaneous theatre projects was his collaboration with Ed Wynn for a grandiose Ziegfeld opus called *Simple Simon*. The only simple thing about the show was its title; there were enough Joseph Urban sets to fill Cain's Theatrical Scenery Storehouse. Wynn insisted on rewriting every syllable (his famous "I love the woodth!" originated in this show); Florenz Ziegfeld insisted on throwing out every substantial song that Rodgers and Hart wrote, including "Dancing on the Ceiling," and dragging in interpolations, which infuriated the composer and lyricist. The only standard they were able to save was a show stopper: Ruth Etting's magical rendition of "Ten Cents a Dance."[2]

Finishing off the Ed Wynn project, Guy boarded the *Majestic* for Europe, where he visited Marguerite and Peggy briefly and collaborated with Ian Hay on *Song of Sixpence,* a Scottish comedy of no particular distinction and moderate success that opened at Daly's on March 17, 1930.

Then, it was back to New York for his fifth and last project of the year, an Aarons and Freedley musical for which George and Ira Gershwin were to supply the music and lyrics, and on whose book he was to collaborate with John McGowan, a former singer for Aarons and Freedley who had authored the book for *Flying High*—a musical that would cause them all a load of problems.

*Girl Crazy,* the title upon which Guy and McGowan and the producers agreed, was an indication that this was yet another pre-*Show Boat* type musical comedy, the kind that Guy could write with one hand, and frequently did. It was to be the next-to-last orthodox musical comedy that George and Ira Gershwin would write. They, like Jerry, were prepared to push the frontiers of the American musical into still more uncharted territory. But in the meantime, the tried-and-untrue would do them no harm and make them a lot of money.

The show would mark two debuts: one, that of a young singer named Ethel Merman, who had auditioned a year earlier for *Top Speed*. She strode to center stage then, sang a few bars, and Bert Kalmar turned disgustedly to Guy. "God, she's too loud! We can't use her!" he shouted, behind his hand.

Rejected by Kalmar and Ruby, Merman went on to an engagement at the Brooklyn Paramount, where Vinton Freedley caught her act, and she caught his fancy. He signed her for *Girl Crazy,* and the rest became Broadway history.

The other debut was that of Willie Howard, who was brought in after Bert Lahr became unavailable. Lahr, thought by Aarons and Freedley—and Lahr himself—to be trapped in a sure disaster, *Flying High,* would be the comic lead. But on the road, carpentry turned *Flying High* into a high-flying hit, and Aarons and Freedley thereupon hired Willie Howard, heretofore half of a nightclub brother act, to fill the role. Howard came to *Girl Crazy* reluctantly, extracting the promise from the producers that he could bring his imitations of Jolson, Jessel, Chevalier, and Cantor with him. Guy and McGowan obliged, leaving holes in the script for Howard's routines.

Ginger Rogers, fresh from *Top Speed,* was hired to play Molly Gray, the postmistress of Custerville, Arizona, and the Gershwins convinced their good friend Fred Astaire to help her in the dance department, a place in which she was notably deficient.

Ira and George wrote arguably their best score for a classic musical comedy, full of lush ballads and driven by the nervous, exhilarating jazz sounds that would set the show firmly into the period and the Gershwin canon. George himself always conducted on opening nights, and to give his music the energy it demanded, he hired Red Nichols and his band, which included Benny Goodman, Jimmy Dorsey, Glenn Miller, Gene Krupa, and Jack Teagarden.

It was obviously going to be a major undertaking, but Ira Gershwin, recalling September 29, 1930, at the Shubert Theatre in Philadelphia, remembered a maddeningly casual Guy. Both stood at the rear of the orchestra, gauging responses, making notes. As the curtain fell on the first act, which was three-hours long, Ira caught a flash of white silk scarf out of the corner of his eye. It was Guy, carefully buttoning his overcoat over it.

"Going for a drink?" asked Ira.

"No," answered Guy. "Going home."

"Home? There's another act!" said Ira, trying not to let his voice rise.

"It's eleven o'clock, Ira," said Guy, his brown eyes placid and comforting. "We'll work tomorrow."

That was the way Ira Gershwin remembered it, and he was not given to either backbiting stories or exaggeration. Guy was simply exercising his status, thereby causing consternation among his collaborators, a not uncommon occurrence in the 1930s.[3]

*Girl Crazy* was a huge success, and Ethel Merman recalled a luncheon on October 14, the day after the opening, on the terrace of George Gershwin's West Side penthouse. The personnel: Merman, George and Ira Gershwin, and Guy Bolton. She was looking forward to a long run; they were planning their trip, in three weeks, to Hollywood, where Guy and the Gershwins had been signed by Fox Films to write *Delicious* for America's screen darlings, Janet Gaynor and Charles Farrell.

. . .

Jerry's first trip to Hollywood was far less sanguine than either Plum's or Guy's. He and Otto Harbach were signed by First National to write the music and lyrics for *Stolen Dreams,* a musical about World War I aviators which united flying and music, the two most popular film subjects with 1929 and 1930 audiences. The composer and lyricist/librettist carved out work space in a bungalow that Jerry, Eva, and Betty had rented at the Beverly Hills Hotel and worked cheerily, completing the assignment by the end of August 1930.

But Jerry had scarcely made it back to Bronxville before the film and his score were subjected to the sort of butchery for which Hollywood was famous. First the title was changed to *The Man in the Sky;* then it was decided that public interest in all-talking, all-singing, all-dancing movies was waning, and the entire film was rewritten, the score dropped entirely, and the title changed to *Men of the Sky.* Not a note of Jerry's music was heard when it was finally released in 1931.

A summer vacation in Europe followed by a second vacation in Palm Beach indicated that there was not a great deal of work for the man who had revolutionized the American musical theatre. But it was the deepest part of the Depression, and although this tragic scourge didn't affect Jerry's lifestyle very much, it shrank the size of Broadway audiences dramatically. Theatres shuttered, and those that didn't slashed their prices.

Gone were the white-tie-and-tails, bejeweled and begowned opening nights of the Princess in New York and the Winter Garden in London; gone, too, were the riotous black-tie nights of the twenties. Audiences still dressed for the theatre, but their tuxedoes were beginning to show signs of wear, and there were considerably fewer jewels in evidence. Audiences demanded either total escape or scathing social comment. It was a new world.

But then again, Jerry had had a hand in creating the musical part of it, and this time, his experiment would carry him still further along the path he had set for himself.

In the early summer of 1931, a young, former vaudeville agent, lately the producer of the Arthur Schwartz-Howard Dietz review *The Band Wagon,* insinuated himself into a dinner party at Max Dreyfus's home in Bronxville. His name was Max Gordon, and he spent an evening alternating between hope and despair, as Jerry, at his most erudite, witty, and energetic, dominated the conversation and the evening, ranging in his delivery from history to sociology to politics to art but rarely to musical comedy.

Later that evening, Jerry summoned Gordon to an upstairs bedroom, shut the door, and talked serious business. He and Otto Harbach were already far into a new experiment, he told Gordon. "We've been talking about eliminating chorus girls, production numbers and formal comedy routines," he told the young producer. "We're striving to make certain that there will be a strong motivation for the music throughout."[4]

The result would be *The Cat and the Fiddle.* Max Gordon would produce it, and it would go into rehearsal in August and open at the Garrick Theatre in Philadelphia on September 23, 1931, to generally favorable reviews. It was serious theatre, a play in which the music did nothing but enhance and propel the story. About two eventual lovers who represent opposite spectrums in music—he for its pure aesthetics, she for popular accessibility in popular songs—it was romantic but substantial and therefore just the sort of property Max Gordon loved.

Although not entirely puritanical, Gordon hated the obscenity with which he felt contemporary theatre was top heavy, and so he was an easy prey for one of Jerry's practical jokes. Sometime during the Philadelphia run, Jerry wrote an absolutely obscene scene, brimming with scatalogical references. Giving the sides to the leads, Doris Carson and Eddie Foy, Jr., he instructed them to insert the scene into that afternoon's run-through.

Gordon seated himself in his usual place in the darkened auditorium. The rehearsal began, ran unobtrusively, and then suddenly erupted into the dirty talk of Jerry's interpolation. Gordon shot from his seat, slammed down the aisle, and was about to pillory the poor actors, when he noticed Jerry convulsed in laughter, tears streaming down his florid face.

It was the sort of relaxation a show in good shape could afford, and the company felt confident when it opened in New York at the Globe Theatre on October 15, 1931. The reviewers were noticeably cool, particularly to the book and the players. But they couldn't ignore a score that contained "She Didn't Say Yes" and "The Night Was Made for Love."

The next day, at Dinty Moore's Restaurant, Jerry defended Otto Harbach against the critics and at the same time offered the most succinct summation of his ambition yet: "A composer never should compose unless he has something to say," he said. "The characters wrote the music; I only placed the notes on the paper. That is why it is the most direct, uncompromising thing I have accomplished. . . ."[5]

Jerry would go on to develop this approach with Oscar Hammerstein, who returned in 1931 from his own junket of disappointment to Hollywood. The result was *Music in the Air,* a slightly more orthodox musical that veered toward operetta and contained two more immortal Kern melodies, "I've Told Ev'ry Little Star" (which Jerry swore he composed after hearing a bird sing outside his bedroom window at the Nantucket home of his cousin Walter Pollak)[6] and the surging "The Song Is You."

Produced by A. C. Blumenthal, who took over the 1932 revival of *Show Boat* after Florenz Ziegfeld died, it opened at the Alvin on November 8, 1932, and became a resounding success, running for 342 performances in the depth of the Depression. It was, in many respects, the melodious escape Depression-weary theatregoers needed.

But Jerry, having accomplished this, moved on, to a musicalization of Alice Duer Miller's novel *Gowns by Roberta.* This time Otto Harbach was his librettist and lyricist and Max Gordon the producer. A musical wrapped around a fashion show, it sported a stellar cast—George Murphy, Bob Hope, Tamara, Fay Templeton, and, in an entertainment-within-the-entertainment, Alan Jones imitating Morton Downey and Fred MacMurray imitating Rudy Vallee. The songs were breathtaking and rich—"Yesterdays," "You're Devastating" (the old "Do I Do Wrong" from *Blue Eyes*), "The Touch of Your Hand," and "Smoke Gets in Your Eyes," to name the most popular. Not since *Show Boat* had Jerry composed a score of such uniformly high quality.

*Roberta* opened at the New Amsterdam on November 18, 1933. Max Gordon had spent $115,000 on the production—a huge amount in Depression dollars—and, as with *The Cat and the Fiddle,* the critics found the music rewarding but the book boring. The public disagreed, demonstrably. Although the box office began slowly, it sustained itself through 295 performances, much of it based upon word-of-mouth that *Roberta* was the smart musical to see.

Now, following an interesting pattern, Jerry turned back to Oscar Hammerstein for his next show. The two toyed with the idea of a Chinese musical—a dangerous thought, as the failed *East Is West* and *The Rose of China* should have taught them. *Golden Bells* was explored and shelved by Jerry and Oscar Hammerstein in 1933.

Shortly thereafter the Theatre Guild approached Jerry and Oscar and offered them the job of turning DuBose Heyward's *Porgy* into a musical which would entice Al Jolson back to Broadway, in blackface, in the title role. The two had the taste to turn it down, thus clearing the way for America's first folk opera.[7]

The show that Jerry and Oscar eventually wrote was *Three Sisters,* which was presented not in New York but at the Drury Lane in London. Starring Adele Dixon, Stanley Holloway, Victoria Hopper, and Charlotte Greenwood, it was a seventy-two-performance failure, producing only one Kern standard, "I Won't Dance."

It had been four years of steady development, if not altogether successful results. Broadway was in the tight grip of financial stress, reflecting the state of the union. Only one location in America was behaving as if the Depression didn't exist, and it was there that Jerry determined he was going to settle. Asked by Oscar where he was heading after he sailed for America, Jerry replied, economically, "Hollywood, for good!"[8]

> "There is something about this place that breeds work. We have a delightful house—Norma Shearer's—with a small but lovely garden and a big swimming pool, the whole enclosed in patio form. The three wings of the house occupy three sides, a high wall, looking on to a deserted road, the other. So that one feels quite isolated. I have arranged with the studio to work at home, so often I spend three or four days on end without going out of the garden: I get up, swim, breakfast, work till two, swim again, have a lunch-tea, work till seven, swim for the third time, then dinner and the day is over. It is wonderful. I have never had such a frenzy of composition."[9]

So wrote Plum to William Townend in June of 1930. He and Leonora, who accompanied him, had plunged into Hollywood at its frenzied height, its most glamorous moment. When he first arrived, Plum spent most of his time writing, and the remainder either with Leonora or with, as he put it, "other exiles—New York writers, etc. Most of my New York theatre friends are here."

There was also a British colony in Hollywood which included Basil Rathbone, Ronald Coleman, Nigel Bruce, Leslie Howard, Maureen O'Sullivan, and C. Aubrey Smith. The Wodehouses were welcomed with solemn warmth, and when Ethel arrived in July, the parties began, much to Plum's dismay. "Heather Thatcher has turned up to spend a couple of months with us," he would write to Townend later in his Hollywood stay.

> We gave a big party for her yesterday, which I found rather loathsome, as it seemed to pollute our nice garden. There was a mob milling round in it from four in the afternoon till eleven at night. About twenty people in the pool at one time. The only beauty of having a party in your own home is that you can sneak away. I went upstairs to my room at five and only appeared for dinner, returning to my room at eight sharp. (The perfect host.)[10]

It was work for which Plum lived, and he was immediately put to it by MGM, rewriting *Those Three French Girls,* which would star George Grossmith,

Fifi d'Orsay, and Ukelele Ike. It was like old times. He not only added the Wodehouse touch to the work of a multitude of other writers, but he began work on a new novel, *If I Were You*, and completed a dramatization of *Leave It to Psmith*, which he had begun with Ian Hay before leaving England. It opened in the West End on September 27, 1930, and ran 156 performances.

MGM liked his work in Hollywood and extended his contract, handing him, of all things, *Rosalie,* which it had just bought for Marion Davies. His routine was to work at home and then, eschewing the studio cars that were regularly sent to fetch him, walk the six miles from his home in Benedict Canyon to the studio in Culver City. It never occurred to him to make use of the preposterous perks that others of his stature enjoyed regularly. He gladly accepted whatever money was handed to him, but always with a little bemusement and a remarkable lack of concentration upon it, two characteristics that were to get him into a certain amount of trouble.

On June 7, 1931, Alma Whitaker, a reporter for the *Los Angeles Times,* interviewed Plum, and he disingenuously unburdened himself to her. Asked about MGM's financial arrangement with him, he replied:

> They paid me $2,000 a week—$104,000—and I cannot see what they engaged me for. They were extremely nice to me, but I feel as if I have cheated them. You see, I understood I was engaged to write stories for the screen. After all, I have twenty novels, a score of successful plays, and countless magazine stories to my credit. Yet apparently they had the greatest difficulty in finding anything for me to do. Twice during the year they brought completed scenarios of other people's stories to me and asked me to do some dialogue. Fifteen or sixteen people had tinkered with those stories. The dialogue was really quite adequate. All I did was to touch it up here and there.
>
> Then they set me to work on a story called *Rosalie,* which was to have some musical numbers. It was a pleasant little thing, and I put in three months on it. When it was finished, they thanked me politely and remarked that as musicals didn't seem to be going so well they guessed they would not use it.
>
> That about sums up what I was called upon to do for my $104,000. Isn't it amazing?

The effect of the published interview was a little like setting off a ton of dynamite at the MGM guard gate. The studio's New York bankers, outraged, rolled heads in the West. And again, Plum lived simply, blissfully on, apparently unaware of the thunderous effect of his gentle words. It would be the first of two such incidents in his life.

By the time the *Los Angeles Times* article appeared, Plum had been joined by

Guy, who came west again in November of 1930 in one of several private railroad cars that George and Ira Gershwin had rented for their first trip to Hollywood. Guy moved in with Plum; the Gershwins rented a Spanish-Moorish home in Beverly Hills that had belonged to Greta Garbo.

Although George Gershwin would never truly like Hollywood and would always miss the brittle and driven tenor of life in New York, he did take to the gathering-driven atmosphere of California. Within days, he became the center-piece of party after party at which he would play the piano until the last weary guest departed. Myrna Loy told this author of one party she gave at which Richard Rodgers and Jerry began the evening, but at which George Gershwin outlasted everyone except the hostess. Still loathe to leave, he sat with Miss Loy on the back steps of her house, talking and watching the sun rise.

Still, the Gershwins had the time and the peace in their driven lives to spend quiet moments with Plum. Ira's wife recalled their first party in Hollywood, at the Wodehouse's. Everyone was in voluble evidence except George, Ira, Plum, and Guy, who spent most of the evening in Plum's upstairs study, away from the merrymakers and in their own selected world. Later, when the Gershwins gave parties, she remembered Plum arriving in a topcoat—an oddity in California—stopping at the entrance, removing his coat, rolling it into a ball and stuffing it behind the front door, so that he could, at any moment, beat a hasty, unnoticed retreat.

June was in Hollywood during the first months of Guy's stay, too. The two doubtlessly met and spent time together, but out of the public eye. Marion had finally agreed to a divorce, and he was taking no chances on scotching it.[11]

Guy and the Gershwins toiled on with *Delicious* at Fox. The score was patched together from previous shows—"Blah Blah Blah" from the late and unlamented *East Is West;* "Delishious," written months before; even "Mischa, Jascha, Toscha, Sascha," a party song the two had written in 1921. The startling new piece of music was Gershwin's Second Rhapsody, composed for a Manhattan dream sequence. The plot, stitched together by Guy and Sonya Levien, was another Cinderella story.

The critics and the public loathed it. "Civilization hasn't had such a setback since the Dark Ages," was the opinion of the critic from *Outlook and Independent.* But by that time the Gershwins were back in New York and deeply into their Pulitzer Prize-winning political satire, *Of Thee I Sing,* and Guy was well into his own checkered future.

At one of the parties the Gershwins gave in Hollywood, Guy was introduced to a petite and marvelously configured, auburn-haired former chorus girl. Her name was Virginia DeLanty, she had danced in *Topsy and Eva,* and she had been married—twice—to Lee Duncan, the trainer of Rin Tin Tin. The two took to each other immediately, and now Guy had two love affairs—this one and June—to hide from Marion and her lawyers.

Fox Films was apparently undaunted by the failure of *Delicious*; in 1931, Guy wrote the scripts for two successful Fox features: *Ambassador Bill,* a vehicle for Will Rogers, and *Transatlantic,* a shipboard romance starring Edmund Lowe, Lois Moran, Jean Hersholt, and Myrna Loy.

The title of the last story was appropriate, for throughout the 1930s, Guy would beat a steady and rapid path between Europe and Hollywood. Virginia left Lee Duncan (she had always been frightened of Rin Tin Tin anyway) and she and Guy rented a house at 401 North Rodeo Drive, in Beverly Hills, where they lived with an audacious parrot that proceeded to bite Bert Kalmar on the nose and Jerry on the finger. From there, in 1931 and 1932, he wrote five more film scripts and two London musicals. For Fox, he completed *Careless Lady,* a musical starring Joan Bennett and John Boles; *Devil's Lottery,* a dramatization of a novel by Nalbro Bartley, starring Elissa Landi and Victor McLaglen; *A Painted Woman,* a South Sea Islands romance starring Peggy Shannon and Spencer Tracy; and *Pleasure Cruise,* a comedy starring Genevieve Tobin and Roland Young. At Paramount, under the pseudonym of George Broxbourne, he wrote *Ladies Should Listen,* a comedy starring Ann Sheridan and Cary Grant.

On the European end of his whirlwind travels, he and Fred Thompson contributed the librettos for *Song of the Drum,* with music by Vivian Ellis and lyrics by Desmond Carter, a huge spectacle at the Drury Lane starring Bobby Howes and Clarice Hardwicke; and, with Weston and Lee, *Give Me a Ring,* a Hippodrome show with music by Martin Broones and lyrics by Graham John, starring Evelyn Laye, who was highly praised while the show was roundly thrashed. The reviews apparently had little effect on attendance; it ran from June through November with, first, Adele Dixon and then Binnie Hale replacing Evelyn Laye.

In early 1933, the divorce from Marion began with the signing of the separation agreement. It would be four years before it would become final, and during that time Marion would continue to bring various suits against Guy for modification of the separation agreement, for more money, for more stocks, for attachment of some of his royalties. The only income Guy was able to hide from her was the fifty percent of Plum's lyric royalties which Plum would slip him on a regular basis, also out of sight of Ethel. With the success of "Bill," after its *Show Boat* appearance, this continued to be a sizable amount. [12]

Guy and Virginia, by this time, were husband and wife in every way but a legal one, and Guy brought Peggy, who was by now a striking seventeen, to Hollywood to stay with them. While he was there, he convinced Arthur Hornblow, Jr., to give her a screen test at Paramount. But Peggy had no aspirations whatsoever to be in films. As ravishing as she was—and she was a traffic stopper, combining the best physical qualities of both Guy and Marguerite—she was and would remain forever unconvinced of her own remarkableness. Rather than inheriting the flamboyance of her mother, she was intimidated by it.

Namara was the toast of the Continent by now; she had made the first operatic film, *Gypsy Blood* (which she later privately renamed *That Bloody Gypsy*), a film treatment of *Carmen,* at British International Pictures in Elstree and at the bull ring in Ronda, Spain. Sir Malcolm Sargent conducted the London Philharmonic, and the film brought her even more attention on the Continent.

She had left Harry Lochman and had taken as a lover a stunningly handsome man named Mindret Lord. Tall, slim, possessed of the same chiseled features as Guy but in a more refined form, he claimed to be a nephew of the Indian poet Tagore, but his last name was actually Loeb, and he was really related to the Loeb of Leopold and Loeb fame. Mindret Lord wrote strange, surreal stories, which were admired by, among others, Carl Van Vechten, F. Scott Fitzgerald, and James Thurber, who was instrumental in getting some of them published in *The New Yorker.* He and Namara spent much of their time at Juan les Pins, taking Peggy with them in the summer, mixing with the rest of the international set that inhabited the Villa America, Gerald and Sarah Murphy's haven at La Garoupe.

Namara took painting lessons from Monet, who in return had a piano shipped to his studio in Giverny from Paris so that she could play and sing to him. She was a frequenter of La Colombe d'Or, where Rouault, Picasso, and a dozen other Post-Impressionists and Modernists paid for their lodging and their meals with their works. Peggy went along and lounged on the beach at Juan les Pins and attended her mother's concerts. Namara would deliver her encores on a tiny spinet, whose white keys were black and whose black keys were gold filigree and whose cover was laced with autographs of Caruso, Debussy, de Falla, Stravinsky, Noel Coward, Cole Porter, Isadora Duncan, F. Scott Fitzgerald, Ernest Hemingway, Stokowski. . . .

"Namara, you should never drink. You were born tight," said Noel Coward to her, and all the while her daughter Peggy wished, as she put it, ". . . to be like everybody else. I didn't want a glamorous mother. I wanted a mother who cooked things in the kitchen and had nice fat red cheeks and wore an apron."

In school in Switzerland, Peggy displayed a picture of her mother in a nun's costume for *Thais* and referred to "my mother the nun" who was so grieved over her divorce from Peggy's father that she took the veil. And she was believed, until one spring day, when parents came to take their children to lunch in Montreux. Peggy was ill and was compelled to entertain her family in the dining hall, under the scrutiny of teachers and classmates whose parents didn't make the trip.

She was terrified. She knew her mother would make nothing less than a grand entrance, and her fears were justified. Fashionably late, Namara swept into the school's courtyard in an open car. She was wearing, rather than a nun's habit, a giant picture hat that made her seem three times life-size. Boisterously accompanying her were Noel Coward, Elsa Maxwell, and Harpo Marx. They took the school by storm.

And so, in Hollywood, though she captivated many men, Peggy didn't become a film actress or anything near it. [13]

In Bronxville, Betty Kern Miller announced to Jerry that she thought *she* might like to become an actress. It was during one of the long and intense talks they had in his library, often later at night than most girls her age stayed up. He would let his eager and embracing mind race through a multitude of topics, challenging her, informing her, tutoring her.

He thought for a moment, then said, in measured tones, "You're intelligent, and so you'll give an intelligent performance. You'll be acceptable. But you'll never be great."

It was the truth as he saw it, delivered as gently as he could, and his daughter heeded his words. [14]

As for his work: Broadway, still in the grip of the Depression, offered little for him. But RKO had tendered him work in Hollywood. He wasn't feeling all that well, and his spirits were given no elevation by his personal physician, Dr. Forster Kennedy, who informed him that he possessed the same pernicious anemia that had been the cause of his father's death.

And so, once again, he left New York for the healing sunshine and proliferating work of California.

. . .

Guy passed through New York in 1933 with Virginia, heading in the opposite direction. They settled in at the May Fair Hotel in London, and Peggy came from Switzerland to spend some time with them. It was Guy's plan to have Peggy be presented at Court and therefore be an especially good catch for a wealthy man. She listened to him carefully, realizing that this might be the way she could finally draw closer to her father. She was aware that his love affair with Virginia was something quite different from that with her mother and with the other women of his life, for instead of becoming restless in time, as he usually did, he was more and more devoted to her. And it was obvious that Virginia was not easy; she was high strung, determined, and very, very possessive of Guy. She wouldn't easily accept Peggy, but Peggy was willing to try, and so she went off to a castle in Scotland, owned by a Mrs. Burroughs—an impoverished aristocrat who took young girls and taught them how to arrange flowers and curtsy before the king and queen.

Meanwhile, Guy and Virginia found a flat at 8 Orchard Court, and a 600-year-old, thatched roof cottage with heavy beams and a constantly surprising garden near the sea in Sussex. Called Thyme Cottage, it would be their weekend and summer refuge for the next six years, where they would entertain Alma and Alfred Hitchcock, Terence Rattigan (as a young genius), Laura LaPlante, Miriam and Tim Whelan, and Arthur Hornblow, Jr. and Myrna Loy, on a prenuptial honeymoon.

But it wasn't for entertaining that Guy sought out Thyme Cottage. It was to work once again with Plum on a new assignment from Aarons and Freedley. It would be the last time Guy and Plum's name would appear side by side in a new Broadway musical, and it would be a smash hit whose creation was equally as dramatic as its success.

*Chapter*

# 19

# Duet

## 1933–1939

Plum, after his not very rewarding sojourn in Hollywood, settled comfortably into a country house on 100 acres in Provence, in the south of France. Down the road from H. G. Wells and called *Domaine de la Freyere*, it was a refuge in which he pounded out novels and short stories at a comfortable rate.

That was one of the reasons that Plum chose to live temporarily outside of America. The other was an equally compelling one, and Guy, ever mindful of money, would eventually follow his friend's example. In December of 1932, Plum had received the shocking news that the IRS was officially certain that he owed them $187,000 in back taxes. His American accountant felt he could reduce it to $70,000, and so, in 1933, Plum wrote to William Townend, "My scheme is to imitate dear old France . . . and sit tight. . . . I shall be glad to be settled in England. . . . This country is fine but we are too far away. . . . And if one lives in Cannes there is the constant temptation of the Casino."[1]

While Plum sat tight, his American tax obligations climbed, with penalties, to $300,000. And so began a long feud between Plum and the tax authorities in both America and England.

From Provence, the Wodehouses moved to Paris, and it was there that Guy caught up with them. He had in hand the offer from Aarons and Freedley to write a shipboard musical with Cole Porter. For Plum, it was too much of a delight to pass up; it was the theatre again, and it would be working with the man with whom he would rather work than anyone else in the world.

The problem was Paris. Guy hated Paris and refused to work in it. Porter loved it, as he would later say in song, but Guy was adamant. They had to search for a middle ground.

Plum and Ethel, with Guy's help, found it in Le Touquet, a seaside resort on the coast of Brittany dominated by a golf course and a casino and just across the English Channel from Guy's cottage in Sussex. Ethel found a house called Low Wood, which Plum likened to their home in Great Neck, and the two moved to Brittany in June of 1934.

"At first I didn't like the place, and then suddenly it began to get me," Plum wrote to Townend, "and it struck both Ethel and me that, as regards situation, it was the one ideal spot in the world. I can get over to England by boat in a few hours and by plane in one hour. It is only two and a half hours from Paris and within motoring distance of Cherbourg."[2]

The house needed an enormous amount of fixing up, and for a while, Plum and Ethel stayed at the Royal Picardy and then the Golf Hotel. But both knew that Low Wood would be their home for a long time.

Now that they'd agreed upon a mutual location, Guy and Plum got to work on the musical—and a straight play, simultaneously. The straight play was to be a dramatization of Plum's novel *If I Were You,* retitled *Who's Who.* The musical went through several title changes as well as plot transformations. It began life as *Crazy Week,* then became *Hard to Get,* and finally resolved itself into *Anything Goes.* Guy stated, in some notes left in his study after he died, that he and the Gershwins had thought of doing a musical called *Bon Voyage* early in the 1930s. But then he went on to say that George Gershwin died in the middle of working on it, thus muddling the chronology and placing the statement under heavy suspicion.[3]

At any rate, by July, they had a preliminary script ready for Aarons and Freedley. Porter had already composed "You're the Top," "Blow, Gabriel, Blow," and "Easy to Love," (which was later replaced by "All Through the Night," when William Gaxton couldn't navigate its range), and two songs that never made it to the New York production: one, "There's No Such Thing as Love," which has disappeared from the Porter treasury without a trace, and "To Be in Love and Young," which was dropped from the show in Boston.

Ironically, in the first version of the script, "To Be in Love and Young" was reprised no less than three times, indicating that Porter, Plum, and Guy had high hopes for it.

The first version of *Anything Goes,* which still retained the title *Hard to Get* for its second act, was an antic Hollywood satire. According to penciled notations on the script by Guy, "Freedley objected to the Hollywood satire, [despite the fact that] George Oppenheimer read this script and said it was the funniest Hollywood satire yet written." The second part of the statement is also suspect, since George S. Kaufman and Moss Hart's benchmark Hollywood send up, *Once in a Lifetime,* had already opened, in 1930.

Still, Hollywood was very much in the recent memories of both Plum and Guy, and they had riotous fun with it. In this version, the juvenile is named Jimmy Crocker, rather than Billy Crocker, as he later became; Reno Sweeney is Jennie Prentiss; Hope Harcourt is Barbara Frisbee; and Moonface McGee — Public Enemy Number Thirteen — is Elmer Purkis, a former scenario writer who introduces himself cinematically: "I'm a fugitive from a chain gang."

Although Guy's notations indicate that Ethel Merman had not yet been hired, the Jennie Prentiss part was obviously written with her in mind. In fact, Merman's name in parentheses follows the character's first appearance, as do Gaxton and Victor Moore's for their projected roles.

In its broad outlines, the plot was set from the beginning: Jimmy has been fired for buying the wrong stocks for his boss, who is the father of a girl whom Jimmy once met and with whom he's fallen instantly in love. Barbara/Hope is sailing on the *Columbia* to Europe to marry Sir Evelyn Oakleigh, who is also aboard. Jimmy/Billy has a friend — Jennie/Reno — who gets stuck on board when the boat leaves New York.

Jimmy/Billy tries everything he can to win Barbara/Hope and eventually gets thrown into the brig for his efforts, but, after Purkis and Jimmy escape from the ship by playing strip poker with two Chinamen and donning their outfits, they expose Oakleigh as the father of an illegitimate Chinese child. The mother, Plum Blossom, has been changed by Oakleigh "from Plum Blossom to Plum Tart," and she has thrown herself into a volcano, leaving behind little Orange Blossom, which makes him "the father of a Pekingese." Oakleigh is thus bested, and it all turns out happily at the final curtain, which is pure Princess formula, featuring a wedding and a two-page tie-up of the plot's multitude of loose ends.

It's in the details that the script differs wildly from its final form. Jennie, unlike Reno, is not a takeoff on Aimee Semple McPherson but experiences a conversion during a bomb scene and thus launches into "Blow Gabriel Blow."

Jimmy/Billy doesn't merely bump into Barbara/Hope at a party; he's saved her life when her horse ran away—down Fifty-ninth Street in Manhattan. After the rescue, he even talked a traffic cop out of giving her a ticket for speeding and reckless driving. Purkis/Moon is escaping, not from jail, but from Hollywood, and this gives rise to the multitude of references and send ups.

Commenting on a detective following them, Purkis states "That wasn't a detective. That was Myron Selznick." Jimmy moans, "My whole future depends on stopping a girl from getting married." "It isn't Gloria Swanson, is it?" asks Purkis. "No!" exclaims Jimmy. "Oh, then you've got a chance," concludes Purkis. When the plot of the play gets muddled, Purkis thinks it's ". . . great Clara Bow stuff."

There's much talk of the writer's lot in Hollywood, and Purkis reveals that a book called *Plotto* was chained in his hutch at the studio. It was organized in slices, designed to be fit together in various combinations. Part way through the second act, the ship's captain, officers, and sailors sit down and conduct a Hollywood story conference, during which Elmer Purkis comes up with the idea of Public Enemy Number Thirteen, his own later incarnation.

Guy's particular obsession, and one that he would carry with him for the rest of his life, was the bomb scene. In it, Jimmy and Purkis plot a ruse that will make Jimmy a hero. They find a dumbbell in Oakleigh's cabin and saw it in half so that it looks like a bomb. Next, they spread the story that there's a bomb aboard. Jimmy produces the phony bomb, throws it overboard, and wins the admiration of Barbara. It works miraculously, until a crew member finds the other half of the dumbbell, whereupon Jimmy is clapped into irons.[4]

The first script was rejected by Freedley for its Hollywood treatment, not its similarity to the tragic fire at sea of the liner *Morro Castle,* as has been historically accepted. Nor would he blanch at the second version because of its continued treatment of a catastrophe at sea. It would be because the second version was a hopeless mess.

The only surviving copy of that script was, alas, blown to bits during World War II, when a direct hit from a German bomb demolished Guy's flat on Onslow Square. Unlucky enough to be located down the block from M.I.5 headquarters, Guy and Virginia's lodgings, containing priceless memorabilia and scripts, received several tons of explosives intended for M.I.5.

However, Guy reconstructed it in outline form several years later, insisting that his and Plum's first and second submissions to Freedley were "challenge" plays, that is, plays in which the hero says he will do a certain thing in a limited amount of time and makes it a sort of a wager. Or, as Plum waggishly put it,

". . . like the fairy stories when the Prince has to bail out a lake with a thimble with a hole in it in order to win the girl."[5]

According to Guy's notes, the second version opened this way: "Billy Crocker, a breezy young man, comes to the sailing of an Atlantic liner in New York to wish bon voyage to an old girl friend with whom he is still on affectionate terms. He runs into his boss, an irascible individual, in a filthy temper after being defied by his daughter who is sailing for England, together with a genial johnny whom she intends to marry on their arrival."

The father, now named Elisha J. Whitney, leaves; Billy runs into Hope, whose name he doesn't remember. She's the boss's daughter, and he climbs aboard the ship to be with her.

So far, the plot of the second version was almost identical to that of the first. But now, it began to diverge:

Once aboard, Billy runs into a ship's gambler masquerading as a clergyman. (Guy claimed he had met just such an individual on several crossings of his own and patterned the character after him.) The police come to arrest the fake Reverend Moon, but Billy leads them astray, and so Moon and Reno, in gratitude and friendship, respectively, agree to try to get Hope, the boss's daughter, away from her betrothed and into Billy's arms.

Moon gives Billy the passport and ticket of a famous thief known as the modern Raffles and then, in order to concoct a heroic action that will make Billy look wonderful in Hope's eyes, starts a rumor that there's been a bomb planted aboard the ship as part of a gangland vendetta. He'll build the bomb, he assures Billy, and at the proper dramatic moment, give it to him. Billy will then appear with it and jauntily throw it overboard. He guarantees that it won't explode.

The rumor that there are bombs aboard circulates, and this in turn causes rampant evangelical fever. Reno, a graduate evangelist, stages a prayer meeting. At the height of it, Billy appears with the bomb, tosses it overboard—and it explodes. Billy and Moon are arrested and thrown into the brig for carrying bombs. End of act 1.

Act 2 was so complicated, even Guy had difficulty remembering it in later years. As nearly as he could recall, it opened with the passengers finding out that Moon and Billy weren't really going to bomb the boat and hijack it and set the crew and passengers adrift. Once realizing this, they freed the two pseudocrooks and proceeded to treat them like two movie stars. But, when news arrived that the *real* Raffles had been arrested in New York, the passengers abandoned the two, and once again, Billy and Moon were tossed into the brig.

They escaped by playing a strip poker game with two Chinese converts of a missionary who was arrested in New York in place of Moon. The boss, flying to England to head off his daughter's marriage, denounced Billy as a con man, Billy again disguised himself as a Chinaman to escape his boss's wrath and coincidentally elope with Hope, Reverend Moon disguised himself as a woman to escape the police, Reno carried off the original bridegroom, and the chorus sang the finale.[6]

Freedley was no happier with this version than the first, but there was time to rewrite. *Anything Goes* was not scheduled to go into rehearsal until October of 1934, and this was still the beginning of August.

Guy had planned to come to New York to shepherd the book through rehearsals, but by the time Freedley received the script, Guy was in a nursing home in Worthing and would remain there for three months, recuperating from the effects of a burst and gangrenous appendix.

Writing later that autumn from Bluepoint, Ferring-on-Sea, Sussex, to his sister Ivy, he recalled it: "I never told you quite how near I was to slipping off into the beyond," he wrote. "I had a gangrene appendix that burst five hours before I was operated on. Why I didn't get peritonitis is, my doctor says, the nearest thing to a miracle he has ever seen. I still feel very thankful when I look at the sunshine sparkling on the sea from this window where I am writing. The world is such a pleasant place. I'm not at all anxious to go exploring for quite a while yet."[7]

"I've just returned from a hurried visit to England, but simply couldn't get a moment to get in touch with you," Plum wrote to Townend from Le Touquet. "I had a phone call from Ethel saying that Guy Bolton had been rushed into hospital at Worthing with acute appendicitis and nearly died, and I had to spend my time travelling up and down. He seems to be all right now, thank goodness, but it was a near thing."

The letter is dated July 23, 1936, but the followup notes by Townend talk of Low Wood being ". . . in the hands of the builders and occupied by Madge, the cook, and her husband. . . ." Low Wood was under construction in 1934, but had long since been finished in 1936. Thus, Plum must have misdated the letter.[8]

As the years went by, Guy would lengthen the hours until he was operated on from five to seven and give himself peritonitis and pleurisy. It was unnecessary; he was in dire straits and far too ill to travel to America in the summer of 1934.

As for Plum, his tax problems totally precluded his coming back to America, and besides, he had to finish up *Who's Who* all by himself for its imminent opening, on September 24, at the Duke of York's Theatre. (It would be an abysmal failure, lasting only nineteen performances.) Besides this, he was writing *The Luck of the Bodkins,* editing a volume of his favorite humorous stories for *Hutchinson's* and writing a 16,000-word story for the *New York Herald Tribune.* He was, simply, as in the case of *Sally,* fourteen years earlier, unavailable.

So, contrary to theatrical legend, which blames the *Morro Castle* disaster for the massive rewrite of *Anything Goes's* libretto, the reasons were considerably more complex and extensive. Faced with a rehearsal schedule and the empty Alvin Theatre, Freedley turned to his director, Howard Lindsay, and Lindsay's friend, Buck Crouse, to salvage the book. This they did, cutting and shaping it, bringing in bits of business such as a comedy scene of Moon winning a clay pigeon shoot with a tommy gun, stealing the boss's glasses so that he won't recognize Billy, and Billy cutting the hair off a Pomeranian to make a beard to disguise himself. And they threw out Guy's beloved bomb scene.

The show opened and was an enormous success, largely because of Cole Porter's score and the performances of Merman, Moore, and Gaxton. It would run for 421 performances in New York and even ring up 250 performances in a Charles B. Cochran production at the Palace Theatre that gave no credit at all to Lindsay and Crouse and featured Jeanne Aubert in the Reno Sweeney—changed to Reno La Grange—role. Miss Aubert's kilometres-thick French accent totally obscured Porter's lyrics, laying waste particularly to "You're the Top"—but audiences came anyway. And for the rest of their lives, Plum and Guy would be able to live better than they might have, had *Anything Goes* not been the smash success it was.

In 1934, the book, still credited to Plum and Guy with an assist from Lindsay and Crouse, was mostly overlooked by audiences and critics.

Guy and Plum, on the other hand, did nothing *but* notice the book. They were furious about the wholesale changes made in their "challenge play." "The story was largely ruined," Guy wrote later in life, "by the rewriting of the lads hired to take Wodehouse's and my place at rehearsals." He adds, unkindly at best, "Crouse at that time had had no connection with the stage and Lindsay, his buddy, was an actor and stage director—not a writer. The play succeeded, despite its defects because of its great score, the casting of Victor Moore and Merman and the great choreography, which was novel, and a chorus line containing solo performers."9

• • •

Hindsight can well be the rear echelon of reason; perhaps if Guy had been there, the book would have been better, but that's open to speculation, judging from the first two versions. It was, ultimately, sad that Guy and Plum would never rejoice in the fact that their last produced musical was such an abiding, soaring hit.

It was in 1935 that Jerry suggested to Oscar Hammerstein that it would be a fine idea to do a Princess-style musical for Broadway. He remembered Bessie Marbury with particular affection, and his plan was to capture her character in a musical that would also re-create the tradition established by her imprint and her vision.

Oscar Hammerstein was sympathetic to the scheme, but it would have to wait three years for fruition. There was much to accomplish on the West Coast, and having made the decision that this was where he should conduct his professional life, Jerry proceeded with plans to settle in California. Nineteen-thirty-five began with an offer to Jerry and Oscar to compose the score for a new Jeannette MacDonald-Nelson Eddy operetta, tentatively titled *Champagne and Orchids* — "unless," Jerry wrote to a friend, "the bright boys in the sales and distributing dept. consider that censorable these pure days."[10]

It was not the production code that aborted the work; failure to develop a suitable script was the culprit, and the only work in Hollywood with which Jerry would mark his fiftieth year was a solitary title song for a Jean Harlow film, *Reckless.*

With no immediate work in prospect, Jerry, Eva, and Betty headed East for a holiday, only to be called back by RKO. This time, the assignment was for a film that would introduce opera diva Lily Pons to the movie-going public. Jerry's lyricist would be a tall and witty woman who would become not only one of his favorite wordsmiths but a constant, bright presence in the Kern household.

Jerry had worked with Dorothy Fields the previous year, when RKO asked for two additional songs for its screen version of *Roberta.* She rewrote Oscar Hammerstein's lyrics for "I Won't Dance" to fit a scene in the movie involving Fred Astaire and Ginger Rogers and supplied the lyrics to a new, marvelously succinct, sixteen-bar Kern melody. Legend has it that the lyrics went into the picture without Jerry's approval, and he heard it first in a screening room full of quaking junior executives who knew of the composer's outbursts. But their trembling was for naught; Dorothy Fields's lyrics to "Lovely to Look At" charmed Jerry, as they would much of the world, and from that point forward, they became fast, creative friends.

The Lily Pons film, *I Dream Too Much*, was a success, and Jerry was immediately offered three more projects: composing additional music for Universal's 1936 screen version of *Show Boat*, writing the scores for a new film for Astaire and Rogers called *I Won't Dance*, and, back at Universal, *Riviera*.

Jerry and Oscar composed five songs for *Show Boat*, only three of which made it past the editors. "I Have the Room Above Her," was a ballad given to Allan Jones to sing to Irene Dunne in a duplex scene aboard the *Cotton Blossom;* "Galavantin' Around," was a blackface solo for Irene Dunne, and "I Still Suits Me," was a good-natured confessional for Paul Robeson.

*I Won't Dance* became *Never Gonna Dance* and then *Swing Time.* It was one of Jerry's richest scores for Hollywood, and Dorothy Fields's lyrics gave a bright lilt to "A Fine Romance," "The Way You Look Tonight," "Never Gonna Dance," and "Bojangles of Harlem."

And so, with work an apparent certainty without end in Hollywood, Jerry and Eva bought property at 917 North Whittier Drive, a newly developed part of Beverly Hills, and began to construct their West Coast home. Although bereft of the terraces of Bronxville, it would resemble their Westchester home in its exterior, white-with-black-trim appearance and in the decoration of some of its interior rooms. The highly personalized, working library would be duplicated by Hammond Ashley, a master carpenter recommended by Dorothy Hammerstein, the patio would be patterned on that of Irene Dunne's, and the swimming pool would contain, at its bottom, a droll octopus.

All that remained was to transfer the contents of Bronxville westward, and that they did in 1937. The piece of furniture with which Jerry exercised the greatest planning was his favorite piano, a Bluthner. Though the Kern living room contained a Steinway, it was the Bluthner that was accorded the private abode of the library, and that Jerry used for composing. Thus, it had an almost mystical significance to him. He made sure that the Steinway company crated and carted it, along with their piano, from Bronxville to Beverly Hills.

On the early July day that the two pianos arrived on North Whittier Drive, Jerry met the movers and watched carefully as they carried the two valuable musical instruments into the house and began to uncrate them. The Steinway was in pristine condition. It had made the trip as if it had been cradled in soft arms.

Jerry and the workmen turned confidently to the container housing the Bluthner. The movers proceeded to gently remove the packing screws. All loosened easily, as they had when they had unveiled the Steinway. All except one. It moved reluctantly, as if it were going through more than the walls of the crate.

And then the horrible reason presented itself. The packers in Bronxville had driven a screw directly through the sounding board of the Bluthner.

Jerry let out a bellow of pain and rage. He turned ashen. The movers might as well have driven a screw through his heart, for, being a betting man, and an imaginative one, he imagined bad luck now, the departure of the precise conditions he had spent a lifetime setting for the writing of his music.

Six mornings later, as he was about to sit down to a bridge game, he complained of feeling ill, rose, and collapsed. He was rushed to Cedars of Lebanon Hospital, suffering from a severe heart attack, complicated by either a stroke or an embolism. It was reasonable to assume that the shock of the damage to his piano, his own high-strung temperament, and the genes of his father converged that calamitous July morning.

It would be a long convalescence. Eva called Oscar and Dorothy Hammerstein home from abroad, and they rushed to Jerry's side. Complete isolation, quiet, and freedom from stress were prescribed, and he would spend the next three months in a private room at the hospital.

The Hammersteins and his own family insulated Jerry from troubles and shocks. The worst of these, one they felt they had to absolutely hide from him, took place on July 11 in the same hospital in which Jerry was confined. George Gershwin, rushed to Cedars of Lebanon to be operated on for a brain tumor, died, just two months short of his thirty-ninth birthday.

In late August, Jerry heard rumors that something was wrong with George, and Eva told him he was ill. Later that same week, Jerry heard a radio playing Gershwin music. The announcer referred to the composer in the past tense. Jerry asked Eva if his discovery, colleague, and friend was indeed dead. She affirmed it, as gently as she could.

It was a greater tragedy than the one that had conceivably brought on his own heart attack, and he absorbed it quietly and sadly. The world would never be quite the same again, even though Jerry would recover and continue to write. Something had gone out of it and out of Jerry, too.[11]

Across a continent and an ocean, Guy and Plum continued to congregate regularly. Le Touquet was just the sort of tonic they needed. There was the golf course on which to roam, the country lanes on which to stroll. And for Ethel, there was the casino, which she frequented regularly.

Peggy, there on holiday with Guy and Virginia, recalled a sunlit summer morning in June. Rising early, packing a lunch, she walked to the beach. She had just spread her blanket, preparatory to a day in the sun, when suddenly she looked up and there, traversing a nearby dune, was Ethel. Still dressed in evening finery and jewelry, she was on her way home from an all-night gambling session at the casino.

"I broke the bank at the casino one night," Ethel later recalled. "I'd been gambling, all night, and I came in, and Plummy was already at work, and he looked up, and blinked, behind his glasses. And he said, 'Oh, you poor darling. You've lost all your money!' And he reached into his pocket and took out all the bills he had and handed them to me. And there I was, with my purse bursting with all the francs I'd won."[12]

Aside from this, it was a low-key life in Low Wood and thus a refuge from the rest of Guy's life, which continued at its accustomed frantic and peripatetic pace, punctuated by mad visits from Marion. At one time, in Hollywood, she strode down the aisle of a theatre during a preview and began to beat Virginia about the shoulders; once, she threw a brick through the window of their home in Beverly Hills; once, she climbed over a guard fence and through the window of their flat in London. And all the while, poor Guybo, conceived in passion and born in bitterness, was subjected to the constant renewal of a soul-searing hurt. At the eye of a self-renewing emotional hurricane, he had no chance at all for normalcy.

Meanwhile, Guy was fast becoming as famous and sought after in the West End as he had been on pre-Depression Broadway. And it was just as well. The American musical theatre was acquiring an intelligence and an edge and a social awareness that were unnatural to Guy and Plum.

The essence of the Princess Musicals was smartness and polish; *Of Thee I Sing, Let 'Em Eat Cake, The Cradle Will Rock,* and *Pins and Needles* were gritty evocations of the spirit of the Depression. But on the London musical stage, time had stopped. It was still the 1920s, and Guy was as much in demand as he had been a decade earlier in New York.

Fred Thompson was his constant collaborator now, and the two ground out, by any age's standards, an extraordinary amount of work in a brief amount of time. Their whirlwind assault on the London stage began with *Seeing Stars,* a vehicle for Leslie Henson, produced by Firth Shephard at the Gaiety Theatre on October 21, 1935. Its minimal book, about Jimmy Swing (Henson), a financially embarrassed hotel proprietor who disguises himself as an Oriental fortune teller and is saved by marrying a princess, was merely a rack upon which to hang the talents of Henson, Fred Enmey, and Louise Brown. The music by Martin Broones—whom Guy had recruited by letter and wire in New York—and the lyrics by Graham John received mild notices. But audience reaction convinced both Firth Shephard and Leslie Henson that Bolton and Thompson were right for the Gaiety.

At the beginning of 1936, Guy collaborated with Clifford Grey on an orthodox operetta set in Balleroo, Australia, and titled *At the Silver Swan.* The music was by Edmond Samuels and the lyrics were by Clifford Grey; it opened for a short run at the Palace Theatre on February 19, 1936, starring Magda Kun, Delysia, Bruce Carfax, and Marta Labarr.

For the next few months, Guy joined Fred Thompson in cranking out no fewer than three shows destined to open within days of each other in the autumn of 1936. First, there was Firth Shephard's annual Gaiety show for Leslie Henson. This time it was called *Swing Along,* all about a certain Maxie Mumm, who, having been cleaned out at Monte Carlo, is induced to impersonate the notorious Xabiski, chief of the Yellow Shirts, whose life is sought by the renegade No Shirts. Douglas Furber joined Guy and Thompson on the book, and the music and lyrics were again by Martin Broones and Graham John. After an August tryout at the Opera House in Manchester, it opened on September 2 at the Gaiety and remained there throughout the 1936–37 season.

Thirteen days later, *This'll Make You Whistle,* which had been tried out at Christmastime, 1935, at the King's Hall, Southsea, and found wanting in the book department, opened at the Palace. Starring Jack Buchanan and Elsie Randolph, it told the suspiciously *Oh, Boy!–Oh, Kay!*-like story of Knightsbridge playboy Bill Hopping, anxious to rid himself of his old sweetheart, the sporty, horsy Laura Buxton (Sylvia Leslie) so that he can pursue the more essentially feminine Joan Longhurst (Jean Gillie). His friends were a roisterous and dissipated lot, headed by artist's model Bobbie Rivers (Elsie Randolph), and through deceptions that included nude pictures, empty liquor bottles, and a deserted baby who turned out to be black, love conquered all at the Hotel Britannique in Le Bouquet (read: Le Touquet). The music and lyrics, this time, were by Maurice Sigler, Al Goodhart, and Al Hoffman, and the show also remained through the season, closing shortly before *Swing Along.*

Three weeks after *This'll Make You Whistle* opened, on October 8, 1936, Arthur Riscoe and Clifford Whitley presented *Going Places,* with a book by Guy and Thompson and music and lyrics by Vivian Ellis, at the gigantic Savoy Theatre. A Parisian romp that starred American dancer/singer June Knight— who was cheered by the gallery on opening night, and whose curtain speeches were the only ones the audience cared to listen to—it featured Arthur Riscoe, Peggy Rawlings, Olga Baclanova, and the fourteen-year-old Mawby Triplets. It wasn't the season's strongest entry; the *Times* complained that "Mr. Vivian Ellis's music deserved a better book."

Nonetheless, Guy could boast of no fewer than four musicals running simultaneously in the West End in 1936 and 1937. It was an achievement to remind him of the heyday of the Princess. Back then, though, he hadn't had Hollywood calling him.

Sometime in the midst of this, he went back to California for consultations on a sound remake of his R. B. Trevelyan masquerade, *The Dark Angel.* The new adaptation, by Lillian Hellman and Mordaunt Sharp, was again produced by Samuel Goldwyn and starred Frederic March, Merle Oberon, and Sidney Franklin. Pronounced by *Variety* a "sockeroo woman's picture," it sustained Guy's fortunes in Hollywood while he was being feted in London.

Marguerite had now left Mindret Lord and married George Hoye, a world-renowned landscape architect who would remain her husband to the end of her life. They had moved back to California; Peggy had adopted Hollywood as her home and had married Jimmy Stack, the brother of movie star Robert Stack. It would be a glamorous but short-lived marriage, punctuated by a round-the-world honeymoon and high life in glamorous places. It was not a match of which Guy approved. It was all well and good for Hollywood to give him money, but his plan for Peggy had been for her to marry into money elsewhere. Jimmy Stack had neither a sustainable fortune nor non-Hollywood credentials, and Peggy and he were met with cool receptions by Virginia and Guy in Sussex. [13]

Meanwhile, in Hollywood, Betty Kern was also entering her first marriage, to Richard Green, the younger brother of composer and Hollywood musical director John Green. It was no more fated for success than Peggy's; in fact Betty apparently realized her mistake before the marriage, but Green's insistence that it would be humiliating to suffer a public broken engagement forced her to go through with it. From the perspective of today, this seems a suspect story, and yet those were different times, even in Hollywood.

Recovered from his heart attack and its accompanying stroke, Jerry returned to the writing of film scores, with Oscar Hammerstein and Dorothy Fields. *High, Wide and Handsome,* the Universal project with Oscar, contained one of his most beautiful melodies, "The Folks Who Live on the Hill," and his next, RKO's *The Joy of Living,* written with Dorothy, contained two more memorable gems, "You Couldn't Be Cuter," and the too-seldom heard "What's Good about Good-Night?"

By the end of 1937, Jerry felt it was time to return to Broadway. He united with Oscar Hammerstein and Otto Harbach on a piece of Americana titled *Gentlemen Unafraid.* So dedicated was Jerry to this project that he rejected, out of hand, an offer to write the music for MGM's projected version of *The Wizard of Oz.*

*Gentlemen Unafraid,* set during the Civil War and dealing with love and Union vs. Confederacy loyalty, was a monster production and demanded epic production ideas and facilities. Jerry and Oscar and Otto determined to open it not at the Forrest Theatre in Philadelphia but at the outdoor Municipal Opera of St. Louis.

Still too weak to travel, Jerry was forced to remain in Beverly Hills. But Oscar and Otto oversaw rehearsals in St. Louis. Anticipation ran high; Max Gordon came to St. Louis as a potential producer; Louis A. Lotito, manager of the Martin Beck, was there; John Kenneth Hyatt, manager of Rockefeller Center, which at that time included the mammoth Center Theatre, was there, as was MGM's Kenneth McKenna.

Nature refused to recognize the importance of June 3, 1938 to Jerry and Oscar, and declined to cooperate; it rained hard until 9:30, and after the curtain rose at that hour, it continued, off and on, for the entire performance. But it wasn't the rain alone that dampened the spirits of audience, critics, and potential producers. The musical itself was in dire book trouble, a victim of its own elevated ambitions. To add to the problems, an under-rehearsed chorus did nothing to present Jerry's music in its best light.

*Gentlemen Unafraid* lived and died in St. Louis in June of 1938, and only one of Jerry's songs, the exquisite ballad, "Your Dream (Is the Same as My Dream)" survived, finding a niche in Jerry's next picture, *One Night in the Tropics.*

But the show's failure failed to deter Jerry and Oscar. Returning with increased strength and enthusiasm to the original idea of re-creating a Princess show and educating the present public about the place in history of Bessie Marbury, they set to work fashioning what would be Jerry's last musical for Broadway, *Very Warm for May.*

Max Gordon, in Hollywood at the time, heard some of the songs that Jerry and Oscar had already written and insisted on producing the show during the 1939–40 season. Oscar and Jerry agreed, and during the summer of 1939 worked in Norma Talmadge's Santa Monica beachhouse, rented for the purpose by Oscar. By August 28, Oscar was in New York to begin rehearsals. As in *Show Boat,* he would direct the book scenes. Vincente Minelli would design the show and stage the musical numbers. Jerry, still without his full strength, arrived in New York on September 25.

By October 10, *Very Warm for May* opened at the Wilmington Playhouse to unabashed enthusiasm. Betty Kern Miller recalls it as a triumph, a lovely evening, in which everybody concerned knew that a hit was in the making. The story involved a summer stock playhouse at which May (Grace McDonald), the daughter of William Graham (Donald Brian), is hiding out from gangsters with whom her father has become involved and who are threatening her life unless he works with them. The playhouse is owned by the eccentric Ogdon Quiler (Hiram Sherman)—a representation of Ray Comstock—and is located on the property of a gloriously fey matron, Winnie Spofford (Eve Arden)—the Bessie Marbury character.

Comic complications, musical comedy crooks a la Plum and Guy, and a neat Princess solution with appropriate youngsters and appropriate oldsters marrying each other ended a charming evening that was enriched by the best score Jerry had written since *Show Boat*. It fairly burst with treasurable, inventive melody, from the lilting "Heaven in My Arms," "That Lucky Fellow," and "All in Fun" through the sostenuto waltz "In the Heart of the Dark" to "All the Things You Are," which has been called by countless composers and musicians either "the one perfect popular song," or "the greatest song ever written."

All was well and exuberant in Wilmington until two days after the opening of *Very Warm for May*. And then, Max Gordon appeared upon the scene. He hated everything he saw and heard. And so began a tumultuous tryout tour, during which Vincente Minelli was fired and replaced by Hassard Short, Albertina Rasch was flown in from California to revise Harry Losee's choreography, and Oscar Hammerstein was ordered to make massive rewrites in the book.

"They kept rewriting it and rewriting it and ruining it and ruining it," Betty Kern Miller recalls. It was a tragic and foolish mistake, and the result was one of the most wasteful failures in the American musical theatre.

*Very Warm for May* opened on November 17, 1939, at the Alvin Theatre in New York, and the universal disdain with which it was greeted sealed its quiet doom. "*Very Warm for May* very cold for November" one headline writer put it, and Brooks Atkinson summed up the reasons pointedly: "The book is a singularly haphazard invention that throws the show out of focus and makes an appreciation of Mr. Kern's music almost a challenge," he wrote. It was the most eloquent argument yet against creation by committee, particularly one chaired by a producer.

Gordon tried to sustain the run by lowering ticket prices, but nothing would entice audiences to *Very Warm for May*. It expired after fifty-nine performances. If only the producer had stayed out of Wilmington, Jerry's last Broadway musical, his tribute to the trio's Princess Theatre origins, might have been the triumph it should have been, rather than the flop it was.

In London, Firth Shephard kept the team of Guy Bolton and Fred Thompson busy churning out just the sort of talent racks that allowed Leslie Henson to pack the Gaiety. Their September entry in the 1937–38 season was called *Going Greek*. A tale of a modern Greek bandit gang, it gave Henson space and some reason to cavort as Alexandros Saggapopolous, Fred Emney to accompany him as his second banana, Pallas Pollicapillos, and Louise Brown to do her ballet turns.

A month later, Guy and Fred were represented, with Douglas Furber, by *Hide and Seek*. The music and lyrics were mostly by Vivian Ellis, and it was destined for the Hippodrome. Starring Bobby Howes, Cicely Courtneidge, and Ian Maclean, it had an unusually ambitious book that veered from 1937 to 1890 and back again, chronicling the fortunes of a Pierrot troupe and its star, Sally (Cicely Courtneidge), who falls in love with an American gangster (Ian Mac-Lean). Paralleling and sometimes interlacing this was a story concerning Sally's mother (Cicely Courtneidge again), who is a barmaid, and present-day Pierrot, Tommy's (Bobby Howes) father (Bobby Howes again), who is a jockey. Talk about complexity.

Still, *Hide and Seek* marked Cicely Courtneidge's return to the stage after an absence making films, and audiences took her, Bobby Howes, and the show to their collective hearts, for a long stay.

With all of his success in London musicals, Guy had not forgotten his straight play beginnings and aspirations; in fact, the other two-thirds of his output in 1937 concerned just that, with a twist. He and Virginia had finally made it legal; they were married in Brighton that year, with Plum, Ethel, and Leonora in attendance. Ethel had taken to Virginia as she hadn't taken to Marguerite. She and Virginia were two women in love with two men whose first and abiding affection was and would always remain writing. But they were willing, for the numerous benefits it provided, to take second chair, knowing that once the writing was over, these men were devotedly theirs.

Even Guy was behaving himself, penning love notes to Virginia, who was, alternately, "The Little Thing" and "His Five O'Clock Girl"—a reference to the time of afternoon they had met secretly in Hollywood while she was still married to Lee Duncan and he to Marion. Her nickname for him was "Hook"— a reference to Captain Hook of Peter Pan fame, who had stolen her away from Rin Tin Tin and his owner.

So, from Sussex, after conferring with Plum about his continuing and stubborn tax dealings with both America and Britain, Guy determined a way to save himself some tax money too: he invented an alias for Virginia—Stephen Powys—made it well known among various agents and managers that it was merely an alias for Virginia Bolton—and set up a separate tax account.

The two straight plays Guy wrote in 1937 bore the name Stephen Powys as their author. Both were comedies of manners. *Wise To-Morrow,* produced by Firth Shephard, opened at the Lyric Theatre on February 17, 1937, starring Nora Swinburne, Esmond Knight, Diana Churchill, and Martita Hunt. It was a solid success.

Even more of a triumph and a money-maker for decades to come was *Three Blind Mice,* produced by Shephard at the Duke of York's Theatre on April 26, 1938. The story of three young girls in search of wealthy husbands, it drew raves from every London critic ("I have no doubt that if in 1948 I am still on earth I shall see, flaming in the forehead of the Piccadilly sky the words 'Three Blind Mice' now in its tenth year," applauded James Agate in the *Sunday Times*), and audiences filled the Duke of York's for two seasons.

But that wasn't the end of *Three Blind Mice.* It was bought by Hollywood, where it was first made into a straight comedy starring Loretta Young, Marjorie Weaver, Pauline Moore, David Niven, and Joel McCrea. Three years later, in 1941, it was renamed *Moon over Miami* and musicalized by Twentieth Century Fox. Starring Carole Landis, Betty Grable, Charlotte Greenwood, Don Ameche, Robert Cummings, and Jack Haley, it was one of the highest grossing musicals of that year. Five years later, it was again renamed *Three Little Girls in Blue* and recast as a turn-of-the-century musical, starring June Haver, Vivian Blaine, Celeste Holm (in her first screen role), and George Montgomery. From such small beginnings, great fortunes are made, and Guy would attempt for the rest of his life to repeat this one.

Meanwhile, Peggy and Jimmy Stack had parted, and she had married Jimmy Burrowes, an executive with the Nestlé Company. The two had settled in Switzerland, and Guy was overjoyed. "Peggy's found herself a nice and wealthy young man who's not in the film business," Guy wrote to his father that year. His advice, both personally and on the stage, paid off bountifully in 1938.

Nor was the musical stage bereft of his name and work. First, to inaugurate the 1938–39 season, there was a new Vivian Ellis show, *The Fleet's Lit Up,* produced and directed by George Black and starring Frances Day, Stanley Lupino, Adele Dixon, Enid Lowe, Arthur Rigby, and Geraldo and his band. Guy and Fred Thompson delivered the script, a sketchy book at best that barely supported specialty turns by the stars, in early June, and by July the show was in rehearsal at the Hippodrome in Brighton, where it opened on Monday, August 1, the August Bank Holiday. Opening night ran nearly four hours, and cuts were made, but not in the book, which was miniscule anyway.

Guy and Fred Thompson were at their lighthearted best in it, with such exchanges as one in which Stanley Lupino held Frances Day in his arms so tightly that she let out an alarmed exclamation. "How fast your heart is beating—" she whimpered. "It sounds like a drum."

"Yes, dear, that's the call to arms," he answered. "Will you marry me?"

"Why, you're only an apology for a man!" she sniffed.

"Well," he rejoined, "will you accept an apology?"

*The Fleet's Lit Up* still ran three and a quarter hours when it opened at the London Hippodrome on August 20, 1938. James Agate, in the *Sunday Times,* pronounced it ". . . a nautical, vortical, piratical, fanatical extravaganza . . . ," which it was, and cluttered, besides.

But by this time, Guy and Fred were busy elsewhere with *Bobby Get Your Gun,* another elaborate show with an elaborate plot presented by Jack Waller and starring Bobby Howes. Its book was by Guy, Fred Thompson, and Bert Lee; the lyrics were by Clifford Grey, Bert Lee, and Desmond Carter, and its music was by Jack Waller and Joseph Turnbridge. It featured, in addition to Bobby Howes, David Burns, Diana Churchill, Bertha Belmore, and, in her first starring role, an American, sultry-voiced, sexily-contoured singer, Gertrude Niesen.

*Bobby Get Your Gun* went through an extensive tour and rewrites, opening first in Glasgow on August 27 and finally arriving at the Adelphi on October 7, 1938. Its combination of lost birth certificates, flashbacks to 1925, musical comedy crooks, and confused peers delighted audiences; Bobby Howes was canonized; Gertrude Niesen stopped the show with a conga and an outrageous burlesque of Cleopatra; at the thunderous ovation on opening night, Jack Waller and Bobby Howes thanked the audience, Gertrude Niesen thanked it a million times, and Diana Churchill thanked it two million times.

Now, with *The Fleet's Lit Up* a solid, sold-out success, and *Going Greek* still on tour at Wimbledon, Guy turned his attention to that season's Gaiety show. This time, he and Firth Shephard supplied the plot—involving film stars being kidnapped by other film stars to be shipped off to China—and Douglas Furber wrote *Running Riot*. The music and lyrics were by Vivian Ellis. Frederick Ashton was called in to stage the Chinese ensembles, Louise Brown again danced, and, once more, Leslie Henson knocked audiences flat with his frightened penguin routine. It was, as usual, a smash hit.

By Christmas of 1938, Guy was ready to introduce his fourth show to the West End season. It was *Number Six,* a mystery adapted by Gerard Fairlie and him, and it was based upon the Edgar Wallace novel of the same name. Guy had lived next to Edgar Wallace in Beverly Hills; he and Virginia played golf with Wallace and socialized continually with him; it was an idea that came to quick fruition. As produced by Firth Shephard, it was an exciting cat-and-mouse evening in which the elite of the French and British detective forces were deployed to capture a master criminal. The mastermind had contempt for all of them except one—Number Six, whose identity was kept secret until the final scene. To lighten the goings on, Shephard added entr'actes played and sung by the Delroy Somers Aldwych quartet.

Starring Gordon Harker, Bernard Lee, Michael Logan, Rosalyn Boulton, and Margey Caldicott, *Number Six* opened at the Aldwych on December 21, 1938, and ran for two years.

Guy's fifth and last show of that bubbling London season was a reconstruction job. Producer-writer Eric Maschwitz called Guy and Fred Thompson in to salvage an operetta called *Paprika,* which was designed as a comeback, after two years, for Binnie Hale. The two librettists bravely waded into a Hungarian stew.

They redid Maschwitz's original book, spicing up its dialogue and trimming long scenes of self-agonizing by a young man who runs away to Hungary and falls in love with a Gypsy violinist-cum-actress. Harold Purcell was brought in to fix up Maschwitz's lyrics to music by George Posford and Bernard Grun.

Retitled *Magyar Melody,* it was only moderately better than it had been in Glasgow, when it opened at His Majesty's Theatre in January. It only survived until April.

But 1938–39 was the sort of season Guy hadn't had since the Princess days. Small wonder that he made his decision in the 1930s to become the toast of the London stage.

What he couldn't know was the disturbing, hidden news that the 1930s and all that had gone before them were about to be shut down forever, at the very height of that high-spirited season. East of London, across the Channel, a war was building. And it would, in a matter of months, consume much of the world, even its most insulated and apolitical writers of humorous verse, musical comedy libretti, and comic novels.

# 20
# War Scene
## 1940–1944

That ceaseless sunlight of childhood, which lasted for the Western world until the 1930s, illuminates all of Plum's novels and all of Guy's plays, even those he thought of as serious.

But the forties were a different matter. And Plum, who had created a world of fiction so real that he and Ethel inhabited it, would be the one to suffer most from this cataclysmic collision of fact and fiction.

The thirties had been an extraordinarily productive and rewarding decade for him. In June of 1936, he received the Mark Twain Medal "in recognition of [his] outstanding and lasting contribution to the happiness of the world . . ." and in October, having squared up, he thought, with the American tax authorities, made his second trip to Hollywood.

There, he, Ethel, and the pekes settled in at 1315 Angelo Drive, in Beverly Hills, in a huge mansion they rented from Gaylord Hauser. Back at MGM, he was faced with déjà vu and a familiar project — *Rosalie.* Once more, he manfully plunged in, and once more, MGM rejected his work, stating that they were turning the whole project over to William Anthony McGuire. This time, they failed to renew his contract, but it bothered him not at all; he was busy enough with work for the *Saturday Evening Post* and multiple offers from various other studios.

During his unhappy stint at MGM, he received the disquieting news that his brother Armine had died suddenly. Committed to a deadline that eventually proved mythical, he nevertheless had to remain in Hollywood while Ethel went back to England to see what could be done for the family. She returned at the end of 1936.

Meanwhile, Plum turned down offers from both David Selznick and Walter Wanger and went to work at RKO turning his *Damsel in Distress* into a musical for Fred Astaire and Ginger Rogers. The prospect of once more working with George and—particularly—Ira Gershwin lured him, though by the end of June, he had cooled somewhat on screenwriting. Hollywood and Ethel's incessant parties (he wrote to Townend in June of one that would involve seventy guests) had begun to wear thin, and he longed for Low Wood and his chums.

"I want to see you," he wrote to Townend, "and I can't, and I want to see Guy Bolton, and I can't, and I have to put up with substitutes. . . ."[1]

*Damsel in Distress* was completed at the end of August, and Plum plunged into work on a new film immediately, with an old acquaintance from before the war, Eddie Goulding. Goulding, now a director in Hollywood, was, by all accounts, a fairly imperious man who insisted on rewriting practically everything Plum handed him. By the end of September the partnership had come apart, and the project was abandoned. On October 28, 1937, Plum, Ethel, and the dogs—increased by a new pup named Wonder—sailed for Europe.

In London, Herbert Jenkins was busily publishing *Blandings Castle and Elsewhere* followed rapidly by *Lord Emsworth and Others*. Back in Low Wood, Plum toiled on two new novels, *The Code of the Woosters* and *Uncle Fred in the Springtime*. He had, by the beginning of 1939, completed 12 plays, 30 musical comedies, 247 short stories, and 42 novels. He was world famous, widely read, and even revered. Oxford presented him with an honorary degree in recognition of his services to literature. James Agate referred to him in print as "P. G. Wodehouse, whose works I place a little below Shakespeare's and any distance you like above anybody else's." The world he had created for his readers and himself was solid and indestructible, or so it seemed.

But while Plum worked on and the literary and academic worlds extolled him, that same something that was about to destroy Guy's world had already established itself, and within a matter of months, it would make even the impermeable world of the imagination subject to demolition.

The previous September, Prime Minister Neville Chamberlain transferred the Sudetenland to Adolf Hitler in exchange, he thought, for peace. But within six months, Hitler invaded Czechoslovakia, and on September 1, 1939, his armies invaded Poland. Two days later, England and France declared war on Germany, and World War II began.

In Sussex and in London, where Guy and Virginia now owned two flats, one at 4 Benting Street and one at 4 Onslow Square, the war was becoming very real. Sand bags appeared around government buildings; blackouts descended; by January of 1940 rationing became a reality. The United States Government was advising all of its citizens to return home, and as transatlantic liners were transformed into troop and cargo ships, space to America began to shrink.

Guy and Virginia crossed to Le Touquet and urged Plum and Ethel to come with them to London and from there to America. It was a decision they had made with great difficulty; Guy had never been more popular or more in demand than he was in London. But that was all coming apart now. Men were being conscripted; theatres were closing; the war was changing lives moment by moment. Guy was as fond of fiction as Plum. But he also had a strong practical streak, reinforced by Virginia, who was nine-tenths practicality. It was either stay and retain part of his popularity in the West End with whatever he could write, or be safe to write another day. Germany was poised to invade Norway and Denmark; the Netherlands would be next, and France was certain to be the target after that.

In Le Touquet, British and American families were packing up, closing their homes, and leaving. Guy and Virginia and the legendary and retired George Edwardes heroine Gertie Miller pleaded with Plum and Ethel to join them. Gertie Miller even risked missing her own boat to safety by making one last return trip to Le Touquet to entreat Plum and Ethel to depart. Leonora, now married to Peter Cazelet and concerned with her own family that included their daughter Sharen, also crossed to Le Touquet to plead with her parents to leave while they still could. But, as Guy later wrote, they were both intractable. There was a chance the Germans would be defeated, a chance they would hold off the invasion of France, that the Maginot Line would hold. There were so many rumors it was difficult to separate them.

"Plum was woefully ill-equipped to deal with crises and this became painfully evident as events gave warning of Hitler's preparations for war," wrote Guy. Decades later, in his early nineties, he planned a book called *Lyrics by P. G. Wodehouse*. It would recount their writing, their lives, themselves.

"Bolton begged him to pack up and come to London," Guy continued, "while their next door neighbor, Lady Dudley, went to the length of crossing back to Le Touquet to convince them of their danger once war was declared. The trouble was the dogs, they would have to go into quarantine which Ethel found unthinkable. Also she had bought a collection of hams at bargain price and these were hanging from the kitchen ceiling. The famed Gertie Miller returned to England defeated."[2]

"It was the damned dogs," recounted Guy in his late years. "Neither one of them wanted to leave them, and that was the reason they were captured."[3]

All of this was true, but it was more than that.

It was the innocence, the belief that life behaves like a musical comedy. It was what had brought Plum and Guy together. It was what made them a phenomenon to everyone whose lives they touched, and it was what made them forever ill-equipped to deal with the disorderliness of reality.

Frustrated, Gertie Miller and Leonora returned home, and Guy and Virginia went back to London to await Peggy and Jimmy Burrowes. Nestlé had advised them to leave while they could. Switzerland planned to remain neutral, but it could not guarantee the safety of Americans if America entered the war. The Nazis were already starkly in evidence in Switzerland.

On Saturday, March 20, 1940, Guy's last play for the duration of the war opened in London. Firth Shephard presented Guy and Vernon Sylvaine's farce, *Nap Hand,* with Ralph Lynn, Charles Heslap, Bertha Belmore, Kay Walsh, and Valerie Tudor. A tale of British male quintuplets rivaling female Canadian quintuplets, it was pronounced, by the *Times,* "One of the jolliest evenings in blacked-out London at the present time."

But Guy had little time to bask in this unlit glory. In April of 1940, while Germany was laying waste to Denmark, Peggy and Jimmy Burrowes set out across northern France in their automobile. The scene there was one of consternation and confusion. Refugees lined the roads. Food was scarce and gasoline scarcer. Rumors of Germany already invading France stalked them like wild beasts. Miles from Calais, they ran out of gas and walked the rest of the way to the Channel crossing.

Virginia and Guy, frantic over Peggy and Jimmy's lateness, met them at Dover, and the four dashed to Southampton, where they waited as liner after liner, filled beyond capacity, left. Finally, they boarded one of the last to leave and sailed for America, as Germany moved inexorably into France.[4]

The impregnable Maginot Line crumbled in days under the assault of modern Nazi weaponry, and now in Le Touquet the hysteria of imminent occupation chilled the air. There were still some British citizens in residence, and in all fairness there was so much confusion among British officials at Boulogne that messages and warnings they received were muddled. Those disposed to stay felt that the 85th Squadron of the Royal Air Force, stationed in the area, and the personnel at the British Military Hospital at Etaples would protect them.

Ethel, knowing beyond opinion that she was doing the right thing for the war, entertained Royal Air Force and Army personnel at repeated dinner parties, using the hams she had found, and Plum wrote on. They and the pekes, they thought, would be safe until told otherwise.

But as May unfolded and both Winkie and Boo, the older pekes, succumbed to tick fever and died, the sounds of gunfire and explosions went from intermittant to constant. Nightly bombings by the Germans increased in intensity and ferocity. There was more and more military activity on the roads between Etaples and Le Touquet, and it became apparent that the time had come to leave.

On May 20, Ethel went to the commanding officer at the hospital at Etaples and asked if occupation was indeed imminent. His answer was as vague as it had been for the past weeks. She went home and continued their preparations. That day, she took several satirical articles Plum had written about the Nazis and burned them; if the German Army overran the town, she reasoned, Plum would surely be shot.

They slept uneasily that night. On the morning of May 21, they packed Wonder and some of their belongings into their large automobile, a dated Lancia. Their other, smaller car was given to Miss Unger, the Swiss governess of their neighbor, Lady Furness.

The Germans were coming from the north; the refugees decided they would set out toward the Somme, in the south. But the Lancia, which had been in an accident two months before, stopped dead after two miles and refused to budge. Plum and Ethel unloaded the car and, in the small car, returned to Low Wood, which was now crowded with a gathering of neighbors preparing to flee. There were two more vehicles, a car belonging to and carrying Le Touquet's golf pro Arthur Grant, his wife Ruth, and their daughter Jacqueline, and a Red Cross van belonging to another neighbor, named Kemp.

The convoy set off, with the small Wodehouse car in the lead, followed by the van and the Grants' Simca. They all reached the junction with the main road to the Somme safely, though the scene, as reported by Jacqueline in her journal, appalled them: "There was a sight we had none of us seen before—cars, carts, bicycles, every form of transport, and people walking, all in the same direction, away from Le Touquet. . . . [The refugees] were carrying all they possibly could, and many cars had the family bedding strapped on the roof. It turned out handy, when they were machine-gunned from the air."

But the crossroads were as far as the van made it. It broke down there, and Jacqueline was sent off in the Simca to the airfield and the Royal Engineers, who, they all reasoned, might be able to fix it.

The Wodehouses were miles ahead and, if they had kept inching on through the swarm of refugees, might have made their freedom. But, as miles passed, and there was no sign of the Grants behind them, they turned around and drove back. At the crossroads, they rejoined the rest of the party, plus two Royal Engineers who were repairing the van.

Evening had begun to descend, and the group decided to return to their homes and make a fresh start the next morning. It seemed to be a wise decision. For the first time in weeks, there was quiet. The German bombing had stopped.

Its reason became apparent with first light. As Jacqueline Grant described it: "Before the dew was off the rosemary bushes edging the lawn, through the green forest they rolled. First, the motorcycles, noisy, brutal and fast, then car after car in which the grey-green officers seemed to sit in tiers, all facing forward, two or three below, two or three on the folded hood."

It was Wednesday, May 22, 1940. Le Touquet was occupied and all of its occupants were prisoners of war. It was a terrifying morning, and the weeks that followed, though calmer, bore a sharp edge of uncertainty. And yet, Plum, like many of his fellow Englishmen during World War II, was fully equipped to adopt a stiff upper lip.

From breathing the freedom of world acclaim and wealth, Plum and Ethel were suddenly plunged into the vacuum of the absence of freedom. It was a long, rapid fall, signaled first by members of the German labor force appropriating their bathroom for daily baths and their back porch for parties afterward.

Plum, so intensely private and shy that, on his solitary walks in the woods near Le Touquet, he would hide behind a tree rather than greet a stranger, was appalled and disoriented. "Mentally I seem not to have progressed a step since I was eighteen," Plum would later write to William Townend, in a deeply self-revelatory letter. "With world convulsions happening every hour on the hour, I appear to be still the rather awkward lad I was, when we brewed our first cup of tea in our study together, my only concern the outcome of a rugby football match."[5]

As May gave way to June and June to July, more and more of their belongings were confiscated. A strict 9:00 P.M. curfew was imposed. In July, the order came down from the German Command that all British subjects were to report each day at 9:00 A.M. to the *Kommandantur* in Paris Plage. It became an appointed routine for Plum (Ethel wasn't required to report) until Sunday, July 21, when he was peremptorily told that, along with twelve other male aliens, he was to be committed to an internment camp.

He was given a short amount of time to gather together a few necessities—a copy of the complete works of Shakespeare was Plum's choice as one of these necessities—say goodbye to Ethel, and present himself back at Paris Plage.

And so, Plum and Arthur Grant, Jeff, the golf club's starter, and Max, the caddie master, two bar owners, Algy of Algy's bar on the rue St. Jean in Le Touquet, and Alfred, of Alfred's bar on the rue de Paris, Charlie Webb and Bill Illidge, who ran garages, and five other Englishmen were loaded onto a bus and taken to the prison at Loos, a suburb of Lille, some seventy miles from Le Touquet. With numerous stops along the way to pick up more internees, the trip took seven hours.

At the end of a week, all of the men who had reached their sixtieth birthdays were set free, according to a September 9, 1939, regulation issued by the German Ministry of the Interior. Plum was near but not close enough. Since he was only fifty-nine, he and 44 others were loaded on a truck and taken to the Lille railroad station, where they were met by 800 other male internees and herded into cattle cars, 50 men to a car, and transported for nineteen hours to Liege, in Belgium, where they were imprisoned in the former Belgian army barracks.

After a week, they were again loaded into cattle cars and moved to Huy, where they were imprisoned in the Citadel, a medieval stone fortress. It was a primitive, nearly barbaric situation. They slept on straw spread on stone floors for six weeks.

On September 8, 1940, they were again ordered to gather their belongings and prepare for another rail journey. This time they were loaded into regular passenger coaches, eight to a compartment, and given one sausage and half a loaf of bread. Thirty-two hours later, they were given another half loaf and a ration of soup. It would be all they would have to eat for three days and nights.

Finally, they reached their destination: a former insane asylum in the village of Tost, in Upper Silesia. There Plum would stay, for forty-two weeks, until his release on June 21, 1941, after—and because of—his sixtieth birthday.

News of P. G. Wodehouse's imprisonment reached America, and Guy and Virginia set to work immediately to secure his release. All through the summer of 1940, Virginia stalked the offices of the magazines for which Plum had written in America—*The Saturday Evening Post, Colliers, Liberty, Ladies' Home Journal, Cosmopolitan* and the *New Yorker*—collecting names, prominent if possible, on a petition to the German Government to turn him free. She continued on to the officers of the Players Club, the Lambs, the Authors League, the Century Club, the Lotos Club, the Dramatists Guild, and the editors of the major New York newspapers.

She and Guy prevailed upon Bob Barbour, a long-time friend upon whose yacht they had spent and would spend endless summers in Palm Beach, to enlist the aid of his father, U. S. Senator W. Warren Barbour, who instantly obliged, collecting the signatures of fifty U. S. senators.

The United States was not yet at war with Germany, and Barbour submitted the petition to the German Chargé d'Affaires in Washington, Dr. Hans Thomsen, who received it sympathetically and forwarded it to the German Foreign Office and the Propaganda Ministry. In addition, Plum had German champions pleading his case, including Baron Raven von Barnikow, a former member of the Richthofen Squadron in World War I and a Hollywood friend of the Wodehouses.[6]

Dr. Paul Schmidt, Ribbentrop's aide in the Foreign Office, received the petition and immediately set in motion a plan to release Plum with worldwide publicity. This would, he reasoned, aid in keeping the United States neutral and out of the war. And anyway, Plum would reach his sixtieth birthday on October 15 and would be automatically freed.

But it never came to pass. The Gestapo blocked the release, maintaining that P. G. Wodehouse was a prisoner of war and would be treated as such.

Now, the mechanism that would plunge Plum into further darkness was set in motion. Another Paul Schmidt suggested to the Foreign Ministry that it might be an effective propaganda ploy to have P. G. Wodehouse record a series of humorous shortwave broadcasts to America and the United Kingdom, not as an expression of support for Nazi Germany but to show how humane and intelligent and understanding his captors really were.

Thus, Plum's release from Tost on June 21 and his removal to Berlin, where at the end of July he was reunited with Ethel and Wonder, were the result of both the efforts of the Foreign Ministry to set him up for the broadcasts and his arrival at and passing of his sixtieth birthday.

While Plum was at Tost, he received no special privileges, although a private room was offered to him in deference to his age and international reputation. Interestingly, he turned it down, saying that he preferred to remain in the dormitory with the other men. He spent most of the long hours there either reading Shakespeare or working, in a recreation room, on a new novel, *Money in the Bank*. Work was his salvation, as it was Guy's. They could, apparently, weather anything, even imprisonment, so long as they could work.

When he arrived in Berlin, Plum was taken to the Adlon Hotel. There, as he was crossing the lobby with his escort and his luggage, he encountered Baron von Barnikow, who had been told of Plum's imminent release by a mutual Hollywood friend, Werner Plack, now an official in the German Foreign Office.

Plum had lost forty-two pounds, and the hardships of his imprisonment were undeniably stamped on him. Von Barnikow immediately offered to find some fresh clothes and far more comfortable lodgings some seventeen miles away, at *Degenershausen,* the home of his cousin and fiancée, Baroness von Bodenhausen. Plum, dazzled by his good fortune, mumbled a thank you, and von Barnikow left to get the clothes.

Suddenly, with a punctuality that, in retrospect, reveals its long-term planning, Werner Plack appeared. Apparently coached by Schmidt, he inquired of Plum about contact with the States. Plum answered readily and easily, effusing about the petition and the hundreds of letters from his American readers that had reached him at Tost.

Wouldn't it be appropriate, Plack gently suggested, to put these readers' minds and hearts at ease by broadcasting his experiences, reassuring them, in a way that only P. G. Wodehouse could? Plum, in his naiveté and belief in the inherent good and simplicity of human beings, assented, enthusiastically.

The very next day, he was driven to Plack's office, where he was told that he would be making five shortwave broadcasts to America and that he could write them, submit them for censorship of course, and then read them himself.

On June 26, he was again summoned to Plack's office. This time, a correspondent for CBS, Harry W. Flannery, was there to interview him. It was all unfolding capitally, thought Plum. Now, he could finally let his friends in the rest of the world know his whereabouts and his well being, which seemed to be increasing by the minute.

Flannery and Plum went to an empty office, and there the correspondent interviewed him. And, as he had in Hollywood, eleven years before, Plum talked generously and ingenuously, trusting his interviewer not to embarrass him. That night, Flannery wrote a script, which was submitted for censorship, and the next day, he and Plum sat down and read the script over the air. Plum, placing himself in the care of everyone, merely skimmed the script before reading it over the air. They were his words, all right. He recognized them.

But he failed to recognize the impact they would have on the British public, now undergoing blitzkrieg, the horrors of Dunkirk, the instant famine and consuming terror of total war.

Asked about his accommodations in Berlin, Plum jovially answered, "I'm living here at the Adlon—have a suite on the third floor, a very nice one, too—and I come and go as I please. . . ."

"Do you mind being a prisoner-of-war in this fashion, Mr. Wodehouse?" read Flannery.

"Not a bit," replied Plum. "As long as I have a typewriter and plenty of paper and a room to work in, I'm fine."

It wasn't enough to raise the hackles of the British yet, though the comparison of his living style to theirs must have begun to bother some listeners. It was the heart of the exchange, couched in Flannery's prose, that sent shockwaves through London. In the course of explaining his writing at the internment camp, Plum remarked, "I'll tell you something about the war and my work which has been bothering me a good deal. I'm wondering whether the kind of people and the kind of England I write about, will live after the war—whether England wins or not. . . ."

They were the scattershot words of an innocent reminiscing about his Edwardian past, about Dulwich and the theatre of Seymour Hicks and life at Emsworth. But that was in his mind and not in the words rewritten by the American journalist.

And if this weren't enough to insult the sensibilities of the bombed-out Londoners tuning in, Plum's answer to Flannery's question, "Anything you'd like to say, Mr. Wodehouse, about the United States?" was. "I'd like to be back there again," blithely admitted this British subject who had been awarded a degree at Oxford. "You see," he continued, "I've always thought of the United States as sort of my country—lived there almost all the time since 1909—and I long to get back there once more. But I guess there's nothing I can do about that now, except write stories for you people. I hope you continue to like them. Well, goodnight, everybody."[7]

The groundwork had been laid for a firestorm. Aside from the almost anti-Wodehouse phraseology, the sentiments, while undeniably true, were just what the battered people of the United Kingdom didn't want to hear.

And so, Plum proceeded from debacle to disgrace. The five German broadcasts were made within a space of two weeks. And now, with the sort of preface the CBS interview gave them, their jocular tone drew, instead of laughs, outrage. In all probability, most listeners barely heard the beginning apologia of British Civilian Prisoner Number 796: "It's just possible that my listeners may seem to detect in this little talk of mine a slight goofiness, a certain disposition to ramble in my remarks," he began. "If so, the matter, as Bertie Wooster would say, is susceptible of a ready explanation. I have just emerged into the outer world after forty-nine weeks of Civil Internment in a German internment camp and the effects have not entirely worn off. I have not yet quite recovered that perfect mental balance for which in the past I was so admired by one and all. . . ."

What practically no one passed over were such statements as "It has been in many ways quite an agreeable experience. There is a good deal to be said for internment," despite the fact that it was followed immediately by, "It keeps you out of the saloons and gives you time to catch up with your reading. . . ."

"Young men, starting out in life, have often asked me, 'How can I become an Internee?'" Plum went on. "Well, there are several methods. My own was to buy a villa in Le Touquet on the coast of France and stay there till the Germans came along. This is probably the best and simplest system. You buy the villa and the Germans do the rest."[8]

It was Wodehouse the humorist, at his best. But to many in Britain, it was Wodehouse the traitor, at his worst. Southport Public Library immediately removed ninety Wodehouse books from its shelves and destroyed them. Other public libraries refused to buy any more books by Plum (though over 450,000 of his novels and collections were sold in the United Kingdom between 1941 and the war's end). The BBC banned all his works.

It was, however, the harsh and virulent attack on July 15, 1941, upon Plum by William Connor, a—in the apt words of Iain Sproat—"brilliantly sulphorous journalist," who signed his column for the *Daily Mirror* "Cassandra," that brought the anti-Wodehouse feeling in Britain to a boil. "I have come to tell you tonight of the story of a rich man trying to make his last and greatest sale— that of his own country," Connor began. "It is a sombre story of honor pawned to the Nazis for the price of a soft bed in a luxury hotel. It is the record of P. G. Wodehouse ending forty years of money-making fun with the worst joke he ever made in his life. The only wisecrack he ever pulled that the world will receive in silence."

"Cassandra" went on, with paragraph after paragraph of vituperation, rising to evangelical heights ("And Dr. Goebbels taking him into a high mountain, showed unto him all the Kingdoms of the world . . . and said unto him: 'All this power will I give thee if thou wilt worship the Fuhrer.' Pelham Wodehouse fell on his knees.") and proceeding to accusations of treason ("Fifty thousand of our countrymen are enslaved in Germany. How many of them are in the Adlon

Hotel tonight? Barbed wire is their pillow. They endure—but they do not give in. They suffer—but they do not sell out.").

The speech was an echo of denunciations in Parliament. Five days before, Foreign Secretary Anthony Eden had accused Plum of having "lent his services to the Nazi war propaganda machine," Quintin Hogg, M. P., called him a traitor, comparing him to "Lord Haw Haw," and announcing, ". . . while he was clowning, British boys were resisting the Germans, and there can be nothing but contempt for the action of a man who, in order to live in a hotel more comfortably than his fellow-prisoners, did that kind of thing against his country. . . ."

A. A. Milne, a respected friend, and Sean O'Casey, who had his own ax to grind over the Oxford doctorate, joined the attack in letters to the *Daily Telegraph*. On the other hand, those who knew Plum, like Ian Hay and William Townend, rose to his defense. But they were, at the moment, a minority.

Meanwhile, in Germany, Plum wrote on, oblivious to the storm in the outside world. At the villa in the Harz Mountains, he was polishing *Money in the Bank* and beginning a Blandings Castle novel, *Full Moon*.

At the end of July, Ethel arrived, bearing his partially completed manuscript of *Joy in the Morning* and news of the effect his broadcasts had had in the outside world. Plum was appalled and shaken. He had never, in his wildest imaginings, intended this. "Plummy lives in the moon most of the time," Ethel had once said of him, and now he was being brought down to earth very hard.

He immediately wrote a statement to the British Government, in his own words, ". . . explaining how the blunder had occurred and reaffirming my loyalty." He applied for permission to return to England via Palestine and was refused. He applied for passage through Lisbon and was refused. He applied for passage through Sweden and was again refused. To anyone who would listen or read his letters, he reiterated his realization that the talks were "a ghastly blunder, and that I was a complete fool to have made them. But I simply had no idea," he continued, "that they could be mistaken for anything other than what I intended them to be—a gesture of gratitude to my unknown friends in America."[9]

Ethel, while bringing perspective to Plum's and her detention in Germany, now proceeded to compound their troubles with their native country. The opposite extreme from Plum's retiring and self-effacing personality, she insisted, often loudly, upon their rights and privileges, which were often bought with the sale of her jewelry. She disliked the quiet isolation of the Harz Mountains and eschewed it for the bustle of life in Berlin, with its attendant world publicity.

When the winter of 1941 arrived, she was happy to return to the Adlon, and when spring again came, Plum went alone to *Degenershausen,* while Ethel remained in Berlin.

The Adlon management forebade dogs; Ethel demanded and received special favor for Wonder, and she flaunted the favor by openly walking the peke through the main lobby at crowded hours.

In one incident witnessed and reported by Allied correspondents, she created a monster scene in the Adlon restaurant at lunchtime. Werner Plack arrived at their table and in a strident voice she commanded, "Werner, will you please tell the head waiter that I have been waiting to be served for an hour and a half! An hour and a half! What's more, this table wobbles!" To drive her point home, she scooped up a white bread roll, which was rationed and scarce and highly valued, and jammed it under one of the table's legs.

To her, it was probably defiance. To Allies, for whom the war was then going badly, it was one more item of evidence of the Wodehouses' collaboration with the Nazis.[10]

Plum and Ethel remained in Berlin and its outskirts for two years. But by 1943, the fortunes of war had turned, and Berlin was receiving carpet bombings night and day, every night and day. Plum prevailed upon Plack to have them transferred to Occupied Paris. Plack obliged and went with them. There, in the Hotel Bristol, they remained until the liberation of Paris. It was a momentary explosion of joy for them. But merely momentary. The next day, they were placed under house arrest by the French police, to await interrogation by M.I.5 for charges of possible treason, an offense that carried the death penalty.

The first British officer to visit the Wodehouses was Major Malcolm Muggeridge. In *Chronicles of Wasted Time,* his book of war reminiscences, he described their state. Plum, he recalled, was "a large, bald, elderly man, wearing grey flannel trousers, a loose sports jacket and what I imagine were golfing shoes, and smoking a pipe; a sort of schoolmaster's rig. [Ethel] turned out to be a spirited and energetic lady trying as hard to be worldly wise as Wodehouse himself to be innocent."

Muggeridge was to keep an eye on the Wodehouses until Major Edward Cussen of Military Intelligence could interrogate them. He brought with him the worst news he could possibly have carried. The previous May, Leonora, having difficulty conceiving a third child, had entered London Clinic for a routine operation. She was just under forty and in excellent health, and yet the night after the operation, she died, alone in her hospital room.

Muggeridge recounted the details as gently as he could. When he finished, there was a long silence. Then, Plum raised his stricken face and said softly, "I thought she was immortal."

Major Cussen arrived, and a long ten days of intense interrogation began. Ethel, too distraught by the news of Leonora's death to cooperate, remained in her bed. Cussen pressed on with Plum and filed his report. His final conclusion was that "Wodehouse must be exonerated of everything but foolishness and one or two minor technical offences." However, he recommended that the Wodehouses be "kept out of the Jurisdiction." By the Jurisdiction, he meant England.

Advice from Muggeridge and Plum's publishers reaffirmed this, but they were mere redundancies. Plum had made his mind up soon after the news that Leonora had died that he would never go back to England. And he never would, for the rest of his life.

Malcolm Muggeridge wrote, later, that Plum's attitude was "like that of a man who has parted, in painful circumstances, from someone he loves, and whom he both longs and dreads to see again."[11]

It was more than this. Several years later, Plum himself would set it down in a letter to Peter Hastings. "My England's gone," he said. "Blandings Castle, Bertie, Pongo, Lord Em—they're all gone. Some people think they never existed. I don't know. I was frightfully fond of them anyway. . . ."[12]

The British continued to treat him with short shrift. The Bristol, with its location on Fauberge St. Honoré, was a hotel preferred by the British diplomatic corps. Told that the Wodehouses were living there, Duff Cooper, who had been one of the first to attack Plum in Parliament, suggested to Muggeridge in a telegram that ". . . the Hotel Bristol . . . is supposed to be reserved for the Corps Diplomatique. . . . In view of the difficulties that might arise if the press were to get hold of the story, I am trying to arrange for Wodehouse to be moved to another hotel."

Muggeridge had them installed in the Lincoln, on the rue Barand. No sooner had they settled in than they were arrested again by the French police and hauled, in the middle of the night, to the Palais de Justice on the Quai d'Orléans. That night, at a dinner party, Luiset, the *Préfet de Police*, had been chided by an English guest for allowing two such notorious traitors as the Wodehouses to roam at large through Paris. And so Luiset had given orders for their immediate apprehension.

Arriving the next morning at the station, Muggeridge found that, as he later wrote, ". . . no one seemed to know why M. and Mme. Wodenhorse (as they appeared on their warrant) were there, and I had no difficulty in arranging for Ethel's immediate release. It appeared that, using her highly individual and idiosyncratic French at its shrillest, she had reduced the whole station to a condition of panic, aided and abetted by her Peke, Wonder, whom she had insisted on taking with her when she was arrested. By the time I arrived on the scene, the police, I could see, were desperately anxious to get Ethel and Wonder off the premises as soon as possible."[13]

And so Ethel returned to the Lincoln. Plum, however, ran squarely into the barbed wire of French bureaucracy, and the only way Muggeridge could arrange for his release was on the grounds of health. So Plum was taken to the sole available hospital space, in a maternity home, and there he remained for two months.

From these bizarre locations, the Wodehouses moved into the summer home of the de Fonscolombes, with whom Plum had been corresponding ever since Berlin. In Barbizon, it was warmer than Paris in the winter, and food was in somewhat greater supply.

By March, Plum and Ethel were back in the Lincoln but were later forced to move several times, since most hotels in Paris became requisitioned, at one time or another, for military or diplomatic use. It was difficult to live anywhere in Europe in 1944 and 1945; although Paris had been spared the bombing and burning and gutting that other European capitals had suffered, poverty and lack of supplies held it in their grasp. By December 1945, Plum and Ethel moved into an apartment at 36 boulevard Suchet, in the Sixteenth Arrondissement.

"The new apartment is proving a tremendous success," Plum wrote cheerily to de Fonscolombe. "We are very comfortable, though of course it is cold except in the one room which we are able to heat with wood fires. That was supposed to be my workroom, but I never can work in a room which is not entirely my own, so now my wife has fixed up my bedroom as a study for me, which is ever so much better. I have an electric heater which keeps me quite warm enough at present, while the weather is reasonably mild. What will happen if we get another cold spell, I don't know!"[14]

And so the Wodehouses stayed on in Paris, in virtual exile. Low Wood had been trashed and would have to be completely rebuilt if they were to return there. There were still angry voices raised against Plum in London—Quintin Hogg, M. P., had, despite intelligence reports, called for Plum's prosecution; Plum's letters from Townend informed him that the opinion at Dulwich was running highly against him.

There seemed to be no alternative but to return to America, a decision Plum had made months before. Yet, the time was still not right. Anti-Wodehouse feeling ran high in America, too. *The Saturday Evening Post*, Plum's solid meal ticket, refused to accept any of his stories. Besides that, out of the blue, the IRS now decided to check on the returns of writers filing tax returns from 1921 through 1925, and had found that Plum owed them $120,000. Better to remain where he was, he felt, correcting page proofs on *Joy in the Morning*, collecting what royalties could be sent to him, and depending upon the kindness of his friends to keep him in contact.

This his friends did, supplying Ethel and him with canned goods and condiments they were denied in the indigent postwar years of Paris. Guy, Townend, and Ira Gershwin were his most constant correspondents, and they cheered Plum up by reawakening a happier, theatrical past.

But it was a moodier, more subdued Plum who wrote to Townend. He had come to certain conclusions about his work that gave him peace and an anchor. "It's a funny thing about writing. If you are a writer by nature, I don't believe you write for money or fame or even for publication, but simply for the pleasure of turning out the stuff," he ruminated. "I really don't care much if these books are published or not. The great thing is that I've got them down on paper, and can read and re-read them and polish them and change an adjective for a better one and cut out dead lines. . . ."[15]

In his sixties, Plum was able to take the long view on his life, both professional and otherwise, and find that, although there was pain present, it did nothing to diminish his antic prose. Commiserating with Townend over having lost a maid, he commented that "we still have one whom Ethel fires on Mondays and Thursdays. On Tuesdays and Fridays she gives her own notice. On Saturdays and Sundays she goes home. So our big day is Wednesday. This is the time to catch us."[16]

For all of this, their troubles persisted. The IRS finally settled for less money, and it was now possible to leave, but they had to secure visas. It would take time, and so they stayed on in France, in first one location and then another, while authors like George Orwell argued for Plum's defense and finally won it.

But it would never be quite the same as it was before the war. "Plum!" wrote Denis Mackail in *Life with Topsy*. "The most industrious author that I had ever known. But the war couldn't go on without hatred, and Plum hated no one. That was his crime."

*Chapter*

# 21

# Finaletto

## 1940–1945

Broadway in wartime was a bustling street. There were some shortages and a noticeable increase of military uniforms on it, but, except for the European community, the impact of the war had not yet reached either the people or the entertainment industry in 1940.

Guy and Virginia were happy to be safe; they immediately found a home in Great Neck, which they named The Wyckwood, and Guy went about reasserting himself on Broadway. He was armed with two strong weapons. First, there was *Three Blind Mice,* which the Shuberts were interested in musicalizing. They were delighted to have him back in the country, and he joined Parke Levy and Alan Lipscott in fashioning the book for Johnny Mercer's lyrics and Hoagy Carmichael's music. First called *The Gibson Girls,* with Simone Simon, Mitzi Green, and Mary Brian playing the three fortune hunters, it changed its title on the tryout trail to *Walk with Music,* and Kitty Carlisle and Betty Lawford replaced Simone Simon and Mary Brian.

But the show was a throwback to the twenties, with formula scenes and parades of showgirls covering dull stretches of plot. *"Three Blind Mice* hangs around the neck of *Walk with Music* like a stricken albatross," wrote Brooks

Atkinson in the *Times,* and most critics agreed that the plot severely interfered with the audience's enjoyment of Hoagy Carmichael's inventive music. Opening at the Ethel Barrymore Theatre on June 4, 1940, it closed after fifty-five performances, a solid flop.

But Guy was already at work on yet another throwback musical set to open the 1940–41 season. Titled *Hold on to Your Hats,* it would mark Al Jolson's return to Broadway from the movies, and if ever there was someone who could write the kind of star vehicle that Jolson knew and loved, it was Guy. This time, he worked with Matty Brooks and a taxi driver he met who had a million jokes, Eddie Davis. Burton Lane supplied the music and E. Y. Harburg the lyrics for a crazy Western spoof of one of that era's favorite radio creations, The Lone Ranger. All about The Lone Rider and his Russian-accented Indian scout, Concho, it sported not only the considerable talents of Jolson but those of Martha Raye and Jinx Falkenburg in roles suspiciously parallel to those of Ethel Merman and Ginger Rogers in *Girl Crazy.* In addition, there was Bert Gordon, the Mad Russian from the Eddie Cantor radio show, as Concho, Jolson's second banana, and the considerable dancing and singing talents of veteran Jack Whiting.

The show opened to rave reviews on September 11, 1940, at the Shubert Theatre. The score sparkled; the book was pronounced hilarious; Jolson was welcomed back with open arms.

It could have run for the rest of the season. But Jolson, once the first blush of adulation wore off, grew tired of the routine he had helped establish. Claiming an inability to stand cold weather, the star left the show for the sun of California, and *Hold on to Your Hats* quietly collapsed after a mere twenty weeks of business.

The second weapon Guy brought with him from abroad was a major one. While in London, he had convinced Somerset Maugham that his novel *Theatre* was a natural for a play. And so began a long-distance collaboration that would eventually result, in the 1941–42 season, in *Theatre,* essentially a vehicle for Cornelia Otis Skinner. About a Lunt-Fontanne–like couple who have separated, then are reunited by their mutual devotion to the theatre, it offered a plum of a part to the leading lady, and Miss Skinner abandoned her wildly popular and profitable one-woman show to appear in it. Produced by John Golden, it opened at the Hudson Theatre on November 12, 1941, to favorable reviews.

But Cornelia Otis Skinner, like Al Jolson before her, tired of the role quickly and longed to return to the much more satisfying and lucrative pursuit of monodrama. She forced *Theatre* to close after only sixty-nine performances.

If *Hold on to Your Hats* proved that musical comedy of the past was not dead and *Theatre* proved that, given the right material, Guy could still write a hit for Broadway, his other straight play of that season proved that he still could not deal with serious subject matter convincingly. *Golden Wings* was an unmitigated disaster. Perhaps it suffered from opening on December 8, 1941, the day after the Pearl Harbor attack. But probably not. *Golden Wings,* which Guy's old Princess friend Robert Milton produced and directed, was all about the RAF, its flyers, and the women who either loved or seduced them. Despite a winsome performance by Fay Wray as the good girl and a steamy one by Signe Hasso as the seductress, the play, which Guy wrote with William Jay, was as realistic as an arcade war game. "Apparently," John Mason Brown wrote in the *American,* "bad dialogue, poor direction and a silly plot can prove as dangerous to pilots as fogs, ice or enemy planes." *Golden Wings* crashed after six performances.

Guy wasn't discouraged. There would be musicals enough for him, he felt. And he waited for calls from producers. But few came. A new and younger crop of writers was creating musicals with messages and reality, something Guy neither liked nor understood. And to add to this, two of his colleagues from the 1920s were about to create an earthquake called *Oklahoma!*

Even Hollywood, the last bastion of unreality, was affected by the war. Once the U. S. entered it, megastars enlisted or were drafted. Bond and USO tours consumed more and more of the time of top talents. And motion pictures—even musicals—were either written or rewritten to contain war themes, war scenes, and patriotic messages.

The first song that Jerry and Oscar Hammerstein wrote together after the demise of *Very Warm for May* was a reaction to the June 14, 1940, fall of Paris. "The Last Time I Saw Paris" was the uniquely conceived link between Jerry and occupied France, where Plum was, at that moment, being transported more deeply into his imprisonment.

Still hampered somewhat by the effects of his stroke, Jerry found that his energy was diminished but not his habits nor the agility of his mind. He read avidly, continued to baffle his guests with *Guggenheim,* continued to keep inordinately late hours, continued his endless searches for valuable furniture, books, and art works.

And the famous mercurial Kern temper was still available to him, as producer Leonard Spigelgass, the boy wonder charged with elevating Universal Pictures from imminent bankruptcy, found. Summoning Jerry to his offices, he laid out what he thought was a fair proposition: The score that Jerry had written for *Riviera* in 1937 could, he felt, be shoehorned into a film version of Earl Derr Biggers's novel, *Love Insurance.* And since Jerry had already been paid for the work, all he had to do was sign over permission for Universal to utilize the score.

Jerry responded in what Spigelgass later described as "icy rage," a state that usually preceded a well-chosen, articulate, and scathing verbal attack on the person responsible for it. But before Jerry could speak, the telephone on Spigelgass's desk rang. It was his secretary, telling the producer that his mother had been rushed to the hospital.

Jerry's anger evaporated as quickly as it had formed, and he offered to drive Spigelgass immediately to the hospital. It was a fleeting moment that revealed, more than a thousand pages of analysis, the true depths of the famous Kern tantrums and the kaleidoscope of facets in this little, still-pixyish, still-powerful genius. [1]

Later that week, Jerry agreed to the transfer of the *Riviera* score but not without a healthy additional fee, which Universal grudgingly agreed to pay. The film, renamed *One Night in the Tropics,* starred Allan Jones, Robert Cummings, and Nancy Kelly, and introduced the comedy team that would ultimately solve Universal's bankruptcy problems, Abbott and Costello. It contained not only the songs Jerry and Dorothy Fields wrote for *Riviera*—including "Remind Me," that staple of every cabaret singer in the world—but "Your Dream (Is the Same as My Dream)," his collaboration with Oscar Hammerstein from *Gentlemen Unafraid.*

Though it was a fallow period for film scores for Jerry, it was a full one for his prestige. Artur Rodzinski, the conductor of the Cleveland Orchestra, asked him to compose a symphonic scenario formed out of themes from *Show Boat.* It was the sort of challenge Jerry's revered friend George Gershwin had accepted almost two decades before, when he decided to do his own orchestration for *An American in Paris.* Unlike Gershwin, Jerry had no Ravel with whom to consult on the fine points of orchestral coloration, but he did have Miller and Harm's resident orchestrator, Eli Gerstenberger, and the original Robert Russell Bennett parts upon which to draw.

The result was charming and effective, with the *leitmotif* of "Ol' Man River" rolling through it, building and rising to a crashing, stirring climax.

Broadway, then, had left neither the Kern lexicon nor life. Once more turning his voracious appetite for reading into the inspiration for a musical, he interested playwright John Van Druten in adapting Leonard Merrick's obscure collection of Paris stories into a unique musical that would be as sunlit, inventive, and stylized as the Post-Impressionist painters his music would use as models. "The music *must* resemble the exciting technique of the post impressionist and modern boys and gals—you know—from Cézanne, Van Gogh, and Gauguin, through Utrillo, Rouault, Laurencin, Pascin and Chagall, etc.—must employ this technique even though we depict the genre of our particular, pleasant, placid period," he wrote to Van Druten, with unbridled enthusiasm. But the musical would, alas, never be written.[2]

However, a revival of *Music in the Air* by Edwin Lester and the Civic Light Opera of Los Angeles did come to popular fruition and brought Oscar Hammerstein to the West Coast. Oscar was in a depressed state. The failures of *Gentlemen Unafraid* and *Very Warm for May* were only two in a long string of flops for him. He was beginning to feel that his career would end long before his ability to create.

Jerry, in a cheerful state, helped in no small degree by Betty's divorce from Dick Green and her imminent marriage to Artie Shaw, a man whose music and mind he admired, attempted to buck up Oscar. It was then, according to Jerry's biographer Gerald Bordman, that Oscar suggested an intriguing collaboration. According to Bordman, Hammerstein confided to Jerry that he had been reading Lynn Riggs's 1931 play *Green Grow the Lilacs* and thought it could be turned into a musical. Was Jerry interested in doing the music? Jerry wasn't, and so *Oklahoma!,* the musical that would do for Broadway in 1943 what *Show Boat* had done for it in 1927, was passed up. And by the man whom Richard Rodgers had studied and to whom he owed—as he openly acknowledged—his own gift for melody.

It makes a neat and symmetrical story, but reality is less structured, and Richard Rodgers's recollections, in his autobiography *Musical Stages,* are probably nearer to the truth. According to Rodgers, Teresa Helburn and Lawrence Langer, his Connecticut neighbors and the founders of the Theatre Guild, gave *him* a copy of *Green Grow the Lilacs,* which he read and liked. He thereupon suggested to Lorenz Hart that they musicalize it. Hart turned it down and Rodgers turned to Hammerstein, and that is *that* version of *Oklahoma!*'s genesis.

Whatever the facts or the reason, Jerry and Oscar Hammerstein didn't work together in 1943 or 1944. Jerry instead did a Fred Astaire film for Columbia with a young and rising lyricist, Johnny Mercer. *You Were Never Lovelier* paired Astaire with Rita Hayworth and produced still more Kern classics, including the title song, "Dearly Beloved" and two contemporary, swinging, up-tempo tunes, "On the Beam" and "The Shorty George."

Meanwhile, *Oklahoma!*'s thunderous success on Broadway rolled westward. Universal, anxious to capitalize on the subject if not the substance of this landmark, contracted with Jerry and E. Y. Harburg to provide the music and lyrics for an adaptation of Samuel J. and Curtis B. Warnshawksy's novel, *Girl of the Overland Trail*. Jerry would be assured of having his music sung well: Deanna Durbin and Robert Paige had been signed for the leads.

He plunged into the project enthusiastically and produced an astonishing score, rich in variety and stuffed with soaring, sustained melodies. *Can't Help Singing* contained two unforgettable ballads, "Any Moment Now" and "More and More," an exuberant moving-on song, "Elbow Room," and a possibly whimsically intended, three-quarter takeoff on "Oklahoma!," "Californ-i-ay."

In New York, Guy absorbed the shock of *Oklahoma!* by ignoring it. New York was overflowing with GIs, waiting to be shipped overseas or getting off basic training at Fort Dix. The Stage Door Canteen not only fed and entertained servicemen, it awakened their interest in Broadway, what with its biggest stars serving them donuts or dancing with them. *Oklahoma!*'s wholesome Americana appealed to servicemen, but so did shows with lots of girls in minimal costumes—the old "leg shows" of the 1920s, in other words. And Guy would be partially responsible for the books for two of these in the 1943–44 season.

The first was a property he first sold to Vincent Youmans for production with—it was rumored—Doris Duke money.[3] When Youmans abandoned it, Vinton Freedley took over *Jackpot,* concerning a girl putting herself up as first prize in a bond-selling rally and being won by three marines who spend the rest of the show fighting over her. Guy was engaged to write the libretto, Vernon Duke was hired to compose the music and Howard Dietz to supply the lyrics. After a few weeks, it became apparent to Freedley that Guy was simply not up to writing the book for a contemporary musical comedy, no matter how old fashioned its structure.

He suggested two young fellows who had been enthusiastically recommended to him by George Balanchine, who had worked with them on an enormously successful revival of *The Merry Widow*. One, Ben Roberts, was in the Army and stationed at Fort Hamilton, Brooklyn; the other, Sidney Sheldon, was in the Army Air Corps, had finished his primary training, and was waiting assignment. Both were twenty-four years old and very much in tune with the times.

Guy readily acquiesced to the partnership; he was happier collaborating than working by himself anyway. And so Roberts and Sheldon, eager to work with an icon of the musical theatre, joined Guy in converting his concept into a workable script. Freedley had presented them with a perhaps wartime, perhaps Freedley-induced condition. At the end of the 1942–43 season, the producer, Dietz, and Duke had fashioned a show for Mary Martin called *Dancing in the Streets.* He still had the sets for the show, which had closed out of town. They could write what they wished, but whatever they wrote would have to take place on *Dancing in the Streets's* sets. Freedley was not about to lose his investment.[4]

That year, Guy and Virginia left Great Neck and moved farther out on Long Island to Remsenburg, a quiet and lushly green hamlet on the rim of the Hamptons and the edge of the water. Virginia, who had friends in the area, found a home on Shore Road into which they immediately settled. It would be their abode for the rest of their lives, though at the time, those lives had begun to turn stormy.

Guy, with little to do in the theatre, had begun to wander again. About to enter his sixties, he refused to acknowledge it and began to spend time in New York with younger actresses upon whom his roving eye fell. Virginia was twenty-three years his junior, and until that time had been all of the young women he could possibly desire. But Virginia had a drinking problem. In later years, she would blame Guy's philandering for her alcoholism, but it was merely an aggravation of a long-time, continuing affliction.

At any rate, when Sidney Sheldon, who had greater freedom of movement than his sidekick Ben Roberts, went out to Remsenburg to work with Guy that summer, he found a gracious but generally boozy Virginia, a cool but efficient Guy, and oftentimes a young lady of the theatre.

On one summer weekend, the resident young actress was Wendy Barrie, to whom Sheldon was mightily attracted, especially after one moonlit stroll along the shore during which she confessed that her current boyfriend beat her up regularly and she needed guidance. The young and romantic and moonstruck writer offered her immediate and succinct advice: "Leave him."

"Yes," she said, relief scissoring through her tears. "I should. I will."

Greatly encouraged by the double-barreled effect of his advice—a decision for her and a possible date for him—he asked her out for several dinners in New York.

Two weeks later, after one of these dinners, a close friend of his, who had just chanced to run into them, called Sheldon. "Sidney," he said, "do you like your life? Do you want to live?"

"Of course I do," the young writer answered.

"Do you know who Wendy Barrie's boyfriend is?"

"No."

"Bugsy Siegel!" the friend exploded.[5]

Sheldon had no more dates with Miss Barrie, nor did Guy. Anyway, by now, *Jackpot* was consuming the time of both of them, and both Sidney Sheldon and Guy accompanied it to New Haven and then Philadelphia.

Despite the contemporization of the book by Sheldon and Roberts, and a cast headed by Allan Jones, Jerry Lester, Benny Baker, Nanette Fabray, Mary Wickes, and Betty Garrett (and, in a bit part, a very young and unknown Jacqueline Susann), the show failed to snare the attention and attendance of wartime New York. It opened at the Alvin Theatre on January 13, 1944, and closed on March 11, a sixty-nine-performance, expensive flop.

Again, Guy was off and running on another venture which would prove far more profitable. His second and last show of that season was an out-and-out girlie show. Produced by Dave Wolper, it reunited Guy with Fred Thompson, who had followed soon after from London to New York, and Eddie Davis, who had by now vacated his taxi license and was living the more lucrative life of a gag writer.

It was the Gaiety and 1930s London all over again. The book, technically about the efforts of burlesque queen Bubbles LaMarr to take over the Spotlight Canteen, was a wispy confection designed merely to connect a string of specialty acts and leggy dances by an underclothed chorus. Even the cast was familiar. Bubbles LaMarr was played by none other than Gertrude Niesen, who had stopped *Bobby Get Your Gun* cold in 1938. In *Follow the Girls,* she did the same, with "I Wanna Get Married," a sexier-than-ever number written by Dan Shapiro, Milton Pascal, and Phil Charig.

*Follow the Girls* was a constant magnet for GIs, who kept it running for a solid two years.

But that would be it for Guy on Broadway for four years. His attention in early 1945 was drawn elsewhere. Shortly after *Follow the Girls* opened, he presented himself at MGM in Hollywood. Arthur Freed planned to do a musical "biography" of Jerry. Jerry had resisted it vigorously at first, but finally agreed when Freed convinced him that it would be fictitious and only marginally approximate the real events in the composer's life. The one script writer who could do this convincingly, Jerry suggested, was Guy Bolton. He had been there, after all, when the American musical theatre got its start from the trio of musical fame. He was part of it, and yet apart, as he always seemed to be. It was only appropriate, perhaps even poetic, that he should be the one to write a biography of Jerry that was in the spirit of the man and his time and yet mostly fiction.

Jerry himself was busily at work on another Harry Cohn project at Columbia, *Cover Girl,* which would star Gene Kelly, Rita Hayworth, and Phil Silvers. Produced by Arthur Schwartz, it was essentially a wartime romance. This time, Jerry's lyricist was Ira Gershwin.

The two would produce one of Jerry's all-time gems, "Long Ago and Far Away," for the film, but with some difficulty. First, Jerry wrote a melody which he played for Schwartz. Schwartz's reaction caused Jerry to immediately pen three letters on the manuscript: "A. D. L." Translation: "Arthur doesn't like."

Next, Jerry wrote another melody and played it for Schwartz in such an ornate arrangement that the producer/songwriter was unable to tell if he liked it or not. At the conclusion of the first rendition, he asked Jerry to play the melody with one finger. He did, and Schwartz immediately approved its flowing beauty.

So much for the music; now came the problem of the words. Ira Gershwin was notorious for his painstaking, lengthy agonizing over lyrics. Jerry, growing impatient, sent him his own dummy lyric, which began, "Watching little Alice pee. . . ." It goaded Gershwin into producing, first "Midnight Music," and finally, "Long Ago and Far Away."

The film was a success; Kern particularly loved working with Gene Kelly, presenting him with a photo at the end of shooting that was inscribed, "To G. K. who's O.K. with J. K."[6]

At the beginning of 1945, much of his old energy had returned, and he was ready to begin a new assignment for Twentieth Century Fox, the music for another Americana musical, *Centennial Summer.* He proposed the audacious idea of composing the entire score in three-quarter time, to give it a period flavor. Studio officials turned it down out of hand, and the idea would have to wait twenty-eight years, for Stephen Sondheim to do exactly that in his score for *A Little Night Music.*

The lyricist assigned to the film was Leo Robin, a careful worker in the Ira Gershwin mode who had the additional problem of being in awe of Jerry. It made for slow going, and in frustration, Jerry submitted some trunk tunes with lyrics by Oscar Hammerstein and E. Y. Harburg. It had a similar effect upon Robin as Jerry's dummy lyric had on Ira Gershwin. He speeded up his output but, unlike Ira Gershwin, lost sole lyric credit. "All Through the Day," the film's best-known ballad, was the Oscar Hammerstein song, and "Cinderella Sue," a specialty for dancer Avon Long, had a lyric by Harburg. "I Got Up with the Lark This Morning," another favorite, did carry Robin's lyrics, as did the remainder of the score.

Once this project was finished, Jerry turned his attention to the MGM biography and the musical numbers that were being recorded, even before the script was submitted. Freed planned to feature thirty-five Kern songs; this figure eventually escalated to forty-three. One that was planned had to be dropped because of lingering legal entanglements: "Ka-lu-a" failed to pass muster with the MGM legal department, since Fred Fisher, long ago, had won a law suit concerning it.

Jerry was not happy with the staging and arranging of his music, but by the time it was ready for recording, he was on his way to New York. Two new projects on Broadway thrilled him enough to elicit a confession that, should these two succeed, they might be enough to draw him back to New York for good.

The first was an offer by Oscar and Richard Rodgers, who had become Broadway moguls and producers, to provide the music for a musical biography of the famous sharpshooter Annie Oakley. Herbert and Dorothy Fields were already at work on the book; Jerry would again be working with Dorothy on the lyrics. Rodgers's eloquent and gallant wire, "It would be one of the greatest honors in my life if you would consent to write the music for this show," swept away any small resentments the composer might have had over Rodgers's assuming Jerry's mantle at the crest of the Broadway composers' hierarchy. Jerry accepted with enthusiasm and was already bursting with ideas.

The second New York lure was the first full-scale revival of *Show Boat* in thirteen years. Jerry and Oscar had, long distance, written a new song, "Nobody Else but Me" for the second act, and Jerry was anxious to once more be part of the preparations for a show for which his affection had never dimmed. He immediately plunged into all of the details of the production, passing on costumes, giving encouragement to Jan Clayton, the young singer/actress who would play Magnolia's daughter and sing "Nobody Else but Me."

Interestingly enough, he had no complaints with the dramatically altered form of the show. Gone were the dark overture and the hard edges of the original orchestration. Out of evidence was the social comment. It was now a romantic excursion down Ol' Man River, paralleling the 1936 movie vision that Oscar Hammerstein had put on screen. An older, less mercurial, and more accommodating Jerry apparently felt it was all right to present it this way.

Or perhaps his acquiescence came from the fact that he was feeling more tired than usual. He and Eva arrived on Friday, November 2, 1945, and moved into their suite at the St. Regis Hotel. Jerry left immediately for the Ziegfeld Theatre, where *Show Boat* had opened in 1927, and where it was now in rehearsal. He spent a joyful day with the production and fell into bed that night happily exhausted. There was a Saturday morning rehearsal which Jerry also attended. He and Eva were invited to go to a show Saturday night, but Jerry declined and retired early. The following day, he and Eva drove to Westchester to visit his parents' graves and attend a dinner party in Scarsdale.

There was no morning rehearsal on Monday, November 5, and so Jerry kept a luncheon date with Guy at the Lambs Club. They discussed much that early afternoon, the sadness of Plum's absence and how much he would have enjoyed this sunny afternoon in New York, the changes that had come about in their lives and in the life of Broadway, and, according to Guy, the possibility of doing another show together, once *Annie Oakley* was safely on the boards.[7]

They shook hands warmly, two old companions who had had their disagreements and differences but who now, entering the autumn of their years, were ready to count their blessings and their accomplishments and leave the rest to the historians. Guy went to his office over the Golden Theatre; Jerry turned east and then north, toward Ackerman's, where he planned to inspect and perhaps buy an antique breakfront he had seen in their catalog.

At the corner of Park Avenue and Fifty-seventh Street, he paused, wavered for a moment, and fell to the sidewalk. New York City policeman Joseph Cribben, on traffic control, saw him fall and, elbowing his way through the crowd that began to collect around the prostrate, deathly pale man, tried to rouse him. Jerry refused to respond.

Dashing to a pay phone, Cribben called a city ambulance, which took the still unconscious Jerry to City Hospital, on Welfare Island in the middle of the East River, beneath the Fifty-ninth Street Bridge.

Dr. Henry Greenberg, the physician on duty, concluded immediately that Jerry had suffered a stroke, and he suggested that his next of kin be notified. But the only identification on the comatose man was an ASCAP card with a number. The hospital contacted ASCAP. They checked their records and, to their horror, found that the owner of the card was Jerome Kern.

When the news spread, a tremor ran through the staff at City Hospital. A screen was drawn around Jerry's bed, isolating him from the long, white, clattering men's ward in which he had been placed. ASCAP tried to contact Eva at the St. Regis, but she was out, at lunch with Dorothy Fields. The *Show Boat* company at the Ziegfeld, concerned about Jerry's absence from that afternoon's rehearsal, called the St. Regis and left a message. ASCAP phoned Oscar Hammerstein's home, but he was at the St. Regis, at a meeting of the Dramatists Guild.

There, ASCAP finally tracked him down, and he in turn gathered Eva, who had just returned from lunch. They rushed to the hospital, where Jerry lay, still unconscious. But at 3:15, as a tearful Eva and Oscar hovered over him, he briefly regained consciousness and recognized them. It was only a momentary reversal. He immediately lapsed back into a coma.

The Kerns' New York physician, Dr. Harold Hyman, summoned by Oscar, arrived and examined Jerry. The composer had suffered a cerebral hemorrhage, he concluded, and it was either terminal or terribly debilitating. A phone call was made to Betty in California, advising her to fly east immediately. She did.

On Wednesday, November 7, the family and Dr. Hyman decided to move Jerry to Doctors' Hospital, where he could rest more comfortably and receive more dedicated care. A steady flow of friends visited the mute and sleeping composer both on Welfare Island and at Doctors' Hospital. Betty arrived and was inconsolable, as were Eva and Oscar, who seldom left his friend's bedside.

It was a tragic week, reminiscent of one eight years earlier, at Cedars of Lebanon in Los Angeles. At Doctors' Hospital, on a different floor from Jerry and unaware of his presence, the forty-seven-year-old Vincent Youmans lay, debilitated by the tuberculosis and bodily deterioration that would kill him in one year.

Now, Jerry slipped further and further away. At 1:00 P.M. on Sunday, November 11, Oscar entered the room. Jerry's breathing was labored, despite the oxygen within the tent that covered his upper body. Oscar recalled that Jerry particularly loved "I've Told Ev'ry Little Star." He lifted the edge of the oxygen tent and softly, sweetly, sang the song they had written into Jerry's ear. He replaced the tent flap and straightened up. It was 1:10 P.M. on November 11, 1945, and there was no movement. Just seventy-seven days short of his sixty-first birthday, Jerome Kern was dead.

Chapter

## 22

# Reprises

## 1945–1961

And so now the trio was a duet, with its two remaining members separated by an ocean. The letters flowed from Remsenburg to 78 avenue Paul Doumer and back and, later, to and from 35 boulevard Suchet. In the summer, Guy complained that both Peggy and Joanie were living with them. Peggy's marriage to Jimmy Burrowes was in trouble, and Joanie was ill and looking for a home in Westhampton, next to Remsenburg. (Eventually, both she and Dickie would move to Westhampton.)

In July, Plum asked slyly if Guy couldn't manage to smuggle Ethel and him to America. Even though the *Saturday Evening Post* still refused to publish any Wodehouse stories, he longed to be close to his old friend. [1]

In 1945, Guybo was a sergeant in the Army. He had spent a year at Rutgers and worked for a while as a librarian at the University of Connecticut. After the war, he went to Cambridge, where he met Françoise Rostand, who was an instructor, and they were married. For a while, his life seemed to gain a structure. He had a family, finally. He went on to work for some insurance firms and grew old rapidly. At the age of thirty-five, he would have his gall bladder removed. Eventually, he and Françoise would move to Paris with their two children, Patrick and Catherine.

Guybo was an intense and intensely sad young man. When he and his family were in America, he was more welcome at his grandfather's home than at his father's. Reginald had never forgiven—and would never forgive—Guy for divorcing Marion, and when he died, in 1944, he left Guy $1.

Through the rest of 1945, Guy worked with a battalion of writers, which included at one time, Marc Connelly, Jerome Chodorov, and Fred Finklehoffe, on shaping and reshaping the film biography of Jerry, which had now become a tribute. Originally titled *Look for the Silver Lining,* it eventually became *Till the Clouds Roll By,* and after weathering the storms created by the Breen office, which objected to Otto Harbach's lyric for "She Didn't Say Yes" and Plum's lyric for "Cleopatterer," the film opened at Radio City Music Hall in New York and established a record high in attendance and income.

It was a time for retrospection, an occupation that would consume much of Guy and Plum's life from that time forward. By the end of 1945, Guy was determined to have *Oh, Boy!* revived, with "Flubbydub" dropped and "Bungalow in Quogue" and the melodrama trio from *Miss Springtime* added. It was a pattern that he would establish for years, for he and Plum had written their last successful and original musical for Broadway.

Still, Hollywood had not forgotten Guy. Buoyed by the success of *Till the Clouds Roll By,* MGM was anxious to film a fictitious life of Rodgers and Hart. And so Guy went to work on *With a Song in My Heart,* which, in its own time, would become *Words and Music.*


In Paris, Plum fretted. He wrote to Ira Gershwin, wondering if Broadway would accept him back. Ira said yes. Plum, relieved, replied, "I'm glad that you think I shall be able to get back to the lyric writing game. That is what I'd like to do. Guy rather scared me by saying that musical shows are being rather rough these days; I'm sure that is true only of some. . . ."

Encouraged by Ira, Plum decided that it would be like the old days when he returned. "I was asked to do a book and lyrics for a show from Vienna in which Grace Moore is to star, and Hassard Short is to direct about Madame Pompadour," he wrote to Ira.

> I was torn between the desire to get in on what would presumably be a big production and a hit (especially since I was an old beach bum trying to make a

comeback after 30 years) and the desire to put on a false beard and hide somewhere till the whole thing had blown over.

I imagine you feel the same as I do when asked to work on a period musical show—a sort of deadly feeling that you are going into it with one arm strapped to your side and hobbles around your ankles so that you won't be able to use anything in the nature of modern comedy lines or ideas, and are robbed of your best stuff.

When I write a lyric I want to be able to work in Clark Gable or Grover Whelan's moustache and corned beef hash, but you can't when you're dealing with la Pompadour.

Besides, on these unfortunate occasions [I think of the time] I helped to write *Kitty Darlin'*, the ghost of which always rises before my eyes when people mention Period Pieces. [2]

It was easy to fantasize from a distance; it always is. Plum was visualizing a Broadway sunk in the teens and twenties. Guy was dealing with the reality of the late forties, and, with the slow return to normalcy after the war, he made plans to go back to London. Of course, he knew it wouldn't be as it had been in the previous decade, but he did have fond memories of his last musical triumphs there.

In July of 1946, he wrote to Plum that he and Virginia were coming to Europe. Plum wrote back that Ethel and he were thinking of rebuilding Low Wood, but he secretly hoped that Ethel, once she got back to America, would want to stay.

Guy arrived in London and found a profoundly different world. The devastation was appalling. In the West End, some of the old managers were still there, but there was very little money and very small shows playing. London was busy rebuilding itself. Nevertheless, he had ideas. He would write a play about the Shelleys, and he did, called *The Shelley Story.* He sent a copy to Plum, and Plum loved it. But nobody would produce it.

He went to see Plum and Ethel in Paris, and while there, he began negotiations to buy the rights to a Sacha Guitry play which he and Plum would ultimately translate into *Don't Listen, Ladies!* But that was it, and Guy returned to New York to fulfill an ironic assignment, the updating of the Oscar Straus operetta, *The Chocolate Soldier.* After all of this time, after what the Princess had accomplished, he was back in operettaland.

And, at the same time, nostalgia hit Plum squarely in the creative process. "Listen," he wrote to Guy,

I've suddenly got the most terrific idea—a book of theatrical reminiscences by you and me to be called

BOOK AND LYRICS

BY

GUY BOLTON AND P. G. WODEHOUSE

I only got the idea an hour ago, so haven't thought out anything about the shape of the thing, but I believe we could make a big thing out of it. You have an enormous stock of theatrical stories and I have a few myself. My idea would be to make it a sort of loose saga of our adventures in the theatre from 1915 onwards, studded with anecdotes. Think of all the stuff we could put into it! I remember you telling me a priceless story about Bill McGuire, but I've forgotten the details, and between us we must have a hundred unpublished yarns about Erlanger, Savage, etc. Do you think in your spare time you could dictate a few to a stenographer—quite in the rough, just the main points for me to work up? Meanwhile, I'll be trying to shape the vehicle. Don't give away the title to a soul, as it seems to me a winner and somebody might pinch it. . . .[3]

It was also time for Plum to take stock, to express the heretofore unexpressed. "I have always thought," he wrote to Guy in June of 1946, "what a miracle it was that I should have been able to work with about the only chap in the world I like to be with."[4]

On March 12, 1947, Hans Bartsch, the German producer, opened Guy's new version of *The Chocolate Soldier* at the Century Theatre in New York, with Keith Andes, Frances McCann, and Billy Gilbert in starring roles and George Balanchine providing the choreography. It would have a moderate run of seventy performances and close for the summer, with a promise for a fall reopening which would never be fulfilled.

Guy, meanwhile, took up with Yolanda May, a Hollywood actress of considerable beauty but few credits, while Virginia, drinking more heavily than ever, was beginning to show the physical effects of long, sustained alcoholism.

He and Virginia set out for Europe in the early spring of 1947. Guy was determined to close negotiations with Guitry on *Don't Listen, Ladies!* He did, but it was the only positive accomplishment in an otherwise disastrous trip.

First of all, he and Virginia missed Ethel and Plum, who, on April 18, 1947, boarded the *America* for New York. Their return had been delayed for months, first by a dock strike and then by Ethel's determination that she couldn't possibly leave for the United States without having first bought an entirely new wardrobe. Guy offered them the Remsenburg house for the summer, and they tentatively accepted.

Once Guy and Virginia arrived in London, and once they had settled themselves into a rented flat, Guy disappeared. Yolanda May magically appeared, and they traveled to Portofino, from where Guy sent periodic notes to Virginia. It was a time for contemplation, he told her, and she apparently took it to heart. She cut back on her drinking dramatically and began to regain the beauty that had first attracted Guy and that drinking had ravaged.

At the same time, Guy was having second and third thoughts. He was in his sixties now, and most men didn't live to be much older than that in the 1940s. He found that the sweetness of the company of young and beautiful and adoring women was no longer satisfying. Yolanda and Portofino began to lose their charm. But should he go back to Virginia? He agonized for weeks, and while he agonized, his hair turned pure white.

Finally, he made a decision. He returned, chastened and considerably older looking, and Virginia and he made a pact that would carry them through the rest of their lives together. She would indulge his dalliances, realizing that they would have less and less chance of consummation as the years accumulated. He would remain as true to her as he could, for he realized that she was the deepest love of his life, the one that aroused in him forgiveness for her weaknesses, too.[5]


Meanwhile, in New York, Plum and Ethel settled into the Weylin Hotel, while Plum submitted himself to several radio and television interviews to publicize the imminent publication of his novel *Full Moon*.

Within a few weeks they moved into a penthouse apartment on East Sixty-sixth Street. Peggy and Marguerite were in New York that summer, and Plum eagerly accompanied them on a memory trip to Great Neck, to relive some of the best of the Princess and Kensington years.

Marguerite was as glamorous as ever. Her high and pure soprano voice had, through neglect and misuse, descended. Still, as a contralto, she was giving well-attended concerts.

It was one of the happiest days Plum spent that summer, for he found that both before and after it he was lonelier and more lost than he had ever been. Guy had been mild in his warnings about the changes that had occurred in the theatre. Plum wrote in distress to his old friend: "I can't get used to the new Broadway. Apparently you have to write your show and get it composed and then give a series of auditions to backers, instead of having the management line up a couple of stars and then get a show written for them. It's so damned difficult to write a show without knowing who you are writing it for. It's like trying to write lyrics without a book. I feel lost without you."[6]

And later, to Ira Gershwin, he would write plaintively, "It's tough these days breaking into the lyric game. Every composer seems to have his own lyrist. I feel like a caged skylark."[7]

Still, offers came to him. Ferenc Molnar, so pleased with Plum's adaptation of *The Play's the Thing* that he stopped the roulette wheel at the casino in Cannes once to offer public homage to Plum in French—which Plum didn't understand at the time—specified that he wanted the Wodehouse sensibility to translate two of his latest works, *Arthur* and *Game of Hearts*. They would never be produced, but they would keep Plum busy that summer, hoping and writing.

And then, in October, Guy and Virginia returned to America, scooped up Plum and took him off to Remsenburg. Guy indeed had a collaboration for them: the deferred *Don't Listen, Ladies!* It would occupy them that winter, and it would be like old times. Guy and Virginia remained more and more in Remsenburg, but Ethel found a spacious apartment with a terrace at 1000 Park Avenue for Plum and herself.

Still, the two writers, as in the old days when Jerry lived in Bronxvile, Plum in Bellport, and Guy in Manhattan, collaborated with ease and success. They turned out a first rate script, full of marvelous wit, crackling with comprehensible characters and situations, constructed with all of the architectural wizardry of the best of their musicals.

Exhilarated, Guy took *Don't Listen, Ladies!* to London and there, authored, supposedly by Stephen Powys (Plum and Guy thought that Plum's name would still scotch success in England), it opened on September 2, 1948, at St. James's Theatre. It was a smash hit and would run for 219 performances.

Now, Plum and Guy thought, would be the time to make their grand reentrance on Broadway. Plum's name was no longer associated with the war in America, and so there was no fear of it being made visible.

However, Sacha Guitry's name was another matter. He had willingly collaborated with the Nazis during the war, "the silly son of a bitch," as Plum put it.[8] And columnist Walter Winchell, publicly patriotic to the roots of what was left of his hair, had already written several columns attacking Guitry.

Guy allayed Plum's fears about Winchell and convinced Lee Ephraim to bring the show to New York, with Jack Buchanan and a new, young star, Moira Lister, in the leads. He shepherded the move and boarded the *Queen Elizabeth* with the cast for America.

What happened next was as much a comment on the unreality of the two survivors of the trio as it was on the new ways of the world. Moira Lister related it in detail to this author. "They were going to do the play just as it was done in

London," she said. "So there was no rewriting. But Guy was there all the time, and watching, and being very charming. He never struck me as being of that sort of tough theatre world. He was such a gentleman. He was so what the French call 'douce.' And there was a lovely atmosphere always. There was never nasty fighting, or anything."

Just like the Princess.

The production, under Jack Buchanan's direction, formed itself. The gowns, by Harde Ame, were opulent, again redolent of the Princess. The sets would be first rate, as they had always been at the Princess.

The play opened in early December in Boston in a snowstorm, and the audience came and loved it in spite of the weather. The cast and creative staff were certain they had a hit.

But meanwhile, back in New York, Walter Winchell was preparing a column attacking Guy and Plum and Jack Buchanan and the entire company for daring to bring in a play by the noted Nazi collaborator, Sacha Guitry. "I mean," recalled Moira Lister, "he hadn't even seen the play, which was so wicked. He prepared everybody before we came in that it was something one shouldn't see."

When they got to New York, the column had not yet appeared. "When we arrived," Moira Lister remembered, "because of Jack being so popular, as he was, we were feted up hill and down dale. My suite at the [Plaza] hotel was filled with every kind of proffering—cases of . . . whiskey, cases of tissues, and flowers, and just every kind of thing. And people gave incredible parties for us."

And then the column appeared.

How dare they do this, crowed Winchell. "I hope Guitry chokes on his royalties!"

The reviews were scathing. Audiences shrank, then diminished, then nearly disappeared. The closing notice went up, but Jack Buchanan, bewildered and hurt and hopeful that it would all pass, poured his own money into the show.

"We kept it open six weeks," recalled Moira Lister, "and Guy was there all the time. Being very warm and consoling. And saying, 'It's not your fault,' and all that. But for actors to be—" she waved her hands hopelessly and eloquently. "People didn't come to see the play, which was awful, and awful for Jack, because he'd never been in a failure before, and to look out at a half empty house the way we had to, night after night—

"And those people who had feted us at the beginning, those same people when we saw them, turned their backs on us.

"It was the first time I had ever been to America," she added, "and I was shocked by it. It was nothing to do with us, you know, but there was this feeling that only success must breed success, and you mustn't be seen with anything that's a failure, because failure breeds failure.

"Well," she sighed, "but that's New York, the kind of tough commercialism of it. There's nothing greater than being the toast of New York. And there's nothing worse than being a failure in it."

Her words went to the heart of it, leaping decades. They expressed feelings that had begun for Guy when he had first become famous at the Princess and that deepened as age overcame him and failure became first a possibility and then an unfriendly but constant visitor. Feted in triumph, he too was beginning to be ignored in failure. But even then, buoyant, bolstering a bewildered cast, he seemed to the world the very image of ceaseless success.

Moira Lister would never star again on Broadway, though she would return to London and become a star there. And of course the entire episode would constitute only a pause in the constantly ascending spiral of Jack Buchanan's career.

Guy, feeling his British roots more strongly than ever, now decided to set them down in London, just as Plum had convinced Ethel it was in America that he wanted to spin out his final days. Guy and Virginia formed VB Enterprises, Ltd., and bought an apartment at 4 Lowndes Court, which they would rent out, they decided, when they were not in London.

It was a noble enterprise, but it would never make them any money, despite their purchase and selling of several other apartments. The fatal flaw in the scheme was that they themselves would always take over the apartments during the peak seasons—in the winter when Guy had a play on and in the summer when he didn't. Nevertheless, it gave Virginia a sense of importance, one that Ethel seemed to have built into her bones.

Back in New York, Plum looked in on a revival of *Sally,* starring Bambi Lynn and Willie Howard, who had replaced Morey Amsterdam in rehearsals. Amsterdam had had the audacity to boast that Guy and Plum were a couple of old fossils and needed him to bring them into the present. It got him a one-way ticket out of the show, which managed to make it through the season, after receiving mixed reviews.

Its success acted as a tonic to both Plum and Guy, who wrote back and forth, suggesting that they form their own management to revive their own shows. Nothing came of it; Guy was busy making contacts in Europe, and Plum was pressing forward with two books of theatrical reminiscence: *Bring on the Girls,* the new title for his and Guy's book, and *Performing Flea,* his own private mirror on the past, told through his letters to William Townend.

Guy, in London, was able to interest Wauna Paul and A. T. Smith in a slight rewrite of his and Somerset Maugham's 1941 hit *Theatre,* now retitled *Larger than Life.* Sparked by the twin presences of Reginald Denny and Jessie Royce Landis, who was imported from America for the occasion, it opened at the Duke of York's on February 7, 1950, and enjoyed a healthy run, thus reinforcing Guy's contention that Broadway was a past dream and London a present actuality. What he failed to notice was the recurring theme in the play's reviews, that ". . . it has nothing to give but pure entertainment."9 Even the London stage, it seemed, was looking for something more in the 1950s than the formulas of the 1920s and 1930s.

That same year, Guy again tried his hand at old operetta, with disastrous results. *Music at Midnight,* a play about and featuring the music of Offenbach, with lyrics by Harold Purcell, and starring Genevieve Guirty, Andrew Osborn, and Joan Heal, opened at His Majesty's Theatre on November 10, 1950, and closed swiftly. "The story is old fashioned, dull and not even very clear," the *Times* reviewer said and continued, damningly, "the dialogue is flat, and even fatuous."

Indefatigable and predictable, Guy, at the same time, was developing a mystery, double-murder play that he and Plum had worked on the previous year. It was tried out in Worthing and received a decidedly lukewarm response, and Guy could find no management willing to bring it into the West End. Very well; he ricocheted back to operetta, writing *Rainbow Square,* with music by Robert Stolz and lyrics by Harold Purcell and himself.

This was a Prince Littler production destined for the cavernous Seville Theatre, which had a supportable reputation as a house of flops. But this time, under the master management of Prince Littler, it would be utilized as it never had been before. "The setting is as realistic and immense as anything in London since the war," gasped the *Observer* the morning after *Rainbow Square*'s opening, on September 9, 1951.

And it certainly was, encompassing different parts of contemporary Vienna—a bombed and scaffold-enclosed church, a hotel restaurant, three-story houses with picture postcard fronts. At one point, a steam-traction engine hauled on the brightly striped caravans and prop wagons of a traveling fair. Strolling players strolled. Children played. A brass band blared its way across the stage. A donkey drew a cart on. Real rain fell. After dark, the buildings were bathed in illuminations while an aerialist cavorted on a high wire. The Viennese, apparently unperturbed by occupation troops, danced and sang at the least provocation—or none at all.

The music was melodious, in the Strauss manner that Stolz had inherited. And the talent, led by the tall, langorous beauty, flowing hair, and full American voice of Martha King, the abundant soprano of Gloria Lane (lately of Menotti's *The Consul*), the manliness of Bruce Trent, and the comedy of Sonnie Hale, was strong and effective.

But for all of this, Guy's book was pronounced "old fashioned, with deplorably old fashioned humor." "It emerges as a series of musical comedy clichés rather than as a dramatic unity," said the *Times*. "Everyone plays it so safe in presenting a 'typical' British musical that burlesque often results."[10]

*Rainbow Square* lost a fortune for Prince Littler, but he apparently didn't hold it against Guy. He in fact asked Guy to advise him on the redecoration and choice of paintings for his new home, and for years afterward, Guy and Virginia were welcomed at the Littlers', until one terrible night years later, when a hopelessly drunk Virginia, accompanied by a similarly intoxicated friend, arrived at a formal dinner party, disrupted it with their conversation, and threw up at the table.

But Prince Littler was one of the last of a generation of prewar producers, too. When *Rainbow Square* opened, *Oklahoma!* had already been to London, *Carousel* and *Kiss Me, Kate* were playing in the West End, and *South Pacific* was on the way from America. Guy and Plum's musical theatre, absolutely absent from Broadway, had begun to disappear from London, too.

Plum found comfort here and there. He saw *Gentlemen Prefer Blondes* and confessed to Ira Gershwin, "[It's] a terrific hit which is encouraging, as it looks as though the old fashioned musical comedy, where the heroine doesn't die of tuberculosis in Act II may be coming back."[11]

He was busily and happily at work turning his novel *Spring Fever* into a play, when a strange dizziness suddenly struck him. One set of doctors diagnosed it as the result of a brain tumor; a second, after further tests, cancelled this evaluation and confessed that they could find no plausible cause. Plum processed the information and concluded to Townend that it was the onset of his seventies. "The score, then, to date," he wrote jovially,

> is that I am deaf in the left ear, bald, subject to mysterious giddy fits, and practically cockeyed. I suppose the moral of the whole thing is that I have simply got to realise that I am a few months off being seventy. I had been going along as if I were in the forties, eating and drinking everything I wanted to and smoking far too much. I had always looked on myself as a sort of freak whom age could not touch, which was where I made my ruddy error, because I'm really a senile wreck with about one and a half feet in the grave.

My doctor, by the way, summing up on the subject of the giddy fits and confessing his inability to explain them, said, "Well, if you have any more, you'd better just have them." I said I would. [12]

Guy complained of creeping rheumatism. Age was upon them both, and they had better get their memoirs down, he advised. And so they devoted more and more time to *Bring on the Girls.* It was a place in which Guy could expect a positive reaction to his writing, in contrast to the opinions of the New York and London critics. "I am stunned by your genius," Plum wrote to his friend and collaborator in February 1951.

So, simultaneously, the collection of Townend letters, *Performing Flea,* and *Bring on the Girls* began to take shape. All were suspect history. "I think," wrote Plum to Guy about *Bring on the Girls* that same month, "we shall have to let truth go to the wall if it interferes with entertainment." [13]

It was not inconsistent; it had been a rule they had followed on the stage; it was only proper that it should happen between the pages of a book, too. And so they happily revised their theatrical pasts and simultaneously tried to collaborate on a theatre piece in the old way. Picking Edward Everett Horton as their gentleman's gentleman character, they began to write *Phipps,* which later became *Kilroy Was Here.*

But Horton was not impressed with the script ("I hope he chokes," wrote Plum to Guy), [14] and Guy endeavored to interest Joe E. Brown in it. Brown evinced some curiosity, so Guy and Plum set about revising it for him. But he would ultimately refuse it. They then interested Dennis Price briefly in the play, pursued him, and rewrote again. But it was for nothing. *Phipps/Kilroy Was Here* would never find either a star or a stage.

And so, though their theatrical enterprises were meeting with less and less acceptance, they were forming a closer relationship than they had ever experienced before. One day in March, Guy suggested still another Jeeves play, and all four of them—Guy, Plum, Virginia, and Ethel—journeyed from New York to Remsenburg so that the two writers could have some sustained time together, not only blocking out the play, but walking the long and winding lanes of Remsenburg and getting in a few rounds of golf at the nearby Westhampton Country Club.

On one of these days, Ethel disappeared. That evening, she returned and announced that she had bought a house a short distance away, on Basket Neck Lane. It was actually much more than a house; it was a twelve-acre estate that stretched back to the bay and forward to the shaded lane on which the house sat.

Behind it was a garden in tangled disuse, and the house itself would have to be fixed up. But it was homey enough to be their American Low Wood, and that was exactly what she was determined to make of it.

Ethel remodeled the sun porch that gave onto the garden, sound proofing part of it and turning it into a bedroom and a study for Plum. They settled in soon after, first spending their summers in Remsenburg and their winters at 1000 Park Avenue and then, after three years, all of their time in Remsenburg. While Plum worked, Ethel turned the garden not only into a proper English one, but into a refuge for as many diverse animals and/or birds as cared to cross or inhabit it.

Guy continued to write plays and doggedly tried to interest managements in reviving the Princess shows. He would rewrite them, discuss the changes with Plum, extract, cut and paste songs from one to the other, to form what both of them felt were fresh new shows, but management interest remained maddeningly cool.

Before the war, Joanie had met Roger Vasselais, a young and ambitious Wall Street broker whom Guy rejected out of hand because he was poor. But Guy was shortsighted. Vasselais proceeded to become enormously successful and wealthy and bought a huge amount of property in Remsenburg, where he and Joanie settled. They had two children, Tony and Peter. Tony, by the 1950s, was happily married. But Peter, born in 1941, died at the age of nine of polio. Guy mourned the loss of his first grandson, and it was the first full expression of loss that those close to him could recall. [15]

More concerned than ever about his precarious financial state, Guy now became more and more tenacious in going after his proper share of Plum's lyric royalties. His industry in this matter dazzled Plum, who left this sort of thing to his agents and Ethel. It made enemies for Guy of men who were normally enemies with no one. But it was, to Guy, merely survival, only collecting debts owed, to keep even with Marion's alimony payments, to allow Virginia and him to live as they properly should in increasingly harder times. Of course, it never occurred to either Virginia or Guy to modify their lifestyles. Whenever they made one of their multifarious crossings, they always went first class. When they stayed at hotels, the hotels would be the Savoy or the May Fair or the Splendide or the Georges V. It was a way of preserving the world that Guy, through years of hard labor and dedicated work and attendant fame, had earned.

And, as if in fulfillment of this, the lightning of good fortune struck, twice. On one of his European junkets, Guy approached Merielle Perry, the young French girl who had graced *Sons O'Guns* in 1930, about extracting yet more mileage from *Theatre*. A failure as *Larger than Life,* it could, he reasoned, be given a new future and a new title and a new translation into French. A young playwright, Marc-Gilbert Sauvajon, would do the translation, the new title would be *Adorable Julia,* and Mme. Perry would be the producer.

The play opened at the Théâtre du Gymnase in Paris on September 20, 1954, with the exquisite French star Madeleine Robinson in the lead and became, immediately, a monster success, exceeding both Guy and Mme. Perry's wildest expectations. "Cher ami," she wrote to Guy, who was in America when it opened, "Votre pièce . . . votre magnifique pièce vieut d'être criée à Paris avec un immense succès! Hélas! Ce n'ést pas moi qui la joue! C'ést Madeleine Robinson. . . ."[16]

*Adorable Julia* would remain in Paris for over 1,000 performances, travel to South Africa, be translated into German, and play for months in Germany. It would provide a comfortable income for Guy for years to come, and he would never cease to talk about its success to anyone who would listen. It dots his correspondence like punctuation to the end of his life.

But in 1954, he was not resting on one laurel. He had already launched *The Guardian Angel,* all about telephones and love affairs and based upon a play by Alfred Savoir called *Passy 0851.* Originally titled by Guy *Give Me a Ring*— perhaps in homage to his salad days of the thirties in London—it found a home in the provinces, but not in the West End. Undaunted, he again gave it over to Marc-Gilbert Sauvajon, who translated it into French, retitled it *Ne Quittez Pas* (Hold the Line, Please) and once more, a translated play ran respectably—but only respectably—in Paris.

*Give Me a Ring/Guardian Angel/Ne Quittez Pas,* however, was only a momentary calm between *Adorable Julia* and Guy's last important work for the Broadway stage, *Anastasia.*

The impetus for writing this version of the story of the missing Romanov princess who supposedly (and, it has now been proved, fictitiously) escaped death in a cellar in Russia at the beginning of the Revolution, had its genesis in either of two years. It was either 1951, when Guy happened upon a French play by Marcelle-Maurette called at that time *The Unknown.* Or, if Guy's recollections are to be trusted—a risky assumption—it began considerably earlier, in 1928, when he was invited by Elsa Maxwell to a party for some charity in some posh hotel in New York City. As Guy would tell it to the *Boston Post*:

> What I do remember quite vividly was a girl, a thin, undistinguished figure, who was seated in a corner listening, it so appeared, to Armand

Vecsey's orchestra playing his own score from "The Rose of China," a work for which P. G. Wodehouse and I had supplied book and lyrics.

As I stood talking to Elsa, a woman made a sort of crouching run toward the girl in the corner and dropped on her knees in front of her.

"What's all that about?" I asked Elsa.

"The girl in the corner? She's the Czar's daughter, the Grand Duchess Anastasia. Her cousin, Princess Xenia of Greece brought her. Anastasia is staying with her down at Oyster Bay."

"But surely," I protested, "the entire family were killed in a cellar from which escape would have been impossible."

"She was rescued by two guards from the pile of dead bodies awaiting burial. There's been a lot about it in the papers but I suppose you only read the theatrical news."

I have reproached myself since with not having asked to be presented. I was a bit put off by that kneeling business. Also I gleaned that whatever chitchat might occur would be in a language of which I had the merest smattering. And then I had no inkling that the Grand Duchess was destined to play a part of some importance in my career. . . .

By the time Guy had rewritten the reminiscence for the *New York Times,* he had eliminated Elsa Maxwell and Armand Vecsey and changed some other details markedly, so this account, while dramatic, may well be in the *Bring on the Girls* vein of autobiography.

What certainly happened after Guy's discovery of the script of *The Unknown* in 1951 was that he took it to Toby Rowland, who worked for Prince Littler and would eventually inherit that production- and theatre-empire, and Toby Rowland referred him to literary agent Miriam Howell in New York. Guy wrote a letter to her in July of that year, detailing the defects he found in the original play and enclosing an outline of it as he envisioned it.

He worked in his flat in London at 1 Braynston Court, off George Street, that summer and early fall, taking time off to go to Stuttgart, Germany, where, in a shack at the edge of the Black Forest, Anna Anderson, the supposed Anastasia, resided in some squalor, but with lawyers at the ready to stop any attempt to impinge upon her forthcoming autobiography.

That would eventually be a problem for future producers, but in the summer of 1951, Guy was only interested in capturing the central character in his next play, which he had already retitled *Anastasia.*

Meanwhile, Miriam Howell moved the work between several producers, eventually selling the rights to Irene Selznick, who optioned it. But in the meantime Guy embarked on a practice that would get him into trouble and create still more enemies. Frightened, perhaps, of not selling the script, he not only toured the theatres in London and gave scripts to various leading ladies, including Eileen Herlie and Margaret Leighton, but placed it with several agents without telling them that it was being carried by others. Thus, at one time, *Anastasia* was represented by Miriam Howell, MCA England Ltd., Jan van Louen, and the Tommy Banyai agency in Paris, which represented Marcelle-Maurette. There was much confusion, a carload of bad feeling, and a few threats of lawsuits, but not enough to keep Guy from continuing this practice for the rest of his life. [17]

On through 1952 the script made the rounds, going to Siobhan MacKenna, Ingrid Bergman, Sybil Thorndyke, Jennifer Jones, even to Alexander Korda with the purpose of obtaining Merle Oberon. Finally, in early December.of 1952, Irene Selznick allowed her option to run out.

In 1953, Robert Fenn, at MCA, interested producer John Counsell in doing a production at the Windsor Theatre with Mary Kerridge as Anastasia and Helen Haye as the dowager empress. It was during this time that the BBC, under Cecil Madden, moved most of the Windsor production into their studios and did a TV version, which was highly successful. That same year, Laurence Olivier, faced with declining audiences for a season of poetic plays at the St. James's Theatre, approached John Counsell to let him do *Anastasia* at the St. James's as a vehicle for Vivien Leigh. Counsell agreed to let him do the production, but with Mary Kerridge, and it lasted for twenty-one performances, enough for Olivier to later share in the film rights. Both productions were viewed as possible inducements for larger, West End producers. But nothing occurred, although Michael Powell was interested, provided Guy and his agents could come up with a superstar for the lead.

On the search went, through Ann Todd, Vivien Leigh (who was suddenly not available), and Wendy Hiller. And it would continue into 1954, when finally, thirty-eight-year-old Elaine Perry, the daughter of Antoinette Perry, the American Theatre Wing's founder, brought to life what a score of more established producers did not or could not. [18]

*Anastasia,* with an achingly beautiful Viveca Lindfors as the possibly lost princess and a stately and unforgettable Eugenie Leontovich as the dowager empress, premiered at the Lyceum Theatre in New York on December 29, 1954. Although most critics detected the eternal Bolton problem of mixing the strange bedfellows of musical comedy with tragic seriousness, every one of them lauded the seventeen-minute recognition scene in the second act, ". . . in which," as Walter Kerr wrote in the *Herald Tribune,*

Eugenie Leontovich, as the ancient but mettlesome Empress, confronts
Viveca Lindfors, the fragile and uncertain pretender who may, after all, be
her granddaughter. The two meet in icy hostility. Miss Lindfors is not even
certain that she wants her identity returned to her; it will force her to face
the horrors of her own life once more. Miss Leontovich is a disbelieving
tigress, taunting and scoffing and closing her mind to the evidence. As
these embittered figures circle one another, startle one another with echoes
of the Winter Palace and the Chinese Island, stir in one another fires that
have been ruthlessly banked, "Anastasia" is suddenly gripping and moving
theatre.

They were the finest seventeen minutes Guy would ever write. And the play
would last 272 performances on Broadway, be revived and re-revived and have a
television life on the Hallmark Hall of Fame twelve years later with Julie Harris
and Lynn Fontanne in the leading roles. By the time it opened, it had already
been sold to Twentieth Century Fox for the astonishing sum, in 1954, of
$500,000, and it would succeed miraculously there, bringing Ingrid Bergman
out of exile and pitting her against Helen Hayes in the recognition scene. Guy
would be called to California to write the screenplay but would soon be replaced
by Arthur Laurents. With his share of the sale plus his screenwriter's fee, he
netted nearly $400,000, and his dismissal from the film bothered him not
at all.

Times were good again. Plum and Guy's theatrical myth-reminiscences,
*Bring on the Girls,* was published and selling well. Their Jeeves play, first called
*Derby Day* and then *Come on, Jeeves,* was given a performance at Worthing, but
never made the trip to the West End. Plum, ever mindful of good material—or,
at least, material he loved—turned it into his sixth Jeeves novel, *Ring for Jeeves.*
What the novel readers missed was his eloquent, Wodehousian tribute to the
partner with whom he would, in the next fifteen years, plan at least a dozen
projects—most of them revivals—but with whom he would actually collaborate
on a new work only once more: "What is so remarkable about [our collabora-
tion]" he opined,

> is not the excellence of the work it has produced, though this is considerable,
> but the fact that after forty years of churning out theatre-joy for a discriminat-
> ing public we are not merely speaking to one another but are the closest of
> friends. If Guy saw me drowning, he would dive in to the rescue without a
> moment's hesitation, and if I saw Guy drowning, I would be the first to call for
> assistance. How different from most collaborators, who in similar circum-
> stances would merely throw their partner an anvil. [19]

Guy, buoyed by *Anastasia's* success, invested more in VB Enterprises in England, bought countless art works, many of which would end up in storage warehouses forever, and continued to journey back and forth across the Atlantic. Plum, writing to his friend from Remsenburg, where he and Ethel had now settled permanently, complained of Ethel's unceasing social program. "I have just refused my third cocktail party invitation," he wrote. "Virginia will applaud this, but you may shake your head. But I simply can't go through these orgies. . . ."[20]

Still, for all her excesses, Plum would never dream of asking Ethel to stop inviting people over—or gambling his money, or arranging his contracts. She could have robbed banks, and he would have wondered why but would never have questioned her right to do it. Though Guy gave equivocal answers when asked if Plum cared deeply for Ethel, it seemed to even the unpracticed eye that he loved her unquestioningly, served her, and sanctified her from the moment he met her until the instant he died. She was the rock upon which reality broke. And he needed that rock more than practically anyone in the world.

Back on Broadway, Guy let little time elapse between *Anastasia's* premiere and the next time his name appeared on a marquee. Back in 1953, he and Eddie Davis had begun work, sporadically, on a musical they called *Ankles Aweigh.* Plum was delighted with the title and prevailed upon Guy not to change it to *Maiden Voyage,* as the producers and Guy wished. Guy nevertheless thought his title (which he abandoned) was more appropriate for their story about a Hollywood starlet on location in Italy, trying to conduct a honeymoon with her naval officer husband despite the demands and annoyances of her studio and his branch of the armed services.

*Ankles Aweigh,* produced by Howard Hoyt, Reginald Hammerstein, and Fred Finklehoffe, with music by Sammy Fain and lyrics by Dan Shapiro, opened at the Shubert in Boston in March, four months after *Anastasia's* triumph. It was received politely by the Boston critics, who had particularly warm words for Betty and Jane Kean, and some tolerant ones for Sonny Tufts, who played the naval man married to Jane Kean.

But Boston was a long way from New York, as the notices of the Manhattan critics on the morning of April 19, 1955 attested. Not one of them who had attended the previous night's premiere at the Mark Hellinger Theatre had a kind word for *Ankles Aweigh.* "A throwback," "ancient," "dated," and "claptrap" were a few of the pejoratives they used. And it was all of this, packed with the customary Bolton-Davis wisecracks, given to Lew Parker and Gabriel Dell as low comic relief, a leggy chorus line, and several out of nowhere tap routines. It was a conscious attempt to bring back the old days of mindless musical comedy.

It might have succeeded. It certainly had enough help from Manhattan's gossip columnists. They rallied to the defense of *Ankles Aweigh,* insisting that the broad arms of Broadway in the 1950s had room for what they remembered with nostalgia and fondness. Arthur Godfrey, Milton Berle, and Jackie Gleason added their voices to a chorus that was conducted by none other than Walter Winchell, the man who shot Guy's *Don't Listen, Ladies!* down in flames. Their efforts kept the show open for twenty-two weeks, which was not enough to pay off its investment.

Still, Plum and Guy blamed progress for their inability to absorb Broadway as it was. Plum saw *South Pacific* and loathed it, saw *My Fair Lady* and hated it, pronouncing it "the dullest, lousiest show I had ever seen," and, later, when he was invited to see Ethel Merman in *Gypsy,* he wrote to Guy, "I wouldn't see it if you paid me."[21]

In *Over Seventy,* which he published in 1957, he wrote:

> . . . if you ever catch me in a pensive mood, sitting with chin supported in the hand and the elbow on the knee, like Rodin's "Thinker," you can be pretty sure that I am saying to myself, "Whither the New York musical-comedy theatre?" or, possibly, "The New York musical-comedy theatre . . . whither?" It is a question that constantly exercises me. I can't see what, as the years roll by and costs continue to rise, is going to happen to the bally thing.

Plum satisfied himself mightily now by sticking to novels and collections. His dizzy spells persisted, and after consultation with Dr. Leray Davis, who had become the family doctor for both the Boltons and the Wodehouses, he concluded that his heart was not what it once had been. But his daily dozen and his walks with Guy kept him on an even path and perhaps even a little bit more. Although his output of words was decreasing, his skill was not.

He was happy in Remsenburg, more at peace than he could imagine, and in 1955 he made the twenty-minute drive to Riverhead, the county seat, and became an American citizen. Great Britain had still not completely exonerated him, and so he adopted the country that had.

In January of 1956, Marion was diagnosed as having cancer, without hope of survival. Guybo, about to receive his degree from Cambridge, was called home and so missed yet another chance of fulfillment and accomplishment.

In her tiny apartment in New York, Marion lingered until September. For the entire nine months, Guybo kept the reality of her cancer from her, sustaining her with the same spinning out of fantasy at which his father was so skilled.

Now, relieved of his anchor and responsibility and reason for rationality, Guybo became more lost and homeless than ever. Although he was married and had children, he utilized the sizable inheritance he received from his mother to travel extensively. He worked for a while in maritime insurance, but soon left that.

He called Peggy frequently. She had divorced Jimmy Burrowes and was now living in Switzerland with a new love, Claude Schlup. Their telephone conversations would sometimes last for two hours. "He was desperately lonely and unhappy," said Peggy to this author. "He wanted so much for Daddy to love him, and he wouldn't. And he began to feel that he had all these physical things wrong with him. And he drank. And he took librium. And it was so sad."

Guy, unaware, labored on now, adapting Henry James's *Wings of the Dove* into *Child of Fortune.* Jed Harris agreed to rewrite it and produce it, and on November 13, 1956, it opened at the Royale Theatre in New York, with a cast that included Pippa Scott, Mildred Dunnock, Edmund Purdom, Martyn Green, and Betsy von Furstenberg. It was roundly thrashed by the critics and closed soon thereafter, but Guy kept the play alive, reworking it, retitling it *Wings of the Dove,* taking his name off it, and turning over another rewrite to Christopher Taylor. It was finally brought, with Susannah York, James Donald, and Wendy Hiller, into the Lyric Theatre in the West End in December 1963, where it succeeded, and moved to the Theatre Royal Haymarket in April of 1964. Success in the theatre, it seemed, had become a series of plodding, barely surviving ventures.

And then, something else happened to make Plum and Guy believe in theatrical miracles. In reaction to rising costs on Broadway, the phenomenon of Off-Broadway gathered force in 1958, and, as it had in the twenties, when it was the launching pad for a young Eugene O'Neill, Greenwich Village became the center for a series of small playhouses willing to experiment at little cost to either producers or patrons.

Two young producers, Joseph Beruh and Peter Katz, leased the tiny Sheridan Square Playhouse, a 182-seat venue with a thrust stage that put its audiences intimately in touch with the casts who performed there. No spectacle, demanding distance, could survive in it, any more than an extravaganza or an operetta could have been shoehorned into the intimacy of the Princess. And so the producers contacted Plum and Guy, received the rights, and announced a new production of *Leave It to Jane*.

It was a marriage made at the Princess. The limitations of the theatre and the salaries paid the actors (non-Equity chorus members received a whopping $15 a week and Equity feature actors $40) were straight out of the Comstock era.

What was not quite historically correct was the book. A compilation of the 1917 and 1927 scripts and George Ade's *The College Widow*, from which Guy had fashioned his original script, it had song transitions and some added lyrics by stage manager and ultimately-principal actor Bert Pollack. Plum, consulted on these lyric changes, acquiesced cheerily, and the entire enterprise resulted in a happy, magical return to the Princess. [22]

*Leave It to Jane* became an extraordinary hit, charming audiences up close and intimately, as it was meant to do, for 842 performances. It was a pure tonic of renewed hope for the two septuagenarians, and one that was reinforced the very next season, in yet another, intimate Off-Broadway theatre, the tiny York Theatre on Manhattan's Upper East Side. Under the aegis of Ethel Watt, a revival of *Oh, Kay!* buzzed merrily along for eighty-nine performances and closed, not because of its failure, but because of prior commitments of the theatre.

The success of these two shows caused Guy to work all the more vigorously on rewrites of the old Princess and Gershwin musicals. If *Leave It to Jane* could be revived with such wild success, what about *Oh, Boy!*? Or *Oh, Lady! Lady!!*? Guy and Plum dug into the files, and while Guy tried to update the books, Plum revised lyrics. They were as enthusiastic about these projects, which would continue in spurts for the rest of their lives, as they had been back in the original Princess days.

The only problem was that, instead of improving upon the books, Guy worsened them. His desire to interpolate all sorts of songs from all sorts of shows caused some friction with old collaborators. And the dividends were few. Joseph Beruh evinced some interest in reviving *Oh, Boy!*, but nothing came of it. Guy's revised *Girl Crazy*, with Danny Churchill turned into a television star, received a West Coast tryout and bombed abysmally.

No matter. The glimmers of success were enough for the two aging gentlemen. It gave them hope. And it also woke memories. In April of 1960, Guy wrote to George Middleton with tenderness and precision and more regret than he would reveal to most of the world. "Dear George," he wrote

> I always *love* to hear from you. I wish I had had you at my side throughout my career—God, how much better off I would be!

I am, as you may have detected long ago, a careless fellow. I used to fall in love with women and buy them jewels and mink coats and furnish apartments and generally make a thoroughgoing fool of myself. I used to write the wrong shows when I might have been busy with you writing better ones. Every now and again my good angel has come along and put me back on the easy street I have been all too ready to consider my home.

Now here I am in my middle seventies trying to get that one more "strike" that will enable me to live on my savings without having to shut myself up with a pad or a typewriter seven or eight hours a day. . . .

I want to leave Virginia comfortably provided for—as for my four brats I don't care. Guy has two charming kids but he also has my life savings (via Marion) and so can support himself and family without working. *I* can't— which is somewhat ironical. My two elder children are also pretty well off and it is only Peggy (Marguerite's child) who needs a hand out. I shall leave my money, after Ginny, to her. [23]

That same year, he tried to turn the Hungarian uprising into a play, *Fireworks in the Sun.* He was too far from it, chronologically, culturally, and professionally. He was unable to sell it.

Later, he translated Colette Audry's play *Soledad* into English and from his flat at 43 Green Street tried to sell it, without success. For years, he would attempt to circulate a musical version of Jean Canolle's 1958 French comedy *Lady Godiva.* Vivian Ellis, talked by Guy into writing music and lyrics, was uncomfortable with the entire project, particularly after he noticed that Guy had appropriated huge chunks of the Canolle play wholesale, without credit.

Plum wrote merrily on, a book a year now, instead of the many he had once managed. *How Right You Are, Jeeves, Ice in the Bedroom* (his "eightieth birthday book") and *Service with a Smile* were published between 1959 and 1961, and in 1960, Simon and Shuster published a definitive omnibus, *The Most of P. G. Wodehouse.*

Guy, sensing that the day of successful productions of his plays was at last over, started to write novels, too. They were essentially novelizations of plays that never got on. The first, *The Olympians,* was a rework of his Shelley play; the second, *The Enchantress,* was another play put between covers rather than on the boards. To find the proper setting, he and Virginia went with Peggy to Vevey on Lake Geneva, where Peggy tended to their needs and he sat on the shore of the lake, writing, and perhaps trying to find the sort of peace that Plum enjoyed all of the time.

He was aware of that discrepancy; Virginia's drinking had escalated to debilitating dimensions. Her arms and legs were the wasted toothpicks of the chronic alcoholic. She was hardly ever sober. Her equilibrium was so upset she had fallen several times and had broken ribs in one of the falls, and from that time forward she would suffer from alcoholic ataxia, which made her stagger as if she were very drunk, whether she had been drinking or not.

In London that year, she attempted suicide by taking an overdose of nembutal and alcohol. She would have died if Guy hadn't contacted their London physician, Dr. Andrew MacLellan, who had her pumped out immediately. "She had taken a dose which, had she not been treated, could have been lethal," Dr. MacLellan told this author. "And it made a great difference to her. After that, she was glad to be alive. After that, she never drank again."

If surviving the suicide attempt began to cure her drinking, the sight of Joanie, when they returned to Remsenburg, sobered her still more. Peter had died of polio, Tony would die in 1966 of throat cancer, and now Joanie, separated from Roger Vasselais, spinning out an unhappy life that bitterness had shaped and shaded, an alcoholic who had matched Virginia drink for drink and sometimes outlasted her, was in the final, agonized throes of cirrhosis of the liver. She moved in with Guy and Virginia and wasted slowly away, finally slipping into a coma that necessitated her removal to Southampton Hospital.

Dick and Wynnie lived nearby in Westhampton; Peggy was in Europe with Claude; Guybo was in many places, most of them unknown to Guy. Finally, realizing that his hardness of heart against his son might, after all, have been responsible for Guybo's lifelong misery, Guy tried to reach out to him through letters. But it was too late. Guybo had given all he had to give, and he stuffed all of the letters he received from his father, unopened, into a drawer.[24]

He seemed to be coming irrevocably apart. Even Françoise and his children only heard from him intermittently, and she kept in touch by letter with Guy and Virginia. The only person with whom Guybo communicated regularly was Peggy. Wherever he was or wherever she was, he would continue to call her and pour out the contents of his injured heart over long- and short-distance telephone lines. At the beginning of the summer of 1961, she urged him repeatedly to join Claude and her on vacation in Spain. It was warm there; he could heal there.

But he refused, telling her he had to follow up on some vague sort of job that was developing in the natural gas industry. He declined to tell her exactly what it was, only that he had to go to America to conclude negotiations.

On August 6, a cable reached Virginia and Guy at the Dudley Hotel in Hove,

Sussex, where they had gone after Joan had entered the hospital. It was from Dick. Three days earlier, Guybo had been found dead in a disarrayed room at the Croyden Hotel, on East Eighty-sixth Street. The New York City police had called Dick, who had driven immediately to New York. There, he found a room in wild confusion, a graphic depiction of the person who had inhabited it. There were empty liquor and librium bottles near the bed.

The police had only given the room a cursory inspection and had failed to find the suicide note that Dick discovered and pocketed. The obituary in the papers the following day would list the cause of death as a heart attack.[25]

Guy immediately tried to phone Peggy in Spain but could not get through. He sat down and wrote to her. Françoise had been contacted through the State Department and was flying to America, he said, and Dick was going to write with the details.

"Poor Guy—" he concluded, with a final burst of understanding. "With all his faults he seems a tragic figure. He never seemed sure of himself, of what he was or wanted to be, of his relationship to other people, to you, to me. All his mysteries were really concealments. He wanted to seem more than he was because he actually felt inadequate. . . ."

But then, Guy's internal switch, the ability that Marguerite detected that would seal him away from a tragedy as near as the suicide of his own son was thrown. "I think Marion did him a disservice with the money," he went on. "If he had been obliged to make his way he would have had self-confidence through a degree of achievement. She made it too easy for him to drift and to fake."[26]

By the time Guy wrote to Plum, on August 13, the shutters had closed. "As you say," he wrote, "one is sorry but that is all. There are very few people who really mean anything in one's life, and it's no good pretending there are."[27]

On September 14, Joan died and was buried in the little churchyard at the top of Basket Neck Lane in Remsenburg. Within six weeks of each other, two of Guy's four children had died. This time, he wrote to no one.

# THE
# NEAR PAST

"Trouble is," says Plum, shaking his head, "I can't work as I used to. A page now when there were four then."

"Was it ever easy?" Guy stops and blows his nose. Squeaky wags his tail impatiently, sensing home.

"Must have been, chap. Otherwise we wouldn't have begun."

"Well, the world changed."

"Did it?"

Guy is silent. He doesn't know. At this point, he honestly doesn't know. But he thinks so. [1]

# Chapter
# 23
# Finale Ultimo
## 1961–1979

"Yogurt and prunes," Guy advised Plum when, in their eighties, his friend complained of a creeping sciatica that gave him wobbly legs and a general feeling of malaise. "It's the secret to good health and longevity," Guy added. And he religiously prepared his own breakfast every day, eating in addition to yogurt and prunes, wheat germ and fresh fruit in season. He would linger over this breakfast before sitting down to write, whether he and Virginia were in Remsenburg or in London, on Green Street, Lowndes Square, Onslow Square, Eaton Street, Orchard Street, or one of the other flats they owned and ultimately sold. [1]

Back in 1957, Archie Thomson, the man responsible for *Gigi,* had approached Guy and Frank Loesser with the idea of turning *Anastasia* into a musical. Loesser was not only a composer but a publisher. His company, Frank Music, set to paper the work of Robert Wright and George Forrest, the men responsible for *Song of Norway* and *Kismet,* two hit operettas that utilized the music of, respectively, Grieg and Borodin. It was Thomson's idea to turn them loose on the music of Tchaikovksy and the plot of Guy's play.

Bob and Chet, as they were known to each other, or "The Gremlins," as John Murray Anderson named them, or "The Boys" as Guy and Plum would forevermore refer to them, weren't interested. They had had estate problems with the other two composers, and they were sure, that with Tchaikovsky's popularity, they'd run into similar difficulties. But when Rachmaninoff was mentioned and Frank Loesser offered to handle the estate clearance, they perked up considerably.

Guy was delighted and plunged pad first into the project, working with Allen Whitehead on the book of what was first called *I, Anastasia* and then *Anya.*

Guy, as usual, was balancing several projects simultaneously. First, he had *Anya.* Then, there was *Severine,* based upon *La Mandarine,* a novel by Christine de Rivoyre, which would never be produced. And then there was *The Third Kiss,* a musical project proposed by Brooklyn Federal Court Judge Fred G. Moritt, based on the lives and love of Robert and Elizabeth Barrett Browning.

*The Third Kiss* would become a year-long repository of disaster and ill-feeling. The judge's first theatrical project was apparently shepherded through name and script changes by Guy for almost a year. And then, a split developed between the two collaborators, necessitating the intervention of the Dramatists Guild. Eventually, the show would, as *Robert and Elizabeth* "from an original idea by Fred G. Moritt" but rewritten by Ronald Millar and Ron Grainer, open in London with John Clements, June Bronhill, and Keith Michell in leading roles. Guy's name and words would be nowhere visible.[2]

And so, loaded up with these multiple projects, his work on everything suffered. He was no longer, in his eighties, able to juggle what he could with aplomb in his thirties and forties. "He would be given pages to do and would deliver them the next day, rewritten, and just the same," Allen Whitehead told this author. "No improvement. It went on that way for months, until Frank Loesser finally gave up."

It was a little more complicated than that, but those, essentially, were the facts. Allen Whitehead finally stated unequivocally to Guy that the script needed massive revisions and a full-time collaborator, and he listed nineteen possible people:

> William Inge
> Harry Kurnitz
> Lillian Hellman
> Abe Burrows
> Joe Masteroff
> Edward Albee

Garson Kanin
Ira Levin
Paul Osborn
Jean Kerr
Wolf Mankowitz
Dore Schary
Jerome Lawrence and Robert Lee
Howard Lindsay and Russell Crouse
Dorothy Fields
George Abbott
Robert Anderson
Herb Gardner
William Gibson

George Abbott was Guy's choice, and Mr. Abbott agreed, provided he could also direct and produce. He was of the same tradition as Guy. Impeccably attired, thoroughly experienced, gracious, noble, he was the personification of the dignity and the energy of the musical theatre at its professional best.

Mr. Abbott poured all of this professionalism into *Anya*, plus his own razzmatazz, lightning-paced style. But the George Abbott touch was apparently not what *Anya* really needed. Mr. Abbott found *Anya*'s glamour but neglected her heart, and the glittering production that opened at the Ziegfeld Theatre on November 29, 1965, after seven years of development, was to practically nobody's liking. Constance Towers, John Michael King, and Lawrence Brooks sang the Rachmaninoff melodies with lyric skill, and Lillian Gish was a convincing grand duchess. But the show never coalesced, and it closed after two weeks.

Ironically, Guy's *Rio Rita* was the Ziegfeld Theatre's first tenant, and his *Anya* was its last. The wrecking ball that demolished Joseph Urban's magnificent manifestation of Florenz Ziegfeld's dream soon after *Anya* closed destroyed more than a building. An era that had taken the lifetimes of, among many, the trio of musical fame to construct, crumbled to dust in several days of gathering darkness.

George Abbott blamed himself for the disaster that was *Anya*. Eleven years later, he would write to Guy, "After the many gross mistakes I made in the producing [of] a musical Anastasia, I should not expect you ever again to trust in my ability. Why these lapses happen to us I don't know, but I look back with regret to my errors in Anya and wish I had it to do over again. . . ."[3]

"I guess the thing is," said Wright and Forrest to this author, "you respect George Abbott so much . . . it hurts *you* for him to be wrong."

*Anya* was a bitter and puzzling experience that really shouldn't have happened. But within months, Guy had restored what he had written, and in 1967 the Brunswick Summer Theatre at Bowden College, in Brunswick, Maine, presented *A Song for Anastasia.* It was essentially *I, Anastasia* before it became *Anya.* The Maine critics loved it; the reviewer for *Variety* pointed out essentially the problems that Allen Whitehead had discovered years before. Its first act moved glacially, its plot was too complex for a musical, although the reinsertion of the recognition scene did wonders for the restoration of its heart.

It would never reach Broadway again. To this very day, Wright and Forrest, to whom Guy gave the rights, have revised and reworked and redistributed it; its present identity is *Anastasia Affaire,* a chamber musical scored for two pianos.

Though he was nearing ninety in the late 1960s, Guy was still afire with new projects. He ground out several not very good plays — *Nine Coaches Waiting* and *The Girl in the Swing,* for instance — but his major attention was lavished on a play about the Churchills. Virginia and he continued their perambulations, now going to Nantucket, now to Hobe Sound in Florida to visit their longtime friend Bob Barbour, now to London, where they settled into a flat on Eaton Square that they rented from Diana Churchill, who was no longer the glamorous actress of Guy's *Bobby Get Your Gun.* The years had been no kinder to her than to most, but she remained totally loyal to the memory of her father, Winston. Her small studio apartment contained memorabilia by the pound and the yard, and Guy became genuinely and enthusiastically fascinated by the love story of Winston and Clementine Churchill.

He followed them from 1908 to 1964, creating a huge canvas, and it must have been exhausting for Guy in his eighties to create and support it as he did. For years he pursued *A Man and His Wife* as if it were his best dream, shepherding it through its opening on October 21, 1969, at the Alexandra Theatre in Birmingham, with Emrys Jones and Sheila Brownrigg in the leading roles. The critics received it respectfully, and it seemed as if either a West End or American production was imminent.

The play was quickly picked up by a South African management and given a production that toured from Durban to Dundee, with Emrys Jones re-creating his Churchill role and Barbara Kinghorn playing Clementine. But midway through the run, the first of a string of disasters struck. Emrys Jones was felled by a heart attack onstage during a performance and died. The play was without a strong leading man.

Guy wrote to everyone he knew who might play the principal roles—Alfred Lunt and Lynn Fontanne, Hume Cronyn and Jessica Tandy, Rosemary Harris, Katherine Hepburn—but no one could quite generate the requisite enthusiasm for it. And then, director Michael Benthall became vitally interested in *A Man and His Wife* and undertook in 1974 to mount a production starring Nigel Stock and Barbara Jefford. Simultaneously, Joan Kemp-Welsh directed a production at the Pitlochry Festival, featuring Roger Hume and Beth Ellis.

The closed-end Pitlochry production was highly successful, but not destined to go beyond its environs. The Michael Benthall production was designed to open at the Theatre Royal in Brighton and then move on to the West End. But at the beginning of rehearsals, Benthall began to hemorrhage. Before rehearsals were over, he was dead of cirrhosis of the liver, and the production, under-rehearsed and directionless, failed. It seemed to Guy that the play was jinxed, as well it seemed to be.

And so he returned, partly, to his and Plum's favorite occupation: revising the old musicals, with some success. A revival with one of his numerous rewritten books, of *Oh, Kay!* opened in London. It was received—as usual—respectfully.

Now, Virginia proceeded to take increasing charge of Guy's life. He was growing frail, although he would still dress impeccably every day and never leave the flat in London or the house in Remsenburg looking like less than a haberdasher's model. In contrast to Plum, who shambled about in a cardigan sweater and a golf cap, and in emulation of his memory of Jerry, Guy retained his sartorial splendor and seemed to draw as much energy and youth from it as he did from his yogurt-based breakfasts.

But he did grow distracted at times, particularly in London. They had rented so many flats, he would sometimes leave for a walk and forget which flat they were inhabiting. He would sometimes disappear for hours while he went from address to address, usually by bus, rarely by taxi, for he felt that taxis were wanton extravagances.

Ethel, in contrast to Virginia, demanded more and more of Plum. While Virginia cooked Guy omelettes and soufflés, Ethel retired to her room upstairs, coming out to tend to the animals but hardly ever to tend to Plum. They had invested in an animal shelter at the Bide-A-Wee Home in Westhampton, and Ethel spent time on its board and delivering food to the animals, a practice that eventually led to an angry confrontation with the shelter's management.

On Thanksgiving, she was determined to deliver turkeys and chickens to the animals. The management patiently explained to her that the bones in the birds would kill, not nourish them, but she took it as a personal affront, and withdrew her support and her self, including a $300,000 bequest to be given to them upon Plum's death.

Still, Plum and Ethel's twelve acres thrived as a wildlife refuge, and their home became a shelter for multiple cats and dogs. Plum deferred to Ethel constantly, responding to her repeated demands that he climb the stairs to her room to bring her various knicknacks or goodies or merely to keep her company. She probably never realized that it would be bad for a man in his eighties, with arthritis, sciatica, and a bad heart, to repeatedly climb the long staircase to her room. Calling upon him was her own expression of love, perhaps, for she did love him. She was, as Malcolm Muggeridge put it, "a mixture of Mistress Quickly and Florence Nightingale, with a touch of Lady Macbeth thrown in."

In her later years, she was still the coquette of her youth. Every man who entered the Wodehouse home had to kiss her. She was as agile and light and flirtations as a young, trained debutante.

The high points of Plum's day were the hours between one and three, when he and Guy would walk the woods of Remsenburg. (He had become addicted to soap operas on television, and the two timed their walks so that he could be back for *Edge of Night.*) The perambulations were tonics for both of them, and when they missed them, they felt only half alive.

"It is a heavenly day and there are carpets of crocuses in Hyde Park but all the same I wish I were back taking a walk with you," Guy wrote Plum from Eaton Square in 1971.

"I miss you sadly on my walks," Plum wrote to Guy that same year. "It'll be fine if you don't get too involved with rehearsals in September. It's extraordinary how dull that round is without you. I do it twice daily, but I don't enjoy it."

"I didn't think I would ever be homesick for America" Guy wrote to Plum the following year, "but despite my love of England in the early Spring, I am. The people who matter in your life matter more than budding hedgerows and rolling landscapes. . . ."4

In the 1960s, Plum's output slowed, but he still managed an average of a book every two years. Considering that he was, as was Guy, in his eighties, this was remarkable, for each of these books was evidence of undiminished charm and uncurtailed skill. *Service with a Smile,* published in 1961, was a favorite with the public, and *Do Butlers Burgle Banks,* published in 1968, when he was eighty-seven, was a favorite of both Plum and Guy. Once more, musical comedy crooks were their joy and inspiration.

And now, in his eighties, Plum was beginning to have books written about him, analyzing, eulogizing, all but canonizing him. He suffered interviews. Longevity had done nothing to alleviate his shyness. He respected the work of Richard Usborne, who approached the Wodehouse canon and the Wodehouse persona with a steady hand and a scholarly eye. Usborne also had an understanding that was not always present in the work of others trying to sum up a lifetime that was copious beyond belief and still pouring forth its literary largesse.

One of the secrets of Plum's continued success, besides his comic genius, was his satisfaction with the world he created. Very much like the world he himself inhabited, it was good enough for his readers and good enough for him. Fifteen years earlier, he had written to William Townend, "The impression [I have] is the rather humbling one that I am a bad case of arrested mental development. Mentally, I seem not to have progressed a step since I was eighteen. . . ."

Guy, on the other hand, tried to catch up with the present. In 1966, he published *Gracious Living Limited,* a delightful, comic novel that was written with one thought in his mind: to convince Margaret Rutherford and Disney Productions that it would be just the right film vehicle for her.

A year later, he persuaded Plum that their 1934 disaster, *Who's Who,* which only survived nineteen showings at the Duke of York's, would make a good rock musical, Off-Broadway. Guy worked with composer-lyricist Johnny Brandon on it, as it went in title from *Who's Who, Baby* to *What's Happening, Baby* to *Come Along 'A Me* to *Look What's Happening.*

Brandon, a talented man who would be better known in 1969 for his Off-Broadway musical *Billy Noname,* also had his own ideas about the show, and when Guy and Plum went to New York one spring afternoon and sat in on one of the late rehearsals, they were so appalled by what they saw, they immediately withdrew their names—but not their financial interest—from the show. It failed, instantaneously.

"I think if we could add a few dirty words and sex perversions to our old musicals we might make it on Broadway these days,"[5] Guy jokingly wrote to Plum, and taking his own cue, he set out to write a racy *roman à clef* about Ziegfeld, Olive Thomas, Jack Pickford, Marilyn Miller, various gangsters, and various chorus girls of the 1920s. His model was Jacqueline Susann's *Valley of the Dolls.*

The first draft of *She Walks in Beauty* kept the names of its major characters intact, which Plum's agent Scott Meredith thought a bad idea. And so Guy went back and further fictionalized the characters. But the more he worked on the book, the quainter and more innocent it became, until eventually it resembled a mulligatawny of faintly lurid sex and period Princess innocence. He would never finish it.

What Guy and Plum really needed was for time to stop, or at least for an opportunity to come along so that they could do the stopping. And that opportunity arrived. In 1965, Peter Cotes produced, and Ian Carmichael starred in "The World of Wooster," a BBC television special series that was received with enormous warmth in England. Plum wrote to various friends that he hated it, but Guy looked at the popular success of his friend's adapted work in an entirely different light. Whether or not it was a vision of Jeeves and Bertie that Plum and he had was not nearly so important as the popularity of the series, he reasoned. A whole new generation was becoming aware of Plum, and so it might be time to do a revival of, say, *Come On, Jeeves.* Guy wrote to Peter Cotes about it and later had multiple meetings with the producer in London.

At the same time, Frank Loesser was struck by the same idea.[6] In ill-health, he was spending more and more of his time in Remsenburg, in his home not far from Guy and Plum. The three met socially, and sometime in 1965, Loesser planted the seed in their minds of writing what they did best—a Princess-style show. No matter that Frank Loesser had pushed the frontier of the American musical theatre ahead himself in the past decade; he saw in these two ageless gentlemen a tradition that needed to be revived.

It was what Plum and Guy wanted, too. Nothing could be better than to have one more chance to work together as they had with Jerry, fifty years before. But who would supply the music?

Frank Loesser suggested Wright and Forrest, and contacted them, inquiring if they would be willing to supply only the music, for this would be not only in the Princess tradition but done as the Princess shows were done, with lyrics by P. G. Wodehouse. And the subject? Bertie and Jeeves, of course. They had been made popular by television; they had never been musicalized. And who better to do this than Plum himself, aided by his constructionist of old?

Wright and Forrest accepted, eagerly, and so began a joyful series of meetings. Plum and Guy would work on the book, writing and walking and talking and writing, alternating acts and rewriting each other's words, fitting character to song, counting back pages and counting forward pages, and working out scenes.

"It's a darling show," Frank Loesser told Wright and Forrest when he first interested them in it. "And it needs simple, very simple music which sounds no younger than the 1920s."

They went to Frank Loesser's home on mornings that spring and summer and worked in his den, a yellow and brown refuge with windows that gave onto the bay, a huge desk, and a Yamaha grand piano. "I remember a tremendous amount of yelling, because Guy and Frank were very very excitable, and noisy, and vocal in their remarks," Jo Loesser, Frank Loesser's widow, told this author. "But it was always over by lunchtime, because they all took naps in the afternoon."

"We worked at Frank's house, because he had a piano," Wright and Forrest recalled, "and these two charming old men would work with us, so patiently, so wonderfully. We did some songs, and Plummy would supply the lyrics. And it didn't take long for us to see how Plummy was working. He couldn't sing, but in his head, *he was hearing old Jerome Kern music! And all of his lyrics were set to it!*"

And so life, in some cyclical way, was providing a finale they had hoped for and would have written if they could, but which, until now, had seemed impossible. It was all as neat as a Princess show. At the end, they were at the beginning. Writing as they had when they first started, they had become, once more, in some ghostly way, the trio of musical fame.

Guy's book abounded in clever, appropriate touches. Plum was just as handy with interior rhyme and charm in his love song verses as he always had been:

> I wonder whether
> 'Twas fate brought us together;
> I can't help thinking that it must have been.
> For miracles don't half work
> Without efficient staffwork
> By Kismet pulling strings behind the scene.

His divine sense of the absurd was unimpaired:

> When the African sun is sinking low
> And shadows wander to and fro
> And everywhere there's in the air
> A hush that's deep and solemn,
> That's when great Abugassa lurks
> To give the crocodile the works,

And hopes to see its name in the
Obituary column.
On the banks of the Zambesi,
Where the mud is thick and greasy,
There the crocodiles take it easy in the sun.
You can see them in their dozens,
With their uncles and their cousins,
Blowing bubbles, which is their idea of fun. . . .

His taste for historical subjects was undulled:

Oh, I love to hear the tales of old
About the days when knights were bold
And every kind of enemy defeated.
Wild dragons they would slay in droves
And though they looked like kitchen stoves,
They knew just how a woman should be treated.

The cadences were Jerry's, straight out of *Sitting Pretty* and *Leave It to Jane*. His presence echoed through them as surely as if he were there. And when Plum finally came to the finale, in the Registry Office, where, in true Princess style, a wedding was about to take place, the echoes became the song itself. And the past rushed back without revision:

To the registry office,          Dear little, dear little
That dear little office,          Church Round the Corner
Where so many lives have begun, Where so many lives have begun,
Where folks without money        Where folks without money
See nothing that's funny          See nothing that's funny
In two living cheaper than        In two living cheaper than
one . . .                          one . . .

*The Little Thing* had come home again.

It would be neat and nice to report that *Betting on Bertie,* as the show became known, went on to be produced to great popular acclaim. But life isn't a

Princess show, either. The musical would have a troubled history and never find a stage.

Guy would take it to London, and it would go through Teddy Holmes and Harold Fielding, who would be interested, but not enough to launch into a full-scale production. Still, enthusiasm remained high in translating the works of P. G. Wodehouse to British television, and in 1967, BBC-I launched a six-part series titled, again, "The World of Wodehouse", this time subtitled "Blanding's Castle." Ralph Richardson, Stanley Holloway, and Meriel Forbes starred. And it, too, became a popular success.

But *Betting on Bertie* could find no producers. Guy turned away from it to *A Man and His Wife,* and while that play was making its ill-fated tour of South Africa he met composer George de Jongh and Jill Fenson at Cecil Madden's flat in London. Miss Fenson, who had the flat across the hall, was looking for a vehicle not only for her performing talents but her lyric-writing ones. Madden put her together with composer George de Jongh, and Guy offered *Don't Listen, Ladies!* The result was anything but laudable. The charm of the original was there, but the score was nothing to either whistle or cheer about. Later, Miss Fenton married the president of the Natal Performing Arts Council, and so *Don't Listen, Ladies!* as a musical had a life in South Africa. But only in South Africa. [7]

Back in Remsenburg, Plum wrote on, first from an armchair and from there to his not altogether trusty Remington portable. "I did four pages in the armchair yesterday," he wrote to Guy,

> and can always improve them when I type. The novel [probably *No Nudes Is Good Nudes,* known in England as *A Pelican at Blandings*] is coming out fine so far, and I think it will be all right to the end, but the blood sweat and tears are awful. When I remember that I wrote the last twenty-six pages of *Thank You, Jeeves* in a single day, I sigh for the past. Pretty darned good if I get three done nowadays. [8]

Guy himself was working more slowly, too. Although he would follow his lengthy, healthy breakfast by setting up his writing implements on his desk, either in his study in Remsenburg or a flat in London or a room in Nantucket, he would invariably fall asleep several times during his writing sessions. Nevertheless, he was able to accomplish an extraordinary amount of work, most of it revisions of the books of old musicals or suggestions for changes in *Betting on Bertie* and *Don't Listen, Ladies!* It was an insular, leisurely existence.

And then, the more accelerated outside world arrived for both Plum and

Guy in a shiny Rolls Royce containing Andrew Lloyd Webber. The *wunderkind* of both pop music and musical theatre, Lloyd Webber and his lyricist Tim Rice had only two works to their credit at the time, but these works were both formidable and biblical. In 1968, their minimusical *Joseph and the Amazing Technicolor Dreamcoat* had, through its recording, brought them into the orbit of impresario David Land, who had increased their incomes mightily. The 1969 recording of *Jesus Christ Superstar* and its later, multiple stage productions had cemented their positions as the wealthiest creators of music then known.

The London production of *Superstar* was currently a sellout, produced by the Robert Stigwood organization with Bob Swash in charge of production; now, they wanted to turn from matters religious to matters irreligious. Lloyd Webber, particularly, had a great affection for Plum's work and had decided to write a musical using Jeeves and Bertie as its main characters—exactly as Guy and Plum and The Boys had done. The only difference was that Lloyd Webber's musical already had a commitment for production by the Stigwood organization.

Plum, impressed and flattered, agreed to sell the rights to Andrew Lloyd Webber and Stigwood. Guy, realizing that they would have to placate Wright and Forrest, who would be understandably outraged at what would amount to a final burial of *Betting on Bertie,* placed all the blame on Plum. "He was dazzled by the *Superstar* boys, with their Rolls Royce and everything," he would tell The Boys, but this was whole cloth fiction. Guy was as impressed and excited about the prospect of an Andrew Lloyd Webber-Tim Rice *Jeeves* as was Plum, and signed on as a coproducer. Still, he believed in burning no bridges. In an apparent effort to smooth over the situation, he turned over the rights to not only *Betting on Bertie* but *Anastasia* and *Anya* to Wright and Forrest.

For all their enthusiasm and skill, the collective judgment of Lloyd Webber, Stigwood, Plum, and Guy proved to be faulty. Tim Rice, never as enthusiastic as Lloyd Webber about the writing of *Jeeves,* bowed out early as librettist and lyricist, and Alan Ayckbourn took his place. "It will be a 1972 *Jeeves and Bertie,* with a 1923 feeling," said the publicity for the show, and perhaps that was its central problem. Jeeves and Bertie were locked forever in the 1920s, as was their creator. To try to modernize any of them was an impossibility, to take them seriously was a disaster.

Furthermore, although Plum often referred to his novels as "musical comedies without the music," they were, in fact, intricately plotted. He relied upon Guy to pare the plots down to the essentials needed for a musical comedy libretto. Ayckbourn, though one of England's greatest writers of comedies for the theatre, simply could not reduce the convolutions of happenings enough to fit the truly lovely and nostalgic music that Andrew Lloyd Webber provided.

Under-rehearsed, running far too long, but gamely acted by David Hemmings as Bertie and Michael Aldridge as Jeeves, *Jeeves* opened at His Majesty's on April 22, 1975, and immediately crashed. To those who were there for one of its handful of performances, it was an excruciating theatre experience. And it did, indeed, bury *Betting on Bertie*. No producer wanted to even hear of it from that point forward.

Andrew Lloyd Webber confessed in a 1991 interview that he still carried within him a special affection for *Jeeves*. "It's one of the very few scores I've buried, that I haven't pillaged, because one day I would like to see if anything could be done with it," he said. "Certainly we didn't get over any of the affection I have for that material. We didn't get any of that kind of rather sort of cosy English showbusiness quality in it. . . ."9

For that, they would have had to import two old gentlemen, who, in their nineties, were intimately acquainted and articulately conversant with that "cosy English showbusiness quality."

Plum continued on, turning out the last of his ninety-six novels, *The Girl in Blue, Jeeves and the Tie That Binds, The Plot That Thickened, Bachelors Anonymous, The Cat Nappers,* most of *Sunset at Blandings.* Collections and reissues swelled the ranks of Wodehouse books on personal and library shelves.

The Goodspeed Opera House in East Haddam, Connecticut, planned a revival of *Very Good Eddie,* and that brought forth another rush of collaboration between Guy and Plum. If *Very Good Eddie* could make it, what about Plum's favorite Princess show, *Oh, Lady! Lady!!?* They went at it with a fever, moving songs around, revising lyrics, bringing in other Kern melodies, while Guy tried to tug the book into what he perceived to be the present.

Late in the midst of this, Dick, playing tennis one summer day in Westhampton, suffered a torn Achilles tendon and a deep cut on his ankle. It was a painful but ordinary injury, but somehow, the first aid people who helped him from the court tied a tourniquet too tightly around his leg. A blood clot formed, raced through his system, hurtled into his brain, and he died. The senseless suddenness of it seemed to diminish Guy. He said little, but the shock of three of his four children dying was now visible on his face.10

• • •

Late in 1975, the New Year's Honours List was announced, and Pelham Grenville Wodehouse's name appeared on it. He was about to become a Knight Commander of the British Empire. It thrilled Ethel beyond belief, liberating her from her room, sending her bustling about, readying them both to go to London to receive the honor. It would be their first trip home in forty years, and she couldn't wait.

But Plum was hesitant. He had, after all, made his home in America. Remsenburg was where he lived, not England, where the complete records of his interrogation after imprisonment had still not been released, and his name had yet to be altogether cleared.

He was grateful for his impending knighthood. He was honored by it. He discussed it with Guy on one of the rides through Remsenburg in Guy's car that had now supplanted their walks. Plum had had a couple of falls, which may have been minor strokes, and he walked with difficulty and a cane. The talks continued in front of the fire in the Wodehouse living room, while Ethel remained upstairs.

Plum also consulted his family physician, Dr. Leray Davis. Although essentially a country doctor, Dr. Davis was also a specialist in coronary problems, and he knew that Plum's heart was his weakest link with life. "Should I go?" Plum finally asked Dr. Davis.

"If you do, I'm afraid it'll be a one-way trip," he told Plum.

The ninety-three-year old author nodded and broke the news to Ethel. She was furious and forbade Dr. Davis to speak to or treat Plum ever again.[11]

On the day he received his knighthood, long distance, Plum also received the world press. It was an annoyance, another party from which he would rather have been absent. But he endured it graciously, then went back to his soap operas and conversations with Guy. Ethel loved every celebrated moment of it, entertaining with charm and enthusiasm. And when the journalists left, she retired upstairs to her room, summoning Plum, who climbed the stairs with great unsteadiness, responding to her command.

In February of 1975, Plum contracted an annoying and life-threatening skin disorder called pemphiguf—a name, as Frances Donaldson, Plum's biographer, correctly pointed out, ". . . he might have invented himself." Its painful blisters could best be treated by doses of steroids, and his skin specialist, Dr. Bernard Berger, suggested hospitalization at Southampton Hospital. Plum packed up the manuscript of *Sunset at Blandings* and went to Southampton.

What occurred on February 14, 1975, is unclear.[12] Guy said that Plum's constant writing while Ethel was in the room angered her so much that she ripped the pencil from his hand, gathered up his papers, and flung them against the walls of his hospital room. He got out of bed to retrieve them and collapsed.

Dr. Berger, called by Ethel to his room, discovered Plum sitting peacefully and lifeless in the room's armchair.

Whatever the cause, the fatal heart attack that Dr. Davis had predicted and which he would now only hear about through a television announcement had occurred. It had been a long way to this sunlit room, and Plum departed it quickly and quietly, without pain.


Guy was distraught, and Virginia closed protectively around him. "How much longer can we go on?" Plum had asked him less than a year ago, and Guy had answered, "I don't know, but we'll try."[13] Now it was Guy alone, and the afternoons would turn endless and unpleasant, for Guy suddenly realized that the fifty-fifty royalty splits of much of the Wodehouse output beyond their collaborations that he and Plum had shared were not in writing, and although Ethel had learned of it long ago, there was no guarantee now that the money would continue to come in.

A conversation with Ethel soon after Plum's death gave Guy no comfort whatsoever. Once the massive outpouring of grief that arrived in Remsenburg had abated, she began to think about the distribution of the estate after she died. They had a gardener who was extraordinarily faithful and had been with them for years. "I'm thinking of leaving him "$20,000," she said to Guy and Virginia.

"That's very generous. Very nice," agreed Guy.

Time passed, and the conversation veered back to the gardener. "Perhaps $20,000 is a rather large amount," said Ethel. "I think 5,000 would be better."

"Well, it's entirely up to you," Guy rejoined. "He's served you for a long time, and very well, and he'd be most appreciative."

The conversation continued, and then Ethel concluded, decisively, "I've been thinking again," she said. "I'm going to leave him the garden tools." And she did.[14]

From Plum's death to her own, Ethel released none of the moneys owed Guy; he knew she wouldn't. It wasn't going to be an easy time, he decided, and he and Virginia began to divest themselves of the flats they owned in London and some of the works of art he had bought to collect and to decorate them. In 1976, *Very Good Eddie*, a huge success at the Goodspeed, was transferred to Broadway and became a moderate hit. Six months later, it moved to London and was a bigger hit. Guy went to opening night and posed, smiling joyfully, for a photograph onstage with the cast. It was the past, coming back to adulate him, and he loved every glorious minute of it, although he was having great difficulty remembering some of the details.

Virginia was his memory, as she was his protectress. He had a habit of changing his mind precipitously, particularly about travel arrangements. He would make and cancel reservations a half dozen times before finally leaving for either America or England. He had logged sixty-four Atlantic crossings by now and a handful of international airplane flights. But they weren't made easily, and they were always first class. He and Virginia continued to travel in style and to live in style, although their money was running out more rapidly than they had hoped. Still, it was a way of life to which Guy had grown accustomed for nearly sixty years, and he was not about to change it.

Even in his nineties, his habits remained constant and unshakable. He still prepared his own healthful breakfast, still wrote in the mornings, and still had an eye for young, feminine beauty. He noticed a dancer on the Dean Martin television show and, using his theatrical contacts, discovered that her name was Tara Leigh. He contacted her, and when Virginia and Guy went to New York, she would have lunch with them. It was all very proper and correct, almost Edwardian, and Virginia watched it with detached amusement. Any infidelities Guy could possibly commit would only be in the mind now, and if he derived pleasure, as he always had, from being in the company of beautiful young women, why not?

Virginia herself had an adopted son. Sueo Miyajawa, a Japanese-American who had, one summer years ago, been part of a group rental across the street from Guy and Virginia in Remsenburg and who shared their political views and horror at the coming into power of Richard Nixon, had become a part of the household, helping Virginia, talking with her in the long silences when Guy slept during the day, and generally becoming her lifelong champion and companion.

Only Peggy was intermittently unwelcome in Virginia's presence. Perhaps it was the lingering memory of Marguerite Namara, who, with George Hoye, her husband, had spent a string of Christmases in Remsenburg with Guy and Virginia and Peggy in the 1960s. Still glamorous, still charismatic, even in her eighties (while Virginia was merely in her sixties), Marguerite had flirted outrageously with Guy, infuriating Virginia and delighting Guy. And so now, repeatedly, Virginia would abruptly throw Peggy out of the house or lock herself in her room, often for days, if she caught father and daughter laughing or talking privately together.

It would distress Peggy to tears and bother Guy, for he had at last found the value of loving a child. There was nothing not to love about Peggy, and he realized it. She was totally disingenuous. She loved him. She was vitally interested in all sorts of metaphysical theories that intrigued him, the closer he moved toward the end of his life. He would never wholly accept her faith in reincarnation, but he would try. [15]

Peggy had her lost moments, too. If he could help her to find herself, he might atone for the lifetime of neglect that had driven all of his children from him. But it was too difficult for Peggy to stay too long in Remsenburg, and so she went back to Europe, to settle into a small town above Montreux, in Switzerland, where she had gone to school. From there, she roamed through Europe with her father's plays under her arm and letters of introduction from him to various agents and managements. Too old now to make the rounds, he sent her on the eternal quest for productions of the nearly one hundred plays he had written.

As for the future: he settled into two projects, one old and one new. Determined to bring the *Oh, Lady! Lady!!* revival upon which he and Plum had been working to a stage, he wrote to George Abbott in Florida. Mr. Abbott wrote back, apologizing again for his role in the *Anya* debacle. "So I would like to make amends by doing better on something of yours," he went on. "I would like to read Oh Lady Lady. But. . . ."[16] He was going into rehearsal with a new Richard Adler-Will Geer musical, *Music Is,* and would not be able to take it on immediately. He never did, but *Oh, Lady! Lady!!* did enjoy a small, moderately successful Equity Library theatre production, directed by Clinton Atkinson.

The second project was, at its core, another attempt by Guy to set the present to paper and prove that he was contemporary, after all. This time, he picked as his subject Legionnaire's Disease and spent long hours discussing it with Dr. Andrew MacLellan at the Sutton Bay Hotel in Dorset.[17] Satisfied, after the conversations, that he knew the effect of the disease, he locked several people in a room after a supper and made Legionnaire's Disease their nemesis.

But what he wrote was more an album of clippings from the past than a new play. Instead of creating an original work, he cut and pasted together various pieces of past works, including the mass hypnosis story from *The Long Arm* and the entire recognition scene from *Anastasia,* delivered in a penultimate moment by the young actress character—named, of course, Tara.

"In his flat near Sloane Square," Dr. MacLellan recalled to this author, "he had a back room, which he called his study, and he'd got his typewriter there, and a table and a chair and so on. He was nearly always asleep. He'd have the paper in his typewriter, and he'd have stuff all over the table, and he'd always be asleep, but he was still trying to write a play."

After dinner, however, Guy would sit down with Dr. MacLellan, who could jog his memory, too, since he was the physician for scores of actors and actresses, including Cicely Courtneidge and Jack Hylton, and even the Duncan Sisters, who were among his first patients. Then, Guy, the master raconteur, would reappear with assists in details from Virginia.

It went on that way until late in 1977, when Virginia complained to Dr. MacLellan of a small swelling in her salivary gland. It was a malignancy, brought on by years of smoking three packs of cigarettes a day. Dr. MacLellan referred her to a surgeon who operated and got it all, he felt.

She recovered well, and she and Guy left for America.

Nine months later, back in London, she again called Dr. MacLellan. Convinced of her cure, she had failed to heed the doctors' warnings never to smoke again. The tumor had returned, and this time it was treated with radiation. "But," recalled Dr. MacLellan, "[the cancer] went like a prairie fire through her entire body. Lungs, liver, bones . . . She wasted away. Simply wasted away."

Sueo, summoned from America, recalled that she weighed no more than forty pounds, and he could lift her with one hand. But she wanted to return to America. She didn't want to die in England, and Guy assured her that he would get her back.

But it was too late. She passed away in their furnished flat near Sloane Square on April 22, 1979.

Guy came apart. She was not only the love of his life but the sustainer of it. He sat in a chair, motionless and silent.

Sueo did what he could; Peggy arrived immediately from Switzerland and added her ministrations. Guy's only specific directions were that Virginia be buried properly, in an English country churchyard. Trevor Passmore, his attorney, was given the task of finding one and arranging the funeral. He went to Harrods, who set out to find the site and prepare the ceremony.

But it was Margaret Greenhill, the secretary in the Passmore office and the liaison between it and Guy, who came up with the site, a peaceful pocket of greenery, in the tiny village of Mickleham, in Surrey, less than an hour from London. Overseen by a stone church, its roof a gentle mound in a slate gray sky, the graveyard was a soft and lovely place away from the frantic world, and Miss Greenhill immediately set about making the arrangements.

Two days later, Virginia was buried peacefully and with great grace by Harrods pallbearers and officials. Guy wasn't there. Dr. MacLellan, watchful of him, advised him not to go, and he readily accepted the direction. For once, the internal switch refused to respond, and he was shaken to his very depths.

Within a few days, his energy began to return. He would, he said, go back to

America now and sell the Remsenburg house. Then, he would return, buy a house in the English countryside, and spend the rest of his years in the place he loved the most.

In May of 1979, Peggy moved into Remsenburg with him, and he went back to work on *The Supper Party*. He was determined to take it personally to London and sell it to a producer, and he became as dedicated to it as he had been to *A Man and His Wife*. But it was slow going. He slept with increasing regularity and awoke irritable. His hearing began to deteriorate. He tried a few hearing aids but found none of them to his liking.

By August his health had begun to fail markedly. The house in Remsenburg had not sold, but he was determined to go to London anyway, to place his one hundredth play and put himself under the care of Dr. MacLellan.

It was the height of the tourist season, and all of the first class cabins aboard the *Queen Elizabeth II* had been taken. He pressed Peggy to get them passage, no matter what the accommodations. There were two tourist class cabins left, widely separated by decks and location. She got them.

Dr. Davis was not at all happy with Guy's plans to travel, but, unlike Plum, Guy refused his American doctor's advice. In his heart of hearts, he knew he had only a little time left, and he wanted to return to England. And so, Peggy and Guy set sail on what would become his last transatlantic crossing.

It was a nightmare journey. Two days before they were to leave, Guy's legs gave out, and Peggy pushed him aboard the *QE II* in a wheelchair.

It was like entering a strange maelstrom. Guy was unused to the crowds, the shoving, the less than elegant dining, the hordes of people who not only didn't know him but had never heard of the theatre he represented. Peggy, as easily distracted as Guy, often lost her way trying to find his cabin, but when she found him, they would make their way to the overpopulated and noisy sun deck, where he could, at least, enjoy the warmth and fresh air.

When they arrived in London, Dr. MacLellan took one look at Guy and immediately suggested that they go to Devonshire, to the Deerpark Hotel. It was near the doctor's home, and he would begin the proceedings to have Guy admitted to the Thames Bank Nursing Home in Goring on Thames. It was beautiful and very close. He was convinced that the end was near, and he determined that Guy should spend that short time in the luxury and beauty to which he was accustomed and which gave him comfort.

And it was an idyllic spot, enhanced by a soft English summer, flooded with sunlight. Boats drifted by on the river; swans swam in it; the garden was dotted with flowers and peacocks.

For a while, Guy seemed to rally, eating well, having a gin and ginger beer before dinner, sitting and sleeping in a wheelchair in the sun in the garden. Still, at times, he became fearful. "What do you think will happen?" he asked Peggy one afternoon.

"There's nothing to worry about," she said, soothing him, smoothing his hand. "There's a lovely transition, and you're going to be met by Virginia, because of your great love. Love is the link. And she's going to take you across. It's so beautiful on the other side."

He seemed to be comforted, but then when he drifted off to sleep, as he often did, he would cry out, "God forgive me. Oh, God forgive me!"

In his waking hours, he appeared to be at peace, remaining outdoors as much as he could, wearing a robe and Plum's golf cap.

Then, his appetite and his spirit began to diminish. On September 4, he asked for a nurse's pad, and in a hand that erupted his writing into jagged surges, he wrote:

Peggy, my darling,
I am dying and much as I long to see you, I doubt if I should put you through the pain of a parting which I have just endured.
I shall try to make a proper will. . . . I have no idea how much money there is but there [will] be enough. Ginnie was very careful.
I love you dearly but am in pain and can write no more.
   Good night, my dear one
   Daddy

On the next day, September 5, 1979, at the age of ninety-six, Guy went peacefully and lastingly to sleep.

Two days later, he was taken to the tiny country churchyard where Virginia was buried, and laid beside her. "It was a lovely day," Dr. MacLellan remembered. "The sun shone. And of course there couldn't have been very many friends left who could have gone. But at the graveside, there were only eight of us. It's extraordinary, how a person can serve the public so well and so loyally, for so long, and nobody will take the time to pay a tribute to him."

Aside from the sun shining, it was not a true Princess ending. That had taken place a decade before, in a study on a bay in Remsenburg, during the writing of a musical. Then, the three men who had begun it all in the American musical theatre had come together for one final collaboration, reuniting in a ghostly, melodious, and altogether appropriate way.

### EXIT MUSIC

*It is vain to remain and chatter*
*And to wait for a clearer sky.*
*Helter skelter, we must run for shelter,*
*Till the clouds roll by.*

# Musicals and Plays

## BY BOLTON AND WODEHOUSE AND KERN

*Miss Springtime*
music also by Emmerich Kalman; lyrics also by Herbert Reynolds
September 25, 1916; New Amsterdam; 227 performances

*Have a Heart*
January 11, 1917; Liberty; 78 performances

*Oh, Boy!*
February 20, 1917; Princess; 475 performances
January 27, 1919 (as *Oh, Joy!*); Kingsway, London; 167 performances

*Leave It to Jane*
August 28, 1917; Longacre; 167 performances

*The Riviera Girl*
music also by Emmerich Kalman
September 24, 1917; New Amsterdam; 78 performances

*Miss 1917*
music also by Victor Herbert
November 5, 1917; Century; 48 performances

*Oh, Lady! Lady!!*
February 1, 1918; Princess; 219 performances

*Sally*
lyrics also by Clifford Grey
December 21, 1920; New Amsterdam; 570 performances
September 10, 1921; Winter Garden, London; 383 performances

*Sitting Pretty*
April 8, 1924; Fulton; 95 performances

## BY JEROME KERN AND GUY BOLTON

*Ninety in the Shade*
lyrics by Michael Rourke and Guy Bolton
January 25, 1915; Knickerbocker; 39 performances

*Nobody Home*
book, music, and lyrics also by Paul Rubens; lyrics by Lawrence
Grossmith, Otto Motzan, Schuyler Greene, Harry B. Smith, Paul
Rubens, and Guy Bolton
April 20, 1915; Princess; 135 performances

*Very Good Eddie*
book also by Philip Bartholomae; lyrics by Schuyler Greene, Harry B.
Smith, Jack Hazzard, Herbert Reynolds, Henry Kailimai, and Ring
Lardner
December 23, 1915; Princess; 341 performances
May 18, 1918; Palace, London; 46 performances

*Zip Goes a Million*
lyrics by Buddy De Sylva
December 8, 1919; Worcester Theatre, Worcester. Mass.; closed in
Washington

*Blue Eyes*
book also by Graham John; lyrics by Graham John
April 27, 1928; Piccadilly, London; 276 performances

## BY JEROME KERN AND P. G. WODEHOUSE

*The Beauty of Bath*
book by Seymour Hicks and Cosmo Hamilton; music also by Herbert E.
Haines; lyrics also by Charles H. Taylor
March 19, 1906; Aldwich, London; 287 performances

*The Cabaret Girl*
book by George Grossmith and P. G. Wodehouse; lyrics by Wodehouse
September 19, 1922; Winter Garden, London; 462 performances

*The Beauty Prize*
book by George Grossmith and P. G. Wodehouse; lyrics by Wodehouse
September 5, 1923; Winter Garden, London; 214 performances

*Show Boat*
book and all lyrics except those of "Bill" by Oscar Hammerstein II
December 27, 1927; Ziegfeld; 572 performances

## BY GUY BOLTON AND P. G. WODEHOUSE

*See You Later*
music by Jean Schwartz and Joseph Szulc
April 15, 1918; Academy of Music, Baltimore, Maryland; closed there

*The Girl Behind the Gun*
music by Ivan Caryll
September 16, 1918; New Amsterdam; 160 performances
May 20, 1919 (as *Kissing Time*); Winter Garden, London; 430
performances

*Oh, My Dear!*
music by Louis Hirsch
November 27, 1918; Princess; 189 performances

*The Rose of China*
music by Armand Vecsey
November 15, 1919; Lyric; 47 performances

*Pat*
　lyrics also by Billy Rose; music by Vincent Youmans
　1922; unproduced

*Oh, Kay!*
　lyrics by Ira Gershwin and Howard Dietz (uncredited); music by George
　Gershwin
　November 8, 1926; Imperial; 256 performances
　September 21, 1927; His Majesty's, London; 213 performances

*The Nightingale*
　music by Armand Vecsey
　January 3, 1927; Jolson; 96 performances

*Rosalie*
　book by Guy Bolton and Bill McGuire; lyrics by Ira Gershwin and P.
　G. Wodehouse; music by George Gershwin and Sigmund Romberg
　January 10, 1928; New Amsterdam; 335 performances

*Who's Who*
　September 20, 1934; Duke of York's, London; 19 performances

*Anything Goes*
　music and lyrics by Cole Porter
　November 21, 1934; Alvin; 420 performances
　June 14, 1935; Palace, London; 250 performances

*Don't Listen, Ladies!*
　September 2, 1948; St. James's, London; 219 performances
　December 28, 1948; Booth Theatre; 15 performances

*Phipps (Kilroy Was Here)*
　1951; unproduced

*Come On, Jeeves*
　1954; unproduced

*Betting on Bertie*
　music by Robert Wright and George Forrest
　1965; unproduced

# Notes

## PROGRAM NOTE

1. Private Collection. Each of the crossovers is, of course, fictitious, but the dialogue is based upon real sources. This one comes from a letter from Wodehouse to Bolton shortly after the publication of *The Olympians*.

## CHAPTER 1

1. Bolton Papers. 2. Private Collection. Postcard to Ivy Bolton (undated). Bolton, alas, never dated his letters. 3. Quoted in Frances Donaldson, *Wodehouse*. 4. The two contending biographers are Gerald Bordman and Michael Freedland. 5. See note 2. 6. This and foregoing material from interviews with Peggy Bolton. 7. Bordman, *Jerome Kern*. 8. Peggy Bolton interview. 9. Private Collection. Letter to William Townend. 10. Donaldson. 11. Jasen, *P. G. Wodehouse*. 12. Donaldson. 13. Freedland.

## CHAPTER 2

1. These and other Jerome Kern lyrics are in the private collection of Betty Kern Miller, Jerome Kern's daughter. Reprinted with her permission. 2. Quoted in Bordman, *Jerome Kern*. 3. The London theatre season information here and elsewhere from the Theatre Collection, Victoria and Albert Museum, London. 4. Private Collection. 5. Jasen. 6. Jasen. 7. This anecdote is told in detail in Michael Freedland's Kern biography. Its authenticity was supported by Alfred Simon, to whom Kern reiterated it. 8. Jasen. 9. Donaldson.

## CHAPTER 3

1. Donaldson. 2. Courtesy of Betty Kern Miller. 3. Wodehouse, *Performing Flea*. 4. Jasen. 5. Material mostly from Andrew Lamb, *Jerome Kern in Ed-*

*wardian England.* 6. *New York Clipper* review. 7. Bordman, *Jerome Kern.* 8. Bolton Papers. 9. *New York American.* 10. Quoted in Bordman, *Jerome Kern.* 11. *New York Sun.*

## CHAPTER 4

1. George Middleton Collection, Library of Congress. 2. Bordman, *Jerome Kern.* 3. Bolton Papers. 4. Bolton Papers. 5. *New York American.* 6. For example, the *Vogue* article. 7. Private Collection.

## CROSSOVER

1. Material from Bolton and Wodehouse's suspect memoir *Bring on the Girls.* This part of it is true.

## CHAPTER 5

1. Quoted in Jasen. 2. Wodehouse and Bolton, *Bring on the Girls.* 3. Comstock Collection, Museum of the City of New York.

## CHAPTER 6

1. Comstock Collection. 2. Comstock Collection. 3. Jerry's daughter, Betty Kern Miller, also avers that the incident did happen and that her father told her of it. Of course, he, like Guy, was a peerless raconteur. 4. John McCabe, *George M. Cohan.* 5. Bolton Papers. This and other Bolton scripts are in this private collection.

## CHAPTER 7

1. *New York Times* interview. 2. All material from interviews with family and friends of Marguerite Namara. 3. A legend repeated often enough becomes the truth, but further reflection strengthens Bordman's point of view. Although Bolton and Wodehouse and Kern stuck to their story about the *Very Good Eddie* meeting, it seems almost certain that they really met ear-

lier, possibly after the opening of *Tonight's the Night,* which would account for the presence in the Kern apartment of most of its cast members. Still, the legend is a better story. 4. Bolton Papers. The files bulge with references to this agreement; Guy used it to buttress his claims for percentages later in life, when times became more straitened.

## CHAPTER 8

1. Bolton Papers. Guy's recollection is partly recorded in *Bring on the Girls,* partly in an unfinished manuscript. 2. Wodehouse and Bolton. 3. Wodehouse and Bolton. 4. Small wonder that the family of Marguerite Namara disputes the details of this. But interviews with Peggy Bolton and Robert Hiden confirm all of the details except the gun story. That, they admit, was something Guy alone repeated. 5. Rodgers, *Musical Stages.* 6. Wodehouse and Bolton.

## CHAPTER 9

1. Private Collection. 2. Wodehouse and Bolton. 3. Middleton Collection. 4. Private Collection. 5. Quoted in Craig Zadan's *Sondheim and Co.* and the narrative of *Side by Side by Sondheim.*

## CHAPTER 10

1. Namara material in this chapter is contained in the Toye family papers, generously made available to the author. 2. Details of the Great Neck experience from interviews with Peggy Bolton and Keenan Wynn, whose memory was particularly sharp—or perhaps the proper word is keen. 3. Reconstructed from material in the Bolton Papers. 4. Bolton Papers. 5. Repeated on paper in a later letter to Guy from Plum. Private Collection. 6. Bolton Papers. 7. Middleton Collection. 8. Bolton Papers. 9. Guy's recollection, in an uncompleted manuscript in the Bolton Papers. 10. Quoted in Jasen. 11. *Philadelphia Evening Bulletin.* 12. The incident appears in Bordman's *Jerome Kern* and was confirmed and detailed in an interview with Vivienne Segal.

CHAPTER 11

1. Marguerite Namara is referred to by the initial *M* in Isadora Duncan's autobiography, *My Life*. 2. Interview with Keenan Wynn. 3. Recollections of Peggy Bolton. 4. Bolton Papers. 5. Bolton Papers. 6. Betty Kern Miller Collection. 7. This is from the script version in the Bolton Papers. 8. Interview with author. 9. *Cleveland Plain Dealer*. 10. Jasen, and confirmation in interviews with Wodehouse family and friends. 11. Bolton Papers. 12. *New York Times,* Unsigned, but Guy Bolton swore it was George S. Kaufman, and Anne Kaufman Schneider, Kaufman's daughter, vouches for her father's authorship.

CROSSOVER

1. Material based upon letters in the Bolton Papers.

CHAPTER 12

1. Bolton Papers. Guy's nervousness about money matters turned to obsession later in life; the files are rife with letters to lawyers, agents, and collaborators focusing on this single subject. 2. Charles Schwartz, *Gershwin: His Life and His Music,* and interviews with Betty Kern Miller. 3. Jasen. 4. All quoted material from *See You Later,* plus Guy's penciled notation regarding Jerry, are in a typescript in the Bolton Papers. 5. Middleton Collection. 6. Plum and Ethel's travels at this time are chronicled in Donaldson. 7. The tale found its way into *Bring on the Girls* and was repeated, in varying forms, by several interviewees in New York, Remsenburg, Hollywood, and London. The author chose to follow the two versions and the lasting effect of the incident given to him by Peggy Bolton. 8. *Ibid.* 9. Private Collection.

CHAPTER 13

1. Interview with the author. 2. Interviews with Robert Hiden, buttressed by the biographical outline prepared by Laurel Baker Tew. 3. The letters between Guy and George Middleton in this chapter are in the Middleton Collection and the Bolton Papers. 4. Quoted in *Performing Flea.* 5. Bolton Papers. 6.

Bolton Papers. Several copies of this survive. 7. Middleton Collection and Bolton Papers. 8. George Middleton, *These Things Are Mine.* 9. Middleton.

## CROSSOVER

1. The anecdote was told to the author by Keenan Wynn, whose father Ed told him.

## CHAPTER 14

1. Most of the Ziegfeld material in this chapter came from the Keenan Wynn and Vivienne Segal interviews, clipping files in the New York Public Library's Billy Rose Collection, Randolph Carter and Marjorie Farnsworth's books on the *Follies* and its creator, Warren Harris's life of Marilyn Miller, *The Other Marilyn,* and Wodehouse and Bolton. 2. These plot details from Bordman's *Jerome Kern.* 3. Interviews with Peggy Bolton. 4. Max Wilk, *They're Playing Our Song.* 5. In Laurence Bergreen's Berlin biography, *As Thousands Cheer.* 6. Private Collection. 7. Quoted in *Performing Flea.* 8. Middleton. 9. Private Collection. 10. Bolton Papers. 11. Marilyn Miller Collection, New York Public Library. 12. Middleton Collection. 13. Interview with Peggy Bolton and Chaplin's *My Trip Abroad.* 14. Bordman, *Jerome Kern.* 15. The recollections of Dorothy Dickson are contained in the BBC Programme 3 profile of Miss Dickson.

## CHAPTER 15

1. Quoted in Donaldson. 2. Bordman, *Jerome Kern.* 3. Donaldson. 4. *Performing Flea.* 5. Private Collection. 6. *Performing Flea.* 7. Donaldson. 8. Interviews with Peggy Bolton. 9. The incident and the quote are from a combination of interviews and Stanley Green's *The Rodgers and Hammerstein Story.* 10. Bolton Papers. 11. Bolton Papers. 12. Bolton Papers. 13. *Performing Flea.* 14. *Performing Flea.* 15. *Performing Flea.* 16. Bordman, *Jerome Kern.* 17. Bordman, *Jerome Kern.*

## CHAPTER 16

1. Schwartz. 2. Theatre Collection, Victoria and Albert Museum.
3. Schwartz. 4. This story is recited again, in greater detail, in Tommy
Krasker's notes for the definitive CD version of *Strike Up the Band,* issued
by Elektra Nonesuch. 5. Gerald Mast, *Can't Help Singin',* and others. 6.
Repeated by many interviewees but not by Betty Kern Miller. 7. Interview
with Betty Kern Miller. 8. Interview with Gerald Bordman. 9. Interview
with Leonore Gershwin. 10. Jablonski and Stewart, *The Gershwin Years.* 11.
Many interviewees, including Alfred Simon. 12. Harris. 13. Bolton Papers.
14. Middleton Collection. 15. Bolton Papers. 16. Private Collection. 17.
*Performing Flea.* 18. Wodehouse and Bolton. 19. Both legends—or truths—
are in Schwartz. 20. Bolton Papers.

## CHAPTER 17

1. Interviews with numerous Bolton friends in both California and
England. 2. Churchill, *The Theatrical Twenties.* 3. *Performing Flea.*
4. Bordman, *Jerome Kern.* 5. Miles Kreuger, *Show Boat.* 6. Kreuger.
7. Kreuger. 8. Details from the BBC Programme 3 profile of Evelyn Laye.
9. Bolton Papers. 10. Middleton Collection. 11. Middleton Collection.
12. This, and all excerpts from June's letters are in the Bolton Papers.
13. Bolton Papers. 14. *Performing Flea.* 15. *Performing Flea.*

## CROSSOVER

1. Bolton Papers. Plum's Edgar Wallace story is taken word for word from
a letter to Guy.

## CHAPTER 18

1. *Performing Flea.* 2. Interview with Keenan Wynn. 3. Interview with
Leonore Gershwin. 4. Bordman, *Jerome Kern.* 5. Bordman, *Jerome Kern.*
6. This and further details of Jerome Kern's life at this time in this chapter are from a series of interviews with Betty Kern Miller. 7. I am, of
course, referring to *Porgy and Bess,* its most eloquent incarnation. Stanley
Green states that Gershwin wanted to musicalize Heyward's novel *Porgy* as

early as 1926 but apparently made no move to secure the property, since a capsule musical version appeared in *Blackbirds of 1928,* with the song "Porgy," music by Jimmy McHugh and lyrics by Dorothy Fields. The writing of *Porgy and Bess* began in 1933, shortly after Jerry and Oscar turned down the project, and culminated in the 1935 Theatre Guild production. 8. Bordman, *Jerome Kern.* 9. *Performing Flea.* 10. *Performing Flea.* 11. The early Hollywood years are re-created from interviews with Guy's and Plum's surviving friends in California, records from the MGM collection at the University of California and the Academy of Motion Picture Arts and Sciences, and from June's autobiography, *The Glass Ladder.* 12. Interviews with Peggy Bolton. 13. Interviews with Peggy Bolton and with Robert Hiden. 14. Interview with Betty Kern Miller.

## CHAPTER 19

1. *Performing Flea.* 2. *Performing Flea.* 3. Bolton Papers. 4. Plum hardly ever kept scripts and didn't keep this one. All of Guy's copies were blown to bits during the blitz of London. The surviving first draft was made available to the author through the kind largesse of Louis Aborn, Guy's longtime friend, agent for his musicals and the president of Tams-Witmark Music Library, Inc. 5. Bolton Papers. 6. Bolton Papers. 7. Bolton Papers. 8. *Performing Flea.* 9. Bolton Papers. 10. Bordman, *Jerome Kern.* 11. Interview with Betty Kern Miller. 12. Interview with Lady Wodehouse. 13. The London and Hollywood material in this chapter comes from interviews with Guy's associates and friends in London at the time, particularly his secretaries, Alison Covil and Vivian Byerly, the Victoria and Albert Museum Theatre Collection, and Peggy Bolton.

## CHAPTER 20

1. Private Collection. 2. Bolton Papers. 3. Repeated by Peggy Bolton and just about every Bolton friend or associate interviewed. 4. Interview with Peggy Bolton. 5. Private Collection. 6. Complete records of the efforts of Virginia and Guy Bolton on behalf of Plum are in the Bolton Papers. 7. The CBS broadcast is quoted in full in Iain Sproat's exhaustive and valuable book on the Wodehouse internment, *Wodehouse at War,* from which much of the detail in the chapter comes. 8. This and other excerpts from

the broadcasts are from full transcripts in the Bolton Papers. 9. Sproat. 10. Sproat. 11. Muggeridge, *Chronicles of Wasted Time.* 12. Private Collection. 13. Muggeridge. 14. Private Collection. 15. *Performing Flea.* 16. *Performing Flea.*

CHAPTER 21

1. Bordman, *Jerome Kern.* 2. Bordman, *Jerome Kern.* 3. Bolton Papers. 4. Interview with Sidney Sheldon. 5. Sheldon interview. 6. Bordman, *Jerome Kern.* 7. Bolton Papers.

CHAPTER 22

1. Private Collection. 2. Private Collection. 3. Bolton Papers. 4. Private Collection. 5. Interviews with Peggy Bolton, Olive O'Neill, Miriam Whelan, and Bolton's secretaries in London. 6. Bolton Papers. 7. Private Collection. 8. Bolton Papers. 9. Victoria and Albert Museum. 10. Victoria and Albert Museum. 11. Private Collection. 12. *Performing Flea.* 13. Bolton Papers. 14. Bolton Papers. 15. Interview with Roger Vasselais. 16. Bolton Papers and interview with Merielle Perry. 17. Guy's friends and colleagues in London all attest to this, with sadness and wonder. 18. Cecil Madden, Vivienne Byerly, Alison Colvil, Mrs. Toby Rowland, and correspondence in the Bolton Papers pieced this odyssey together. 19. Bolton Papers. 20. Bolton Papers. 21. Bolton Papers. 22. Interviews with Bert Pollack and Ray Tudor, who played Bub in the revival. 23. Middleton Collection. 24. Interview with Françoise Bolton, Guybo's widow. 25. Interview with Peggy Bolton. 26. Bolton Papers. 27. Bolton Papers.

CROSSOVER

1. Plum's words come from his memoir, *Over Seventy.*

CHAPTER 23

1. Interview with Peggy Bolton. 2. Bolton Papers. 3. Bolton Papers. 4. Private Collection. 5. Private Collection. 6. This and all that follows re-

garding *Betting on Bertie,* comes from interviews with Robert Wright, George Forrest, and Jo Loesser and from the various versions of the show in the Bolton Papers. 7. Interview with Cecil Madden. 8. Private Collection. 9. Arts and Entertainment Network Special. 10. Interview with Peggy Bolton. 11. The foreclosure remained permanent, and my father, Dr. Leray B. Davis, learned of Plum's passing on the evening news. 12. Guy's version is from interviews with his secretaries, Peggy Bolton, and various Remsenburg friends; Dr. Berger's is from an interview with the doctor. 13. Bolton Papers. 14. Bolton Papers. 15. Interviews with Peggy Bolton. 16. Bolton Papers. 17. The final material about Guy and Virginia's last years comes from extensive interviews with Sueo Miyajawa, Margaret Greenhill, Peggy Bolton, and Dr. Andrew MacLellan.

# Selected Bibliography

Amory, Cleveland, and Frederick Bradlee, eds. *Cavalcade of the 1920s and 1930s.* London: The Bodley Head, 1960.

————. *Vanity Fair,* New York: Viking Press, 1960.

Applebaum, Stanley. *The New York Stage.* New York: Dover Publications, 1976.

Atkinson, Brooks. *Broadway.* New York: The Macmillan Company, 1970.

————. *The Lively Years 1920–1973.* New York: Association Press, 1973.

Bergreen, Laurence. *As Thousands Cheer: The Life of Irving Berlin.* New York: Viking Press, 1990.

Bordman, Gerald. *American Musical Theatre.* New York: Oxford University Press, 1978.

————. *American Operetta.* New York: Oxford University Press, 1981.

————. *Days To Be Happy, Years To Be Sad: The Life and Music of Vincent Youmans.* New York: Oxford University Press, 1982.

————. *Jerome Kern: His Life and Music.* New York: Oxford University Press, 1980.

Burton, Jack. *Blue Book of Broadway Musicals.* Watkins Glen, N.Y.: Century House, 1952.

Carter, Randolph. *The World of Flo Ziegfeld.* New York: Praeger Publishers, 1974.

Chaplin, Charles. *My Trip Abroad.* New York: Harper and Brothers, 1922.

Churchill, Allen. *The Theatrical Twenties.* New York: McGraw-Hill Book Co., 1975.

Donaldson, Frances. *P. G. Wodehouse: A Biography.* New York: Alfred A. Knopf, 1982.

Duncan, Isadora. *My Life.* New York: Liveright. Reprint, 1972.

Ewen, David. *Complete Book of the American Musical Theater.* New York: Holt, Rinehart and Winston, 1959.

Farnsworth, Marjorie. *The Ziegfeld Follies.* New York: Bonanza Books, 1961.

Flanner, Janet. *London Was Yesterday, 1934–1939.* New York: Viking Press, 1975.

Fordin, Hugh. *That's Entertainment: The Freed Unit at MGM.* Garden City: Doubleday, 1975.

Freedland, Michael. *Jerome Kern: A Biography.* New York: Stein and Day, 1978.

————. *Irving Berlin.* New York: Stein and Day, 1974.

Gänzl, Kurt. *The British Musical Theatre.* Hampshire, England: Macmillan Press, Music Division, 1988.

Gershwin, Ira. *Lyrics on Several Occasions.* New York: Viking Press, 1959.

Green, Stanley. *Encyclopedia of the Musical Film.* New York, Oxford University Press, 1981.

————. *Encyclopedia of the Musical Theatre.* Dodd, Mead & Company, 1976.

————. *The Great Clowns of Broadway.* New York: Oxford University Press, 1984.

————. *Ring Bells! Sing Songs! Broadway Musicals of the 1930s.* New York: Galahad Books, 1971.

————. *The World of Musical Comedy.* New York: A. S. Barnes & Co., 1968.

Guernsey, Otis L. Jr. *Curtain Times: The New York Theater 1965–1987.* New York: Applause Theatre Books, 1987.

Harris, Warren G. *The Other Marilyn.* New York: Arbor House, 1985.

Henson, Leslie. *My Laugh Story.* London: Hodder and Stoughton, no date.

Jabolonski, Ed, and Lawrence D. Stewart. *The Gershwin Years.* Garden City, N.Y.: Doubleday, 1958.

Jasen, David. *P. G. Wodehouse: Portrait of a Master.* New York: Mason & Lipscomb, 1974.

June. *The Glass Ladder: An Autobiography.* London: Heinemann, 1960.

Kreuger, Miles. *Show Boat: The Story of a Classic American Musical.* New York: Da Capo, 1990.

Lamb, Andrew. *Jerome Kern in Edwardian London* (monograph). New York: Institute for Studies in American Music, Conservatory of Music, Brooklyn College, 1985.

Laufe, Abe. *Broadway's Greatest Musicals.* New York: Funk and Wagnalls, 1977.

Lerner, Alan Jay. *The Musical Theatre: A Celebration.* London: Collins, 1986.

Marbury, Elisabeth. *My Crystal Ball.* New York: Boni and Liveright, 1923.

Marks, Edward B. *They All Had Glamor.* New York: Julian Messner, Inc., 1944.

Mast, Gerald. *Can't Help Singin': The American Musical on Stage and Screen.* Woodstock, N.Y.: The Overlook Press, 1987.

Mates, Julian. *America's Musical Stage.* Westport, Conn.: Greenwood Press, 1985.

Matthews, Jessie. *Over My Shoulder.* New Rochelle, N.Y.: Arlington House, 1974.

Mattfield, Julius. *Variety Music Cavalcade 1620–1961.* Englewood Cliffs, N.J.: Prentice-Hall, 1962.

McCabe, John. *George M. Cohan: The Man Who Owned Broadway.* New York: Doubleday, 1973.

Merman, Ethel, with George Eels. *Merman: An Autobiography.* New York: Simon and Shuster, 1978.

Middleton, George. *These Things Are Mine.* New York: The Macmillan Company, 1947.

Morley, Sheridan. *Gertrude Lawrence.* New York: McGraw-Hill, 1981.

Muggeridge, Malcolm. *Chronicles of Wasted Time.* Washington, D.C.: Regenry Gateway, 1989.

Perrett, Geoffrey. *America in the Twenties.* New York: Simon and Shuster, 1982.

Pollock, Channing. *Harvest of My Years.* New York: Bobbs-Merrill, 1943.

Rodgers, Richard. *Musical Stages: An Autobiography.* New York: Harcourt Brace Jovanovich, 1975.

Schwartz, Charles. *Gershwin: His Life and Music.* New York: The Bobbs-Merrill Co., 1973.

Sproat, Iain. *Wodehouse at War.* New York: Ticknor & Fields, 1981.

White, Mark. *You Must Remember This . . . Popular Songwriters 1900–1980.* New York: Charles Scribner's Sons, 1985.

Wilk, Max. *They're Playing Our Song.* Mount Kisco, N.Y.: Moyer Bell Ltd., 1991.

Wilson, Edmund. *The Twenties.* New York: Farrar Straus and Giroux, 1975.

Wind, Herbert Warren. *The World of P. G. Wodehouse.* New York: Praeger Publishers, 1972.

Wodehouse, P. G., and Guy Bolton. *Bring On The Girls.* New York: Simon and Schuster, 1953.

Wodehouse, P. G. *Over Seventy.* London: Herbert Jenkins, 1957.

——. *Performing Flea.* London: Herbert Jenkins, 1953.

Ziegfeld, Patricia. *The Ziegfelds' Girl.* Boston: Little, Brown & Co., 1964.

# Index

This book was composed in
Garamond No. 3 with Parisian and
Kuenstler Script Medium by
The Sarabande Press, New York.

It was printed and bound by
Arcata Graphics
on 50# Sebago Antique cream white paper.

The typography and binding
were designed by Mary A. Wirth for
Beth Tondreau Design, New York.